Teresa de Ávila

LETTERED WOMAN

S. Theresia molestas absentium cogitationes
Cælitus agnoscit eorumq; mentem pijs exhi-
larat Epistolis

Arnold. V. Westerhout sc. :

Teresa de Ávila

LETTERED WOMAN

Bárbara Mujica

Vanderbilt University Press

NASHVILLE

13 12 11 10 09   1 2 3 4 5

This book is printed on acid-free paper made
from 30% post-consumer recycled content.
Manufactured in the United States of America

Publication of this book has been supported by a generous
subsidy from the Program for Cultural Cooperation between
Spain's Ministry of Culture and United States Universities.

Frontispiece: Saint Teresa writing a letter while
messenger waits. Engraving by Arnold van Westerhout
(Flemish, 1651–1725), Carmelitana Collection.
Photograph by Christopher Wilson.

Library of Congress Cataloging-in-Publication Data

Mujica, Barbara Louise.
Teresa de Ávila, lettered woman / Bárbara Mujica.
p. cm.
Includes bibliographical references (p.) and index.
ISBN 978-0-8265-1631-2 (cloth : alk. paper)
1. Teresa, of Avila, Saint, 1515–1582—
Correspondence. I. Title.
BX4700.T4M77 2009
282.092—DC22
[B]
2008025852

To my husband Mauro,
to my children and grandchildren,
and to Saint Teresa, with gratitude

Contents

Preface

I became fascinated with Saint Teresa when, during a time of personal difficulty, I felt drawn toward *The Interior Castle*. I had taught early modern Spanish literature for many years, but I had never examined the *Castle* in depth. I found in Teresa a superb guide whose spiritual wisdom, wit, and down-to-earth common sense spoke to me at the profoundest level. The current popularity of Teresa attests to her ability to reach beyond cultural and religious barriers. *Publisher's Weekly* calls her "a mystic for our times" in a review of three new books published early in 2007: *Entering the Castle*, by Caroline Myss; a new translation of *The Book of My Life*, by Mirabai Starr; and my own novel, *Sister Teresa*.[1]

Once I began to read Teresa in earnest, I became intrigued not only with her teachings but also with the woman herself. Much of what we know about Teresa derives from her *Libro de la Vida* (*Book of Her Life*) or from early biographies such as those by Diego de Yepes, Francisco de Ribera, Julián de Ávila, and Jerónimo Gracián. Neither of these sources is necessarily reliable. *Vidas* were nearly always written at the behest of spiritual directors anxious to examine their charges' orthodoxy, and Teresa's was no exception. Fearful that her visions and ecstasies would provoke the scrutiny of the authorities, her confessors—in particular García de Toledo, but also Pedro Ibáñez, Gaspar Daza, and Baltasar Álvarez—ordered her to write an account of her spiritual experiences. She had already produced two *Spiritual Testimonies*, but the confessors were anxious for a more complete report. The resulting book was a combination autobiography, spiritual confession, and prayer manual, which she presented to García de Toledo in June 1562. He read it, perhaps showing it to others, and ordered certain revisions. Teresa added chapters on prayer, spiritual favors, and the foundation of San José. She probably completed the final version in 1565. Eventually the book was submitted to the inquisitional censors in Toledo. Another primary source is Teresa's *Libro de las fundaciones* (*Book of the Foundations* [Kavanaugh uses *The Book of Her Foundations*]), probably requested by her Jesuit friend, Jerónimo Ripalda. The book, which was written during three different periods, narrates the story of Teresa's foundations and contains advice to prioresses on how to run a convent.

It includes suggestions on dealing with depressed nuns, nuns given to extreme mortifications, and spurious visionaries. Much of the book deals with the persecutions of the Discalced Carmelites at the hands of Calced friars. Alison Weber notes that in these chapters Teresa depicts herself as a "picaresque heroine on a series of road adventures" (*Rhetoric* 123). One might also see her as a beleaguered warrior who, with God's grace and guidance, triumphs over adversity. The defensive nature of this material necessarily skews it. Although, as many critics have suggested (Weber, Slade, Ahlgren), Teresa probably enjoyed writing and welcomed the opportunity to defend her spiritual practices and reformist ideas, she was nevertheless aware that her work would be scrutinized by confessors and church authorities, which led her to develop self-protective rhetorical strategies. Consequently, Teresa's books do not necessarily provide an unvarnished view of her character and temperament.

Early biographies—and many subsequent ones—present an equally biased picture. After Teresa's death the church hierarchy and even many Discalced Carmelite friars began to feel uncomfortable with the model of female leadership embodied by Teresa. They sought to reconstruct her image in order to bring it into harmony with acceptable notions of female sanctity. They downplayed her reformist activism and highlighted her obedience, humility, and piety. They promoted Teresa as a spiritual icon, enhancing her saintly virtues while overlooking the messiness of the battles in which she engaged to reform her order. They explained away Teresa's keen psychological insight and pedagogical talent by depicting her as a supernatural phenomenon that by God's grace transcended the natural limitations of her sex. Until the mid-twentieth century most studies of Teresa were hagiographic in nature. More recently, however, scholars have examined Teresa's life and writing with a critical eye. The new perspectives offered by feminism and cultural studies have served as the impetus for a focus on Teresa's own writing for clues to her personality and social reality. Víctor García de la Concha's *El arte literario de Santa Teresa*, Rosa Rossi's *Teresa de Ávila*, Alison Weber's *Teresa of Avila and the Rhetoric of Femininity*, Gillian T. W. Ahlgren's *Teresa of Avila and the Politics of Sanctity*, Carole Slade's *St. Teresa of Avila*, and María Carrion's *Arquitectura y cuerpo en la figura autorial de Teresa de Jesús* provide a more accurate assessment of Teresa's position as a woman, an ecstatic, and a self-aware writer than the idealized images of earlier tomes. In addition, Jodi Bilinkoff's *The Avila of Saint Teresa* offers invaluable insight into sixteenth-century Castilian society and Elena Carrera's *Teresa of Avila's Autobiography: Authority, Power and the Self in Mid-Sixteenth-Century Spain* reconstructs the spiritual climate of Teresa's time.

Yet, to really hear Teresa's voice, we must turn to her letters. As useful and stimulating as her treatises are, it is her letters that reveal her day-to-day struggles, her frustration, her joy, her sense of humor, her temper, her compassion. In her letters we hear her standing up to church officials, cajoling colleagues, teasing friends, and offering advice. Teresa's epistolary writing delineates the different roles she played within the reform: foundress, spiritual director, politician, administrator, legislator, fundraiser, marketer, teacher, disciplinarian, and nurse. It reveals how she used her political acumen to dodge inquisitors and negotiate the thorny issues of the reform, facing off the authorities—albeit with considerable tact—and reprimanding priests and nuns who failed to follow her orders. Her letters bring to light the different strategies she used—code names, secret routing—in order to communicate with her collaborators. They show how she manipulated language, varying her tone and rhetoric according to the recipient or slipping into deliberate vagueness in order to avoid divulging secrets. What emerges from Teresa's epistolary writing is a portrait of extraordinary courage, ability, and shrewdness. Yet, in spite of the extensive attention her other writing has received, until now no book-length study of Teresa's letters has been done. In the sixteenth century, the word *letrado* (lettered) referred to the learned men of the church. Teresa treated *letrados* with great respect and always insisted on her own lack of learning. The irony is that although women could not be *letradas*, Teresa was, as her epistolary collection shows, "lettered" in more ways than one.

Letters have gained prominence in recent years as scholars turn their attention increasingly to nontraditional literary forms. This phenomenon is a natural outcome of postmodern sensibilities. By questioning the boundaries between "high" and "low" forms of expression, postmodernism has "decentered" literary studies, shifting the focus from the canonical to the marginal. Jacques Derrida's attempt to disengage culture from the traditional focal points of Western civilization—Truth, Beauty, Ideal Form, and the like—toward an exploration of the marginalized or repressed Other led scholars to question long-held assumptions about legitimate areas of study. Neglected groups—women, gays, the poor, and ethnic, religious, and racial minorities—achieved validation as generators of culture and cultural products worthy of study. The canon, consisting of works in genres conventionally considered "literary," was forced to expand to include different types of writing, since marginalized groups did not necessarily cultivate prevailing literary forms. For example, few early modern Spanish women cultivated the standard genres (novel, theater, poetry), while countless numbers of them wrote letters. Gabriella Zarri provides a synopsis of the rich medieval treasury of women's letters, from the amorous missives of Eloise to Abelard to the spiritual communications of female religious leaders such as Hildegard von Bingen to friendly letters between laywomen. The advent of humanism nourished this tradition, as in the fifteenth and sixteenth centuries cultured European women engaged in intellectual epistolary exchanges with both male and female acquaintances (Zarri x–xi). Nuns used correspondence as a means of maintaining contact with friends and family and sometimes of receiving spiritual direction. For Teresa, letters were essential tools in the management of the Carmelite reform she launched and the maintenance of cohesion in the order. Unsurprisingly, in recent years feminist researchers have devoted increased attention to epistolary collections. Although relatively little work as been done on women's letter-writing in Spain, several collections of articles focusing on other European countries have been published since 1990.[2]

Epistolary writing is also of interest to modern scholars because of ways in which postmodern decentering has called into question traditional historical knowledge. Rather than limiting themselves to the official view of events as interpreted by the power elite, practitioners of "new historicism" include alternate versions and therefore must turn to unconventional sources, such as letters. Personal correspondence of political and religious leaders such as Teresa reveals the inner workings of history—how decisions were made, what compromises were required, how the personal influenced the public. In addition, letters sometimes provide alternate interpretations of well-known developments. For example, the letters of Carmelite nuns living in the Low Countries during the early seventeenth century afford us with a view of the Protestant Reformation from the perspective of the women struggling to maintain Catholic strongholds in areas quickly losing ground to Protestantism. Both in form and content, letters can also bring new insight to tensions between social classes. In *Correspondence: Models of Letter-Writing from the Middle Ages to the Nineteenth Century*, Roger Chartier, Alain Boureau, and Cécile Dauphin examine the development of epistolary rules and prototypes in France and their role in the maintenance of social order.

While the "new historicism" advanced by Stephen Greenblatt and others during the 1980s explored alternate perspectives and common experience, its focus was largely political—that is, on the workings of the state and the intricacies of power conflicts. "New historicism" is "committed to the value of the single voice, the isolated scandal, the idiosyncratic vision, the transient sketch," explain Catherine Gallagher and Stephen Greenblatt (16). However, this anecdotal data served as a basis for analyzing relationships within hierarchical power configurations. In the 1990s, as Patricia Fumerton notes, the focus began to shift away from the privileged and toward the common—"but the common in both a class and cultural sense: the low (common people), the ordinary (common speech, common wares, common sense), the familiar (commonly known), the customary or typical or taken for granted (common law, commonplace, communal)" (3). This new social historicism—what Fumerton calls the "new new historicism"—"looks beyond (and below) the politics of the court and the state apparatus" to the everyday (4). For the understanding of the everyday, letters are a precious resource. Social historian James Casey cites letters as "one of the most valuable sources of all" for grasping the instability of the early modern Castilian family (193). Teresa's correspondence provides readers with a privileged look not only into the author's personality and the politics of the Carmelite reform but also into everyday life in an early modern convent. Teresa's comments on the size of dowries and the appearance of postulants make it clear that convent life was about more than prayer. References to betrayals, bickering, gossip, and cliques show that even in the regimented Discalced cloister, emotions could get out of hand. Also relevant to the new new historicist are Teresa's comments on convent decoration, entertainments, cooking, household remedies, clothing (including underskirts), family squabbles, and the mail service. Furthermore, Teresa's lively and idiomatic language, her jokes and ribbing, and her quick switches from diffidence to assertiveness provide important clues regarding linguistic usage in the sixteenth century, especially by women. Simply put, Teresa's letters provide a goldmine of information on the spiritual, personal, political, and quotidian in early modern Spain.

My original intention upon beginning this project was to devote the first part of the book to Teresa's letters and the second part to those of her followers, in particular, María de San José, Ana de San Bartolomé, and Ana de Jesús. However, it soon become evident that Teresa's epistolary alone provided material for an entire volume. A trip to Spain during which I examined many of Teresa's autographs and early printed editions of the epistolary confirmed the need to revise my original plan. I decided to divide the project into two books, the first on Teresa and the second on her disciples.

I am grateful to the many researchers whose work on Saint Teresa provided the background for this study. All Teresian scholars have built on the superb contributions of the Carmelite historians Efrén de la Madre de Dios, Otger Steggink, Teófanes Egido, Ildefonso Moriones, and Joachim Smet. More recent scholars such as those mentioned in the paragraphs above have provided new perspectives on Teresa as a woman, a reformer, a writer, and a spiritual leader. Several scholarly papers by Joan Cammarata sparked my interest in Teresa's epistolary themes. I am greatly indebted to Georgetown University for three grants that enabled me to devote time exclusively to this project and to travel to Spain to complete my research. My heartfelt thanks go to several members of the Carmelite community: Kieran Kavanaugh, O.C.D., who made his translations of the second volume of Teresa's letters available to me before their publication; the sisters of the Monasterio de la Concepción in Valladolid, in particular Mother María Capilla de Jesús, who graciously allowed me to examine Teresa's autographs; Patrick McMahon, O. Carm., director of the Carmelitana Collection in Washington, D.C., and librarian Patricia O'Callaghan, who facilitated my research. I also extend thanks to Espiritualidad for granting me permission to reprint seven of Teresa's letters from the collection *Epistolario* (1984), edited by Luis Rodríguez Martínez and Teófanes Egido. I am grateful to Vanderbilt University Press for engaging Dr. Carole Slade, of Columbia University, to evaluate my manuscript. Dr. Slade made many excellent suggestions that greatly improved the book. My graduate assistant, Maureen Chant Russo, deserves special recognition for her outstanding proofreading and constructive comments. I also wish to express my gratitude to the following friends and fellow scholars for their help and encouragement: Teófanes Egido, O.C.D., Ildefonso Moriones, O.C.D., Alison Weber, Christopher Wilson, Thomas Walsh, Héctor Campos, John O'Malley, S.J., Jeffrey von Arx, S.J., and William Watson, S.J. Finally, I am grateful to my husband, Mauro E. Mujica, and my children, Lilly, Mariana, and Mauro, for their love and unswerving support. And, of course, I thank Teresa herself for her guidance and inspiration.

Sources and Abbreviations

SOURCES

Quotations in Spanish of Saint Teresa's works are from *Obras completas*, edited by Enrique Llamas, et al. Quotations in Spanish of her letters are from *Epistolario*, edited by Luis Rodríguez Martínez and Teófanes Egido. Quotations in English of her works are from *The Collected Works of St. Teresa of Ávila*, vols. 1–3, translated by Kieran Kavanaugh and Otilio Rodríguez. Unless otherwise indicated, quotations in English of her letters are from *The Collected Letters of St. Teresa of Ávila*, vols. 1 and 2, translated by Kieran Kavanaugh. Chapters and section numbers are from these editions. For example, *CWST* 1, *Life* 4:7, means *The Collected Works of St. Teresa*, vol. 1, *The Book of Her Life*, chapter 4, section 7. *The Interior Castle* is divided into seven Mansions, and each Mansion is divided into chapters. Thus, *CWST* 2, *Interior Castle* IV:2:7 means *The Collected Works of St. Teresa of Ávila*, vol. 2, *The Interior Castle*, Mansion 4, chapter 2, section 7. The *Constitutions* are divided into articles. *Constitutions* 11 refers to article 11 of the document.

ABBREVIATIONS

CW   *The Complete Works of Saint Teresa of Jesus*. Ed. and trans. E. Allison Peers. 3 vols. London: Sheed and Ward, 1946.

CWST   *The Collected Works of Saint Teresa of Ávila*. Trans. Kieran Kavanaugh, O.C.D., and Otlio Rodríguez, O.C.D. 3 vols. Washington, DC: Institute of Carmelite Studies, 1980–1987.

Letters *The Collected Letters of St. Teresa of Ávila*. Trans. Kieran Kavanaugh, O.C.D. 2 vols. Washington, DC: Institute of Carmelite Studies, 2001, 2007.

Mss.   Manuscript collection, Biblioteca Nacional, Madrid.

WPV   *Way of Perfection*, Valladolid edition. *The Collected Works of Saint Teresa of Ávila*. vol. 2. Trans. Kieran Kavanaugh, O.C.D., and Otlio Rodríguez, O.C.D. 3 vols. Washington, DC: Institute of Carmelite Studies, 1980–1987.

Teresa de Ávila

LETTERED WOMAN

Introduction:
The Pen and the Sword

Teresa de Ávila and her followers were tough, determined managerial types who faced obstacles every bit as daunting as the glass ceiling faced by professional women today. The difference is that for women of Teresa's generation, the glass ceiling was not invisible; it was patent and manifest, proclaimed from pulpits throughout the land in the form of church doctrine and scriptural interpretation. These strong-willed women belonged to a new order, the Discalced Carmelites, that sought to contribute to church reform by promoting a more authentic, personal spirituality than that practiced in most Catholic communities. Although these women were contemplative nuns who belonged to a cloistered order that stressed humility and quiet, they found in the core of their belief system the courage and stamina to confront a patriarchy determined to keep women in their place. In spite of harassment by the Inquisition, the opposition of the church hierarchy, and the hostility of male authorities of their own order, they succeeded in founding convents where, removed from the pressures of a patriarchal, class-conscious society, women could find peace and spiritual sustenance. After establishing religious houses throughout Spain, they went on to carry their movement to the rest of Europe and even to the New World.

Reform and Reformation

Their leader, Teresa de Ahumada (1515–1582), was a Carmelite nun from the town of Ávila, then a bustling commercial center known for wool and silk. Exposed in her early twenties to the reformist ideas that had begun infiltrating Spain from the Low Countries decades before, Teresa rejected the empty, mechanistic Catholicism dominant in Europe in favor of a more personal, authentic spirituality.[1] By the late Middle Ages religious practice had become highly ritualistic and many monasteries had grown lax and corrupt. To counteract these tendencies, during the twelfth and thirteenth centuries new orders formed (for example, the Carthusians and Cistercians) devoted to a simpler, purer spirituality. During the following century, certain mendicant orders divided into "conventuals," who continued to practice the mitigated, laxer lifestyle, and "observants," who returned to the primitive rule.[2]

Around the same time, a new spiritual movement called the *devotio moderna* emerged in the Low Countries. Instead of the mechanical repetition of prayers that had become endemic in Christian observance, the practitioners of the *devotio moderna* stressed recollection—that is, interiority or withdrawal into the inner self—and mental prayer in order to cultivate a more genuine, spontaneous relationship with God. Reformers such as the humanist Erasmus of Rotterdam were highly influenced by the *devotio moderna* and introduced its methods into their spiritual practice. In his *Enchiridion Militis Christiani* (*Dagger for a Christian Soldier*), a best-seller in its time, Erasmus promotes a distilled, Christ-centered faith in which quiet devotion born of contemplation matters more than pomp and ritual. Erasmus enjoyed tremendous popularity in Spain, and Cardinal Francisco Ximénez de Cisneros, Queen Isabella's confessor, not only introduced his teachings at court but even invited him to settle south of the Pyrenees—an invitation Erasmus declined.[3] Teresa writes in her *Life* that she was introduced to recollection, a form of interior prayer associated with the *devotio moderna*, through *The Third Spiritual Alphabet*, by the observant Franciscan Francisco de Osuna, a book she read while visiting her uncle (*CWST* 1, 4:7).[4]

In spite of its acceptance among many religious, the new spirituality met with intense opposition. The tension between reformers and resisters is a complex issue. In the late Middle Ages both men's and women's monasteries in Spain depended in large part on patronage. Rich patrons endowed these houses, provided dowry money for professing relatives, bought artifacts for the chapel, contributed to improvements on the convent property, or donated tracts of land. Elizabeth Lehfeldt explains, "The investments of secular citizens made significant statements about their piety, communal values, and a yearning for salvation" (15). In return for their support, patrons sometimes required nuns to pray for their souls in perpetuity or display their family crest or portrait in the convent. Thus, strong ties were forged between the secular and the sacred. Secular women were often among the most generous of patrons, as charitable donations to religious institutions were one of the few ways in which women could exercise influence. Female donors were allowed to visit convents, penetrating the cloister, and nuns were allowed to visit both men and women to offer spiritual guidance and attend to business matters. Through the system of patronage, some religious houses acquired great estates, and officers of both sexes exercised near-autonomous management of these properties, sometimes even becoming involved in lawsuits. Religious houses sold the produce and collected the rents from rural lands, leased out urban holdings for a profit, and found ways to lend money and charge interest while avoiding the taint of usury (Lehfeldt 50). Several religious houses became tremendously powerful, even controlling entire towns. This meant raising soldiers for the king and collecting royal revenues. In addition, some religious controlled their own money and assets in spite of the fact that they technically relinquished their wealth to the convent upon professing. Management responsibilities often required nuns and priests to leave their monasteries to oversee their property, engage lawyers, and tangle with tenants.

In the case of women, the convent often afforded a financial and social independence unattainable in secular society. It also offered women a chance for an education and meaningful work. In convents, women did the accounting, disciplined their peers, and taught novices and secular schoolgirls. Some nuns laminated manuscripts, painted, or composed music. A few traveled to distant cities to found new convents. Abbesses could wield immense clout. A few directed double monasteries of men and women. The abbess of the Cistercian convent of Santa María de las Huelgas in Valladolid not only named certain municipal officials of the town of Zaratán, which the convent controlled, but oversaw the chaplaincies of the local church and two additional foundations and even designated the parish priest. The abbess of the Cistercian convent of Santa María de las Huelgas in Burgos "enjoyed quasi-episcopal jurisdiction over the towns and monasteries subject to her monastery" (Surtz 2). She and other Cistercian abbesses believed themselves empowered to hear confessions and preach, practices prohibited by a papal bull issued by Innocent III.

It was in this environment that reformers began to clamor for the transformation of monastic life through increased discipline, austerity, and enclosure. Although resistance to reform among priests and nuns is usually depicted as a predilection for easy living over spiritual rigor, Lehfeldt argues that, in some cases at least, opposition stemmed from the reluctance of religious men and especially women to give up the autonomy to which they were accustomed and felt entitled. Many of these women were serious about their vocations and believed enclosure would limit their ability to perform important spiritual duties, such as comforting grieving widows. They did not so much oppose reform as the imposition of change by outside forces.

The papal canon *Periculoso*, written by Boniface VIII in 1298, had prescribed perpetual strict cloister for nuns of all orders. However, the law was unevenly enforced, with so many exceptions made over subsequent decades that it was virtually ineffectual. By the fourteenth century, reform movements again burgeoned throughout the kingdom, this time with the vigorous encouragement of the king, Juan I of Castile (1358–1390). Religious leaders sought to return orders to their original rule, stressing poverty and enclosure. Although there had been attempts at reform before, the movements of the fourteenth century were unprecedented in the sense that they attempted to abolish nuns' revenue-generating activities and to force religious women to adhere to standards different from the ones in existence when they entered the convent. Furthermore, some convents had originated as *beaterios*, communities of pious women known as *beatas* who observed chastity and individual poverty but took no formal religious vows. These women regularly performed public services in hospitals or among the poor, and so were used to circulating freely. When they organized into convents, they often continued to perform the same charitable services. Attempts to impose enclosure met with resistance not only from the nuns themselves, who saw their normal activities disrupted, but also from secular communities that depended on sisters to meet some of their spiritual needs.

The battle for reform extended throughout the fifteenth century, but men and women did not meet the challenge in the same ways. Male orders often responded by restructuring themselves and adopting observant conventions, which were less traumatic for men than for women because even reformed male houses did not necessarily insist on enclosure. Although separation from the world was considered desirable and salutary, it was not required. In fact, certain reformed male orders made active proselytizing one of their objectives. For female religious, the drive for enclosure was far more energetic. Abbesses were supposed to relinquish their financial and administrative authority to male clergy, and many of them did, albeit begrudgingly. Lehfeldt writes, "The fifteenth-century fight had centered on the attempt to carefully demarcate the boundary separating the secular from the sacred—and enclosure had emerged briefly as a near-universal ideal in the attempt to achieve this" (136). However, by the era of the Catholic Monarchs, standards had once again become lax and reformers found it necessary to enforce claustration.

For Ferdinand and Isabella, religious purity was essential to the safeguarding of political unity, and they linked female enclosure to the achievement of this ideal. Convents, in Isabella's view, had become impossibly corrupt. The ideals of poverty, chastity, and communal living had been seriously compromised, and the nation had to be cleansed of religious pollution. "Thus," explains Lehfeldt, "over the course of a thirty-year campaign, ecclesiastical visitors went to convents throughout the peninsula and insisted that they return to observant monastic standards and adopt a posture of passive contemplation" (137).[5] However, many convents did not accept the new regulations willingly but "rejected this program of reform and vigorously protected their corporate autonomy, identities and traditions" (Lehfeldt 137). While many Spanish nuns embraced the new spirituality inspired by the *devotio moderna*, in general the crown's efforts to impose rigorous standards of monasticism met with resentment and resistance.

The Catholic Monarchs tightened their grip. For them, monastic reform was necessary not only for the spiritual health of the country but also for achieving dominion over Spain's dangerously independent religious orders. The king and queen needed to assert their authority. However, the standards were different for men and women. The monarchs charged the enforcement of the reform to male clerics, who were to circulate outside their own religious houses to compel conformity with the new rules, to serve as chaplains, or to attend to church business. Women, on the other hand, were required to observe strict enclosure. Thus, decades before the Council of Trent decreed the claustration of female religious in 1563, the Catholic Monarchs had made it the primary aspect of female monasticism (Lehfeldt 145). *Exposuerunt nobis*, a papal bull issued in 1493, buttressed the crown's efforts, granting the ecclesiastical visitors the authority to impose the standards advocated by the monarchs.[6] Yet, in the end, Ferdinand and Isabella were unsuccessful. Their efforts not only exacerbated tensions between observants and conventuals but failed to completely rein in nuns. As before, in addition to resistance by the women themselves, efforts to enforce the cloister met with opposition from secular communities that supported unenclosed convents, both because they benefited from the nuns' spiritual services and because they had interest in maintaining contacts within the house. And also as before, nuns who resisted reform often did so not because they wished to engage in improprieties, but rather because they desired to maintain their autonomy and corporate identities (Lehfeldt 175).

The Carmelite order, which Teresa entered in 1536, mirrors these same conflicts. The order has its origins in a community of penitent lay hermits founded in the early 1200s on a western slope of Mount Carmel, about three miles south of Haifa. Saint Albert had established a strict rule for the Carmelites—at the time, an all-male order—that stressed hermitic asceticism, poverty, and manual labor. By the fourteenth century, the Carmelites had spread throughout Europe and established friaries in many major cities. Unsurprisingly, they experienced the same tensions that wracked the Franciscans and other mendicant orders. The increased laxity produced by the transition from hermetic to urban life led to disregard for the vow of poverty, and friars not only kept personal belongings in the monasteries but acquired lands and other property. Some purchased their own cells, which they were allowed to possess for as long as they lived. Women were allowed to visit brethren as long as the door was left open. Communal life began to dissipate, and friars took fewer and fewer meals in the refectory. (The Constitution of 1354 required that meals be taken in the refectory only twice a week, although this was later modified.) Doctors of theology were allowed special privileges, such as dispensation from the refectory and the right to keep a servant, whose salary would be paid for by the community. Such benefits led many friars to pursue (or fraudulently obtain) university degrees without having any sincere interest in the intellectual life.[7] In 1432, due to declining membership, Pope Eugene IV relaxed

Saint Albert's original rule, in particular with regard to solitude, fasting, and abstinence.

At the same time, certain convents were insisting on strict observance, although the accomplished Carmelite historian, Joachim Smet, emphasizes that we do not yet know the extent of the Carmelite reform movement in the fifteenth century (1:78). We do know that Fra Jacobo di Alberto initiated a reform in Tuscany, where the Convent of Le Selve, between Pisa and Florence, was established as a "house of observance." Another such monastery was established in Florence, and then another in Mantua, from which the movement, known as the Mantuan Reform, took its name. Jean Soreth (1394–1471), prior general of the order, traveled to Italy and then throughout Europe, attempting to restore observance. He wrote a commentary on the Rule (the *Expositio paranetica*) and published revised Constitutions in 1462. He also established the female branch of the order, supported foundations in northern Europe, and was instrumental in the creation of Third Order, or secular Carmelites. However, it was not until 1562, when Teresa founded the Discalced Carmelites—at first a branch of the Carmelites that observed the primitive rule—that the reform began in earnest.

If at the end of the fifteenth century reformist ideas had found favor among the Spanish aristocracy, by the beginning of the sixteenth, tolerance for new approaches to spirituality was quickly vanishing. In 1517, Martin Luther, an Augustinian monk, attacked the practice of selling indulgences, thereby setting in motion the events that would culminate in the Protestant Reformation.[8] After Luther broke with Rome in 1520, Protestantism spread rapidly throughout northern Europe, provoking a forceful reaction in countries remaining loyal to the Catholic Church. In Spain, church officials clamped down on religious practices considered heretical.

Under Philip II (1527–1598), whose religiosity bordered on fanaticism, the state became an instrument of repression. The king attempted to insulate Spain and its colonies against outside contact. Reform movements that emphasized austerity and interiority became suspect. Philip not only used violence to impose orthodoxy at home and in the American colonies but sent his armies to confront Muslims and Protestants abroad. Philip had succeeded his father, Charles V, as ruler of the Low Countries, and through his half-sister, the regent Margarita de Parma, implemented a policy of brutal repression against the Protestants. When an uprising broke out in the Netherlands in 1567, Philip charged the Duke of Alba with quelling it. However, the cruelty with which the Duke persecuted non-Catholics only served to strengthen Dutch resistance. The Dutch prince William I of Orange (1533–1584), although raised a Catholic, embraced Calvin out of patriotism and led the struggle against the Spaniards, whom the Dutch finally expelled in 1576. But the Netherlands represented only one front in Philip's struggle against "heresy." Although the Spaniards had—at least ostensibly—eliminated Islam from their country, Philip continued to struggle against the Muslims abroad. On 7 October 1571 the Holy League, consisting mainly of Spanish, Venetian, and papal ships under the command of Philip's half-brother, Juan de Austria, won a decisive naval battle at Lepanto—the first major Ottoman defeat by Christian powers. In spite of this resounding victory, the ensuing campaign for control of Tunisia failed, and Spain eventually lost her African holdings.

In spite of his fervent faith, Philip II tried to maintain a degree of ecclesiastical independence from Rome. Charles V had had a rocky relationship with Pope Paul III and warned his son that, although he should always be submissive to the church, he must never allow his deference to prejudice Spain's prosperity and independence.[9] The Council of Trent (1547–1563) gave Philip the opportunity to demonstrate both his obedience and his autonomy. From the beginning of the sporadic meetings at Trent, the pope had attempted to use the council to reinforce papal authority. Certain Catholic monarchs, including Charles V, resisted these efforts. Charles opposed the selection of the intensely anti-Spanish Giovanni Pietro Carafa as Pope Paul IV in 1555. Paul IV was a stern, temperamental, opinionated, and chauvinistic man with a strong sense of papal privilege. Intensely disliked by the Habsburgs, the new pope excommunicated both Charles and his son shortly after Philip's coronation in 1556. The year before he had allied himself with France in order to drive the Spaniards out of Italy, but Philip's victory at St. Quentin (1557) and the advance of the Duke of Alba upon Rome forced him to abandon his French alliance.

Philip's troublesome relationship with the pope did not prevent him from accepting the decisions of the Council of Trent, where Spanish bishops had played a significant role. According to historian Henry Kamen, Philip believed that the council "had a spiritual authority that was completely independent of the pope," and he adopted "a remarkable dual policy, of accepting Trent while questioning papal politics" (Kamen, *Philip of Spain* 104). He championed many of the innovations adopted at Trent, among them the reform of religious orders, regulation of the clergy, education of parish priests, preparation of missionaries, and liturgical revisions. However, these projects could not be implemented without the support of Rome, and the king was not about to allow the pope to dictate policy in Spain without asserting his own authority. He not only delayed the publication of the Canons and Decrees of the Council of Trent for two years but also imposed a proviso that ensured his own influence on ecclesiastical jurisdiction and the selection of bishops. Furthermore, he established a council in Madrid to undertake the monastic reform according to Spanish models. Philip wanted to impose much stricter norms in Spain than those required by the Council of Trent. His goal was to suppress the conventuals and impose the observant life on all the monasteries of Spain. Rome considered this stance disrespectful and rebellious, and it was not until a new pope came into power—Pius V, Philip's own candidate—that the king was able to realize his ambition.

Philip's methods were extraordinarily heavy-handed: "His attempts to reshape the religious orders were no less ruthless than the measures undertaken by reformers in the England of Henry VIII. Monasteries and convents all over Spain were occupied by soldiers and closed, monks and nuns expelled, property confiscated" (Kamen, *Philip of Spain* 105). Teresa used Philip's stance on monastic reform to her own benefit, as we will see, for she repeatedly appealed to the king as a friend and ally. She refers to his support in *Foundations*: "The king is so fond of favoring religious who he knows are faithful to their profession that once he had learned of the manner of life in these monasteries and that we follow the primitive rule, he favored us in everything" (*CWST* 3, 27:6). Carole Slade has shown that Teresa probably overstated her case. "During her lifetime, Philip's support for the Discalced was sporadic, and he probably never took an interest in Teresa herself" ("Teresa of Avila and Philip II" 241). In fact, Philip's rift with Rome actually produced delays in gaining recognition for the new order. However, it did enable Teresa to play one of her favorite power games: pitting one authority against another.[10] She not only claimed Philip's favor but also cultivated the goodwill of the pope, sending envoys to Rome to argue in support of her cause.

Letters as Instruments of Reform

This period of transition and reform saw a surge in epistolary writing. Erasmus spread his ideas not only through publications but also through steady correspondence with humanists throughout Europe. He created a veritable "letter-writing empire," thereby establishing letters as an important instrument of reform (MacCulloch 94). By doing so, he provided a precedent not only for Protestant reformers such as John Calvin and Theodore Beza but also for Catholics such as Carlo Borromeo, chief architect of the Counter-Reformation and author of some thirty thousand extant letters. For the Society of Jesus, perhaps the order most closely associated with the Counter-Reformation, letter-writing was an essential means of maintaining contact and cohesion. Soon after the order was founded in 1540 by Ignatius of Loyola, Jesuit missionaries fanned out across Europe, then went on to India, Japan, and eventually Latin America. Ignatius wrote scores of letters through which he governed his order and provided spiritual guidance for his disciples.[11] After his death, his successors continued his example. Likewise, Teresa wrote letters constantly to conduct the business of the reform and to edify and encourage her followers. In fact, she maintained such an extensive correspondence that Alison Weber dubbed her "the saint of letters" ("Dear Daughter" 243). Over her career Teresa wrote hundreds, perhaps thousands of missives.[12]

While the Spanish crown strove to purify and spread Catholicism by the sword, these reformers had recourse to the pen. For Teresa and her followers, prayer was part of an active apostolate, an effective tool against the corruption and laxity that were eroding the church from within and against the Protestantism that menaced from without.[13] The convents she founded not only provided women with a refuge where they could devote themselves entirely to prayer but also formed a bastion against encroaching threats to the faith. Writing was vital to Teresa's mission, and an enormous amount of writing went on in her convents. Many religious houses were veritable intellectual centers where nuns produced *Vidas* (life stories or spiritual memoirs), chronicles, hagiographies, religious treatises, poetry and plays, and, of course, letters. Letter-writing was essential to the enterprise, for through letters the sisters promoted their cause, transacted business, defended themselves, and maintained cohesiveness within their order. Through letters they boosted each other's morale in times of conflict and illness.

From the beginning of the reform until the end of her life, Teresa wrote letters. Through persistent illness, persecutions, and the grueling work of founding convents, she wrote letters. She undoubtedly produced letters before 1561—in her *Life* she mentions writing to her brothers in the colonies and in a missive to Lorenzo dated 23 December 1561 she refers to previous correspondence—but E. Allison Peers, who spent nineteen years translating Teresa's epistolary writing, conjectures that she probably wrote few letters at Encarnación, since most of her friends lived in Ávila (*Letters* 1:16). She may have written to her brothers in the Americas or to her sister Juana, who moved to Alba de Tormes after her marriage, but these letters have not survived. During the first five years of her career as foundress, her letters were fairly infrequent, since she remained in her native city, but her correspondence intensified after that. Eventually, letter-writing became one of her principal activities, peaking in 1576, one of the most difficult years for the reform. Although only 450 of Teresa's letters are extant, researchers estimate she wrote far more—1,200 (Rodríguez and Egido), 5,000 (Silverio de Santa María), or even 15,000 (Efrén de la Madre de Dios and Steggink).

The correspondence of Teresa and her spiritual daughters provides an intimate look at everyday life in convents, depicting activities such as sewing, cooking, writing, teaching, nursing, and performing music. Many letters reveal warm friendships and mutual support, but others expose the dark side of convent life: jealousy, infighting, cliquishness, and problematic "special friendships." Teresa's letters paint a vivid picture of the difficulties she endured as she struggled to found Discalced convents in spite of violent opposition from Calced or unreformed Carmelites. The letters of her followers (to be explored in volume 2) expose problems as Discalced nuns strove to spread the reform into France and the Low Countries: meddling priests, xenophobia, bitter cold, linguistic barriers. These letters bare the emotional trauma of living in hostile and confusing surroundings engendered by fierce battles between Protestants and Catholics, between Calced and Discalced Carmelites, and between opposing Discalced factions.

Several critics (Cruz, Maiorino, Lázaro Carreter, Rico) have pointed out the relationship among epistolary, confessional, and autobiographical literature, particularly the picaresque autobiographical novel.[14] Since the autobiographical letter is often constructed as a response to a request for information, this type of writing draws attention to the individual and his or her subjective appraisal of events. Weber has pointed out certain picaresque elements in Teresa's *Foundations*, in which the author depicts herself as a picaresque heroine who repeatedly outsmarts the rich and powerful (*Rhetoric* 123). Similarly, taken as a whole, Teresa's letters read something like a picaresque novel in which the narrator, as author of her own story, controls information and molds it for her own purposes. Some of Teresa's long, newsy letters read like picaresque episodes, in which the *pícaro*, traveling from place to place, comments on incidents and people, exposing the immorality of those in authority and justifying her own behavior.[15] As Weber points out, Teresa is shaped by her experiences and represents herself as she wishes to be seen, depicting herself differently to different readers or groups of readers. The image of Teresa that emerges from her epistolary writing is therefore dynamic, not static. Like the protagonist of *Lazarillo de Tormes*, Spain's first picaresque novel, Teresa, by writing, becomes one of the first nonaristocratic protagonists in Spanish literature; she breaks away from the dominant code system, which determines who has a voice in society.[16] By writing letters to people in power, she herself becomes powerful; she assumes authority before church officials and even the king. However, unlike Lazarillo, Teresa does not find her niche by compromising her ideals but by maintaining a clear image of herself as an instrument of God's will and by remaining faithful to her objective: to do God's work, providing devout women and men with refuges where they can devote themselves entirely to God.[17]

Teresa's letters provide an ongoing view of the creation of a new religious order as it unfolds. They are on-site reports. Teresa tells the same story in her *Life* and *Foundations*, but those books were written after the fact and were destined to be read and "corrected" by her spiritual directors. Even if, as Weber argues, Teresa had a collaborative relationship with these men, the knowledge that her work was to be assessed by *letrados*—learned men—necessarily affected both the content and style of her books.[18] In addition, in early modern Spain inquisitional censors reviewed all new publications, and Teresa was careful to depict her experiences in a way that made them palatable to the authorities. The letters, in contrast, were directed to a much smaller audience and not subjected to official appraisal. The epistolary writing shares with *Life* and *Founda-*

tions the subjective, self-fashioning narrator but provides her with a less-restrictive medium than books. Even so, Teresa often could not express herself freely, even in letters, which could always be intercepted by hostile forces. Still, even though she had to exercise caution, she was in greater control of her letters than of her other writing. And, in fact, many of her letters—especially those to personal friends—are surprisingly candid. By examining Teresa's letters, we can watch the Carmelite reform unfold as it was experienced by Teresa herself.

Chapter 1

From Teresa de Ahumada
to Saint Teresa

The woman who spearheaded the movement known as the Carmelite reform was an unlikely hero. Teresa Sánchez Cepeda y Ahumada was born in Ávila in 1515, the daughter of a *converso* silk and woolens merchant. *Conversos*, or New Christians, were Jews who had converted to Catholicism, often due to intense pressure from the crown. Teresa's Jewish ancestry is of more than anecdotal interest. The position of *conversos* in early sixteenth-century Spain made it likely that many of them would become proficient at filing petitions, managing legal documents, and writing letters.

Learning to Write: Converso Spain

In spite of portrayals of medieval Spain as a tolerant society in which Christians, Jews, and Muslims lived in harmony, anti-Semitism has deep roots on the peninsula.[1] Periods of peaceful cohabitation, cultural intermingling, cross-fertilization, and interethnic cooperation did exist from the eighth to the fifteenth centuries, as María Rosa Menocal has demonstrated, and these phenomena contributed to the creation of a rich, vibrant intellectual climate in medieval Spain. However, Joseph Pérez argues that true open-mindedness did not exist: "Tolerance presupposes an absence of discrimination against minorities and respect for the points of view of others. In the Iberia of the eighth century to the fifteenth, such tolerance was nowhere to be found" (1). Similarly, Kamen writes, "The communities of Christians, Jews, and Muslims never lived together on equal terms; so-called *convivencia* was always a relationship among unequals" (*Spanish Inquisition* 4). Rather, the three predominant cultures coexisted, each as a separate community. In spite of periods of peaceful *convivencia*, or coexistence, Jonathan Ray notes that scholars in the field of Jewish studies have challenged the idealized view of Spain as a multicultural utopia, "pointing out the persecutions against Jewish populations under the Muslim Almoravid and Almohad dynasties of the eleventh and twelfth centuries, the widespread Christian pogroms and forced conversions of Jews in 1391, and the cycle of forced conversions, expulsions, and inquisitorial harassment of Jewish and Muslim communities throughout the late medieval and early modern periods" ("Beyond Tolerance" 2). Ray challenges over-simplifications that portray medieval Spain as *either* a period of tolerance *or* persecution for Jews, arguing that most studies are based on attitudes of non-Jews toward Jews.

By examining the writings of medieval Sephardim themselves, Ray shows that during periods when Spanish authorities adopted a laissez-faire policy toward intercultural intermingling, Jewish moralists themselves argued for greater Jewish isolation because they feared that contact with non-Jews, particularly Christians, was leading to acculturation, moral laxity, and conversions to Christianity. The lure of social and economic advancement, the practice of taking Christian lovers, and the predilection for taking legal complaints to Christian—and even ecclesiastical—courts threatened to undermine the integrity of Jewish communities, argued these Jewish thinkers, who complained that Jews were putting their personal advancement above their loyalty to their own group. Ray points out that "Christian legislation aimed at regulating Jewish dress was only loosely enforced, and decrees such as the one issued at the Castilian Cortes of 1268 that prohibited Jews from assuming Christian names reflects Jewish interests in acculturation and integration as much as it does a Christian campaign to exclude them" ("Beyond Tolerance" 10). In response to this tendency, Jewish leaders chided the members of their communities for adopting Christian garb and customs, and for settling outside of established *juderías* (Jewish neighborhoods), even acquiring lands in rural areas. Ray points out that medieval Sephardim do not comprise a fixed, monolithic group, but rather a fluid one that varies from place to place and from one set of circumstances to another. Jews were part of a rich, complex, cultural weave that was influenced by autochthonous as well as external pressures. Ray concludes that "if . . . Spanish Jews continually pursued associations and social positions that closely resembled those of their Christian counterparts, then perhaps we have to revise our notion of *convivencia* as merely a measurement of tolerance" ("Beyond Tolerance" 13). The tension within Sephardic communities between the forces of assimilation and cultural preservation is a significant factor in Teresa's family history and helps to explain the Sánchez-Cepeda conversion to Christianity.

Convivencia might be affected by countless variables. In general, as long as the economy was strong and Christians, Muslims, and Jews did not have to compete with each other, they could live side by side, but downward swings brought persecutions. Similarly, political conflicts, epidemics, and other upheavals produced waves of resentment and hostility among the groups. Early in the fourteenth century the Black Death ushered in a period of hardship, and Christians began to see the plague as punishment for permitting "deicide people" to live among them. Virulent anti-Semitism spread from France throughout Spain. Although many Jews were poor, the stereotype of the rich Jewish moneylender intensified antagonism. Some monarchs did protect Jews: Pedro I of Castile (1334–1369) was dubbed "King of the Jews" by his illegitimate half-brother, Henry of Trastámara, who manipulated Spanish anti-Semitism for his own political advantage.[2] When the nobles of Castile revolted against King Pedro, they accused him of surrounding himself with Jews and Moors; their rebellion unleashed a series of abuses, including massacres.

Several clerics were influential in instigating anti-Semitic violence. Vicente Ferrer (1350–1419) was a charismatic Dominican preacher from Valencia whose fiery sermons helped unleash forced conversions and massacres of Jews during the late fourteenth and early fifteenth centuries.[3] In 1378, inflation and high prices caused widespread deprivation; Fernand Martínez, the archdeacon of Ecija, in Andalusia, preached a string of anti-Semitic sermons that led to anti-Jewish rioting, the demolition of synagogues, and mass murders. The violence, rooted largely in class resentment, swelled to engulf the rest of Spain. As a result, thousands of Jews asked to be baptized. By the end of the period of terror, only about one hundred thousand Jews remained in Spain, about half the original population (Pérez 12).

Twenty years after the massacres, civil authorities, dissatisfied with the rate of conversion, urged measures that would force the remaining Spanish Jews to accept Christianity. Jews were confined to ghettos, outside of which they were banned from practicing certain professions, such as doctor, chemist, druggist, tailor, butcher, cobbler, or tax collector. To make them easily identifiable, they were forced to allow their hair and beards to grow long and to wear red disks sewn to their clothing. Certainly, there were periods of respite. In the early fifteenth century, between 1419 and 1422, King Juan II of Castile and Alfonso V of Aragon repealed many of the discriminatory policies adopted by their predecessors. But the intense campaign for conversion had succeeded in destroying Spain's vibrant medieval Jewish communities.

During the fifteenth century, Spaniards began to distinguish between practicing Jews and *conversos*, many of which now occupied positions formerly held by Jews. *Conversos* became scribes and notaries, counselors and doctors. Many, like Teresa's father, became successful merchants, making a fortune in the silk and woolens trade. Spain's Jewish communities had always placed a high premium on education, and *conversos* from educated families frequently entered the church, where they could devote themselves to intellectual pursuits. However, in spite of their rapid integration into Spanish society, the *conversos* remained suspect. Although the church instructed Old Christians to accept them as equals—and many educated, upper-class Spaniards actually did—resentment grew among the less enlightened. As New Christians began to achieve rank and wealth, moving into positions previously closed to them, such as *alguacil, regidor,* or church official, many people saw them as interlopers and made them scapegoats for whatever evil befell society. An uprising in 1449 in Toledo led to the promulgation of the statutes of *limpieza de sangre*, the doctrine that excluded *conversos* and *moriscos* (converted Muslims) from public offices and benefices.[4] Religious orders soon began insisting on *limpieza de sangre* as well. The Hieronymites, native to Spain and much favored among the aristocracy, began the practice in 1486, and the Franciscans and Dominicans quickly followed suit.

In 1469, Ferdinand of Aragon married Isabella of Castile, uniting two powerful realms. At first, the new king and queen made no move against the Jewish and *converso* populations. In fact, certain prominent *conversos* had aided in the marriage arrangements.[5] However, once they had solidified their position, the Catholic Monarchs, as they came to be known, adopted fervently anti-Semitic policies. A chief agent in the implementation of their agenda was Francisco Ximénez de Cisneros, an Observant Franciscan friar who became the queen's confessor. Diarmaid MacCulloch observes: "In his austere, focused piety and his determination to proclaim his vision of Christian faith to the people of the Spanish kingdoms, he was much more like Luther, Zwingli, or Calvin than his Spanish contemporary Pope Alexander VI" (59).[6] In many ways, Ximénez de Cisneros incarnates the paradoxes characteristic of Spanish religious thought of the period. On the one hand, he was a practitioner of the *devotio moderna*, which he imparted to the queen and her court, and he was a member of a rigorous order that stressed austerity, piety, and withdrawal from the world. On the other, his activism impelled him into the center of power, and he used his authority to ruthlessly impose these new ideas on other clerics and to rid Spain of "heresy," brutally persecuting Jews and *conversos*. On the one hand, he founded the University of Alcalá, established a humanistic curriculum, and funded the printing of some of his favorite mystics, such as Catherine of Siena. On the other, he had thousands of non-Christian books and manuscripts burned.

The initial impetus behind the crown's anti-Semitic policies was political. Unlike France, Spain had no strong centralized government, which allowed nobles to constantly challenge the authority of the king. In order to unite their two kingdoms into an integrated state and rule effectively, the Catholic king and queen took measures to reduce the power of the nobility. They established the *Santa Hermandad* (Holy Brotherhood), a combination of permanent police force, rural constabulary, and judicial tribunal whose purpose it was to assert royal jurisdiction and contain aristocratic power.

Defiant nobles were not the only threat to the monarchy, however. Jews still lived in Spain, although in reduced numbers, and they were suspected of encouraging *conversos* to practice their ancient religious rites in secret. The Catholic Monarchs believed the creation of a new, cohesive Spanish identity required the country to adhere to one faith, and they saw the continued existence of Jews in Spain as a menace to national unity. As Barbara Weissberger puts it, "This national self-concept was disseminated in therapeutic terms, as a purification of the body politic, a purging of alien and contaminating agents that had resided in Spain for centuries. Those threatening aliens were primarily the Jews and Muslims" (*Isabel* xiii). In 1477, Ferdinand and Isabella visited Seville, a city afflicted with widespread unrest. Certain leaders, among them the head of the local Dominican monastery, attributed the city's ills to the Jews, whom they accused of stirring up *conversos* and causing them to revert. B. Netanyahu stresses that, in fact, only a small minority of Sevillian *conversos* were actually guilty of Judaizing, and those who led the campaign against them were motivated by greed and resentment more than true religious zeal—a situation recognized by many honorable Sevillian Christians who strove to quiet the anti-*converso* fervor (807–8).

In the end, the forces of anti-Semitism prevailed. Bolstered by myths of Jewish ritual murders of Christian children and other tales of Jewish cruelty, preachers rallied the masses to the anti-Jewish cause. Convinced that the Inquisition was the solution, Ferdinand and Isabella appealed to Pope Sixtus IV, who issued a bull on 1 November 1478, investing the monarchs with power to appoint inquisitors in all parts of Castile. Two years later, Ferdinand and Isabella appointed two Dominicans as inquisitors for their entire realm, which included parts of Andalusia. Kamen stresses that figures suggesting massive executions by the Inquisition are exaggerations. Although thousands of people passed through the hands of inquisitors, most were "rehabilitated" or "reconciled" to the faith, often by paying a fee. Kamen notes, for example, that although more than eight thousand cases may have been brought before the tribunals in Toledo during the period from 1481 to 1530, "the overwhelming majority of these were not in fact brought to trial; they were disciplined as a result of the edicts of grace, and had to undergo various penalties and penances, but escaped with their lives" (*Spanish Inquisition* 59).[7] Kamen points out that most executions took place during the early years, and even those were sporadic. He concludes, "Taking into account all the tribunals of Spain up to about 1530, it is unlikely that more than two thousand people were executed for heresy by the Inquisition" (60). The Spanish Inquisition was a lumbering bureaucracy, not an efficient killing machine like the ones perfected in the twentieth century by Nazis and Stalinists. Nevertheless, its inefficiency would have been of small comfort to Spain's Jews and *conversos*, who lived in constant fear of being hauled in and thrown on the rack. The use of surveillance by relatives and neighbors, torture, shame, and public punishment made the Inquisition a constant and dreaded menace.

The Inquisition was not a Spanish invention. Motivated by politics, the German king and Roman emperor Frederick II (1194–1250) took a decisive step toward the establishment of the Inquisition when, legislating for northern Italy, he declared death by fire for impenitent members of certain religious sects. In 1231 Pope Gregory IX adopted the imperial legislation and within the next few years established the procedures of the medieval Inquisition. The institution soon spread throughout Italy and to France, Germany, and Aragon. By the time Ferdinand and Isabella decided to implement the Inquisition in Spain, its cruel methods were already well established. Joseph Pérez argues that the Catholic Monarchs turned to the Inquisition not to propagate violence and anti-Semitism, but to eliminate them: "It was their belief that the Inquisition would force the *conversos* to become definitively assimilated," he writes. "Once all the New Christians had renounced Judaism, there would be nothing to distinguish them from other members of society. Anti-Semitism would disappear along with the reasons that had occasioned it" (21). However, the Inquisition soon began to spread its grip across Castile and Andalusia, wreaking both violence and anti-Semitism. The first *auto de fe* (literally "act of faith") took place in Seville on 6 February 1481. An *auto de fe* was a forced procession of penitent or impenitent "heretics" that ended with the public execution of the unrepentant. The excesses of the Spanish Inquisition led the pope to complain to the Catholic Monarchs in a letter dated 29 January 1482. However, Ferdinand and Isabella continued to push on with their projects until inquisitional tribunals were established all over Spain.[8]

In order to eradicate every trace of Judaizing among *conversos*, the king and queen thought it necessary to distance them from the pernicious influence of practicing Jews. The most efficient way to accomplish this goal was simply to remove the Jews. In 1482, Jews were expelled from parts of Andalusia and then, the following year, from the dioceses of Seville, Córdoba, and Cádiz. Attempts to eliminate Jews from other parts of Spain followed, although not all were successful. In its attempt to rid itself of this unwanted minority, Spain was hardly alone. England had expelled its Jews two hundred years earlier, in 1290. Around the same time as the Andalusian expulsions, Jews were also driven out of parts of France and Italy.[9]

In Toledo, where Christians, Moors, and Jews had once coexisted, albeit with episodic uneasiness, anti-Semitism was now on the rise. Juan Sánchez, Teresa de Ahumada's paternal grandfather, had made a fortune as a *converso* merchant. He lived well and had integrated into Toledan society, in spite of his involvement in an occupation considered *vil* (vile) because it was associated with Jews. His first wife, Leonor, was from a prestigious family, that of Simón de Fonseca Pina. When Leonor died after the birth of the couple's third boy, Sánchez married Inés de Cepeda; she was from a less-prominent family, but her father, a merchant from Tordesillas, was an Old Christian and a respectable man. However, in 1485, the Inquisition arrested Juan Sánchez and found him guilty of reverting to Jewish practices. According to the testimony of Inés's brother, Pedro de Cepeda, Sánchez was reconciled with the church *en tiempo de gracia;* that is, he confessed (Egido 187–89).[10] It is possible Sánchez was actually practicing Judaism, but we can't be sure. Teófanes Egido suggests the confession was not voluntary. The *conversos* of Toledo had been involved in a conspiracy against the Inquisition or the monarchy itself. Some of the participants were sentenced to death, but Sánchez was spared, probably in exchange for money. The crown was at war with the Moorish province of Granada and needed funds. Sánchez's " 'rehabilitation' cost him dearly," writes Egido. "One of the lists of the rehabilitated shows that Juan Sánchez . . . paid more than any other *converso* of Santa Leocadia [the district where he lived]" (26). Sánchez was not spared public humiliation, however. He was condemned to march, along with his sons, in a penitential procession to the churches of Toledo on seven consecutive Fridays. It is not known exactly how many sons Sánchez had at the time, but charges were brought only against the father, not against any of his children.[11] Even so, twelve-year-old Álvaro and ten-year-old Alonso accompanied him. Another son, Hernando, fled to Salamanca, where he took the surname Santa Catalina, supposedly because Saint Catherine's symbol was the wheel and he had changed from Jew to Christian and back again so many times that he thought this saint an appropriate patron.

Penitential processions were elaborate and horrendous affairs. Participants were divided into two groups. Those in the first group wore a *sambenito,* a full-length yellow cloak decorated with flames and devils that parodied a monk's robe. The term San Benito was a corruption of *saco bendito* (holy sack), the name of the garment penitents wore. The unfortunate souls in *sambenitos* were headed for execution. They processed toward the stakes, their lines interspersed with rotting corpses of exhumed heretics and effigies of fugitives, all clad in *sambenitos* and mock bishop's miters—the living, the dead, and the gruesome dolls dressed alike. When they reached their destination, they were hoisted up on posts and surrounded by straw. Then some worthy dignitary would light the torch.

Juan Sánchez was one of the fortunate ones in the second group, composed of "rehabilitated" Jews. Each penitent in this group wore a *sambenitillo,* a shorter, knee-length version of the *sambenito,* decorated with black crosses from top to bottom. Sánchez and two of his sons were forced to parade down the road, stopping at every church in Toledo and ending at the cathedral. Neighbors lined the streets, hurling stones at the marchers as they passed. The holy fathers placed the younger children at the end of the line out of kindness; by the time the little ones moved down the road, the neighbors would be almost out of stones. According to contemporary chroniclers, some seven hundred Judaizers were burned at the stake between 1481 and 1488, while five thousand were, like Juan Sánchez, "reconciled" to the church (Edwards 75).

After this mortifying experience, Sánchez left Toledo and moved his family to Ávila, a city with a thriving *converso* community. There he set up a new shop where he once again prospered selling woolens and silks. Jodi Bilinkoff has drawn a vivid picture of Ávila at the beginning of the sixteenth century. Like many European cities, Ávila experienced intense growth during this period, attracting immigrants of different social classes that spurred rapid urban expansion as well as overcrowding. Ambitious merchants and artisans, known as "new men," poured into the city. Bilinkoff points out that "the pressures of rapid expansion also strained relations between social groups, underscoring in particular the aspirations of an increasingly influential group of non-noble merchants, financiers, and professionals. Teresa de Ahumada y Cepeda grew up in this dynamic if sometimes tense atmosphere of demographic and social change in Ávila, in which 'new men' began to challenge the exclusive control of the city's hereditary oligarchy" (*Avila* 53). Sánchez probably thought that in this changing society, he would be able to carve out a niche for himself. He actually spent little time in Ávila, however, since he also maintained businesses in Toledo, Ciudad Real, and Salamanca.

The aspirations of the "new men" to prestige and privilege led to resentment on the part of the old oligarchy, which was fearful of losing its grip on Ávila's political and religious institutions (Bilinkoff, *Avila* 63). In order to secure their positions in society, many merchant-class *conversos* bought their way into the ranks of the lower nobility by means of a legal procedure called the *pleito de hidalguía*. In 1500 Juan Sánchez won a *pleito de hidalguía*, a petition for recognition of his status as a gentleman. This led to the issuance of an *ejecutoria*, or patent of nobility, which attested to the bearer's Old Christian blood. The document was obviously fraudulent, but thousands of *conversos* obtained *ejecutorias* by bribing officials in order to free themselves of the stigma of their Jewish background. Efrén de la Madre de Dios and Otger Steggink suggest that in Sánchez's case, the petition was a business decision, since nobles not only were exempt from paying taxes but also could aspire to the lucrative position of tax collector, which Sánchez managed to obtain (8). There can be no doubt, however, that the document also improved his social standing. He was now authorized to use the title of respect *Don* with his name and to marry his children to Old Christians. This would in fact dilute the "taint" of Jewish blood, since each succeeding generation would be less "contaminated." Just to make sure, he affixed the surname of his wife's brother, Pedro de Cepeda, to his own, which is how Teresa's father came to be Alonso de Cepeda. Yet, in spite of Juan Sánchez's efforts, nearly twenty years later, when four of his sons made their own collective *pleito de hidalguía*, there were still people who remembered his confession of Judaizing to the Toledo tribunal.[12]

During the decade following Sánchez's public penance, anti-Semitism grew more virulent in Spain. For centuries blood libels—stories of ritual murders of Christian children by Jews—had inflamed hatred of this minority throughout Europe. At the end of the fifteenth century, a spectacular and highly publicized murder pushed anti-Jewish sentiment to a new level. The case of the *niño de la Guardia* became a cause célèbre. According to confessions obtained under torture, Jews crucified and tore the heart from the body of a Christian child from La Guardia, a province of Toledo, for use in a magical rite whose objective was to annihilate Christians. A number of Jews and *conversos* were tried for the murder, found guilty, and executed publicly in November 1491 in Ávila, birthplace of Teresa de Ahumada. No doubt the ensuing anti-Jewish frenzy contributed to the crown's decision to seek a solution to the "Jewish problem" once and for all.

The Inquisition had been in place for twelve years yet had not managed to rid Spain of Jewish influence. Since Jews continued to "attempt in various ways to seduce faithful Christians from our Holy Catholic Faith," the monarchs issued an edict declaring that "the only solution to all these ills is to separate the said Jews completely from contact with Christians, and expel them from all our realms" (Kamen, *Spanish Inquisition* 20). As Kamen points out, "The edict was not to expel a people, but to eliminate a religion" (22). Implicit in the document was the offer to allow any Jew who accepted Christ to stay. The clergy launched a concerted conversion campaign, and, in support, Tomás de Torquemada, the inquisitor general, ordered leniency toward recently converted Jews who committed small transgressions in religious matters. Unsurprisingly, many of Spain's remaining eighty thousand Jews accepted baptism. Under the circumstances, it is not surprising that Juan Sánchez thought it essential to acquire a patent of nobility attesting to his *limpieza de sangre*. Although the document probably convinced no one, at least it offered Sánchez some protection against persecution.

However, his sons must have thought its protection insufficient, since in 1519, when Teresa was just four years old, her father and three of her uncles initiated another *pleito de hidalguía* in the village of Hortigosa de Rioalmar, in the hamlet of Majalbalago, which was under the jurisdiction of Ávila. Curiously, none of them lived in Hortigosa full-time—although Pedro owned property and occasionally spent time there. Theoretically, their father's *ejecutoria* guaranteed his and their "pure" blood, so no additional *pleito* should have been necessary. However, certain insinuations made by the peasants regarding the brothers' lineage apparently kindled in the Cepedas a renewed sense of vulnerability. The four brothers—Alonso, Pedro, Ruy, and Francisco—deliberately provoked a showdown with the authorities intended to establish once and for all their Old Christian lineage. This they accomplished by alleging that they were exempt from taxes by virtue of being nobles, thereby instigating a *pleito de hidalguía* at the Royal Chancery of Valladolid (Egido 13–14).

Charles I of Spain, later Charles V of the Holy Roman Empire, was a notoriously unpopular king. The grandson of Ferdinand and Isabella, he ascended to the throne after his mother, Juana la Loca, had been deemed unfit to govern. Born in Gante, Charles hardly spoke Spanish when he ascended to the throne in 1516. Many Spaniards resented being governed by a foreigner and found Charles's fiscal policies odious. In order to finance his wars in Italy, he levied taxes Spaniards considered excessive, thereby creating a climate of widespread resentment against the government. In 1520, the year after the Cepedas initiated their *pleito*, Ávila participated in the Revolt of the Comuneros, a nationwide uprising against Charles's fiscal policies. However, in the case of the Cepeda brothers, the levy was not excessive, only the modest sum of one hundred *maravedíes*. The Cepedas' refusal to pay taxes was clearly a ruse designed to enable the brothers to acquire a new patent of nobility.

The maneuver unleashed a flurry of investigations, testimonies, and affidavits. The Cepedas orchestrated the procedure cunningly, filing the petition in Hortigosa rather than in Ávila, where they actually lived, in order to bribe the village elders and secure a sympathetic prosecutor. The *procurador general de los pueblos y tierras* (prosecuting attorney in charge of towns and lands under the jurisdiction of the city of Ávila) was Francisco de Pajares, Pedro de Cepeda's brother-in-law.[13] The *procurador* hardly bothered to refute the Cepedas' claim, asking only perfunctory questions. The *fiscal de la Chancillería* (public prosecutor for the High Court), who represented the interests of the crown, alleged that the Cepedas were *pecheros*—plebeians and taxpayers—not nobles (Egido 15). It was not in the king's interests to grant exemptions from taxes. However, the Cepedas and their relatives suborned witnesses, turning the case in their favor. Four witnesses who were supposed to testify against the Cepedas suddenly changed their minds. Under interrogation they admitted that Pajares had bought them off, but this disclosure did not derail the procedure.

One by one, witnesses came forward and swore that from "time immemorial," that is, for at least three generations back, the Sánchez-Cepedas had been *hidalgos*. The brothers were connected with more than one influential, Old Christian family by marriage, and these families had a vested interest in establishing the noble lineage of the Cepedas. Hostile witnesses recalled Juan Sánchez's reconciliation with the church and his "vile" occupation of cloth merchant. Nevertheless, on 16 November 1520 the court found in favor of the brothers. Ultimately, the question raised by the *pleito* involved class—that is, the aristocratic origins of the Cepedas—rather than blood. The opposing side appealed, but the original verdict was upheld in August 1522. As Egido has shown, the resulting *ejecutoria*, issued 16 November 1523, was to be of use to the Cepedas for years to come, and, in fact, Teresa refers to it in a 1561 letter to her brother Lorenzo, written forty-one years after the original judgment. Curiously, the family was not entirely satisfied with the ruling and brazenly altered the *ejecuto-*

ria. The original patent included an addendum specifying that the Cepedas' *hidalguía* was valid *only* for Ávila and surrounding communities, but in an extant copy the word "Addendum" is scratched out and the word *especially* has been substituted for *only* (Egido 30–31).

The extremes to which the Cepedas were willing to go in order to prove their "pure" lineage attests to the tremendous pressures felt by *conversos*, who continued to feel marginalized throughout the sixteenth and seventeenth centuries. The Cepeda case is not unique. There were so many *pleitos de hidalguía* during the early sixteenth century that in Valladolid a *procurador* was assigned exclusively to these petitions and a room in the High Court set aside for the purpose of hearing them (Egido 11). Many *conversos* resorted to subornment and other corrupt practices to secure their positions in Spanish society. Acquired wealth was the instrument that enabled *conversos* to buy rank, but it also fostered resentment. In 1551 the Cortes (Parliament) complained that grandchildren of persons condemned by the Holy Office were forbidden from holding office, "but since such people are all wealthy, they obtain validation of their status from Your Majesty by favor" (Qtd. Casey 232). In 1618 the deputy from Ávila to the Cortes grumbled that "the only nobility or *limpieza* in Spain nowadays is whether a man is well liked or not, or whether he has the means and adroitness with which to purchase it" (Qtd. Casey 232). Although the power of merchant-class *conversos* lay in their monetary resources, many, like the Cepedas, gave up the "vile" businesses that associated them with their Jewish past and lived sumptuously, in the manner expected of nobles, only to squander their fortunes and sink into debt.

Teófanes Egido has reproduced 118 documents relating to the *pleito*, covering a period from 1519 to 1537, plus the *ejecutoria*. The volume of paper and ink expended on these petitions attests to the importance of *hidalguía* to Spain's social fabric. One can imagine the household in which Teresa grew up bustling with lawyers and amanuenses, her father Alonso de Cepeda absorbed in litigation. Although Teresa was only seven when the *ejecutoria* was issued and was probably unaware of the issues involved, she would have been conscious from an early age of the importance of the written word. After all, hers was a world in which the difference between *only* and *especially* in a legal document could be monumental. Teresa never mentions her Jewish origin in her writing, and it is remotely possible she wasn't even aware of it; many *converso* families were so sensitive to the "stain" on their lineage that they kept it secret even from their own children. Cathleen Medwick remarks that if Teresa did know the truth about her background, "it was probably not through her father, a man invested in obliterating his past" (14). However, it is futile to speculate about who might have told Teresa about her Jewish heritage. In Ávila's close-knit *converso* community, many knew about the family's background, and the astute and linguistically perceptive Teresa would probably have picked up the signals. As several scholars have noted, Teresa's insistence on detachment from the world, her rejection of the Spanish obsession with honor, and her refusal to investigate her postulants' lineage may well have stemmed from her own sensitivity about her ancestry.[14]

Much has been made of the reading that went on in Teresa's home. The future saint must have learned to read at an early age. She writes at the beginning of her *Life*: "My father was fond of reading good books, and thus he also had books in Spanish for his children to read" (*CWST* 1, 1:1). She attributes her mother's direction and the books provided by her father with guiding her toward virtue when she was a child of six or seven (a path, she says, from which she later strayed). Although in the early sixteenth century most women received no formal education, Teresa grew up in a home in which little girls as well as boys learned their letters—a situation not uncommon among the families of the upper classes and the rising bourgeoisie.[15] However, not all the books Teresa read were of the type considered worthy. Her mother "loved books of chivalry," although her father frowned on these frivolous novels and moralists condemned them.[16] Teresa and her mother felt compelled to read in secret, which undoubtedly heightened the attraction of the forbidden tomes. Teresa became so infatuated with stories of knights and ladies that she read obsessively: "I was so completely taken up with this reading that I didn't think I could be happy if I didn't have a new book" (*CWST* 1, *Life* 2:1). Later, she gave up her chivalric tales and went on to read Saint Jerome, Pedro de Osuna, Saint Augustine, and other authors whose influence would be decisive in her spiritual development.

The Cepedas not only read, they also wrote. Little has been made of the importance of writing in the Cepeda home, but in the atmosphere of constant litigation in which she spent her early years, Teresa must have been aware of her father constantly writing or dictating letters, complaints, petitions, and declarations. In a famous episode in *Life*, Teresa describes how, as a little girl, she and her brother read the lives of the saints and were so impressed with the martyrs that they ran away from home in hopes of being killed by Moors; when that plan failed, they played at being hermits (*CWST* 1, 1:4–5). However, as Egido notes, "[Teresa's] childhood . . . was not filled only with hermitages, lives of saints, and escapades to the lands of the Moors, but with the lawsuits brought by that impenitently litigious family" (10). As late as 1537, when Teresa was twenty-two years old, the Cepedas were still struggling to validate their social status. That year, they filed a petition demanding that they be exempted from certain debts by virtue of having a patent of nobility (Egido 239–40).

Furthermore, before he gave up his "vile" occupation, Teresa's father would have maintained a steady correspondence with buyers and suppliers. He would have had to draw up letters of agreement, contracts, and payment and production schedules. Lisa Jardine notes that in the late Middle Ages, the diaspora of Jewish families prominent in commerce and banking meant that these families had contacts throughout Europe (*Worldly Goods* 110). These people transacted business through correspondence. Jardine cites the case of Francesco di Marco Datini, who exchanged about ten thousand letters a year with his representatives in other cities (*Worldly Goods* 111). The same was undoubtedly true of *conversos* in Spain. Even if Alfonso de Cepeda wrote only a fraction of this number of letters, he must have devoted considerable time to his correspondence. It is possible that Teresa never read a single one of her father's legal documents or a single piece of his business correspondence. Nevertheless, her world was surely filled with legal and business communications. Simply by watching her father, she would have learned the importance of letter-writing. *Conversos* like Alonso de Cepeda did not defend themselves with the sword from the onslaught of persecutions wrought by the crown, the church, and society at large; they defended themselves with the pen.

From Teresa de Ahumada to Fundadora

Like the *converso* businessmen in whose midst she grew up, Teresa understood the importance of writing. She wrote hundreds of letters pertaining to business and legal matters, as well as personal letters through which she kept in touch with collaborators, friends, and relatives. In order to contextualize Teresa's letters and identify her correspondents, it will be useful to summarize the last twenty years of her life, during which she launched the Carmelite reform.

Teresa Sánchez de Cepeda y Ahumada was the eldest daughter of Don Alonso and his second wife, Doña Beatriz de Ahumada. His first wife, Doña Catalina del Peso, had died in 1507 after two years of marriage, leaving him with two children, María and Juan. Doña Beatriz immediately gave birth to two boys, Fernando and Rodrigo. The young parents named their first girl, born on 28 March 1515, for her maternal grandmother, Teresa de Ahumada. It was the custom for some of the children in a large family to take their father's surname while others took their mother's; Teresa used her maternal last name. In the four years from 1519 to 1522, Doña Beatriz bore four more sons: Lorenzo, Antonio, Pedro, and Jerónimo. In spite of Don Alonso's many servants, Doña Beatriz must have been exhausted, but in 1527 she gave birth to another son, Agustín. By the time her daughter Juana was born the following year, the young wife's health was so fragile that she died.

Biographers have sometimes portrayed Teresa as a devout child, but in her description of her early years, she does not depict herself as particularly angelical. She loved reading hagiographies, but these were often adventure stories not unlike novels of chivalry. Besides, in Ávila, a city steeped in religious lore and teeming with churches, it is not surprising that children played at being crusaders or nuns. She does say that she was by nature spiritual, but in adolescence she abandoned her childhood piety and began to keep the company of an unidentified relative, a frivolous girl her mother saw as a negative influence (*CWST* 1, *Life* 2:3). After her mother's death at thirty-three, Teresa came under the influence of this relative, who immersed her in "conversations and vanities," almost setting her on the path to perdition (*CWST* 1 *Life* 2:3). In these first chapters of *Life*, Teresa depicts herself as a girl full of energy and verve, traits that resonate throughout her letters.

A scandal involving one of her male cousins led Teresa's father to place her in a convent. Although Teresa insists that her relationship with this cousin "was in view of a possible marriage," and "having inquired of my confessor and other persons about many things, I was told I was doing nothing against God" (*CWST* 1, *Life* 2:9), some biographers have concluded that she was actually having an affair. Antonio T. de Nicolás, reading a declaration of guilt into a deliberately vague passage, asserts that Teresa "was not a virgin" when she entered the convent (xiv). Victoria Lincoln, although more circumspect, reaches the same conclusion (15). However, given the fact that in early sixteenth-century Spain any breach of decorum could compromise a girl's honor (understood as "reputation"), the issue is irresoluble. Teresa entered Nuestra Señora de la Gracia, an Augustinian convent, as a *doncella de piso*, or boarder, with no intention of becoming a nun (*CWST* 1, *Life* 3:1). Since she was equally opposed to marriage, however, she eventually decided to take vows, reasoning that "the trials and hardships of being a nun could not be greater than those of purgatory" (*CWST* 1, *Life* 3:6). Since Teresa's mother had died after giving birth to her youngest child, Juana, it is possible that fear of pregnancy influenced Teresa's decision.[17] We will probably never know exactly why Teresa opted for the convent, but the anguish she expresses in her *Life* makes it clear she was quite conflicted. Nevertheless, by the time she left the Augustinian sisters in the fall of 1532 because of illness, she had made up her mind.

Don Alonso opposed the plan. Teresa writes in *Life* that she was his favorite child, and he may have been reluctant to part with her. It is also possible that memories of the traumatic *auto de fe* in which he had participated as a child made him wary of relinquishing his daughter to the church. Nevertheless, upon her recovery Teresa snuck out of the house and made her way to the Carmelite convent of La Encarnación (*CWST* 1, *Life* 4:1–11). The chapter of her memoir devoted to the incident depicts her as a cunning, strong-willed girl who from a young age knew how to get her own way, even in the face of opposition. Similarly, letters written years later attest to both her steadfastness and her ability to strategize, maneuver, and sweet-talk her superiors. Teresa had found the Augustinian convent overly strict. While not unusually lax by existing standards, Encarnación was less austere. The Encarnación sisters practiced the relaxed or mitigated rule, which allowed nuns to retain their possessions, even receiving the revenues from property and other sources. Some maintained an active social life, entertaining guests at the grille and leaving the premises for meals.

Early modern religious houses mirrored the stratified society of the outside world, with its concern for social class, ethnicity, and honor. Bilinkoff points out that "social differences, coupled with the pressures of rapid demographic expansion between 1540 and 1560, periodically produced bitter social conflicts" in convents (*Avila* 113). Some prestigious convents attracted whole clans of wealthy, aristocratic women—sisters, cousins, aunts, and nieces, or widowed mothers and their daughters. These women were addressed as *doña* and enjoyed the privileges of their caste. Often they entered with servants and slaves, occupied elaborate cells, ate specially prepared meals off fine china, and slept in feather beds.[18] Noblewomen often formed cliques, snubbing their lower-born sisters. Sometimes convent life degenerated into a morass of shifting alliances and political maneuverings. Most orders had a two-tier system: dowered, black-veiled nuns performed administrative duties and choir recitations, while poorer, white-veiled nuns performed manual labor.

Teresa had money and connections. Her father's *pleito* guaranteed she would be treated like a lady, and indeed, prior to 1562, she signed her letters "Doña Teresa de Ahumada." Her father provided twenty-five *fanegas* of grain or two hundred gold ducats a year and paid her entrance and profession costs. In addition, as a respected cloth merchant, he endowed her with a mattress and bedspread, blankets, sheets, a rug, habits, and cloaks (Bilinkoff, *Avila* 114). Raised in a materialist world, Teresa knew the value of things. Even though she would later found convents where austerity was cherished, her letters show she was a shrewd businesswoman able to negotiate a property contract and raise funds. At Encarnación she occupied a large, two-level apartment, where her sister Juana would eventually live with her as a boarder.

In Teresa's day women entered convents for a variety of reasons. Of course, many were motivated by a sincere desire to serve God, but others were forced by circumstance to take the veil. Even wealthy families were often unwilling to provide costly marriage dowries for more than one daughter. The practice of limiting marriage dowries to one daughter was so common that early in the seventeenth century the Junta of Reform noted: "It has become so much the usage in our Spain for parents to give all their property to one daughter in order to marry her advantageously that they leave the others without any dowry" (Qtd. Casey 200). These families placed daughters not destined for marriage in convents, sometimes at the age of four or five years old, where the required dowry was much lower. Girls encloistered from childhood professed without ever having the opportunity to marry. Their celibacy was crucial to the economic system, since it helped to maintain intact the family's patrimony. (Due to the laws of primogeniture, which stipulated that only the eldest son inherit family land, younger sons were also often forced to take vows.) In addition, the illegitimate daughters of noblemen, widows, deflowered (and therefore un-marriageable) girls, and orphans sought refuge in religious houses. In addition to postulants, convents also took in boarders.

Some women opted for the convent as an alternative to married life, preferring the cell to the risks of childbirth or submission to a husband. As in medieval Europe, convents in sixteenth-century Spain offered women opportunities unavailable to them in secular society.[19] They governed and performed administrative duties, kept accounts, voted in convent elections, disciplined their peers, and taught novices. Some were nurses and phar-macists. Some were choir mistresses, composers, or painters. Some even became pioneers who left Spain to establish convents in the colonies.[20] For women wishing to devote themselves to intellectual pursuits, the convent was usually the only option. Margaret King notes that "nuns made up a great fraction of educated women, and cloistered women were dispropor-tionately literate" (82). Some convents became veritable cultural centers. The exceptionally accomplished seventeenth-century Mexican nun, Sor Juana Inés de la Cruz, was a poet, scientist, and theologian until church authorities put a stop to her activities.

At the time Teresa professed at Encarnación, on 2 November 1536, the place was overflowing. About two hundred women, including servants and nuns' relatives, were living in a house built for less than half that number. Although Encarnación imposed fasting, abstinence, and periods of silence, no time was allotted for mental prayer. Instead, the sisters practiced ritual-ized vocal (recited) prayer. Because the convent was teeming, nuns were encouraged to take meals with their families and accept food gifts from visitors. Bilinkoff notes that "economic resources at la Encarnación be-came so strained that as many as fifty nuns at a time would live away from the convent" (*Avila* 115). Teresa participated enthusiastically in the con-vent's social life but later would come to see this freedom as detrimental to her spiritual development (*CWST* 1, *Life* 7:3).

Shortly after her profession, Teresa once again fell ill. She had been sickly since girlhood and would have problems all her life, which helps to explain the preoccupation she shows in her letters with her own and her friends' health. The exact nature of her infirmity is unknown, but she men-tions fainting spells, chest pain, and "many other illnesses all together" (*CWST* 1, *Life* 4:5). Since local doctors were unable to cure her, her father decided to send her to a famous healer in the town of Becedas, a village in the foothills of the Gredos Mountains, in the province of Ávila.

On her way she spent some time with her Uncle Pedro, who lent her a copy of Osuna's *Third Spiritual Alphabet*, which introduced her to the *devotio moderna*, in particular recollection and mental prayer: "I did not know how to proceed in prayer or how to be recollected. And so I was very happy with this book and resolved to follow that path with all my strength. . . . I began to take time out for solitude, to confess frequently, and to follow that path, taking the book for my master" (*CWST* 1, *Life* 4:7).[21] The prayer of *recogimiento* (recollection), practiced by Observant Franciscans since about 1470, stressed interiority and quiet.[22] Although *recogimiento* was greatly appreciated by Spain's spiritually advanced elite prior to 1520, after the Protestant Reformation the church began to view spiritual illumination unmediated by clergy or sacraments as a menace to orthodoxy—a situation that would greatly impact Teresa's career.

The healer in Becedas turned out to be a quack, and after three months Don Alonso brought Teresa back home to Ávila. She was so ill she could hardly bear the pain: "Sometimes it seemed that sharp teeth were biting into me, so much so that it was feared I had rabies" (*CWST* 1, *Life* 4:7). She fell into a coma that lasted four days. According to her description in *Life*, everyone except her father thought she was dead. The nuns created a *capilla ardiente*, a funeral chamber filled with burning candles, and prepared her for burial. One can only imagine their shock when Teresa opened her eyes and chided them for bringing her back from the other side! It is possible that Teresa includes this episode in *Life* in order to validate her spiritual authority: release from death evokes the stories of Lazarus and even Christ, and the prominence she gives the story in her memoir suggests a typological significance.[23] This, of course, does not invalidate the incident. Teresa was chronically ill throughout her life, and so the story is quite plausible.

When she was well enough, she returned to Encarnación, but instead of following the spiritual path to which Osuna had drawn her, she once again became involved in convent social life and worldly affairs, going "from pastime to pastime, from vanity to vanity, from one occasion to another" (*CWST* 1, *Life* 7:1). However, one day, when engaged in frivolous conversations with another nun, Teresa saw Christ looking at her "with great severity," a vision that left her "frightened and disturbed" (*CWST* 1, *Life* 7:6). Still, she continued to suffer long periods of "aridity" during which she was unable to pray. Although she had introduced her father to mental prayer—a practice favored by many *conversos*, who may have felt more comfortable praying alone in silence than in church—she herself often felt "lost" (*CWST* 1, *Life* 7:13).[24] This was a period of spiritual struggle for Teresa. By nature a sociable person, she felt drawn to the communal give-and-take of convent life at the same time she longed to withdraw in order to experience the kind of intimate dialogue with God Osuna described.

Her father's death in 1543 jolted Teresa into a period of activity. Don Alonso made Teresa coexecutor of his will, forcing her to put her managerial skills to work. Medwick writes: "Whether or not he appreciated Teresa's talents for prayer, Alonso had correctly assessed her talent for administration" (36). Teresa's coexecutor was Martín de Guzmán, her sister María's husband, who immediately filed claims on his wife's behalf against Don Alonso's already heavily indebted estate. Although we have no correspondence from this period, the claims against her father's assets plunged Teresa back into the world of litigation and paperwork she had known as a child. She wrote to two of her brothers in the colonies, coaxing them to relinquish their inheritance in favor of María. Eventually, the case went to court, and most of the remainder of the estate was lost to lawyers (Medwick 36). The episode provided Teresa with decision-making experience that would prove invaluable once the reform got under way.

It is not surprising that our first extant letter of Teresa's is a piece of business correspondence. On 12 August 1546 she wrote to Alonso Venegrilla, who attended to the pigeon house that the Cepeda-Ahumada family owned in Gotarrendura, just north of Ávila, asking him to advance money for ten bushels of wheat to be delivered by a certain Santos García and promising reimbursement from her brother-in-law Martín de Guzmán. Although seemingly a trivial affair, the letter provides an inkling of the kind of administrator Teresa would become: She stayed on top of things. She was a stickler for detail, managing her father's property as attentively as she would later run convents. And she was concerned about money. Although Teresa wrote many personal letters, most of her correspondence is devoted to business—founding, funding, and staffing convents, securing documents, petitioning authorities, and dealing with attacks from enemies of the reform.

In 1553 Teresa's younger sister Juana married Juan de Ovalle in Alba de Tormes. Don Alonso was no longer around to negotiate the marriage contract, and Teresa's brothers were overseas in the New World, where Antonio had died fighting Indians seven years earlier. Once again, Teresa had to assume the role of administrative head of the family. Juana had lived with her at the convent as a *doncella de piso* for about ten years after the death of their father and apparently met Don Juan at the grille. The suitor was a distant relative by marriage; his brother Gonzalo was the husband of one of the daughters of Pedro de Cepeda, their uncle. The Ovalles were not wealthy, and Don Juan's lack of income could have been a problem. However, Teresa saw to it that the elder Ovalle gave Juan a piece of property and an allowance.

But Teresa was not concerned exclusively with worldly matters; during this period her supernatural experiences intensified. In 1554 she had a powerful vision that initiated what came to be known as her "reconversion."[25] One day as she was entering the convent oratory, her eyes came to rest on a statue of the wounded Christ, an *ecce homo* someone had brought in for a special celebration. Distressed at the Savior's suffering, Teresa fell into a fit of sobbing: "Beseeching Him to strengthen me once and for all that I might not offend Him, I threw myself down before Him with the greatest outpouring of tears." (*CWST* 1, *Life* 9:2). After this incident, which marked the beginning of a profound spiritual awakening, Teresa was at last able to practice mental prayer effectively and eventually to reach the highest plane of mystical experience.[26] About 1557 she began to receive locutions, the first of which she describes in the following passage: "Once . . . while reciting the Hours, I came to the verse that says: *Justus es, Domine, and Your judgments*. . . . While I was thinking that You justly permit that there be many . . . who are very good servants of Yours and yet do not receive these gifts and favors You grant me because of what I am, You answered me, Lord: 'Serve me, and don't bother about such things.' This was the first locution I heard You speak to me, and so I was very frightened" (*CWST* 1, *Life* 19:9).[27] She began to experience raptures and visions, sometimes seeing Christ, the Virgin, or even the Devil. But not all her confessors were receptive. She was convinced her experiences came from God, but others dismissed them as inauthentic or even demonic. By now, Teresa was a woman in her mid-forties with some twenty years of experience as a nun, yet learned men refused to take her seriously. She felt isolated: "I had no one with whom to speak. They were all against me; some, it seemed, made fun of me when I spoke of the matter, as though I were inventing it; others said that my experience was clearly from the devil" (*CWST* 1, *Life* 25:15). It was the arrival of the Jesuits in Ávila that changed everything.

At Encarnación Teresa had become friends with Doña Guiomar de Ulloa, a beautiful, rich, and well-connected widow who had two daughters at the convent. Teresa began to leave Encarnación to spend time with Doña Guiomar at her palace, where the lively, devout widow surrounded herself with Ávila's spiritual avant-garde, men and women who were interested in the sophisticated prayer practices—meditation, recollection—that the authorities increasingly considered suspect. Among her friends were Gaspar Daza, Francisco de Salcedo, and Juan de Ávila, all of whom would become Teresa's spiritual guides. Insecure about her supernatural experiences, Teresa discussed them with Daza and Salcedo, who wound up causing her considerable grief by taking the position that her raptures were caused by the devil.

In 1554, the same year that Doña Guiomar was widowed, the Society of Jesus started the *colegio* (school) of San Gil in Ávila, near the Ulloa palace. Founded by Ignatius of Loyola in 1540, the new order stressed public preaching, missionary work, service to the poor, and education. The importance the Society gave to mental prayer and examination of conscience coincided with the ideas being advanced by Ávila's cutting-edge spiritual thinkers, and Doña Guiomar not only began to confess with a Jesuit but encouraged Teresa to do the same. Diego de Cetina, Teresa's first Jesuit confessor, was a young man of about twenty-four, recently graduated from the University of Salamanca and with the Society for only three years. In spite of his youth, Teresa took his spiritual direction seriously. Cetina encouraged her to continue practicing mental prayer and to meditate on the humanity of Christ. He probably also introduced her to the *Spiritual Exercises*, a system of prayer devised by Ignatius of Loyola that calls on the exercitant to engage the senses to recreate mentally scenes from Scripture in order to enter into an intimate dialogue with Christ.[28] It was perhaps the first time that any confessor had really taken Teresa seriously.[29] However, Cetina lacked the authority to reassure Teresa of the authenticity of her experiences. When Francisco de Borja visited Ávila later that year for the official opening of San Gil, Teresa's Jesuit friends arranged for him to examine her.

Borja, of the Spanish-Italian Borgia family, had once been one of the most powerful men in Spain and would eventually become father general of the Jesuit order.[30] He reassured Teresa that "the Spirit of God" was working in her and that she should not try to resist her supernatural experiences but instead "meditate on an event from Christ's Passion" (*CWST* 1, *Life* 24:3). Borja was a man of authority, and his favorable findings undoubtedly increased Teresa's credibility among other Jesuits. After Cetina fell ill, Doña Guiomar introduced Teresa to her own confessor, Juan de Prádanos (1526-1597), also of the Society of Jesus. At twenty-six or twenty-seven, he was a few years older than Cetina, although they had both been in the seminary at the same time. Prádanos turned out to be an excellent spiritual guide. Teresa writes that under his direction she made great progress.

Around this time she experienced her first rapture. Prádanos had told her to recite the hymn *Veni Creator*: "One day, having spent a long time in prayer and begging the Lord to help me please Him in all things, I began the hymn; while saying it, a rapture came upon me so suddenly that it almost carried me out of myself. It was something I could not doubt, because it was very obvious. It was the first time the Lord granted me this favor of rapture. I heard these words: 'No longer do I want you to converse with men but with angels.' This experience terrified me because the movement of the soul was powerful and these words were spoken to me deep within the spirit" (*CWST* 1, *Life* 24:5). This locution, she goes on to explain, gave her the strength to put service to God before all other things and to cultivate detachment from worldly affairs.

In one of her most famous visions, Teresa saw a small, beautiful angel with his face all aflame: "I saw in his hands a large golden dart and at the end of the iron tip there appeared to be a little fire. It seemed to me that this angel plunged the dart several times into my heart and that it reached deep within me. When he drew it out, I thought he was carrying off with him the deepest part of me; and he left me all on fire with great love of God" (*CWST* 1, *Life* 30:13). This "wounding," often referred to as the Transverberation, was immortalized by Gianlorenzo Bernini in his statue

Saint Teresa in Ecstasy, which is suspended in a niche in the Church of Santa Maria de la Vittoria in Rome.[31]

As these mystical occurrences became more frequent and intense, Teresa's fame spread. Many admired her heightened spirituality, but others were skeptical. By mid-century, mistrust of ecstatics was growing. With the spread of Protestantism, the institutional church took a stand against the notion of personal, unmediated religious experience. The concept that through recollection one could enter into an interior darkness in which one might experience God's light smacked of *alumbradismo* (Illuminism), a term applied to a variety of spiritual movements that stressed a personal relationship with the divine and taught that spiritual enlightenment came directly from God. Illuminist groups met in homes, where prayer sessions were sometimes led by laypersons, even women. The movement's emphasis on interiority rather than ritual made it popular among Observant Franciscans and *conversos*. All of these factors—the belief that an individual could enjoy a personal relationship with God without the involvement of clergy, the acceptance of lay leadership, and the participation of women and *conversos*—made Illuminism anathema. The first trials against *alumbrados* were held in 1524 and 1525, and *alumbradismo* soon became a primary target of the Inquisition. By the time Philip II ascended to the throne in 1556, "Illuminism had become synonymous with Lutheranism, a term used in Spain to refer not specifically to Protestantism but generally to any religious belief or practice perceived to undermine the authority of the Roman Catholic Church, including various forms of Erasmian humanism, mysticism, and charismatic movements" (Slade, *St. Teresa* 18). Furthermore, some Illuminists stressed interiority over charitable acts, a position akin to the Lutheran doctrine of justification by faith alone.[32]

The church's attitude toward female mystics exacerbated the situation. The sixteenth century saw a burgeoning of women claiming to have supernatural experiences. In spite the growing disfavor with Erasmus of Rotterdam in the church, the Spanish translation of his *Modus orandi*, published in 1546, achieved great popularity in Spanish convents. The book reflected some of the most radical currents in reformist thought, especially its espousal of mental prayer to achieve an intimate dialogue with God.[33] It appealed to a wide range of readers, in particular to nuns avid to experience the delights of mystical union. So frequent were women's claims to ecstasy that Marcel Bataillon speaks of a kind of mystical epidemic in Spanish convents. However, upon investigation many of the raptures reported by female religious were found to be spurious. It was commonly believed that women were hysterical by nature (*hysterikós* means "related to the uterus" in Greek), and the ecclesiastical establishment saw religious ecstasy in women as the product of mental instability. The church's stand, argues Gillian Ahlgren, undermined women's religious authority: "Since the source of women's authority was external revelation or reflection on experience, and since it rested on a charismatic gift, it had to be examined for validity. As attitudes toward revelation changed, so inevitably did the authority of women's voices" (*Teresa de Ávila* 21). The case of Magdalena de la Cruz, famous in Teresa's day, gave clerics ammunition against female mystics. Magdalena, an abbess of the Order of Poor Clares, was known for her miracles and prophesies.[34] However, on 1 January 1544 inquisitors convinced Magdalena to confess that her raptures were specious and her clairvoyance the result of a pact with the devil. As a result, Magdalena was imprisoned and demoted to the lowest position in her order. The story scandalized all of Spanish society, and from then on the example of Magdalena loomed over every claim to extraordinary religious experience.

Another factor jeopardous to Teresa was her *converso* background. King Philip II was radically hostile to New Christians. According to Slade, "he expressed, and undoubtedly helped to shape, the national sentiment when he attributed all heresies, in effect all his political problems in consolidating the Spanish empire, to *conversos*" (*St. Teresa of Avila* 20). As a result, the Inquisition was suspicious of all converted Jews. Although we cannot know how widely Teresa's ethnic background was known in ecclesiastical circles, in mid-sixteenth-century Ávila there were certainly people who remembered her father's and uncles' *pleito de hidalguía*.

Late in 1558 Juan de Prádanos fell ill, and Teresa found herself in the care of Baltasar Álvarez, a young, insecure Jesuit confessor apprehensive of displeasing his superiors. Daza and Salcedo had spread gossip alleging the demonic origins of Teresa's visions, and since failure to deal with a possessed penitent would reflect badly on her confessor, Álvarez, apprehensive of erring on the side of imprudence, subjected her to terrible mortifications. When the renowned mystic and holy man Pedro de Alcántara examined Teresa and reassured Álvarez that her visions came from God, the young Jesuit desisted for a while. However, Teresa herself had begun to fear her mystical experiences were demonic in origin. She decided to consult the Dominicans at the Royal Monastery of Saint Thomas, where she knew the subprior, García de Toledo. Through García she met the highly respected theologian Pedro Ibáñez. After examining her, Ibáñez wrote a memorandum in 1560 on the state of Teresa's soul in which he concluded that she was not possessed by the devil but blessed with "an admirable clarity of understanding, and an illumination of the things of God." (Qtd. Walsh 167).

That was not the end of Teresa's worries, however. Teresa was ill at ease at Encarnación, not only because some nuns resented her reputation as a holy woman and mystic but also because no time was allotted for mental prayer. In conjunction with a close-knit group of friends that included María de Ocampo, the daughter of her cousin Diego de Cepeda, Teresa came up with a radical solution: She would abandon the convent she had inhabited for some twenty-five years and found a new one where women could strive for spiritual perfection. At first she wavered, but then came to believe that God himself wanted this new convent: "One day after Communion, His Majesty earnestly commanded me to strive for this new monastery with all my powers, and He made great promises that it would be founded and that He would be highly served in it. He said it should be called St. Joseph and that this saint would keep watch over us at one door, and our Lady at the other" (*CWST* 1, *Life* 32:10). After that initial communication, Teresa writes, the Lord spoke to her often about the new monastery, until eventually she became convinced.

The convent she envisioned would adhere to the primitive or unmitigated Carmelite rule. The nuns would devote themselves to prayer and observe strict poverty, relying on alms and on the fruits of their own labor. They would remain cloistered, neither leaving for visits nor receiving guests, except for family members and certain persons known to be holy. They would live in silence, shunning the cliques and gossip that corrupted Encarnación. Teresa envisioned an egalitarian convent in which titles— even *doña*—would be banned. She would not do background checks on her nuns to determine whether or not they were of *converso* background. Although she would accept dowries, no worthy candidate would be turned away for lack of money. (However, she would not abandon the customary two-tiered system of black-veiled and white-veiled nuns.)[35] Slade notes that Teresa's abolition of class and ethnic distinctions constituted a significant act of resistance against social norms: "Teresa . . . intended and indeed effected social reforms—specifically, increasing autonomy for women and integrating *conversos* . . . into Spanish society" ("Social Reformer" 91). The nuns would be called Discalced (Barefoot) Carmelites to signify their commitment to poverty and austerity, although out of modesty they would wear stockings and sandals. In adopting this abstemious, structured lifestyle, Teresa was following the tradition of monastic reform of previous centuries. She had an excellent model in Pedro de Alcántara, who had initiated a similar reform among the Franciscans in 1540 for the purpose of restoring the asceticism embraced by the order's founder, Saint Francis of Assisi.

At a time when the church was challenged not only by tepid religious practice but also by encroaching Protestantism, Teresa was anxious to play an active role in the defense of the faith.[36] Bilinkoff argues that Teresa "deeply envied male priests" because they had the freedom to preach and proselytize. She saw founding convents as a means of achieving an apostolate that she had long yearned for but, as a woman, had been denied ("Woman" 296). Slade points out that Teresa aspired to model herself after Mary Magdalene, whom she saw as an apostle working tirelessly to bring Christ souls ("Social Reformer" 95). On several occasions Teresa mentions her distress over the inroads Protestants were making in France and elsewhere. After hearing about the Huguenots' destruction of churches in France, she experienced a terrifying vision of hell: "From this experience also flow the great impulses to help souls and the extraordinary pain that is caused me by the many that are condemned (especially the Lutherans, for they were through baptism members of the Church)" (*CWST* 1, *Life* 32:6).[37] She also agonized over the unbaptized Indians in the Americas.

The new convents enabled women to do their part in remedying the situation, for by praying constantly they contributed not only to their own spiritual renewal but to the revitalization of the church. Thus, Teresa saw the reform as a form of spiritual activism. "If male clerics engaged in active apostolates, Discalced Carmelite nuns could exercise an apostolate of prayer," writes Bilinkoff ("Teresa of Jesús" 174). Teresa clearly believed that women had both a duty and a right to take an active role in the defense of the faith. In the sixteenth century convents were often supported by wealthy patrons who sometimes demanded that nuns pray in perpetuity for their families. Teresa attempted to avoid accepting patronage, thereby freeing her nuns to pray for the church as a whole, not just for wealthy patrons.

However, it would be erroneous to assume that Teresa's primary motivation in founding convents was to combat Protestantism and paganism. In her letters, she hardly mentions "Lutherans" and Indians. Although, as we shall see in Chapter 5, she wrote to her prioresses extensively about spiritual matters, instructing them on how to monitor their charges' prayer lives, she did not urge them to order nuns to pray for heretics. She seems much more concerned with the nuns' personal spiritual development, the authenticity of their experiences, and their access to appropriate confessors. For Teresa, founding convents and writing manuals such as *Way of Perfection* and *The Interior Castle* were part of the same enterprise: to guide souls—especially her nuns' souls—on their spiritual journey.

In spite of Teresa's efforts to keep her first foundation secret, word soon got out: "Hardly had the knowledge of it begun to spread throughout the city when the great persecution that cannot be briefly described came upon us: gossip, derision, saying that it was foolishness" (*CWST* 1, *Life* 32:14). Outcry came from all sides. The Encarnación nuns were insulted that Teresa wanted to found a new, stricter convent. Wasn't her old convent good enough? Her notion that traditional beliefs about honor and lineage were incompatible with true spirituality irritated these nuns, some of whom were from the noblest families in Ávila. The Carmelite authorities were appalled at her audacity in going over their heads. Doña Guiomar, in great secrecy and in her own name, had applied to Rome for authorization to found San José in the primitive rule under the jurisdiction of the Bishop of Ávila rather than the Carmelite provincial, Ángel de Salazar. Church officials were indignant at her outrageous display of independence, and Teresa was besieged by doubts: "The devil stirred up within me a spiritual battle. . . . He brought doubts to my mind about whether what I had done was wrong; whether I had gone against obedience in having made the foundation without my provincial's orders" (*CWST* 1, *Life* 36:7). She began to wonder if the nuns would be happy living in austerity. "What if they lacked food?" she asked herself (*CWST* 1, *Life* 36:7). Often she wavered.

The greatest opposition came from the city itself. Teresa's decision to found in poverty produced a knotty situation. At a time when outward displays of piety brought benefactors prestige and, supposedly, admission into heaven, it was common for rich patrons to finance religious foundations. Unsurprisingly, sponsors expected to have something to say about the running of the convents they backed. Teresa was reluctant to accept funding from anyone who might later make demands on her. Furthermore, she believed that the new convent would be better off depending on alms than on a sponsor. She actually did not expect her nuns to starve. In fact, she writes in her 1565 book *The Way of Perfection* that she desired that nothing should be lacking in her convents (*CWST* 2, 1:1). She had seen the scarcity of food at Encarnación, and she knew that patrons could prove unreliable or else die without providing for the institutions they had supported. But her refusal to accept a sponsor alarmed the citizenry. Local religious orders and town leaders complained that there were already too many convents in Ávila dependent on insufficient alms.

Ángel de Salazar set out to derail the plan. An opportunity to absent Teresa from Ávila presented itself when Doña Luisa de la Cerda, daughter of the second duke of Medinaceli, lost her husband. The duchess had heard of Teresa and was curious about her. Doña Luisa's children contacted Salazar to arrange for Teresa to visit and comfort the distraught widow at her Toledo palace. The plan ultimately worked in Teresa's favor, however. Apprehensive that Teresa's raptures would provoke an inquisitional investigation, García de Toledo had instructed her to compose a spiritual memoir or *vida* in order to demonstrate the orthodoxy of her prayer practices and justify the reform. Teresa's months-long interlude at Doña Luisa's gave her time to write. Furthermore, the powerful contacts Teresa made in Toledo would later be useful.

Once back in Ávila, Teresa arranged to have her brother-in-law, Juan de Ovalle, purchase a small house in the San Roque district, outside the city's wall, that workmen secretly transformed into a tiny convent. Still, the battles continued. At last she received permission to found the convent, provided it had a patron. Exhausted from battling with the town elders, Teresa wavered: "Finally they came to agree that if it had an income they would . . . let the foundation continue. I was already so wearied of seeing the hardship of all those who were helping me, more so than in seeing my own, that it didn't seem to be a bad idea to have an income until our adversaries quieted down, and then give it up afterward. At other times, wretched and imperfect as I am, I thought that perhaps the Lord wanted this since we couldn't succeed without it; I was disposed to accept the compromise" (*CWST* 1, *Life* 36:19). However, a vision of the mystic Pedro de Alcántara, who had recently died, convinced Teresa that she should not give in.

The Carmel of San José opened its doors on 24 August 1562, with a population of four novices. Doña Teresa de Ahumada dropped her honorific and took the name Teresa de Jesús. She was not permitted to move into the new convent immediately, but eventually she received permission to take her place among its first inhabitants. She was on her way to becoming the mother foundress of a new order.

One of Teresa's first extant letters concerns the little hermitages, or huts, she had constructed in the garden of San José. Addressed to "The Lords of the Town Council" in Ávila, the letter defends the construction of the hermitages, which were to serve as retreats where the sisters could retire and pray. Lázaro Dávila, the city water inspector, had brought suit against the convent, claiming that the hermitages would cast shadows on nearby fountains, chilling them and freezing the municipal water supply in the winter. Teresa's tone is diffident: "Since we received information that the little hermitages constructed on our property would cause no damage to the city's water ways, and the need was very great, we never thought your honors would be disturbed" (*Letters I*, 5 December 1563:3). She expresses her distress at having displeased the councilmen and promises to provide any documentation their lawyers demand to show that she has proceeded in good faith. She argues that the nuns find great consolation in the hermitages and that to remove them would cause distress. In addition, she pledges to pray for Ávila. However, her pleas fell on deaf ears, and she was forced to remove the hermitages. This letter shows that from the very beginning of her career as a reformer, Teresa had to use her letter-writing skills to advance her cause. Although her entreaty to the town council was unsuccessful, with time letters would become one of her most effective instruments of reform.

From Fundadora to Santa Teresa

Teresa remained in Ávila for five years following the founding of San José in 1562. In 1566 she completed the first and probably the second version of *Way of Perfection*, a guide to prayer written for the San José sisters. During the spring of 1567, the prior general Giovanni Battista Rossi, known in Spain as Rubeo, made an official visitation in Ávila. He was anxious to meet Teresa, about whom he had heard. At her urging, Rubeo granted permission to found more Discalced Carmelite convents in Castile. Teresa also requested his consent to found friaries, since she knew that to gain respect and authority for her movement, she needed to include men. Furthermore, the nuns would need confessors trained in the Discalced charism. Rubeo authorized two friaries, provided they were not in Andalusia. The reason for this exclusion is clear. The Andalusian Carmelite friars, notorious for their rowdy behavior, were adamantly opposed to reform. Rubeo had tried unsuccessfully to rein in these ruffians, and he knew that establishing Discalced houses in the south would only provoke them further. In the meantime, Teresa inaugurated a second Carmel in Medina del Campo, where she met her future collaborator Juan de la Cruz (hereafter identified by his English name, John of the Cross).

Teresa made her next foundation in Malagón, on the estate of Doña Luisa de la Cerda. Although Teresa had been determined not to accept patrons, social and financial considerations caused her to change her mind. Doña Luisa was anxious to have a convent on her property, and Teresa was indebted to her for her support of the reform. Furthermore, the town was too small to sustain an unsubsidized convent, and, as Teresa explains in *Foundations*, her advisors informed her that "since the holy Council had given permission to have an income, I shouldn't, because of my own opinion, fail to found a monastery where God could be so much served" (*CWST* 3, *Foundations* 9:4). Teresa made other modifications as well. Although the Constitutions stipulated that nuns were to eat meat only once a week, Teresa changed the rule, since fish was hard to come by in the area. Her flexibility in these matters demonstrates a pragmatism that would serve her well in her career as foundress, although it provided ammunition for detractors who accused her of obeying the rules only when it suited her. The following year, in Valladolid, where she made her next foundation, Teresa instructed John of the Cross about the Discalced way of life, and by the end of 1568 he and Antonio de Heredia had founded the first male Discalced convent in Duruelos.

Through Luisa de la Cerda, Teresa met two women who would have a significant impact on her life. One, María de Salazar, would profess at Malagón as María de San José and go on to become one of Teresa's most trusted friends. The other, Ana de Mendoza, princess of Eboli, would become one of her most vicious enemies. Doña Ana was the wife of the powerful Ruy Gómez de Silva, advisor to King Philip II. Arrogant and irascible, she insisted on having not only a nunnery but also a friary on her property in Pastrana. Although Teresa had serious misgivings, in June and July 1569 foundations for nuns and friars respectively were made in Pastrana. The princess also persuaded Teresa to let her read *Life*, promising not to show it to anyone. However, the treacherous Ana not only shared the book with her friends, but also cruelly ridiculed its contents.

Two other foundations followed Pastrana in quick succession: Salamanca (1570) and Alba de Tormes (1571). These accomplishments did not go unnoticed. Opposition was growing among influential ecclesiastics who resented Teresa's success. For a woman, she displayed extraordinary independence and administrative ability, and some thought she overstepped the limits of decorum or were suspicious of the kind of contemplative spirituality she was fomenting in her convents. Furthermore, the reform was producing tensions within the order. To take her out of circulation, Ángel de Salazar encouraged the apostolic visitator, Pedro Fernández, to name Teresa prioress of Encarnación, the convent she had left eight years before. This would be a difficult job because many of the Encarnación nuns still harbored hostility toward her. Gradually, however, using tact and common sense, she won over her former enemies. During her three years as prioress she introduced many reforms and named two Carmelite friars, John of the Cross and Germán de San Matías, as the nuns' confessors. She also began writing *Foundations*.

But Ana de Mendoza was not done with her. In 1573 the princess was widowed and decided to enter the Pastrana convent along with her mother and servants. Doña Ana had no intention of obeying the rules of the order and immediately insisted on special treatment. Her arrogance greatly irritated the nuns, and she clashed repeatedly with Isabel de Santo Domingo, the prioress. Eventually she left the convent but continued to meddle in the nuns' affairs, once suppressing their revenue—which amounted to starving them—in order to whip them into submission. In 1574, Teresa received permission to found a convent in Segovia and then, finally, to leave Encarnación definitively. When she heard that the princess was making their lives unbearable, she ordered the Pastrana nuns to abandon their convent. During the night of April 6–7 the women stole out of their house and made their way to Segovia, where Teresa received them in her new foundation. However, Doña Ana was not one to be crossed. She took vengeance by denouncing Teresa's *Life* to the Valladolid Inquisition.[38]

During this period Teresa began writing letters in earnest. From the year 1571 only seven extant letters remain, from 1572 there are nine, from 1573 there are ten, but from 1574 there are twenty-two. These are the years during which Teresa tried to run Encarnación while directing the reform from afar. After her release from Encarnación, she continued to write constantly, as the administrative demands of the reform became more complex and the political situation thornier. The year 1575 was a watershed for Teresa. On February 24 she founded a new convent in Beas, which she believed to be outside of Andalusia, for she writes, "if I had known that it was in Andalusia, I would by no means have gone" (*CWST* 3, *Foundations* 24:4). However, as it turned out, although Beas was under the civil jurisdiction of Castile, it was under the ecclesiastical jurisdiction of Cartagena, in Andalusia. In April, Jerónimo Gracián, a young Carmelite thirty years her junior, went to visit her, and it was this meeting, not the foundation, that would change the course of the reform.

Gracián was clearly a young man with promise. Teresa was immediately taken with his charm and reformist zeal, and she came to see him as the future leader of the male branch of the order. Shortly after his profession in 1573 he was named visitor of the Carmelites of the observance in Andalusia. Since all Carmelites were technically observants, it was in this capacity that he found himself with Teresa in Beas.[39] Teresa appreciated Gracian's gentle approach to guiding nuns, so different from the rigorous asceticism promoted by some reformers. She describes him in *Foundations* as "a man of much learning, intelligence and modesty, along with other great virtues" (*CWST* 3, 23:1). She was so taken with him that that she made a vow of obedience to him. He, in turn, promised to consult her on all issues pertaining to the reform.[40]

But Gracián was something of a hothead, and he would soon steer Teresa into a hornets' nest. As apostolic visitor, his duty was to pacify the unruly Andalusian friaries. Prodded by his companion Fray Ambrosio Mariano, he had founded a Discalced monastery at Almodóvar del Campo, thereby overstepping his authority, since his job was to enforce reforms in existing houses, not establish new ones. The provincial, Ángel de Salazar, ordered Gracián and Mariano back to Pastrana, but instead they went to Seville, where Gracián claimed to have personal business. There, he infuriated Discalced and Calced alike by placing some Discalced novices in a Calced monastery. He then went on to establish new monasteries in Andalusia, disregarding Rubeo's express order that no further foundations be made in the south. It was Gracián who convinced Teresa to found in Seville in violation of Rubeo's prohibition.[41]

Teresa explains simply that Gracián thought "that a foundation in Seville would render great service to God" and would be "very easy, for some well-to-do people had asked him and were able and wealthy enough to provide a house at once" (*CWST* 3, *Foundations* 24:4). Although she says she had "very serious reasons against going to Seville," Gracián was her superior, so she "immediately submitted" (*CWST* 3, *Foundations* 24:4). However, we shall see in Chapter 4 that Teresa had other options. If she agreed to obey Gracián, it could have been because his directive coincided with her own desire to spread the reform.

Whatever her reasons, Teresa did found in Seville. She describes in *Foundations* the grueling trip in the Andalusian heat and her disappointment with Fray Mariano's botched arrangements (*CWST* 3, 24:14). (He had failed to obtain a license from the archbishop.) In spite of the setbacks, on 26 May 1575 she inaugurated the Seville Carmel and appointed María de San José its prioress. Later that summer, her brother Lorenzo returned from the New World. She had depended on his generosity to finance the convent of San José in Ávila, and now, once again, he lent his assistance. However, things soon took a turn for the worse. A disgruntled nun accused Teresa and others of unorthodox spiritual practices. Worse still, the Carmelite authorities were enraged at her disobedience. Ángel de Salazar went so far as to excommunicate her, although the excommunication was short-lived. At the chapter meeting held in Piacenza, Italy, it was decided to put an end to the reform. Teresa was to choose a convent in Castile and stay there, making no further foundations.

Teresa decided to go to Toledo, and on 28 May 1576 she left Seville with her brother and his family, arriving about a month later. Although she said that Rubeo had done her a favor because she was tired and needed a rest, she was chafing. She wrote in *Foundations*, "Before I came back from Seville, a general chapter was held. In a general chapter one would think they would be concerned about the expansion of the order, but instead the definitory gave me a command not merely to make no more foundations but not to leave the house in which I chose to reside, which would be a kind of prison, for there is no nun who for necessary matters pertaining to the good of the order cannot be ordered by the provincial to go from one place to the other, I mean from one monastery to another" (*CWST* 3, *Foundations* 27:20). She clearly resented this forced enclosure, since she needed to travel for the good of the reform. Her life's work seemed to be unraveling.

Teresa began a period of intense letter-writing. Immobilized by the Piacenza directive, she had to lead the reform and combat its enemies long-distance. At the same time that she began her masterpiece, *The Interior Castle*, Teresa was writing letters—to ecclesiastical authorities, prioresses, and male collaborators—late into the night. There are twenty-one extant letters from 1575, seventy from 1576, fifty from 1577, and fifty-six from 1578. Tensions between the Calced and Discalced were intensifying. The Calced had circulated rumors about Gracián's supposed sexual improprieties with María de San José and others, including Teresa herself, and threats had been made against his life. Teresa took the audacious step of writing directly to the king protesting Gracián's mistreatment by the Calced, or "friars of the cloth," as she called them.

To make matters worse, Rubeo appointed Jerónimo Tostado as visitator, reformer, and commissary general of the Spanish provinces. An adversary of the reform, Tostado attempted to carry out the policy of the Piacenza chapter, suppressing all the Discalced houses and bringing them under the control of the Calced. Only the intervention of King Philip II prevented him from achieving his objective. On 18 June 1577, the papal nuncio, Niccolò Ormaneto (hereafter identified by his Spanish name, Nicolás), died. He had been an admirer of Teresa's, and his death left the reform dangerously unprotected. He was replaced by Filippo Sega, who manifested his hostility to the reform by supporting Tostado in his efforts to suppress Discalced houses.

Finally, in July 1577 Teresa was allowed to leave Toledo. She returned to Ávila, where she struggled to place San José under Gracián's jurisdiction in order to prevent it from coming under the control of the Calced. But then another complication arose: the prioral election at Encarnación. Teresa had no intention of ever returning to her old convent, but now the same nuns who had made her life impossible six years earlier were campaigning to have her elected. They liked her reforms, and their families were backing them up. Tostado was livid. He threatened with excommunication any nun who voted for her. As a result, Tostado excommunicated fifty nuns and appointed a new prioress. In the end, Teresa worked out a deal with the commissary: she would ask the nuns who had voted for her to obey the new prioress if he would lift their excommunication. But then, the Calced began spreading gossip that the Encarnación confessors, Johnof the Cross and Germán de San Matías, were behind the disgraceful vote. On December 3 the friars of the cloth abducted and imprisoned the two Discalced Carmelite confessors of Encarnación. Beside herself, Teresa wrote to the king, pleading for help, but Juan remained in his tiny prison cell in the Calced monastery of Toledo until August of the following year, when he managed to escape. On 24 December 1577 Teresa fell down the stairs at San José in Ávila, breaking her left arm. The fracture failed to heal properly, leaving her partially incapacitated. In spite of her injury, Teresa continued to write letters, although now with the help of an amanuensis. As we shall see in Chapter 3, Teresa waged an epistolary war against Sega, who, in July of the following year, moved to take away Gracián's responsibilities as apostolic visitor and in October placed all Discalced friars and nuns under the authority of the provincials of the Calced.

But then, unexpectedly, on 1 April 1579 he did an about face. The pope had been unhappy about the behavior of the Calced Carmelite friars for years and wanted to reduce, not augment, their power. Under pressure from Rome, Sega and his counselors deprived the Calced provincials of authority over the Discalced, putting an end to the persecutions. In 1580 the papal brief *Pia consideratione* allowed the Discalced Carmelites to form a separate province, and in 1581 Philip II executed a brief officially dividing the Calced and Discalced Carmelites. The chapter of Alcalá confirmed the Discalced Constitution. In June 1580 a "corrected" version of Teresa's *Life* was cleared by the Toledo Inquisition. The reform had triumphed.

Chapter 2

Teresa de Jesús:
Woman of Letters

The wide variety of people with whom Teresa de Ávila corresponded makes her letters a goldmine of information. She takes the time to write a thank-you note to the mother of a novice for a gift of lard and quince jelly (*Letters* 1, 31 October 1574). With her brothers and sisters she shares gossip and family news. She offers her nuns and friars spiritual advice, encouraging them when they flag. To her collaborators she reveals her fears for the reform, her anger at its enemies, and her exasperation at the impolitic behavior of some of her collaborators. She counsels her prioresses on the running of convents, advocating leniency rather than rigor. To her friends and relatives she complains about her health, admitting to being exhausted by her workload and even close to depression. She writes to María de San José about the intrigues and persecutions instigated by the Calced Carmelites. To Gracián she offers encouragement, spiritual direction, and an occasional reprimand. She maintains an animated correspondence with church and state officials and even dares to write to the king. She groans constantly about the martyrdom of letter-writing. Unfortunately, Teresa destroyed the letters she received from others, making it impossible to reconstruct epistolary dialogues.[1] Even so, her letters create a fascinating picture of the intricacies of the reform and of conventual life in early modern Spain.

Teresa's correspondence reveals her warmth and humanity, but also her political acumen and administrative talents. It provides examples of her speech when she addresses people of different backgrounds for different purposes. Because they are often (although not always) less guarded than her books, Teresa's letters reveal her personality more accurately than her other writing. Still, it would be naive to assume that Teresa's epistolary writing represents a completely sincere, spontaneous expression of her thoughts.

Claudio Guillén shows to what extent an early modern letter writer could use correspondence to advance a particular version of himself. Lisa Jardine argues in *Erasmus, Man of Letters* that the great humanist used correspondence to depict himself as a master scholar, establishing his authority by publishing it in a printed volume. Teresa had no intention of circulating her missives on a large scale, but, as Slade has pointed out, Teresa's letters, like her books, comprise a "project of self-representation" (*St. Teresa* xiii). In her study of the correspondence of early modern Italian women, Maria Luisa Doglio remarks that in a period when every aspect of a woman's life is dictated by men, in letters "woman becomes subject rather than object," an active "maker of her own image" (17).[2] Unlike *Vidas*, letters freed women to express themselves without fear of official censorship. As we shall see, Teresa adopted diverse letter-writing styles in accordance with her purpose, fashioning multiple self-images (authority figure, spiritual guide, obedient daughter, innocent victim, etc.) as suited her needs.

The Public Nature of Personal Letters

In Teresa's time the influence of private correspondence could be far-reaching. Among family members and religious communities, personal letters were routinely shared with others. John O'Malley notes that correspondence was used among the first Jesuits to achieve "union of hearts." As Jesuits spread out from Japan to the New World, letters became a vehicle to maintain cohesion within the order. Rectors wrote to provincials and provincials to the father general as often as once a week. Jesuits wrote unofficial letters for the purpose of edifying each other, and these letters were often passed around or read at table (62–63).

Likewise, the communication network Teresa and her collaborators maintained through letters facilitated their work. In an age when information traveled slowly, the thirst for news was enormous. Letters were often meant to be read not only by the addressee but also by other nuns and male associates. Teresa and her disciples constantly wrote letters to inform, encourage, or instruct others with the expectation that some would become semipublic documents. Sometimes Teresa addresses a letter to a whole convent.[3] These letters were read at mealtimes or at other gatherings, as were sermons or spiritual books. Josefina C. López points out that the custom of reading aloud to groups, widely practiced in the sixteenth century, helps to explain the orality of much of Teresa's writing: "Teresa not only writes, but 'speaks' in her writing and through her writing" to her spiritual daughters (4).[4]

Often Teresa instructs one of her correspondents to pass her letter along to someone else. She writes to María de San José: "The other day I wrote to my *padre* Prior de las Cuevas (Hernando de Pantoja). . . . Read the letter I wrote to Father Garciálvarez, and if you think it's all right, give it to him" (*Letters* 2, 4 June 1578: 8). In a missive to Don Roque de Huerta, an influential royal official and one of Teresa's most important contacts at court, she mentions "the letter from Valladolid that I told you the other day to read and send to our *padre*" (*Letters* 2, October 1578: 6). In another missive to Pantoja, written during the persecutions of the Discalced nuns of Seville, she begs him to let the sisters see her letters before handing them over to the provincial, who could confiscate them, "since it might make [the sisters] feel better to see my handwriting." She also tells him, referring to a letter addressed collectively to the convent, to "please feel free to read the letter I wrote to the sisters" (*Letters* 2, 31 January 1579: 6).[5]

Teresa also shared with others some of the letters she received. In a dispatch to Lorenzo, she notes, "Yesterday my sister María sent me the enclosed letter" (*Letters* 1, 23 December 1561: 7). She writes to María de Bautista, prioress of Valladolid, with regard to the postulant Casilda de Padilla, "Let her read the enclosed letter from her aunt, for I sent her aunt the one Casilda wrote to me" (*Letters* 1, 14 May 1574: 6). To Father Ambrosio Mariano she says, "That you may see whether or not my nuns surpass yours, I am sending you a section of a letter from the prioress in Beas" (*Letters* 1, 21 October 1576: 21). Her assumption that some letters are meant to be shared is clear in her missive to Gracián: "Oh, how happy it makes me to see the perfect way in which you write to Esperanza. For when dealing with letters that will be shown around, it is good that they be written in this way" (*Letters* 1, 9 January 1577: 4).[6] In fact, Gracián's letters were "of so much benefit" for the souls of the nuns that Teresa writes to Gracián's sister Juana Dantisco, asking that, "like sermons," the sisters in Juana's convent read them all together (*Letters* 2, 28 December 1578: 3). (Collections of sermons were especially popular reading among nuns.)

However, Teresa expected her correspondents to be discreet and not show her letters injudiciously. Matters concerning the reform were to be kept secret. When Gracián shares with others a letter in which she divulges confidential business, she chides him, directing him "not to read in public the letters I write to you" (*Letters* 1, November 1576: 3). Committing sensitive information to writing could be dangerous, for letters were often lost or stolen in transit. Inquisitional spies sometimes intercepted letters and used them as evidence against a person. Once the reform was underway, Calced Carmelites waylaid and robbed postal messengers in order to gather intelligence that would enable them to undermine the Discalced movement. In order to avoid information falling into the wrong hands, Teresa often used code names. Gracián was Eliseo or Paul; Nicolás Ormaneto, the nuncio, was Methuselah; the Discalced Carmelite nuns were butterflies; the Discalced Carmelite friars were eagles; and the unreformed Carmelites were cats. Teresa herself was Laurencia or Ángela.

Another strategy she used to outsmart curious and potentially dangerous readers was to send politically sensitive letters to a third party rather than to the person for whom they were intended. On 8 November 1576 she writes to María de San José: "I will put the letters for our *padre* (that is, Gracián) in a wrapping without an address and with your name on it and two or three crosses. . . . And ask him not to address his letters to me but let you address them and mark them with the same sign. Doing this will conceal them better" (8 November 1576: 5).[7] Two and a half years later these precautions were still necessary. Teresa tells Roque de Huerta, "Will you have the letter for the Prior of St. Augustine's given to someone who will deliver it into his own hand without letting it be known that it has come through me or through you? Believe me, if that is known, it may do us harm" (*Letters* 2, 12 March 1579: 9).[8] The extreme care Teresa took in disguising identities and routing mail through clandestine channels suggests that confiding information through letters—especially when political matters were involved—could be extremely hazardous. She also often took the precaution of having letters hand delivered; the letters written after 1576 contain numerous references to hand delivery or else are themselves marked "hand deliver."[9] Sometimes Teresa decides that writing is just too risky: "I'd rather talk to Señor Garciálvarez than write to him because I can't say what I'd like to in writing" (*Letters* 2, 31 January 1579: 9). The semipublic nature of letters and the danger of their interception during this period meant that Teresa's letters often could not be completely spontaneous.

Delivering the Goods: The Mail Service

Even in the best of circumstances, communicating by mail was precarious business. Early in the sixteenth century the first regular postal service in Spain was established between Valencia and Madrid, with riders guaranteed to cover ten leagues a day, or even twenty if they were paid extra (Casey 14).[10] Philip II greatly expanded both the domestic and international postal service so that he could communicate with Rome and with Spanish holdings in the Low Countries more readily. Geoffrey Parker explains:

> Philip II could count on a postal service of unprecedented quality. The Taxis family created a direct courier link between Spain and the Netherlands through France, with 106 relay stations (each provided with at least two horses), soon after Philip of Burgundy became king of Castile in 1504. In 1516 his son Charles signed a contract with the Taxis company that established guaranteed times for various services to link him with his representatives in Germany, Italy, Spain and the Netherlands; and two years later Charles and Francis I of France agreed to accord the service diplomatic immunity, permitting all couriers on official business free passage across their territories in time of peace, and every week scores of messages passed safely along the chain. From 1560, an "ordinary" courier left Madrid from Brussels (and vice versa) on the first day of each month (and later on the 15th also), with additional "extraordinary" mes-

sengers dispatched as necessary, while a similar service linked Madrid
with both Rome and Vienna. In 1567 the duke of Alba established a new
postal chain, with two horses at each relay station, from Milan to Brussels during his march to the Netherlands along what would later be called
"the Spanish Road," providing an alternative link with Spain whenever
civil war rendered passage through France unsafe. In 1572 he began to
send two copies of all his letters to the king: one through France and
the other down the Spanish Road to Italy and from there to Barcelona by
sea. (48)[11]

Although this system was set up for royal dispatches, during Teresa's lifetime it was open to the public. A person could deposit a letter at a postal
house with hopes that it would be delivered to its destination, although
there were no guarantees (Kavanaugh, Introduction to *Letters* 1:21). Postal
messengers left for major cities so frequently that Teresa quotes this refrain
in a letter to her sister Juana: "Wait no longer than a Credo and a messenger leaves for Madrid" (*Letters* 1, 9 March 1573: 2).[12]

In spite of these improvements, letter writers often preferred to entrust
their dispatches to friends or to private carriers who were usually paid by
the recipient, not the sender. These couriers might have to take circuitous
routes due to poor roads, weather conditions, or bandits. In a letter to
María de San José, Teresa complains, "The mail is as slow in getting up
to us as it is in getting down to you" (*Letters* 1, 3 January 1577: 1). At
the time the road to Seville went through Almodóvar del Campo, which
boasted no less than twenty public inns to cater to the traffic between Andalusia and Castile, or else through Extramadura, along the Portuguese
border. Carts also passed through the Sierra Morena, stopping at little
towns that popped up along the way (Casey 13–14). But all of these routes
were slow and could be treacherous in the winter. A letter from Toledo to
Seville could take eight days to reach its destination.

Some of Teresa's correspondence was international, and a letter to
America or Rome could take months. Kamen notes, "In good conditions,
Madrid was four days away from Seville and Lisbon, ten days from Brussels, two weeks from Milan, nearly four weeks from Rome, and possibly six from America" (*Spain* 145). When dispatching a letter to the New
World, one had to first find out when the fleet was leaving and take care to
get one's missive to the port on time. In a letter to her sister Juana, Teresa
remarks, "I have written four times to the Indies, for the fleet is leaving"
(*Letters* 1, 4 February 1572: 1). After the letter crossed the ocean, it had to
travel by land to its destination. Letters from America to Spain were just
as slow. Those from outlying areas had to travel first to capitals and from
there to ports, then to Seville, from where they were distributed to Madrid and other cities (McAlister 207). No wonder Teresa's brother Lorenzo
often sent her gifts via personal acquaintances rather than via the post.

(Teresa mentions in her letter of 23 December 1561 that Lorenzo's monetary contribution to the foundation of San José of Ávila arrived with some merchant friends of his.)[13] Communications to and from Rome could take just as long. Kavanaugh notes that one of Rubeo's letters to Teresa took as many as 150 days to arrive, and another took 374 (Introduction to *Letters* 1:22).

Whenever possible, Teresa entrusted her mail to friends, often traveling friars or nuns. Otherwise, she preferred to send letters along established postal routes or by muleteers, who, although expensive, could carry more than post riders and were willing to go to out-of-the way places. Sometimes she mentions a messenger in whom she has particular confidence. She tells María de San José, "The packages arrived in good condition and that will always be so with Figueredo's services. . . . [He] is a very good man" (*Letters* 1, 13 October 1576: 2).

The price of sending mail was a serious consideration. In another missive to María de San José Teresa writes that she will have to cut down on her letters "because of the cost of the postage" (*Letters* 1, 17 January 1577: 6). When María sends her a package of potatoes, a keg, and lemons, Teresa writes, "Everything arrived in good condition. But the portage cost so much that there is no reason for you to be sending me anything more; it's a matter of conscience" (*Letters* 1, 19 December 1577: 1). Nevertheless, when she had an unusually important letter to send and no friend to transport it, she took care to hire a reliable messenger and encouraged her friends to do the same: "If you cannot find a safe and trustworthy person, engage a private messenger and our *padre* (Gracián) will pay for it" (*Letters* 1, 7 October 1577: 1). Kieran Kavanaugh notes that even though Teresa wrote letters constantly, "correspondence in sixteenth-century Spain was a luxury" (Introduction to *Letters* 1:22). Because of her desire to live in poverty, Teresa disliked having to spend exorbitant sums on mail and abhorred requiring her correspondents to pay postage on her letters. Since the recipient was expected to pay the postage, Teresa sometimes included the amount due in the package in order to avoid imposing the burden of paying on her correspondent. "Enclosed is the postage, for it's expensive," she writes to María de San José (*Letters* 1, 5 October 1576: 11). She also expected others to do the same for her. On one occasion she instructs María de San José to place the money to cover the postage in her package, adding, rather gruffly, "Write on the outside the amount that is enclosed— and don't forget to enclose it" (*Letters* 1, 13 October 1576: 2).

Even well-paid mail carriers were not always trustworthy. Sometimes they ransacked letters in search of valuables or lost them along the way. They could be finicky, too. For example, they did not like to be kept waiting. She tells her sister Juana: "The muleteer is coming . . . thus there is no time to say more" (*Letters* 1, February–March 1572: 1). "The muleteer sent me your letters and is in a hurry for the reply. So you'll have to forgive me, daughter, if this is so short," she writes to María de San José (*Letters* 1, 7 December 1576: 1). Teresa frequently comments that she must dash off a letter without rereading it because the carrier is anxious to be on his way. Sometimes, to save money, she sends a whole packet of letters to one of her prioresses, asking her to deliver them to individual nuns. But messengers could balk; they did not like to accept more letters than they had bargained for: "There are two packs of letters, for we had already sent one when another business matter arose, and this mail carrier would in no way let us add the later ones to the earlier ones" (*Letters* 1, 7 October 1577: 2).

By the 1570s, Teresa was writing letters constantly. Kavanaugh remarks that upon examining Teresa's neat autographs, with evenly spaced lines and a dearth of corrections, one would never guess the haste in which she composed them (Introduction to *Letters* 1:16). Yet an epistle to her brother Lorenzo gives an idea of the slapdash way in which she sometimes worked. In it she admits she does not know whether she answered all the questions from his previous letter because she has not taken the time to reread it. Furthermore, she urges him not to bother rereading his letters before sending them off, since she does not bother rereading hers: "You shouldn't make the effort to read over those you send me. I never reread mine. If some word is missing, put it in, and I will do the same here with yours. The meaning is at once clear, and it is a waste of time to reread them unnecessarily" (*Letters* 1, 17 January 1577: 12). As a result of their hasty composition, many of Teresa's letters are difficult to understand. Words can be missing, sentences can be rambling, and antecedents can be unclear.

The Burden of Letter-Writing

The onus of writing letters day in and day out weighed heavily on Teresa. "The biggest burden is letter-writing," she tells her sister Juana (*Letters* 1, 2 February 1572: 1). To her friend Father Domingo Báñez she complains, "I would . . . like to write at length, but I have many letters to write" (*Letters* 1, January 1574: 1). To Gracián she grumbles: "I can't count the letters that have arrived these past two days. They'll make me lose my mind" (*Letters* 1, 20 September 1576: 6), and then, the following month, "I carry out the orders (to write the *Book of the Foundations*) more eagerly than I do this letter-writing, for all the bustle involved is killing me" (*Letters* 1, 31 October 1576: 1). The bustle included finding reliable messengers and getting her letters ready in time for the courier.

The burden of correspondence sometimes compromised Teresa's health. Sickly since childhood, she suffered from head, stomach, and chest pain much of her life. Squatting for hours by a window ledge to write letters could aggravate her discomfort. She tells María Bautista, prioress of the Valladolid Carmel: "Together with your letter, I have to respond to some letters from Ávila, so I won't be able to send them off until tomorrow at noon. Neither my eyes nor my head are up to doing any better" (*Letters* 1, 14 May 1574: 1). Often she wrote late into the night. She begins a letter to María de San José: "The clock will soon strike two, and so I can't be long, I mean two o'clock in the night" (*Letters* 1, 17 December 1576: 1). At the time, Teresa was sixty-one years old, in poor health, and under virtual house arrest in Toledo, with no way to attend to the affairs of the reform except through letters. Sometimes the workload was so heavy that she made mistakes out of sheer exhaustion: "My head was in such a condition that I don't even know how I said what I did. That day the business matters and letters had so piled up that it seemed, as it does sometimes, that the devil had done this. . . . It was a miracle that I didn't send a letter I had written to Padre Gracián's mother to the Bishop of Cartagena, for I had put it in the envelope addressed to him" (*Letters* 1, 10 February 1577: 12). Because the mail was so uncertain, she often made several copies of her letters and sent them by different routes, thereby further increasing her workload. When, in her later years, the physical demands of letter-writing became too great, she dictated her epistles or had younger nuns copy them. Ana de San Bartolomé testified during Teresa's beatification that she wanted to serve Teresa as her secretary but was unable to learn to write until Teresa finally gave her a few lines in her own hand. Ana copied them, and before the end of the afternoon she had miraculously learned to write (*Obras Completas, Declaración* 100)!

The Art of Letter-Writing

Like nearly every aspect of sixteenth-century life, letter-writing was highly codified. Teresa sometimes mocks the multitudinous conventions that regulate correspondence: "But just for the titles of address on a letter there's need for a university chair, so to speak, to lecture on how it's to be done. For sometimes you have to leave a margin on this side of the page, sometimes on the other; and someone who's not usually addressed as *magnifico* must then be addressed as illustrious" (*CWST* 1, *Life* 38:10). The remark is less outlandish than it might seem. From antiquity, instructions for letter-writing and collections of model letters provided people with guidance in epistolary style, with the letters of Pliny, Symmachus, Sidonius, and others serving as examples to be emulated. From the eleventh century, *ars dictandi*—literally, the art of dictating—was recognized as a new system of rhetoric and began to replace traditional rhetoric in the educational curriculum.[14] It emerged as a response to the requirements of administrative procedure and was primarily intended to provide models for letters and official documents (Curtius 75). By the early sixteenth century, educated professionals needed to know Latin and the rules of *ars dictandi* in order to carry out the bureaucratic duties of church or state.

During the early modern period, the personal letter also began to flourish. For Renaissance humanists, letters became not only a means of communicating information but also a literary genre to be cultivated. Humanists such as Erasmus and Carlo Borromeo transformed letter-writing into an art. Fray Antonio de Guevara composed *Epístolas familiares* filled with wordplay and rhetorical flourishes as well as anecdotes, news, autobiographical data, and material from his readings. It is not clear that he ever intended to send them but rather destined them for a wide audience, publishing them in 1539 and in several subsequent editions. Marc Fumaroli sees this kind of letter as a precursor of the modern essay: "The humanistic letter, from the time of its origin in Italy, is already an 'essay,' in the sense Montaigne uses the word, in which every subject is broached from the perspective of the meditative and central self" (Qtd. Trueba Lawand 45). He calls Petrarch's *Epistulae ad familiares* "a 'portrait' of the intimate self retreating into an uninterrupted interior meditation . . . about friendship, love, death, glory . . . a fragmented autobiography" (Qtd. Trueba Lawand 45). Although many of Teresa's letters reveal inner musings, they do not fit the humanistic pattern exemplified by Petrarch's letters. Teresa did not usually use letters to create reflective treatises, but rather to spur the recipient to action, to communicate information, or to make queries.

Even humanistic letters followed norms. Young men receiving a humanistic education studied epistolary art. Two instruction books devoted to letter-writing that circulated widely in sixteenth-century Europe were Erasmus's *De conscribendis epistolis* (1522) and Juan Luis Vives's work of the same name (1536). A number of such books met with success in Spain: *De conscribendis espitolis liber unus* (1564), by Francisco Juan Bardaxí; Book III of *Arte de la retórica* (1578), by Rodrigo de Espinosa y Sáenz y Santayana; *Dilucida conscribendi espistolas ratio* (1585), by Juan Lorenzo Palmireno; and *Liber de conscribendis epistolis* (1589), by Bartolomé Bravo.[15] These volumes categorize epistles by function and describe the style, parts, and appropriate subject matter of each type. In general, these writers insist that decorum and the rules of rhetoric be respected in any letter. Palmireno and Bardaxí, in particular, follow Vives's lead in emphasizing simplicity of style and flexibility of subject matter.

Style manuals were not limited only to literary letters. By the sixteenth century, literacy was increasing among tradesmen, shopkeepers, artisans, and even journeymen. "Across the length and breath of Europe, a specialized literature came into being, whose aim it was to regulate and control ordinary forms of writing, first by explaining and instilling in people the difficult techniques that writing entailed and then by setting out the rules and conventions proper to each written genre" (Chartier 1). In France *se-*

crétaires or collections of model letters, precursors of the letter-writing manuals of the nineteenth century, provided ordinary citizens with the rules of epistolary style and with examples. In Spain *manuales epistolares* fulfilled the same function.

Although Teresa was well-read for a woman of her time and class, many scholars believe it is not likely that she consulted these manuals. Early twentieth-century critics (Américo Castro, Ramón Menéndez Pidal, Juan Marichal, Helmut Hatzfeld) remark that Teresa was a careless letter writer who broke with convention. She wrote spontaneously, they insist, not for publication but to communicate with personal friends and officials connected with the reform. They comment on her disregard for the epistolary norms detailed in the letter-writing manuals of the day and on her tendency to write as she spoke, full of colloquialisms and refrains. Most laud her freedom of expression, simplicity, and sincerity, although Castro deplores her lack of refinement, her *tendencias vulgaristas* (76–77). Based on Teresa's meticulous use of titles and formulas, Pilar Concejo believes that Teresa actually did consult courtesy books.[16] But either way, she would have had access to information on letter-writing. Slade notes that Teresa "learned some epistolary protocols from well-connected friends and associates, particularly Jerónimo Gracián. . . . Gracián's father, Diego, and his brother Antonio were secretaries to Philip, and brothers Tomás and Lucas published treatises on courtesy" ("Teresa of Avila and Philip II" 231).

It is certainly true that Teresa rejects the kind of epistolary adornments that characterize the writing of a Guevara. She disregards the traditional distinction between personal and official communications, often combining elements of both. (In this sense her letters are similar to those of other reformers of her time, such as Ignatius of Loyola, although Teresa's are far more lively and entertaining than those of the founder of the Society of Jesus.) It is also true that Teresa frequently rambles, jumps from one subject to another, omits words, and is chatty, disorganized, and repetitive. Josefina C. López attributes Teresa's chatty style in her books to her notion of herself as a transmitter of God's message, which she had received through direct communication. Through a style of writing that approximates speech, argues López, Teresa diminishes the distance between her and her readers, in many cases nuns, making her words more accessible and imbuing them with the characteristics of a face-to-face dialogue (3). Although López is referring specifically to *The Interior Castle*, the same is even truer of her letters, in which the need for personalization is greater, since Teresa is usually trying to motivate the recipient to act. As Jane Couchman and Ann Crabb note, women often subverted epistolary convention "to produce their own versions of *decorum* in shaping their letters to the recipients and to the situations" (7). If some critics find Teresa's letters slapdash and shoddy, it is because they are holding her to a set of standards for which she clearly had no use. If Castro found no worth in her letters, he overlooked the warmth, verve, originality, and spiritual wisdom of her epistolary writing.

The free-flowing epistolary form was considered particular to women, who, unencumbered by university education, achieved naturally the kind of flexibility Vives and his followers had recommended. As Europe moved away from medieval Scholasticism, the natural, authentic, and conversational qualities of women's writing was increasingly appreciated. Jean de la Bruyère (1645–1696) noted that women "find at the tip of their pens expressions and turns of phrase that often, in men, are the result of long searching . . . they have an inimitable way of putting words together that seems to come naturally and that is only held together by the meaning" (Qtd. Goldsmith 46). "Women did not have to worry about shedding a scholastic rhetoric that they had never learned, and the only form they had to attend to was the loose structure of polite conversation, at which they were thought to excel" (Goldsmith 47). Teresa's epistolary style shares with that of other European women letter writers the fluidity that rhetoricians denominated "feminine" long before Hélène Cixous attempted to identify an *écriture féminine*. The seventeenth century saw an explosion of women's writing in France, and the majority of that writing was letters.[17] Epistolary writing was elevated to a social art, and women's letters were published in collections—all of which were edited by men—to provide models of unpedantic style. Yet, as editors of women's letters (most of which appeared anonymously) and arbiters of their worth, men remained in control of the epistolary genre.[18]

Teresa's letters differ from these later models in that they were not inspired by the salon environment, nor were they written for the purpose of cultivating the social arts. For the most part, they are working documents; even those that are intensely personal often have as their primary purpose the expansion of the reform. Couchman and Crabb note that for women who wrote prior to 1700, "the goal of the letter is almost always practical, concrete; the writer wishes to bring about some action or reaction on the part of the person to whom it is addressed" (3). Although "women of the early modern period had available to them the same models of the epistolary genre as did men, and the same range of rhetorical techniques and conventions," they usually disregarded them (Couchman and Crabb 7). Teresa's derisive remark on the need for a university chair for letter-writing shows that she was indeed aware of the existence of such techniques and conventions. If she ignored them, it may have been because the practical and often urgent nature of her correspondence left no time to consult manuals or simply because the models they provided were not relevant to her work.

Another factor may have been her position as a woman, with no claim to the kinds of knowledge that highly educated *letrados* had. The distinction between *letrados*, whose authority came from intellectual sources and church tradition, and *espirituales*, who cultivated experiential and intuitive sources of knowledge, was particularly pertinent to women. By downplaying the role of the intellect and stressing mental prayer, *espirituales* such as Osuna, Luis de Granada, and Bernardino de Laredo (all sources of guidance for Teresa) validated the spiritual experience of people, including women, who were not university educated. But as the church attempted to reclaim its hold on individual religious practice, the teachings of the *espirituales* became problematical, since, as Grace M. Jantzen shows, "a person who was acknowledged to have direct access to God would be in a position to challenge any form of authority" (1). Elena Carrera explains further:

> As a wider range of people gained access to spiritual knowledge through books in the vernacular, they also gained power over themselves and over the ways they lived their Christianity, by fashioning their lives in accordance with their "experiential" interpretations during prayer of Christ's life. But when this emerging power over themselves threatened to make people like the *alumbrados* and Lutherans "autonomous" from the Church's structures of power and knowledge, its officials sought to enforce the old forms of knowledge, which relied on the authority of the Church and the texts of Tradition, and thereby ensured that the Catholic Church maintained its power over its Christian subjects. (83)

The growing threat dictated that "those who claimed knowledge of the mysteries of God should be contained within the structures of the Church, since the power of the Church would be severely threatened if it should be acknowledged that access to divine authority was possible outside its confines" (Jantzen 2). Dominican *letrados* such as Juan de la Cruz (not to be confused with the Carmelite saint of the same name) and Melchor Cano actively sought to counteract the influence of Franciscan *espirituales*, some of whom had been found guilty of *alumbradismo*. In his *Diálogo* (1555), Juan de la Cruz criticizes the unsupervised practice of mental prayer and the publication of inspirational books in the vernacular, which, he believed, could lead ignorant people to embrace heretical practices. In his *Censura al Catechismo de Bartolomé Carranza* (1559), Cano attacked the notion that the call to perfection was open to laypeople and the publication in the vernacular of books on contemplation.[19]

In 1559 the Valdés Index of Prohibited Books banned most treatises on contemplation, interiority, and mystical theology, including many of those that had been instrumental in Teresa's spiritual formation. Unsurprisingly, the censors were particularly harsh on books written in the vernacular, as these could be read by unlettered readers, including women, who could easily be enticed by unorthodox doctrines. In *Life* and *Way of Perfection*

Teresa criticizes the proscription of books she had found enriching, and she encourages her nuns to continue to practice contemplation even without the guidance of books. Carrera concludes that ultimately, "the effectiveness of the Index in discouraging the individual practice of mental prayer was . . . limited, since the teachings of books on prayer continued to be practiced by those who had assimilated them and no longer needed books to be taught how to acquire such knowledge. Ordinary individuals like Teresa could resist the power of the Inquisitorial measures by continuing to practice the method of prayer from the books they had read" (85). One of the objectives of her own treatises may have been to provide her nuns with instruction in contemplative prayer to fill the void left by the index.

In this period of intense censorship, Teresa would have been acutely aware of the need to present her ideas in a way that would exhibit full conformity with Catholic doctrine and that would avoid placing herself in a position of authority unsuitable for a woman. Thus, as Ahlgren notes, Teresa was careful to avoid technical terms in her books. Her claim to legitimacy came from the straightforward, humble way in which she describes her mystical experiences, which came directly from God. Since any pretense to theological knowledge on the part of a woman could provoke charges of pride, *alumbradismo*, or even witchery, "she employed a series of rhetorical devices to justify her right to write as an 'unlettered woman'" (Ahlgren, *Politics* 30). Likewise, when writing letters to influential clerics, Teresa presents herself as a humble, unlettered woman who is doing the will of God, thereby bolstering her moral authority and enabling her to advance her cause more efficaciously. In this sense, by subverting epistolary convention, Teresa creates her own "version of *decorum*" that serves her reformist ends.

We must be careful, however, not to assume that Teresa's expressions of humility in letters and elsewhere are mere subterfuge. Humility is a Christian virtue, and Catholics are called upon to be humble before God and his priests, who, as ministers of Christ, receive divinely constituted sacramental power to perform certain offices of divine worship. From her Franciscan and Jesuit sources Teresa would have learned that self-examination led to an awareness of one's sinfulness, making one humble and intensifying one's faith. Carrera synthesizes: "In the Christian tradition humility was seen as a consequence of self-knowledge, which was in turn seen as a step toward knowledge of God" (49). In his *Spiritual Exercises* Ignatius of Loyola describes this traditional Christian virtue as detachment from worldly values to the point "where I do not desire, nor even prefer, to be rich rather than poor, to seek fame rather than disgrace, to desire a long rather than a short life, provided it is the same for the service of God and the good of my soul" (*SE* 165). Ultimately, this will lead to "the most perfect humility," which enables one "to imitate Christ Our Lord and to be actually more like him" (*SE* 166). Ignatius's propensity to describe himself as a "pilgrim" and a "sinner" reflect his attitude of humility. Francisco Javier, one of Ignatius of Loyola's original companions, echoes this attitude when he writes to his companions in Goa preparing to leave for Japan: "Dispose yourselves to cultivate humility, being very strict with yourselves about those things that should instill repugnance in you, making the greatest effort possible to know yourselves interiorily, and in that way you will grow in faith, hope, trust, and love of God, as well as in charity for others, because mistrust of oneself generates a greater, truer trust in God, by which you will reach greater interior humility, which you need in any place, but particularly here (in Japan)" (Kagoshima, 5 November 1549: 21 [*Cartas y escritos*, 347]). Humility was essential for knowing God, and knowledge of God in turn made one more humble. Having read Observant Franciscans on *recogimiento* and been exposed to the Jesuits' *Ejercicios espirituales*, Teresa would have internalized these notions.[20]

For Teresa, humility was more than a rhetorical ploy; it was an essential element of the way of perfection. At the same time, the cultivation of humility and the authoritative texts on which she based her practice of this virtue not only helped to guarantee her orthodoxy but also gave her confidence to pursue her goals: "By belittling himself, the knowing subject acknowledges God's omnipotence, becomes receptive to his teaching, reduces the interference of his own personal preferences, preconceptions or prejudices, and ensures his openness to being corrected. This attitude was crucial in guaranteeing the orthodoxy of people like Teresa, who could only rely on their subjective experience of spiritual truths." At the same time, "she cultivated humility as a way of becoming receptive to God's grace and thereby became increasingly confident that she could attain high things" (Carrera 53).

Humility, in its Christian sense, is not groveling to superiors, but "knowing one's place and taking it." It "avoids excessive devaluation of oneself," but rather "requires a dispassionate and honest appreciation of the self in relationship to others and to God" (McBrien 644). Humble people recognize not only their limitations but also their capacity to serve God within the parameters of their own personal abilities. Although Teresa was conscious of her duty to remain unassuming before God's ministers, she often chafed at the arrogance of priests who presumed to denigrate her spiritual experiences. In *Life* she repeatedly rails against confessors who misjudged and misled her, causing "severe disturbance" (*CWST* 1, 26:22). Paradoxically, humility empowered Teresa, helping her to see the "big picture"—the reform—and her role in it. Humility gave Teresa the self-assurance she needed to confront men of influence and also to discipline disobedient subordinates, as we will see in our examination of her letters in the following chapters.

Epistolary Etiquette

Although the internal construction of her letters does not follow the patterns prescribed by *ars dictandi*, Teresa was, in fact, meticulous in her attention to the external niceties of letter-writing. Even though she was thrifty with portage, she took care to use fine paper and ink for her correspondence. Paper had been produced in Spain for centuries, the first European paper mill having been built at Jativa, in the province of Valencia, in about 1150. By the end of the fifteenth century, paper mills existed in many parts of Europe. The shift from parchment to rag paper in the thirteenth century had facilitated letter-writing by making writing materials cheaper (Eisenstein 125). The introduction of movable type and the importance Luther placed on Bible-reading generated an upsurge in papermaking in Europe.[21] Presses consumed huge amounts of paper, using three reams (fifteen hundred sheets) per press, per day, and France alone had between five hundred and one thousand presses (Jardine 162). Movable type existed in Spain from 1499, and by the early sixteenth century Spanish printers were also using substantial amounts of paper, as Catholic apologists, complaining that Protestants were spreading their heresies through the printed word, demanded that doctrinally correct material be made available.[22] (See, for example, Ignatius of Loyola's letter to Peter Canitius, dated 13 August 1554, in which he complains of the proliferation of Protestant books.) Alliances flourished between the state and the printing industry. Cardinal Cisneros backed the Spanish printer Arnao de Brocar, while Philip II gave Christophe Plantin of Antwerp the monopoly for printing breviaries, missals, and other liturgical books to be used in Spain.

However, by Teresa's time paper had become expensive. Although paper for printing was not of exactly the same fine consistency as that designed for quills and scribal inks, the demand for all kinds of paper produced shortages of raw materials, which, along with regulations governing trade in rags, pushed prices up.[23] It is an indication of the high cost of this product that about two-thirds of the outlay for producing a book was the paper (Jardine 162). Still, Teresa was particular about the paper she used for correspondence. Kavanaugh notes, "Teresa chose paper of the best quality, with its watermark still perceptible. If she inadvertently began on a piece of poor quality paper, she felt no scruple in leaving the rest blank" (Introduction to *Letters* 1:20). In a letter to Gaspar Salazar, one of her confessors, she stops mid-sheet with the instruction to "pass on to the next page, for I got a bad piece of paper" (*Letters* 1, 13 February 1573: 3). A rough surface or a nick would have caused splotches or uneven lines.

Teresa used varying types of paper, but, as was the custom in her day, she preferred large sheets that when folded made four pages of about eight by twelve inches. Envelopes had not yet been invented, so the last page was left blank and the sheet folded in such a way that it could serve as a cover on which the address and the price of the postage could be written. Sometimes letters were sent in a kind of wrapper on which this information appeared. Finally, the letter was fastened shut with wax and stamped with a seal (Peers, Introduction to *Letters* 1:14–15). Teresa had at least two seals, one with a cross and bones and one with the letters IHS, which she mentions in a missive to her brother Lorenzo: "I can't bear using this seal with the skull. I prefer the one with the monogram of him whom I would like to have engraved on my heart as had St. Ignatius" (2 January 1577: 5).[24] She was also careful about the quills she used. She begins another letter to Lorenzo, "Tell Francisco (Lorenzo's son) to send me some well-cut pens. There aren't any good ones around here, they are a nuisance and make my work harder" (*Letters* 1, 27–28 February 1577: 1). Later in the same letter she remarks, "I have changed pens so often in this letter that my handwriting will seem worse than usual" (*Letters* 1, 27–28 February 1577: 12). We cannot know how Teresa managed to pay for expensive paper and quills or how she justified these expenditures, but it is clear from the importance she attached to proper writing materials—and, as we shall see below, to the use of appropriate titles—that she was savvy about worldly ways. In spite of the scorn she repeatedly expresses for social niceties, Teresa knew that in order to gain the cooperation of powerful people, she had to respect certain details of epistolary etiquette.

At the top of each page Teresa usually left an approximately one-inch margin, although larger borders were required for people of rank and influence. When writing to close friends, such as María de San José, however, she often filled the margins and even the outside cover page that served as an envelope with notes and post data, leaving almost no white space at all. Sometimes she would include a personal message in the margin of a letter written by an amanuensis. In the top margin she would write IHS, a slash running through one of the vertical columns of the H to form a cross. This was a common practice for religious letter writers of both sexes. For example, Ignatius of Loyola and Ana de Jesús routinely placed the letters IHS at the beginning of their missives, while Gracián placed a cross over the words "Jhus María." Teresa usually began her letters with the greeting "Jesús," "Jesús sea con vuestra reverencia / vuestra merced" (Jesus be with you), or some similar words of blessing. Often she concluded with a prayer. A letter to Gracián ends: "God deliver us from having a need for creatures. And may it please him to help us see clearly without any other need than for him" (*Letters* 1, 19 November 1576: 5). Another concludes: "May His Majesty watch over you and make you as holy as I beg him to, amen" (*Letters* 1, 7 December 1576: 10). And a letter to María de San José closes: "May God charm you and transport you into himself, amen, amen" (*Letters* 1, 9 January 1577: 10).

Considering the disdain for worldly honor she expresses in her books,

Teresa's scrupulousness about forms of address seems surprising. We have already spoken of her desire to make her convents as egalitarian as possible by eliminating titles. She warns her nuns to "take careful note of interior stirrings, especially if they have to do with privileges of rank" (*CWST* 2, *WPV* 12:4).[25] Inside the convent, she warns, "the one who is from nobler lineage should be the one to speak least about her father. All the sisters must be equal" (*CWST* 2, *WPV* 27:6). She sees "vain esteem for honor and wealth" as detrimental to the pursuit of a life of detachment and prayer (*CWST* 2, *WPV* 12:5). She complains about the importance the world accords to social ritual: "It seems that, like children, we are making houses out of straw with these ceremonious little rules of etiquette" (*CWST* 2, *WPV* 36:3). For Teresa, the convent and the world were, at least in theory, two distinct spaces.[26] The convent was to reflect the ways of God, not the ways of humanity.

But Teresa was anything but naive when it came to social relations. She might abolish the use of *Doña* in the monastery, but she knew that when dealing with the aristocracy, it behooved her to show respect for rank: "We must not approach a conversation with a prince as negligently as we do one with a farm worker," she writes in *Way of Perfection* (*CWST* 2, 22:3). "Is there anyone, however foolish, who when he is about to ask for something from an important person doesn't think over how he should go about asking? He must find favor with this person and not seem rude" (*CWST* 2, *WPV* 30:1). Even when providing guidance on prayer, she remains cognizant of social reality. People must proceed, she says, each "in conformity with his state" (*CWST* 2, *Interior Castle* I, 2:14). She observes repeatedly that a lady must behave according to her station in life, as a nun must with hers. While Teresa drops the title *Doña* from her own name and reprehends her brother Lorenzo for using *Don*, in social situations she is careful to respect common usage. She shows herself to be acutely aware of social differences when she notes that on a visit to Doña Luisa de la Cerda she conversed "with those noble ladies . . . with the freedom I would have felt had I been their equal" (*CWST* 1, *Life* 34:3). She scorns Doña Luisa's friends as slaves to decorum and rank, yet treats them with all the reverence due their status, fretting at first over the proper way to address Doña Luisa. Teresa was much too clever to alienate the people whose support she needed by refusing to treat them as propriety demanded.

Still, we cannot assume that Teresa's use of titles was simply a strategic ruse. Teresa grew up in a highly stratified society whose structure she absorbed. The notion of class was so ingrained in her that even when writing of spiritual matters, she often used metaphors based on it: "[God] is the friend of all good order. Now, then, if we fill the palace with lowly people and trifles, how will there be room for the Lord with His court?" (*CWST* 2, *WPV* 29:12). "If a peasant girl should marry the king and have children, don't the children have royal blood? Well, if our Lord grants so much favor to our soul that He joins Himself to it in this inseparable way, what desires, what effects, what heroic deeds will be born from it as off-spring?" (*Song of Songs* 3:2). For Teresa the reform was about providing women and men with a means to pursue an active spiritual life free of distraction; it was not about starting a social revolution.

Teresa's epistolary salutations—quoted here in the original Spanish to conserve their grandiosity—show her to be adept at handling the elaborate formulas of courtesy of her time. In addressing letters to members of the highest echelons of society, she adopts an appropriately diffident form of address. Her letter of 11 June 1573 to Philip II, in which she seeks the king's support for the reform, begins, "A la sacra católica cesárea real majestad del rey nuestro señor" (To the Sacred, Catholic, Royal, Imperial Majesty of Our Lord King).[27] One of Philip's principal projects was the reorganization of religious orders, but, as we have seen, he distrusted Rome to accomplish this goal.[28] Instead, he instructed the Council of Orders in Madrid to tighten its grip on monasteries. Although Philip was considered a great defender of the faith in Spain, Rome considered him a rebel who exceeded his authority and trampled repeatedly on papal rights. However, in 1566 and 1567, Pope Pius V (whose candidature for the papacy Philip had supported) issued the briefs *Maxime cuperemus* and *Superioribus mensibus*, which allowed Philip to forge ahead with his project to suppress the conventual communities and foment the observant way of life. By addressing the king as *sacra católica majestad* (Sacred Catholic Majesty) Teresa appeals to Philip's self-image as defender of the faith, and by including the adjective *cesárea* (Imperial Majesty), she likens him to the great Roman heads of state, in particular Julius Caesar. She also subtly suggests a relationship between the king and herself, since both are leaders of the monastic reform in Spain. However, in the conclusion, she addresses the king with great humility, stressing his role as champion of Christendom and protector of religious purity, an effective strategy in this plea for support.

In her three subsequent letters to the king, Teresa dispenses with the flowery salutations, beginning simply *Jesús* or directly with a simple prayer, such as "The grace of the Holy Spirit be with your majesty, amen" (*Letters* 1, 4 December 1577). The pressure under which these letters were written perhaps accounts for the omission of elaborate greetings. When Teresa wrote to Philip II on 19 July 1575, she was a virtual prisoner in Toledo. In her letter she begs the king to separate the Discalced friars and nuns into a separate province, with Gracián as its superior, so they will no longer be under the jurisdiction of their tormentors, the Calced. In her letter of 18 September 1577 she defends Gracián against accusations of immoral conduct. In the one dated 4 December 1577 she pleads with the king to rescue John of the Cross, who has been imprisoned in Toledo.

All four of Teresa's letters to the king end with a plea for help from a powerful, magnanimous monarch who is the order's only succor on earth: "Su Divina Majestad le guarde tantos años como la cristiandad ha menester. Harto gran alivio es que, para los trabajos y persecuciones que hay en ella, que tenga Dios Nuestro Señor un tan gran defensor y ayuda para su Iglesia como vuestra majestad es" (May His Divine Majesty preserve you for as many years as Christendom requires. It is a great relief that in its trials and persecutions, our Lord God has such a great defender and help for His Church as your Majesty) (*Letters* 1, 11 June 1573). Her closing, "Indigna sierva y súbdita de vuestra majestad" (Your majesty's unworthy servant and subject), is formulaic and appears at the end of nearly all Teresa's letters to persons of rank.

In other letters to influential nobles and high church officials, Teresa observes the very niceties she mocks elsewhere. She addresses most caballeros and religious officials as *magnífico* or *muy magnífico*, a term reserved for grandees: "Al muy magnífico y reverendo señor el licenciado Villanueva" (To the Very Magnificent and Reverend Señor Licentiate Villanueva) (*Letters* 1, 2 July 1577); "Al muy magnífico señor Antonio de Soria" (To my lord, the Very Magnificent Antonio de Soria) (*Letters* 2, April 1578). She addresses a letter to Don Teutonio de Braganza: "Al Ilustrísimo y Reverendísimo Señor don Teutonio de Braganza, arzobispo de Évora, mi señor" (To my lord, the most Illustrious and Reverend Señor Don Teutonio de Braganza, Archbishop of Évora) (*Letters* 1, 3 July 1574).[29] The use of titles such as *magnífico* and *ilustre* were established by etiquette, although in his 1611 *Tesoro de la Lengua Castellana o Española* Sebastián de Covarrubias notes that *magnífico* is already a "título desusado" (outdated title). The fact that Teresa, writing in the 1560s, 1570s, and early 1580s, adheres to this form of address that is beginning to fade from fashion is an indication of the importance she places on traditional epistolary etiquette. Proper titles are so important to her that when she does not know how to address a letter to the nuncio, she asks Gracián to do it with the help of some lady whose handwriting resembles hers, lest she make a mistake (*Letters* 2, End of August 1578: 1).

When addressing women of rank Teresa is somewhat less ceremonious. Her letters to Luisa de la Cerda, daughter of the second duke of Medinaceli and widow of Antonio Arias Pardo de Saavedra, one of the richest and most titled men in Castile, usually begin simply: "Jesús sea con vuestra señoría" (Jesus be with your ladyship). The same greeting appears in other letters to important noblewomen, for example, Doña María de Mendoza. She usually signs these letters with the formulaic "Indigna sierva y súbdita de vuestra señoría" (Your ladyship's unworthy servant and subject). She addresses most other secular persons of rank, including family members such as her brother Lorenzo or her sisters Juana and María, relatives of nuns, *hidalgos*, and businessmen, as "Vuestra Merced" (Your Honor, Your Mercy). The usual closing for such letters is "Indigna sierva de Vuestra Merced" or sometimes "De Vuestra Merced muy cierta servidora," roughly the equivalent of "Yours truly."

When addressing nuns and friars, even close friends, she normally employs titles of respect such as "Vuestra Reverencia" (Your Reverence) or "Vuestra Paternidad" (Your Paternity), although she sometimes uses "Vuestra Merced." All of these titles carry the meaning "you" throughout the letter. For example, she writes to the Dominican García de Toledo: "En todo haga vuestra merced como le pareciere" (Do whatever you think fit) (*Letters* 1, June 1562). She closes with the formulaic "De Vuestra Reverencia" or, when writing to priests, "Indigna sierva de Vuestra Paternidad" or else "De Vuestra Paternidad hija y sierva" (Your Paternity's daughter and servant). In letters to close friends, especially her spiritual daughters, Teresa shows more flexibility, sometimes addressing them as "Hija mía" (My daughter), "Hija mía y señora mía" (My daughter and lady), or a combination of these terms and the more formal "Vuestra reverencia." In a letter to a layman, perhaps of the minor nobility, dating from before the reform, Teresa begins simply: "Señor Venegrilla." The subtleties of these forms of address are lost in English versions of the letters. Peers omits them entirely, and Kavanaugh translates all these forms of address in the body of the letters simply as "you." However, by examining Teresa's salutations and closings in the original Spanish, we see how careful she was to use the proper greetings.

Teresa's Epistolary Rhetoric

In spite of her care with forms of address, Teresa routinely ignored classical epistolary sequence—*salutatio*, *exordium*, *narratio*, and *conclusio*—ordering her letters in any way she found effective or simply writing down thoughts as they occurred to her. Yet, as suggested above, Teresa's letters were not as spontaneous and artless as some critics believe. In *Teresa of Ávila: The Rhetoric of Femininity*, Weber describes the diverse rhetorical strategies Teresa uses to assert her authority while avoiding the appearance of arrogance. These include the rhetoric of self-deprecation, whereby the subject insists on his or her flaws and deficiencies; the rhetoric of concession, by which the subject confesses a misdeed only to counter the acknowledgment with a statement of self-exculpation; and *captatio benevolentiae*, that is, appeal to a benevolent reader by which the subject manifests deference or self-effacement (as illustrated in expressions such as *paréceme* or *puede ser*, which permeate Teresa's books) (42–76). Although Teresa's cultivation of humility was undoubtedly sincere, the survival of the reform dictated that she use these rhetorical strategies to her own advantage. Her frequent references to herself as *vil* or *ruin* (wretched), to her ignorance, and to the frailty and stupidity of her sex are an acknowledgment of inferiority, which she turns into a defense by asserting that God favors the weak. Ahlgren clarifies that Teresa "acknowledged her limitations as an unlettered woman in her efforts to disarm hostile readers with her humility and lack of pretentiousness" (*Teresa de Ávila* 67). Thus, self-abasement and expressions of uncertainty became tools of empowerment that enabled her to claim spiritual authority without overstepping her bounds.

This analysis gives rise to a number of questions: How conscious was Teresa of manipulating language to serve her purposes? Did she intentionally construct forms of exposition and argumentation based on readings, sermons, and judicial formulas, or were they so ingrained in her mind that she used them instinctively? Is her self-abasement a result of depression (as suggested by Peers), extreme scrupulosity of the kind suffered by other reformers (such as Ignatius of Loyola and Francisco de Borja), or simply her modus operandi for escaping persecution?

Teresa's letters provide a vehicle for studying her verbal expression removed from the constraints imposed by ecclesiastical supervision. In approaching Teresa's letters to peers, subordinates, and superiors, it is instructive to explore whether or not she employs the same kinds of rhetorical strategies she uses in her books. As we shall see in the next two chapters, expressions of self-deprecation and uncertainty are absent from much of Teresa's epistolary writing. Even hard-hitting letters written during the worst years of the reform are usually devoid of self-abasement. However, instances of *captatio benevolentiae* do occur precisely where we would expect them: in letters to spiritual authorities, superiors, and benefactors—those to whom she felt the need to ingratiate herself. She casts herself as a suppliant in need of benevolence when she asks for support, fears she has overstepped her bounds, or wishes to soften a reprimand.[30]

Early in 1574 Teresa writes to Don Álvaro de Mendoza, at the time bishop of Ávila, on delicate family matters about which he was upset. Although she does give her opinion, Teresa refers to herself as a "sinner" and shows appropriate meekness when referring to the noblewomen involved (*Letters* 1, January–February 1574: 4). In her missive to Luis de Granada, the admired author of two influential inspirational books, *Libro de oración y meditación* and *Guía de pecadores*, she refers to her "wretched life" and laments that her being a woman has prevented her from ever meeting him (*Letters* 1, May 1575?: 2). She expresses her satisfaction that a powerful friend, Don Teutonio de Braganza, "has ordered me to write this letter, something I wouldn't have dared to do on my own" (*Letters* 1, May 1575?: 2). Here she has recourse to another tactic she often uses to avoid the appearance of brazenness: claiming that she acts only out of obedience to her superiors. Later, when Braganza is elevated to bishop, Teresa writes soliciting his support for the reform, once again referring to herself as "wretched" (*Letters* 2, 16 January 1578: 3). In a letter to Pedro de Casamonte on her concern for two Discalced friars headed for Rome on behalf of the reform, she calls herself a "miserable creature" (*Letters* 2,

2 May 1579: 6). In 1580 she writes to Don Diego de Mendoza, brother of Don Álvaro, at this time bishop of Palencia, consoling him for having been passed over for a position of authority and referring to herself as "foolish" and "worthless," perhaps in an effort to avoid sounding condescending (*Letters* 2, 21 August 1580).

Teresa most frequently uses the rhetoric of self-depracation in her letters to Gracián. In 1575 Teresa was trying to control a potentially incendiary situation. Nicolás Ormaneto had sent Gracián to Seville as apostolic visitor, but the Calced Carmelite friars rebelled against his heavy-handed efforts to impose reform. Teresa wrote to Gracián instructing caution, but softened her demand by concluding, "I am indeed wretched, and what is worse, I never mend my ways" (*Letters* 1, November 1575: 1). Teresa had to step gingerly. Gracián was impetuous; he was also her superior and the man to whom she had taken a vow of obedience. After lecturing him against rash behavior, she adopts a gentler tone: "Your worries are an affliction to me, and the help you get from me is my wretchedness. . . . May God make me improve" (*Letters* 1, November 1575: 7).

The following year Gracián committed the unpardonable blunder of reading in public one of Teresa's confidential letters. Although Teresa reprimands him in no uncertain terms, she is careful to maintain her position of humility. On the one hand she tells him he has behaved in a stupid and naive manner; on the other she excuses him because his candor is "that of a saint." Once again, she refers to herself as "wretched and malicious" (*Letters* 1, November 1576?: 1). However, the underlying message is that naiveté (saintliness) has no place in politics. In this letter Teresa proves herself a master of doublespeak. The tone and intent of the missive are clear; she is indignant at Gracián's irresponsible behavior. She offers herself as an example of an astute tactician who, although "wretched and malicious," would never make such a dumb mistake. Yet, to avoid sounding arrogant, she censures from a position of humility: "Despite my wretchedness . . . I have gone about with . . . circumspection and vigilance" (*Letters* 1, November 1576?: 2). A few lines later she berates herself for even daring to correct Gracián: "But how tiresome I am! May it not prove a burden to *mi padre* to have to hear these things" (*Letters* 1, November 1576?: 3). Nevertheless, the paragraph ends with a stern scolding.

Similarly, Teresa reprimands Ambrosio Mariano, one of the most active Discalced Carmelites in the reform, for his excessive rigor, then softens her reproaches by referring to herself as useless and "wretched" (*Letters* 1, 12 December 1576: 2). A rough and impolitic Discalced friar, Mariano wanted to impose extreme austerity on the order. In Teresa's view, discipline was a means by which spiritual perfection could be cultivated, not an end in itself. She worried that Mariano's policies might frighten away talented candidates. In her letter she ridicules the notion that "discalced" means they should all go around barefoot: "What was set down was only so as to distinguish ourselves from the other Carmelites. It could be that I said their feet would be just as cold as when bare" (*Letters* 1, 12 December 1576: 5). After chiding Mariano for his excessive zeal, she teases him: "I praise our Lord greatly because he gives you so much light in matters of such importance" (*Letters* 1, 12 December 1576: 8). Through self-deprecation and humor she clarifies her position on monastic asceticism and holds the line on Mariano's harshness. *Captatio benevolentiae* was one of the tools she used to advance her agenda and avoid confrontation.

As in her books, Teresa sometimes demeans herself in her letters by referring to the frail and stupid nature of her sex. In the missive to Teutonio de Braganza of 2 January 1575 mentioned above, Teresa refers to Casilda de Padilla, an aristocratic young woman who joined the Discalced convent of Valladolid against her family's wishes. The incident had caused a scandal and Teresa wanted Braganza to intervene, but in her letter she is careful about how she broaches the subject: "I wouldn't want you to pay attention to what we poor women tell you," she tells him, suggesting he listen to priests or God himself instead (*Letters* 1, 9). Similarly, in an appeal to Rubeo to stop persecutions against the reform and to help John of the Cross, who has been arrested, she remarks, "Even though we women are no good for giving counsel, we sometimes hit the mark" (*Letters* 1, January–February? 1576: 8). She had just rebuked him for ignoring some of her earlier requests for help, but then, as if realizing that her harshness could be counterproductive, she backtracks: "I am fully certain that if I am mistaken in my words, my will does not intend to be" (January–February 1576: 8). By insisting on her own imperfection—that is, her verbal inadequacy—she humbles herself in an attempt to gain Rubeo's support. At the same time, she excuses herself by insisting on the purity of her intentions. This use of the rhetoric of concession—conceding her inefficacy with words while at the same time advancing her cause—is a technique Weber has documented in Teresa's books.

In her letters Teresa used many of the same strategies as elsewhere, and with the same objective: to assert authority without appearing unduly aggressive. However, in her letters Teresa used these strategies very selectively. When writing to powerful clerics or benefactors whose support she needed, she was often careful to maintain an unassuming posture. But as we shall see in the next chapter, when the occasion demanded, she was capable of expressing herself forcefully without resorting to self-deprecation or vacillation, even when addressing men of influence. With male collaborators and prioresses, her language is usually familiar and self-assured. In fact, upon occasion her tone can be mordant. The selective manner in which Teresa uses the aforementioned rhetorical strategies in her letters suggests that she was in fact conscious—at least on some level—of manipulating the language in her books to protect herself from censors. When freed of the millstone of censorship, she was able to write in a much more natural way. In spite of the strain under which she often composed letters, the epistolary collection reveals a Teresa who is sharp, self-confident, and persuasive.

Far from diminishing her, Teresa's humility was precisely what empowered her. Humility brought her closer to God, and the conviction that God guided her actions bolstered her strength and determination. By the time she began writing letters in earnest, Teresa was in her mid-forties and launching the reform. In spite of the opposition of her early confessors, Teresa had won the support of several Jesuits from the Colegio San Gil in Ávila and of Francisco de Borja, who would eventually become father general of the order. She had been examined by such highly respected spiritual men as Pedro de Alcántara, founder of the Alcantarine Franciscans, and the Dominican *letrado* Pedro Ibáñez, who determined her to be spiritually sound. In 1562, when she wrote *Life*, she was confident enough of herself to criticize anyone without spiritual experience who presumed to belittle those who had such experience: "Let him not be surprised or think these things are impossible—everything is possible with the Lord—but strive to strengthen his own faith and humble himself in that the Lord makes a little old woman wiser, perhaps, in this science than he is, even though he is a very learned man" (*CWST* 1, 34:12). In spite of the derisory tone of this remark, Teresa knew she needed the support of *letrados*. The endorsement of men like Ibáñez, who approved her *Cuentas de consciencia* in spite of initial doubts, and Domingo Báñez, who defended her first foundation and then, as inquisitional censor, her *Life*, boosted Teresa's credibility and thereby her authority and self-confidence. This self-confidence is evident in her correspondence. The image of Teresa that emerges from her letters is that of a strong, self-assured woman who, even in times of adversity, maintains not only her focus but even her sense of humor.

Chapter 3

God's Warrior and
Her Epistolary Weapons

The fluid nature of Teresa's letters makes it impossible to classify them thematically. Teresa's tendency to move from subject to subject creates the impression of spontaneity, even in letters that show clear political purpose. When writing to church officials, Teresa often inquires about their health, comments on her own, delivers news about mutual friends, or remarks on spiritual subjects in the midst of communicating the real business of the letter. However, the untidy structure of Teresa's epistolary writing does not signify lack of focus. In spite of her potpourri of topics, her intention is clearly to do God's work by advancing the reform. Teresa saw herself as God's warrior, and letters were weapons in her arsenal. She used them not only to fight her enemies but also to wield control over her collaborators. Even during the movement's darkest hours, when church and Carmelite officials sought to disable Teresa by imprisoning her and reining in her companions, she used the post to influence the decisions of the hierarchy and to spur her lieutenants to action. She was like a general strategizing, maneuvering, and striking from a distance.

The phrase "contemplative in action" refers to a person who is both intimately in touch with God and involved in the choices and decisions of everyday living. A contemplative in action discerns, through contemplation, a proper course of action and proceeds accordingly. Teresa was truly a contemplative in action. Action was central to both her spiritual and her political thinking, which were inseparable from one another. Although Teresa was a contemplative who advocated withdrawal from the world, she was also an activist, not only because she saw prayer as a form of engagement but also because her commitment forced her into a life of action and advocacy outside the cloister. In her masterwork *The Interior Castle* Teresa depicts the soul as a castle made of diamond or very clear glass in the form of seven concentric circles, or "mansions," through which the soul travels inward, into its own center, where God, the king, dwells.[1] The relationship between the soul and the king is a dynamic one, as the soul at first strives to progress toward its secret center until it at last reaches the contemplative state, at which point it ceases striving and rests in God's embrace. For Teresa, one's relationship with God entails an active commitment since embarking on the spiritual journey calls us to lead our lives in purposeful ways. This involves making conscious decisions that bring our acts into conformity with our sense of mission.[2] Her own activism stemmed from her realization that spiritual selfhood leads one to take a stand with regard to one's situation, even to take risks. For Teresa, cultivation of the interior life galvanizes one to act; active service to God through service to others and a dynamic interior life nourish one another mutually. Teresa's commitment to the prayerful life led her to accept the obligation to extend the possibility of such a life to others, that is, to become God's warrior, even facing risks and ordeals.

In fact, throughout her epistolary writing she insists that she welcomes "trials and dangers," since the rewards of martyrdom are great.[3] The notion that trials are a sign of God's love for us and our endurance of them is a sign of our love for God is a leitmotiv in Teresa's letters. She writes to Luis de Cepeda that "trials are the greatest gift that God can give us in life," since they will serve us in the hereafter (*Letters* 2, March 1578: 2). She writes to Gracián that she envies the "martyrdom" of John of the Cross, who was tortured by his Calced captors in Toledo (*Letters* 2, 21–22 August 1578: 2). It is not surprising that future generations often depicted Teresa as a martyr, since she herself saw her ordeals as a martyrdom she suffered gladly for the reform.[4]

The Reform as War

For Teresa, the reform was a war in which God was the supreme commander or captain general, she was a general, her collaborators were lieutenants, and the nuns and friars were soldiers. The vocabulary of war permeates her writing. At the beginning of the reform, she writes to her brother Lorenzo, "We must never stop trying to serve the Lord. Each day we will advance at least a little further, and with fervor. It seems, and so it is, that we are always at war, and until we are victorious, we must not grow careless" (*Letters* 1, 23 December 1561: 5). Later, as calumnies spread about Gracián and the Discalced nuns in Seville, she writes to María de San José, "Now, as in time of war, we need to proceed with more care" (*Letters* 1, 7 December 1576: 1). When Fray Ambrosio Mariano de San Benito, one of Teresa's close associates, became too frank and open about his criticisms of the nuncio, thereby risking the anger of authorities in Rome, Teresa reminds him that he must proceed tactfully, as "all the devils are waging war against us" (*Letters* 1, 15 March 1577: 3).

The military motif is frequent not only in Teresa's letters but also in her other writing. She often urges her nuns to think of themselves as soldiers in God's war: "We must be like soldiers who even though they may not have served a great deal must always be ready for any duty the captain commands them to undertake, since it is he who gives them their salary. . . .

Since the captain sees his soldiers present and eager to serve and has understood the capability of each one, he distributes the duties according to the strengths he sees. . . . And so it is with us, Sisters" (*CWST* 2, *WPV* 18:3–4). Mental prayer was the ammunition with which the Discalced Carmelites would fight the multiple menaces they faced, but in order to use it most effectively, they would have to be placed strategically in convents. Teresa would have to oversee the operation, which meant that she herself needed to be mobile. Although she bristled when Rubeo, the Carmelite general, had her held in Toledo, she continued her work through letters. From 1575, the year of Teresa's detainment, until nearly the end of her life, Teresa wrote letters constantly on behalf of the reform.

General Rubeo and Lieutenant Gracián

Through letters Teresa directed her lieutenants, maneuvered her troops into position, cheered them on, and personally battled the opposition. The worst battle arose over efforts to expand the reform into Andalusia, resulting in a conflict with the Calced friars that forced Teresa into action as never before. As we saw in Chapter 1, Rubeo, the Carmelite general, gave Teresa permission for two Discalced friaries, provided they were not in Andalusia. The south of Spain was politically unstable, and the notoriously rowdy Andalusian Carmelite friars resisted all attempts to reform them. With the impetus of the Tridentine reform, Rubeo had come from Rome in 1566 to whip them into shape, and his investigations revealed countless abuses: physical cruelty, lechery, embezzlement, and total neglect of religious duties.[5] The friars responded to his reprimands by running him out of town. Among the most recalcitrant of the Calced were the infamous Nieto brothers—Melchor, Gaspar, and Baltasar—whose unruliness caused the general to depose Gaspar from his position as provincial in Andalusia. Rubeo was afraid that trying to establish Discalced houses in this volatile region would only aggravate the situation. He thought it would be more effective to implement changes in the existing Calced houses rather than to introduce Discalced monasteries.

Since Philip II had little patience with Rome to effectively reform nunneries and friaries, he implemented his own plan, known as the "King's Reform," which went into effect throughout Spain in October 1567. However, the program was largely unsuccessful, and the pope imposed a new plan: the generals were charged with continuing the work of the reform in their orders, except that the Carmelites, Trinitarians, and Mercedarians were assigned to Dominican papal commissaries. The brief *Singularis*, dated 20 August 1569, named three visitators for the Carmelites: Pedro Fernández for Castile, Francisco Vargas for Andalusia, and Miguel de Hebrera for Aragon and Catalonia.[6]

Fernández, the commissary for Castile, thought the best way to effect change was to place Discalced friars in positions of power in Calced friaries. His intention was not to transform these friaries into Discalced houses but to introduce the new, reformed mentality in order to help them to adhere better to their own Constitutions. Vargas, the commissary for Andalusia, decided he also wanted some Discalced friars for his territory. On 11 November 1571 he wrote to Ambrosio Mariano de San Benito, instructing him to found a Discalced house in Seville, which, he said, would be exempt from the provincial's authority and receive novices only from the laity, not from Calced monasteries. This was decidedly not what Rubeo had wanted when he gave Teresa permission to found friaries. However, the Dominican visitators gave the Discalced Carmelites their unqualified support, and soon other reformed friaries began to appear in Andalusia.

In 1573 Baltasar de Jesús (Nieto) was given power over all Discalced friaries in Andalusia. One of the infamous Nieto brothers, Baltasar had been disciplined by Rubeo in 1566 but was later pardoned with the proviso that he never return to the south. He joined the Discalced Carmelites in 1569 and became prior of Pastrana the following year. Defying Rubeo's order, Baltasar then returned to Andalusia, where Vargas made him visitator for all the Discalced Carmels. On May 19 Baltasar founded a new Discalced house, Los Mártires, in Granada. Another Discalced friar, Gabriel de la Concepción, founded La Peñuela on June 29. However, due to Rubeo's ban, Nieto was unable to continue in his function of visitator and so returned to his priorate in Pastrana. He delegated the role of visitator to Gracián, just out of the novitiate, thus setting the scene for the clash that during the coming years would force Teresa to muster all her strategic, diplomatic, and combative skills. According to Joachim Smet, once Gracián became apostolic commissary and visitator, he assumed that "all things were permitted him in the name of reform" (2:61).[7] Along with Mariano and Juan de Jesús Roca, he would soon lead Teresa's movement on a collision course with the Carmelite hierarchy.

In order to carry out his commission, Gracián resorted to a trick. Mariano had received permission from the provincial of Castile, Ángel de Salazar, to go to Seville on personal business with an unspecified companion. That companion turned out to be Gracián. When Salazar found out he had been duped, he was furious. However, Gracián was now out of Salazar's reach. He flexed his muscles by founding Los Remedios, another Discalced Andalusian house, then wrote a memorandum justifying his actions. Rubeo was not amused. Gracián wrote to Rubeo again describing his activities in Seville.[8] Rubeo lashed back: "You are scarcely a novice; without knowledge of the institutions of the Order you may easily be led along ways and paths that are not good. . . . Your intention is according to God, but because you act against obedience and your conscience is burdened with sanctions and censure, I think you are not acting in the service of God" (26 April 1573. Qtd. Smet 2:62). However, Rubeo's hostility did not crimp Gracián's style; the young Discalced Carmelite went on to create more problems in Andalusia.

Pressure was growing in Rome to curb the Calced Andalusian friars. Pedro Cota, the subprior of the Seville community, had been caught in a brothel, and Rodrigo Curiel, another Calced Carmelite, had been seen wandering around in secular clothes. Some Carmelite friars had taken to wearing buttons and ribbons on their cassocks, and reports of the friars' fighting, profanity, and licentiousness provided fodder for Seville's gossips. On 13 June 1574 Gracián was named vicar provincial of both Discalced and Calced Carmelites in Andalusia, and he was determined to bring the Calced friars into line. For their part, the Calced friars were just as determined to do things their own way. On 25 June the provincial Agustín Suárez informed Mariano, then "president" of Los Remedios in Seville, of the Carmelite general's prohibition on founding Discalced houses in Andalusia. The pope then placed the Carmelite reform in the hands of the papal nuncio Nicolás Ormaneto.[9] Although Philip II was furious that the pope had meddled in the Spanish reform without consulting him, the new directive stood.

Teresa was pleased with the progress Gracián and Mariano were making in Andalusia, but she was concerned about Rubeo's opposition. A letter to María Bautista, prioress of the Valladolid Carmel and a close friend, reflects her anxiety: "Oh, if you could see the agitation going on—although in secret—in favor of the Discalced. It is something to praise the Lord for. And it was all stirred up by those who went to Andalusia—Gracián and Mariano. However, my delight is greatly tempered by the grief this will give our Father General" (*Letters* 1, 14 May 1574: 3). The situation was further complicated by Teresa's own foundation in Seville, made on 29 May 1575 at the behest of Gracián. Under Rubeo's direction, the general chapter, held in Piacenza, Italy, in May and June 1575, suppressed the three Andalusian Discalced friaries, which Gracián and Mariano had made without even notifying the general. This was the same chapter that forbade Teresa from making any further foundations and ordered her to retire to a convent of her choice in Castile. Dealing with Rubeo was the first battle of what was to prove a very long war.

Smet conjectures that Rubeo wrote letters to Teresa, letters that are no longer extant, expressing his displeasure with her conduct (2:66). Teresa responded on June 18, about three weeks after making the Seville foundation. She begins, diplomatically, by mentioning her prayers for him, inquiring about his health, and reminding him of their long friendship; it was Rubeo, after all, who had enabled her to expand the reform after she had made her first foundation. "The nuns . . . never cease being grateful to you for having encouraged us in the beginning," she writes (*Letters* 1, 18 June 1575: 1). To assuage his anger, she assures him that when she established the Carmel in Beas, she did so believing she was respecting his prohibition against founding in Andalusia: "You should know that before coming to Beas I made many inquiries to make sure it was not Andalusia. In no way would I have otherwise considered coming here, for I do not fare well with these people" (*Letters* 1, 18 June 1575: 2).[10] She also shows sympathy for his censure of Gracián, Mariano, and the other Discalced friars: "I cannot help but blame them. Now it seems they are beginning to understand that it would have been better for them to have proceeded otherwise so as not to have been troublesome to you" (*Letters* 1, 18 June 1575: 2). However, she is not willing to take more than a superficial stand against Gracián, her primary lieutenant for the foundation of friaries. Instead, she skews her comments to throw the bulk of the blame on Mariano and Baltasar Nieto: "Mariano and I especially argued a great deal, for he is very impetuous. Gracián is like an angel, and were he alone he would have done otherwise. His coming here was by order of Fray Baltasar [Nieto], who was at the time prior of Pastrana" (*Letters* 1, 18 June 1575: 2). Finally, she reiterates her respect for Rubeo: "You should understand for the love of our Lord that I would not give a thing for all the Discalced friars together if they dared even so much as to brush against your robes. This is a fact, because to cause you the least displeasure would be like striking me in the pupil of the eye" (*Letters* 1, 18 June 1575: 4). There can be no doubt that Teresa was truly distraught at having alienated Rubeo, her former ally. Still, her apple-polishing is preparation for some shrewd defensive maneuvering. In the rest of the letter Teresa employs an "attack-and-retreat" approach, her own particular version of the Fabian strategy—a military strategy by which direct confrontation and pitched battles are avoided in favor of simply wearing the opponent down. As we shall see, Teresa repeatedly used this "attack-and-retreat" strategy in her battles.

One of Teresa's customary expressions of humility precedes the first salvo: "I will now give you my opinion and if it amounts to foolishness, please forgive me" (*Letters* 1, 18 June 1575: 5). However, her self-deprecating tone is merely a feint. What follows is a hard-hitting attack on Salazar, who had ejected Mariano from the Seville friary on the grounds that he had been excommunicated, only to be rebuked by Ormaneto, who took the Discalced friars' side. Teresa mentions the excommunication three times, ramming home the absurdity of punishing men with good intentions: "*Mi padre* and lord, this is not a time for excommunications" (*Letters* 1, 18 June 1575: 6). The next salvo could be construed as a veiled threat. Teresa reminds Rubeo that Gracián is well-connected, with a brother who serves as Philip II's secretary and who might influence the king to side with the Discalced. Furthermore, she implies that Rubeo is a fool to trust the Calced, since they are hypocrites who tell him only what he wants to hear. As proof of their corruption, she offers the news that since her arrival, two Calced have been arrested in a brothel. The "retreat" portion of this "attack-and-retreat" maneuver consists of interspersed snippets of flattery.

After dressing down Rubeo for his naiveté, she writes: "I truly know of your holiness and how fond you are of virtue" (*Letters* 1, 18 June 1575: 6). Still, there is no doubt about where she is going with these arguments. She is mounting a defense of the whole Discalced project in Andalusia, including her foundation in Seville.

Teresa's coup de grace consists of a reminder that Rubeo himself gave her permission to found convents, in a letter dated 6 April 1571, after the pope imposed his new plan for reform: "For the last patent letter you sent me in Latin, after the visitators came, gives permission and says that I can make foundations everywhere." Of course, Teresa does not know Latin, so she rests her argument on the authority of *letrados*. "And this is the way learned men understand it, for you do not designate any house or kingdom, nor are any limits indicated; rather foundations are to be made everywhere" (*Letters* 1, 18 June 1575: 7). She follows this attack with another expression of humility, which she balances with an assertion of her own sanctity. She is "old and worn out" and has been pushed to the limit, she writes; still, the Lord continues to grant her favors—an understated but clear reminder that she is, after all, one of God's chosen.

In her final paragraphs Teresa appeals to authority, arguing that Vargas, Gracián's predecessor, believed that the "the main tool for reform is to have houses of Discalced friars" (*Letters* 1, 18 June 1575: 8). She concedes that mistakes were made but exonerates herself, swearing her loyalty to Rubeo: "If Teresa of Jesus had been here, perhaps this would have been carried out more carefully, for if they even considered founding a house without your permission they would have been fiercely opposed by me" (*Letters* 1, 18 June 1575: 8). She also resorts to name-dropping, mentioning that the king himself supports the Discalced and that the "archbishop argues that they are the only real friars" (*Letters* 1, 18 June 1575: 9).[11] Smet sees Teresa as a master of Realpolitik who cleverly warns Rubeo that the Discalced friars are so popular among the people that they take them for saints (2:68). For her final argument, Teresa assumes her role as instrument of God's will. If Rubeo withdraws his support from the Discalced, she warns, he will displease not only the Lord but also his Blessed Mother.

Perhaps Teresa learned "attack-and-retreat" tactics as a child growing up in a household of brothers destined to fight in the New World, or maybe she learned them playing chess. She is known to have been a clever chess player as a girl, and in *The Way of Perfection* she compares the strategies for achieving perfection with a chess game in which the queen, Humility, conducts "the best battle" against the vanities (*CWST* 2, *CPV* 16:1–2). But whether learned or purely instinctive, Teresa's fighting skills come into evidence when she sees her reform threatened.

Another tactic Teresa used was to jump the chain of command. In July 1575 she sought to gain leverage against the Carmelite hierarchy by petitioning directly to the king for support. Teresa had written to Philip II before. In 1573 she appealed to him from Encarnación, where Ángel Salazar had maneuvered her into the prioress-ship two years earlier, to request an undisclosed favor. In that letter, which is replete with flattery and expressions of self-abnegation, she assures the king that although she prays for him, her "poor prayers" are worth very little, since she is "so miserable a person" (*Letters* 1, 11 June 1573: 1). He, on the other hand, is a champion of Christianity, a "defender and help" of the church (*Letters* 1, 11 June 1573: 2). In contrast, her letter of July 1575, written a little over a month after the Piacenza chapter, dispenses with adulation and gets right to the point.

In order to put a stop to the persecution of the Discalced by the Calced, she implores the monarch to divide them into separate provinces. Her tone is urgent. She knows the Calced friars, she says, and if he does not protect the Discalced, harm will come to them. She appeals to Philip as the protector of the order, assuring him that by acquiescing to her petition, he will be serving Our Lady, since the Carmelites belong to the Virgin.[12] Only at the end does she consider that she may have overstepped her bounds, but she counterbalances her apology with a reminder that the king rules by divine right and acts for God in the realm, which obligates him to defend the reform: "I recognize that I am being very bold. But in reflecting that the Lord listens to the poor and that you stand in his place, I don't think you will become annoyed" (*Letters* 1, 19 July 1575: 4). This forceful petition demonstrates Teresa's ability and readiness to use letters to go over the heads of her superiors to forge an alliance with the most powerful person in the realm. Although there is no record that Philip responded, five years later he would pressure the pope to issue a brief creating a separate Discalced province.[13]

Rubeo's goal at Piacenza was to maintain the unity of the order. At the chapter meeting it was decided that the Reformed Carmelites were no longer to be called "discalced," but "contemplatives" or "primitives," and the term "friar of the cloth" was to be abandoned. Rubeo's stated position was that "no rift should be created in the order by calling some discalced and others 'of the cloth'" (Qtd. Smet 2:68). Rubeo insisted he had no wish to suppress the reformed Carmelites but simply wanted to contain them. However, Smet argues that

> the attitude of the chapter was too unyielding and was designed to exacerbate the conflict. The Andalusian convents, as Teresa had suggested, should have been accepted as a *fait accompli* and the Discalced should have been erected into a separate province with the prospect of forming other provinces as the need arose. Such a measure would not only have met a real need—the mixture of reformed and unreformed was impracticable—but would have exorcised the specter of Discalced fear, real or

imaginary, of being "undone" and perhaps would have created a climate in which the unity of the order might still be salvaged. (2:70)

Instead, the decrees of the chapter, which the Discalced construed as unduly harsh, provoked hostilities between the two groups of Carmelites.

Particularly hurtful to Teresa was the chapter's decision to immobilize her, especially because it was not communicated directly to her by Rubeo but instead reached her through the provincial, Ángel de Salazar, who sent Miguel de Ulloa, prior of the Calced friars in Seville, to inform her. She complains to her friend María Bautista: "I must choose a house and remain there permanently and make no more foundations, for I can no longer go out, because of the Council. Clearly this is due to annoyance over my having come down here. I have reached the conclusion that the mandate came at the request of the friars of the cloth. They think it will do me much harm" (*Letters* 1, 30 December 1575: 3).[14] Although she says she would prefer to settle down in Valladolid, where María Bautista is prioress, she cannot because of "some reasons that cannot be mentioned in a letter" (*Letters* 1, 30 December 1575: 3). Clearly, she fears increased persecutions against the reform and its leaders if her enemies intercept sensitive information. Not only had Salazar made the chapter act public before Teresa had heard about it, but he actually declared her "apostate and excommunicated." Teresa took the chapter's resolution as a personal attack by the "friars of the cloth," as she still called them. She held them responsible for all the persecutions against her order.

At the same time, she was livid over Gracián's high-handedness with the Calced in his role as visitator. Gracián's attempts to bully the mitigated friars into submission by excommunicating them only served to incense them even more.[15] Teresa tried to avoid a standoff, writing to Gracián: "You should hold off, even if they do not obey, from delivering letters of excommunication, so they may have time to reflect" (*Letters* 1, End of November 1575: 4). However, the Calced friars revolted, and Gracián did, in fact, excommunicate them. In a letter to María Bautista, Teresa complains bitterly of Gracián's behavior: "There is no obedience; he has excommunicated them; there is another uproar. I tell you I have had much more suffering than happiness since he has been here; things were going much better before" (*Letters* 1, 30 December 1575: 2).

Teresa finally decided to retire to Toledo. Before leaving Seville, she wrote to Rubeo several times, but her letter to him of January or February 1576 indicates that she did not receive a reply. Although Teresa expresses her anger guardedly in this letter, she is clearly bristling over the events in Piacenza and annoyed at Rubeo's reticence. She uses the same "attack-and-retreat" approach as in her letter to King Philip, although the criticisms she directs at Rubeo are surprisingly blunt. "May God be blessed that the chapter is over," she begins (*Letters* 1, January–February 1576). She gives a brief account of the state of the Andalusian convents and then launches a defense of Gracián and Mariano, who have asked her to serve as their intermediary, since they do not dare to write Rubeo themselves: "Certainly, they are your true sons, and I would dare say that, substantially, none of those who insist they are your true sons would surpass them. . . . I beg . . . that you do me this favor and believe my words" (*Letters* 1, January–February 1576: 2).[16] She argues that Gracián never wanted to be reappointed visitator in the first place. She subtly mentions Gracián's well-placed brother, undoubtedly hoping to increase the pressure on Rubeo to forgive her favorite disciple for his lack of judgment.

Even though Teresa swears her allegiance to Rubeo throughout the letter, she has no qualms about reminding him of her own importance and how indebted he is to her: "When we stand before the judgment throne, you will see what you owe your true daughter Teresa de Jesús" (*Letters* 1, January–February 1576: 3). Throughout the letter she becomes increasingly aggressive: "If these fathers would have listened to me after [Gracián's reappointment and the Calced opposition] had become a fact, everything would have been done quietly and as though among brothers. And I did all I could to foster this attitude" (*Letters* 1, January–February 1576: 5). She praises certain Calced friars and even muses that she would like to have some of them in Castile, but this soft-pedaling does not disguise her conviction that Rubeo managed the rift between Calced and Discalced very badly.

Not only does Teresa urge Rubeo to respond to Gracián, but presumes to instruct him on how to do it: "Do so with gentleness and leave aside the things of the past. . . . It is characteristic of sons to make mistakes and of fathers to forgive and overlook faults" (*Letters* 1, January–February 1576: 7–8). She attempts to shame Rubeo by contrasting his harsh stance against Gracián with God's fathomless mercy: "God never fails to forgive" (*Letters* 1, January–February 1576: 8). Since by giving Rubeo advice she is assuming the roles of spiritual director and theologian, she camouflages her comments in the rhetoric of humility: "Even though we women are not good for giving counsel, we sometimes hit the mark. . . . If I am mistaken in my words, my will does not intend to be" (*Letters* 1, January–February 1576: 8–9). Still, the implication is that she would have known how to handle the affair better than he.

Rubeo's treatment of Gracián is only one source of Teresa's irritation. She is even angrier about his treatment of *her*—first, about his charging Salazar with the task of informing her of her detention, and second, about the detention itself. Still, she expresses her indignation with a degree of circumspection. With regard to Rubeo's making Salazar his intermediary, she writes: "It would have been a great gift and happiness for me if you had sent [the chapter act] to me with a letter to let me know that you were feeling sorry about the great trials I was undergoing. . . . Since I have such great love for you, I could not help, sensitive as I am, feeling hurt that the order should come as though to someone very disobedient and in such a way that Padre Fray Ángel could publish it in Madrid before I knew anything about it, as though they were using force with me" (*Letters* 1, January–February 1576: 12–13). Through these repeated expressions of devotion Teresa apparently hoped to make Rubeo feel guilty for his sneaky way of proceeding.

More serious still was the chapter's attempt to destroy the reform by clipping her wings. Teresa had always moved freely through Spain founding convents. The chapter's decision to detain her spelled a death knell for all she had fought for. The Tridentine canon on strict observance of the cloister provided the friars at Piacenza with the ammunition to restrain Teresa. However, she knew the rules. She countered the chapter by shrewdly declaring its decision illegal: "In these parts they have never understood, nor do they understand, the Council or *Motu proprio* as having taken away from prelates the authority to allow nuns to go outside to do things for the good of the order, for many reasons for doing so may occur" (*Letters* 1, January–February 1576: 15).[17] In this letter she insists that she founded in Andalusia with the permission of the prelate; therefore, Salazar had no right to declare her apostate and excommunicated. To win Rubeo over, she cleverly casts him as her protector against Salazar, the villain. Yet, although Teresa intersperses her reprimands with protests of affection for Rubeo, she is not subtle about berating him and affirming her own primacy: "My rest will have to wait until that eternity that has no end, where you will see what you owe me" (*Letters* 1, January–February 1576: 17). Packed with more attacks than retreats, the letter is, in essence, a scathing censure of Rubeo's bungling of the whole business.

Ormaneto ignored Piacenza and named Gracián provincial, visitator, and reformer of the Carmelites in Andalusia and the primitives (Discalced) in Castile. As Teresa mentions in the letter quoted above, Gracián, fed up with the mitigated friars, opposed this appointment. To confuse matters further, at Piacenza the hierarchy decided that Agustín Suárez would become provincial of Andalusia but that the Discalced would remain under Ángel Salazar, the provincial of Castile. In spite of these complications, Gracián continued to use the title Ormaneto had assigned to him. "Little wonder that the Andalusians balked," writes Smet (2:71). At Teresa's urging, Gracián began his visitations. In September 1575, Teresa met with the Andalusian Calced hierarchy and became convinced they would work with Gracián, provided he handled them diplomatically. However, when Gracián presented his credentials at the Calced monastery in Seville, the friars raised a ruckus and locked him in. Rumors spread that they had killed him. Although they eventually released him, they refused to recognize Ormaneto's authority or to receive Gracián as visitator. Finally, Ormaneto ordered them to obey Gracián under pain of excommunication.

Rubeo's candidate, Miguel de Ulloa, became prior of the beleaguered Calced community, and two of its friars, Pedro de Cota and Luis de Navarrete, left for Rome to petition that Ormaneto be forbidden to intervene in their affairs. They also sought to replace Gracián with the ordinary visitator, Jerónimo Tostado, a friend and confidante of Rubeo's. Cota returned with documents supposedly granting the Calced friars' petitions, although Gracián disputed their validity. On 15 January 1576, Gracián began his visitation and immediately embarked on a program of reform of the male and female convents of Andalusia.[18]

The Battle against Tostado

From the beginning, Teresa saw Tostado as a foe of the reform and advocate of the mitigated friars. Several months before, Rubeo had appointed him visitator, reformer, and commissary general of the Spanish provinces with the task of putting into effect the ordinances of the chapter of Piacenza. Rubeo imposed two restrictions on Tostado: he was not to grant any friar permission to join the contemplatives or to permit contemplatives to found new houses. On 9 May 1576, Teresa wrote to Mariano that Cota had returned from Rome with the dreaded documents and was holed up with Tostado, who would soon be carrying out Rubeo's directives. When Tostado left temporarily for Portugal, Teresa, relieved, wrote to Gracián: "Blessed is the Lord who has so ordained" (*Letters* 1, 5 September 1576: 2). Two days later she wrote to María de San José: "Since God has delivered us from Tostado, I hope in His Majesty that we will be shown favor in everything else. I don't believe there is the slightest exaggeration in accusing him of hostility toward the discalced friars and me, for he gave clear signs of this" (*Letters* 1, 7 September 1576: 3). Like any clever general, Teresa weighed her options and forged alliances that she hoped would tip the balance of power. The king's resentment of Rubeo's propensity to proceed without consulting him gave Teresa hope that Tostado would not enjoy free reign in Spain. She began to see Philip II as her greatest ally.

But the king was not the only powerful man anxious to hold Tostado in check. When the archbishop of Seville, Cristóbal de Rojas, appointed a new visitator for the nuns of his diocese, he required the new appointee to follow the reforms Gracián had initiated, prompting Teresa to write to María de San José: "Tostado is not going to be allowed to proceed, the reform promoted by the discalced nuns will not stop with this monastery alone" (*Letters* 1, 3 December 1576: 2). By April of the following year, Tostado still had not received permission from the royal commission to undertake his duties as visitator, and he was apparently trying to expedite matters through Ambrosio Mariano, who had connections at court. Teresa writes to Mariano: "Tostado . . . will not come without the consent of the one you mention. Thus, he wants to obtain it with your help. I've never seen anything so charming" (*Letters* 1, April 1577: 2).[19] From her cell in Toledo, Teresa was struggling to control the most wayward of her lieutenants, Mariano, and to prevent him from doing anything to help enemies of the reform. At the same time, she was struggling to keep abreast of Gracián, who acted as though he were fighting the war on his own.

While Tostado was on his way to Portugal, Gracián proceeded with his project to form a separate Discalced province, which Teresa considered essential for the survival of the reform. By letters of patent dated 3 August 1576 he created a congregation of Discalced Carmelites composed of existing and future friaries and nunneries in Castile and Andalusia; he also confirmed the three Discalced Andalusian friaries that had been founded earlier. According to Gracián's dictates, Discalced religious of both sexes were to respect the Constitution and customs already in effect, and Discalced were forbidden to practice the mitigated rule under pain of apostasy. At the chapter meeting of Discalced friars in Almodóvar del Campo convoked on 26 August 1576, Gracián established the position of *zelator* (promoter of monastic observance) for the houses and also placed himself at the head of the new province. At that same meeting the friars voted to send two Discalced representatives to Rome to plead their case.

Although Teresa agreed with Gracián's objective, she had not been in favor of convoking the chapter at Almodóvar, for she knew that without official permission from Rome his scheme would fail: "You should know that the members of the Council say that if they are to give the license on the basis of the usual procedure, they cannot do so, for we need to have more convincing reasons. If they see a letter from the nuncio saying that he grants it, they will give it without further discussion" (*Letters* 1, 5 September 1576: 1). Teresa feared the pope's mind had already been poisoned against the Discalced by the friars of the cloth: "if they give this false information to the pope, and there is no one there to counter it, they will get as many briefs as they want against us" (*Letters* 1, 5 September 1576: 4). The only solution was for the Discalced friars to send their own representatives to Rome.

However, Gracián was proceeding according to his own plan, apparently without consulting Teresa. Still, when she heard about his progress in Almodóvar, she was thrilled. Friars returning from the chapter meeting gave her an excellent report, spurring her to write to Gracián: "The members have returned extremely happy about all the good that was accomplished, glory to God! As usual, this time, too, you have not been spared great praise. . . . I was extremely pleased about the appointment of a *zelator* for the various houses. That is a very good step and will prove beneficial" (*Letters* 1, 20 September 1576: 8). She was also relieved to hear that Gracián had attempted to get Rubeo's consent: "I was very happy over the steps taken to strive in every way possible to become a separate province by approaching our Father General, for it is an unbearable battle to have to go about with the displeasure of one's major superior" (*Letters* 1, 20 September 1576: 8–9). That was one battle Teresa was hoping not to fight.

As Teresa feared, Gracián's move met with immediate opposition on the part of both the Carmelite hierarchy and the authorities in Rome. Gracián justified his audacity by arguing that he was only doing the nuncio's will. In a letter of September 1, he states that it was the intention of Ormaneto to form a separate Discalced province, "and that many times we heard him say it" (Qtd. Smet 2:79).[20] Smet remarks: "The nuncio undoubtedly wanted a separate Discalced province, but to want it and to feel authorized to institute it are different matters. In any case he would not have decided so important a matter in such an offhand way. It was typical of Gracián's muddled thinking in the matter of his prerogatives" (2:79). Livid, the pope's secretary, Ptolemy Galli, wrote a memorandum stating that the Spanish houses were to obey the decisions of the general chapter of Piacenza. The memo authorized the punishment of disobedient reformers and the closing of houses founded without Rubeo's permission. Furthermore, Galli reprimanded Ormaneto for naming Gracián provincial, visitator, and reformer without the latter's having completed the requisite ten years of profession, and he expressed his indignation over Gracián's arrogance and disobedience.[21]

In October Gracián resumed his visitations in Andalusia. In January 1577, Galli wrote to Ormaneto again about complaints by the Andalusian Carmelites that Gracián was behaving tyrannically. For his part, Gracián saw himself as a worthy reformer faced with disciplining a pack of incorrigibles. In April 1577, he wrote to Ormaneto: "I have visited almost all of the convents in Andalusia, verifying what needs to be remedied, and I have corrected whatever I could" (*Cartas* 38).[22] He outlines an extensive reform program, citing generalized and particular abuses and painting a dismal picture of the situation in the monasteries. By then, Teresa knew that Gracián was in the wrong. On 18 February 1577 she informs Mariano that Pedro Fernández, the former Dominican visitator of the Carmelites in Castile, has told her that Gracián acted illegally, since commissaries are not allowed to establish new provinces. (Gracián held the position of apostolic commissary.) He had, in fact, overstepped his bounds.

As far as Ormaneto was concerned, Tostado was the problem. He had come to Spain to suppress the Discalced and to oppose the primitive rule. Ormaneto wrote to Galli defending the reformed friars and justifying his decision to appoint Gracián to a supervisory position. Teresa, who shared Ormaneto's view, wrote to her brother: "We still have fear of this Tostado" (*Letters* 1, 10 February 1577: 13). Still, she was cautious with her comments because Tostado had enormous power over the reform. In several letters she insists on his good intentions or on the positive effects of his persecutions, since they have taught the reformers to endure suffering. News that Tostado would return to Spain from Portugal in mid-May made Teresa's troops apprehensive, but Teresa did her best to keep up their morale. She wrote to Mariano: "*Padre*, don't become distressed over the arrival of Tostado. Leave matters to our Lord. . . . What seems hardest is that he is coming just when the nuncio [Ormaneto] is departing, for the commission of our *padre* [Gracián] will then come to an end" (*Letters* 1, 6 February 1577: 3). During the next several months Teresa wrote to Mariano repeatedly, urging him to remain calm, to hold his impetuousness in check, and to avoid making rash decisions. She did not want to rile Tostado, especially since rumors were rampant that Ormaneto would soon be replaced.

As it turned out, rumors of Ormaneto's removal from office were false. However, months later, on June 18, the nuncio died, intensifying Teresa's anxiety about the future of the reform. She writes to her friend Ana de San Alberto, "As you know, the nuncio died, and Tostado . . . is in Madrid. Although the king until now has not wanted him to carry out any visitations, we don't know how things will end up" (*Letters* 1, July 1577: 5). During this period, expressions of incertitude appear frequently in Teresa's letters. "We don't know how things will end up" becomes a refrain repeated over and over from 1576 until 1581, when the Discalced finally became a separate province.

At the same time, Teresa's health was worsening. The constant pressure of managing the reform in the face of mounting hostility was taking its toll. She begins her letter of 28 February 1577 this way: "Because of the illness described on the enclosed piece of paper, I have not been writing to you, waiting until I felt better so as not to cause you grief" (*Letters* 1, 28 February 1577: 1).[23] Starting at about this time, Teresa's handwriting shows signs of deteriorating. In this same letter to María de San José, she appears not to have complete control of her script. Her characters are larger than usual, and some parts are garbled. The words "San Gerónimo" are crossed out and someone else has written "la hermana S Gerónimo" over them. Nevertheless, Teresa took the time to go over this letter and make some corrections. She writes to her brother, "I think this illness will end up serving a good purpose, for I am beginning to get accustomed to having another do my writing for me. I could have already done so in matters of little importance; I will continue doing this now" (*Letters* 1, 27–28 February 1577: 2). However, as Kavanaugh points out, even in this stressful time, Teresa handled almost all her correspondence by herself (*Letters* 1:508n2). In another letter to María de San José, written on March 1 and 2, Teresa's handwriting seems more normal—clipped and tight, with little space between lines—but by April it has once again become a scrawl.

Perhaps the news that Tostado would soon return to Spain worsened Teresa's health. "Tostado is already in Madrid," she writes to María de San José at the end of May. "Pray that my head will get better, for it is still in bad condition" (*Letters* 1, 28 May 1577: 2). A month later, she writes to María: "My head is in a miserable state. . . . There has been some improvement in that some of the weakness is gone. I can write and use it more than usual. But the noise continues and is most unpleasant, and so I use a secretary, except for secret matters or when I am obliged for reasons of courtesy to write the letter myself. So, be patient in this regard as in all else" (*Letters* 1, 28 June 1577: 2–3). Although the first paragraphs of this letter were written by an amanuensis, starting with "El de mi cabeza" ("My head"), the rest is in Teresa's hand. Teresa's doctors had told her not to write herself, but she seems determined not to follow their advice. After she fell and broke her arm on 24 December 1577, all of her letters were written by secretaries for several months, although even then, she often took the pen and added lines in her own wobbly hand. A tough general, Teresa was intent on fighting even when wounded. Besides, in spite of her frequent complaints about the burden of letter-writing, she apparently loved to write.

Ormaneto's death left the question of Gracián's duties unresolved. Rome had instructed the nuncio to terminate Gracián's visitations and send Tostado in his place, but Gracián argued that Ormaneto had never complied. While church officials quarreled over what should be done, Gracián continued his visitations, despite vociferous objections from the Calced. The situation was so dicey that on 14 July 1577 Teresa wrote to Roque de Huerta, who was a friend of Gracián's family and a court official, asking him to serve as a conduit for her letters to Gracián, since so much secrecy was required. She also strove to ensure that no unseemly rumors circulated about her friars, a difficult task given that the Calced friars continued spreading stories not only about Gracián but also about other friends of the reform. Shortly after writing to Roque, she orders Gracián not to let any friars, even confessors, spend too much time talking to nuns, as such behavior gives rise to gossip: "Such goodness can give rise to bad judgments in people with malicious minds, especially in small towns, and everywhere else as well" (*Letters* 1, July 1577: 1). At this point in the war, she seems to be skirmishing on all fronts.

By the end of July Teresa was back in Ávila, released from her captivity in Toledo by King Philip himself. In order to avoid having the Ávila Carmel come under the jurisdiction of Tostado, she applied to the bishop of Ávila, Álvaro de Mendoza, to commit the convent to Gracián. Early in August she writes to Mendoza thanking him for granting her request: "If you had seen how necessary it was for a visitation to be made by someone who knew how to explain the constitutions, and was also familiar with them through practice, I think you would have been very happy. And you would have realized what a great service you render to our Lord and all the good you did for this house by not leaving it under the power of someone incapable of recognizing the way in which the devil could begin to meddle, and indeed had begun to do so" (*Letters* 1, August 1577: 3). Obsequious in tone, this letter reveals Teresa's keen understanding of the workings of the ecclesiastical hierarchy.

In order to counter Tostado, Teresa needed to gain the support not only of the king but of as many other powerful men as possible. In her letter to the bishop she is effusive in her recognition of "the love for us that you have shown throughout your entire life" and wishes "that we had you here and could enjoy your presence" (*Letters* 1, August 1577: 4). (At the time, Mendoza was in Palencia.) She confirms that "we have made no changes, for we are as always your subjects," rather than Tostado's. She also puts in a good word for Gracián, "who seems to have caught the love that we have for you" (*Letters* 1, August 1577: 4). She mentions that Gracián has gone to Alcalá to dispatch the two friars selected by the Almodóvar chapter to plead their case in Rome. Teresa's letter illustrates to what degree ecclesiastical business was carried out through *enchufe* (personal connections). In that same letter she promises to intervene in the nuptials of Don Álvaro's niece, who was apparently staying at the convent of Las Huelgas in Valladolid, where the bishop's cousin was abbess. The following month she writes to Mendoza expressing her joy at his niece's marriage and reassuring him that the difference in age between bride and groom, which had worried the bishop, will actually be an advantage, since "wives are treated much better by someone who is mature in age" (*Letters* 1, 6 September 1577: 1). For Teresa and her contemporaries, the personal, the political, and the tactical were all intertwined.

Ambrosio Mariano: The Wayward Lieutenant

Strong generals know how to discipline their troops, and although Teresa could be humble and self-effacing, she could also be forceful when the situation demanded—and when she thought she could get away with it. With both nuns and priests who crossed her, she could be brutal. Because she had a clear notion of her objective, Teresa never wavered when it came to chastising her lieutenants. One friar against whom she lashed out repeatedly was Fray Ambrosio Mariano, whose arrogance and independence frequently caused Teresa grief. While Teresa was holding down the fort in Toledo and Ávila, Mariano, her own lieutenant, was doing battle against her—or at least that is how she felt.

On 12 May 1576 Castile held its chapter, where it was decided that primitives and friars of the mitigated rule were to wear the same habits (in accordance with what had been decided at Piacenza) and live together in the same monasteries (contrary to what had been decided at Piacenza). After Gracián had created a separate province of Discalced Carmelites for Castile and Andalusia without telling Teresa, Mariano moved to Madrid, also without informing her of his plans or of developments in the south.

She writes to him: "I don't know how we can be at peace, since you give me so much occasion for war. . . . It seems only right that you would have let me know about everything" (*Letters* 1, Beginning of October 1576: 1). A few weeks later she writes to Mariano, asking him to buy a house in Madrid to serve as a business office for the Discalced friars, who do not have their own monastery in the city. She asks him to first get Ormaneto's permission for the purchase so that everything will be done properly. But Mariano, always impetuous, went ahead and bought the house without authorization. Teresa writes to him: "You should know that I thought it would be easy to have a house in Madrid where the friars could stay. And even though the house were not a monastery, it wouldn't be unusual for them to have permission for Mass." However, Gracián opposes the plan, and Teresa changes her mind. She scolds Mariano: "You shouldn't have decided to bring so many friars together and set up a church as though you had permission, which makes me laugh. I never even bought a house until I had permission from the ordinary of the place. You know well what it cost me in Seville for not having gotten this permission" (*Letters* 1, 21 October 1576: 8).

Mariano did know very well about Teresa's problems founding in Seville because he had caused them. When Teresa moved into the Seville convent, she believed that Mariano had obtained licenses for the new Carmel from the archbishop, Don Cristóbal de Rojas y Sandoval. Mariano knew that the archbishop was opposed to founding religious houses in poverty, but both he and Gracián believed Rojas would change his mind when he met Teresa. To avoid a hullabaloo, Mariano decided to remain silent about the proposed Carmel. As soon as Teresa arrived, she realized what Mariano had done. The archbishop announced that although he admired Teresa, he had not licensed the new convent and did not intend to, since there were already over forty religious houses in Seville and no need for more. This was all the Calced Carmelites had to hear to launch their campaign against the new foundation.

When Teresa wrote Mariano about the house in Madrid, she was still in Toledo, suffering the consequences of the mess he had made in Seville. Now he was repeating the same mistake. At the time, he was living with the Calced Carmelites, where Ormaneto, following the directives of the Castile chapter, had ordered him to stay. But Mariano was anxious to found a Discalced friary in Madrid, and since permission was slow in coming, he decided to move out of the Calced house and go to live with secular friends, accompanied by four Discalced colleagues. Teresa rebukes him: "I would like to know how you can be in that city without living with the friars, I mean in the Carmelite monastery, since the nuncio has insisted so much on this. It's only right that we not displease him in anything. . . . Up until now with the expectation of having a house there, any arrangement seemed acceptable. But believe me, *padre*, so prolonged a stay, and with four Discalced friars, doesn't seem right to anyone. . . . I would not want us to provide the slightest occasion for criticism by doing anything that would give the appearance of non-compliance" (*Letters* 1, 15 March 1577: 1–2).

Teresa was especially concerned about Mariano's propensity to shoot off his mouth: "I also beg you to speak with great caution, whether you have any complaints about the nuncio or not. Because of your frankness— with which I am familiar—I fear that you are careless about this; please God nothing will reach his ears" (*Letters* 1, 15 March 1577: 3). By mid-April he was once more back in the Carmelite monastery with the friars of the cloth. Teresa writes to him: "What made me so happy is that you are going to live with the friars, since you have to stay in Madrid. But be careful, *padre*, for they will weigh all your words" (*Letters* 1, April 1577: 2). In the meantime, Gracián was trying to pressure Ormaneto to approve the new monastery. However, Teresa knew that this tactic could backfire. She was so nervous that she wrote to Mariano in code: "I already knew it would be almost useless to try to get Methuselah [Ormaneto] to hurry" (*Letters* 1, April–May 1577: 4). About a week later she writes to him again, cautioning him to be careful about what he says: "Take care, *padre*, to be on your guard, and don't grow careless about anything, for the friendships shown to you could be feigned" (*Letters* 1, 9 May 1577: 4). In the world of shifting alliances that was Carmelite politics, Teresa saw Mariano as a loose cannon whose indiscretion could cause irreparable harm. The Andalusian friars of the cloth were waging a war of calumnies against the reformers, and she was terrified that Mariano would give them ammunition.

The Battle against Sega

Ormaneto died on June 18. He was replaced on August 29 by Filippo Sega, who took an immediate stand against the Discalced. Until now, Tostado had been prevented by the nuncio and King Philip II from unleashing the full extent of his wrath against the reform. Now, under Sega, he decreed that no new foundations could be made and that all Discalced houses were to have a Calced prior. He and Sega considered Gracián a particular irritant. Ormaneto had defied the Piacenza chapter by expanding Gracián's authority in Andalusia, and now Sega wanted to rein him in. He allowed him to continue working but required periodic progress reports, which infuriated Gracián. Sega's campaign against Gracián escalated during the last months of 1577. Eventually Sega would confine Gracián to a monastery in Alcalá, but in the meantime, the Calced Carmelites, angry over Gracián's reforms, began to circulate rumors accusing him of improprieties with nuns.

Through letters to Mariano and Gracián, Teresa sought to fortify defenses against the Calced. She warned both of her lieutenants to proceed with caution: to avoid divulging Discalced secrets or exposing themselves to danger. (The Calced were threatening to poison Gracián). As it turned out, the next attack came not from the Calced but from within Teresa's own ranks. Bitterness against Gracián had been growing among the Discalced Carmelites, some of whom thought he was letting Sega get the upper hand and others of whom resented his overbearing ways and rapid rise to power. One of Gracián's detractors was Baltasar de Jesús (Nieto), who had been prior of Pastrana, where Gracián had entered the novitiate. Nieto left his station as prior at Almodóvar and went to Madrid, where he put himself under the authority of Tostado and formulated a plan in which he embroiled Miguel de la Columna, a mentally slow Carmelite brother who had accompanied Gracián on his visitations. Nieto wrote a letter, which he had Brother Miguel sign, accusing Gracián of immoral conduct with nuns and other women. According to these allegations, nuns in Beas served Gracián sumptuous meals, and a beautiful young sister in flimsy silk veils danced for him. Tostado and certain Calced friars were also allegedly involved in this plot to discredit Gracián. Incensed, Teresa wrote to the king countering the accusations. Unbeknownst to her, Brother Miguel had already retracted his charge and Nieto had written a letter of apology to Gracián.

As in her previous letter to Philip II, Teresa dispenses with niceties and gets right to the point. Curiously, she portrays Nieto and Brother Miguel as victims rather than instigators: "I am astonished at the intrigues of the devil and these Calced fathers. They're not satisfied with defaming this servant of God . . . but are striving now to discredit these monasteries where God is so well served. For this purpose they have made use of two Discalced friars" (*Letters* 1, 18 September 1577: 1). Like a general covering for his men, Teresa explains that evildoers have manipulated Nieto and Brother Miguel for their own purposes. She begs the king to take the matter into his own hands and not to allow the case to go forward: "For love of God I beg your majesty not to allow such infamous testimony to be presented to tribunals" (*Letters* 1, 18 September 1577: 2). Teresa understands the ways of the world. She knows that once news of the accusation gets out, the public will see the reform with a jaundiced eye even if Gracián is exonerated.[24] Therefore, it is necessary to keep the whole affair quiet.

Teresa goes on to defend Gracián, mentioning his service to the church and the order, the persecutions he suffers at the hands of the Calced, the danger in which he finds himself, and his excellent personal qualities, especially "the rectitude and perfection with which he proceeds in everything" (*Letters* 1, 18 September 1577: 4). She slyly mentions his court connections—"he is the son of parents who are in your majesty's service"—and, finally, reverts for an instant to her customary humble stance: "I beg your majesty to pardon me for being so lengthy. The great love I bear you has made me bold and I reflect that since the Lord puts up with my indiscreet complaints, you will also" (*Letters* 1, 18 September 1577: 4–5). However, her retreat—this one notable for its brevity—precedes an attack. In her postscript Teresa hammers Tostado, whom she sees as the mastermind of this scandal. Furthermore, she now distances Nieto from the reform and associates him with the Calced, making direct reference to his shady past: "I suspect that since Tostado will remain in his present position, the visitation will be of no benefit, but rather very harmful, especially since that preacher (Nieto) who was previously a calced friar, and about whose life I beg your majesty to inquire, has linked up with him" (*Letters* 1, 18 September 1577: 7). This letter is as interesting for the image that emerges of Teresa as for her portrayal of Gracián and his accusers. She keeps flattery and expressions of contriteness to a minimum. She presents her defense of Gracián in a logical way. She does not mince words when it comes to the Calced. She names Tostado and attacks him openly. Teresa comes across in this letter as a tough, self-assured warrior. She is fighting for the life of the reform. Since years of combat have given her confidence, she addresses even the king without wavering.

A few days later, on September 23, Sega contacted Philip II about his intentions concerning the Carmelites. Teresa, uneasy about writing to Gracián in this time of plotting and intrigue, sends a pack of letters to Roque de Huerta for delivery: "Since these letters are of the greatest importance they are being sent with a much higher portage. I beg you to have them sent with the usual caution and quickly. If you cannot find a safe and trustworthy person, engage a private messenger and our *padre* (Gracián) will pay for it" (*Letters* 1, 7 October 1577: 2). Teresa's urgency and apprehension are almost palpable. She repeats in a postscript the need for prudence and speed. If the pack is intercepted, her plan to wrest control away from Tostado could be discovered and harm could befall Gracián.

On October 14 Galli sent Sega instructions to allow the "officers appointed by their generals" to proceed with their visitations, relieving them only if they fail to comply with their duties (Smet 2:84). However, the dispute over jurisdictions was not resolved. Sega wrote to Galli on November 25 asking that the visitations of the commissaries appointed by Ormaneto be suspended.[25] In the meantime, the king had shown several prelates memoranda that Gracián had written complaining of "the great disadvantages that occur in the religious orders of Spain when nuncios issue briefs contrary to the ordinances of their superiors" (Gracián, *Anastasio* 38). Those documents later fell into Sega's hands. Furious, Sega forbade Gracián to continue with his visitations and then excommunicated him along with Mariano and Fray Antonio de Jesús, one of their collaborators. "And there we were," writes Gracián, "excommunicated, unable to hear or say Mass (no small sentence), awaiting the punishing bolt that was sure to come" (*Anastasio* 39). Gracián, fearing he would be turned over to the Inquisition and burned at the stake, escaped to Alcalá and then to Pastrana, where he lived in a cave. Gracián's account of these events is far more dramatic than Teresa's—he tended toward histrionics. In *Foundations* Teresa describes this period succinctly and matter-of-factly: "He [Sega] began to act with the greatest severity, condemning those he thought could oppose him by imprisoning them or sending them into exile. Those who suffered most were: Father Fray Antonio de Jesús, who was the one who started the first monastery of discalced friars; Father Fray Jerónimo Gracián, whom the former nuncio made apostolic visitator to the Fathers of the cloth and with whom the new nuncio was greatly displeased; and Father Mariano de San Benito" (*CWST* 3, 28:3–4). In spite of her apparent cool-headedness, Teresa was deeply concerned, as the letters cited below show. Although Tostado was forbidden to visitate in Andalusia and Castile, he continued to exercise his authority elsewhere.

Now back in Ávila, Teresa faced another complication. The nuns of Encarnación Convent were due to elect a prioress, and many of them wanted her to return in that capacity. However, Tostado, who feared Teresa's growing strength, determined that no candidates outside the community would be eligible. On 7 October 1577 the election was held under the supervision of the provincial of Castile, Juan de la Magdalena Gutiérrez. In spite of Tostado's directive, fifty-four nuns voted for Teresa. Gutiérrez declared their ballots null and named prioress Juana del Águila, the choice of the remaining forty-four nuns. When Teresa's supporters protested, he excommunicated them, and Tostado supported his decision. Smet points out that Gutiérrez was acting within his legal rights, but the excommunication provoked fury on the part of the families of the punished nuns, who appealed to the royal council. The council reversed Gutiérrez, and Hernando Maldonado, prior of the Calced monastery in Toledo, granted an absolution. Nevertheless, the election was deemed valid and Juana del Águila remained prioress. Teresa paints a dramatic picture of the balloting in a letter to María de San José:

> I tell you that what is going on at the Incarnation is of a kind, I think, never before seen. By orders of Tostado the provincial of the Calced friars came here fifteen days ago for the election with threats of great censures and excommunications for anyone who might cast a vote for me. Despite this, they paid no heed, and as though he had said nothing to them at all, fifty-five nuns voted for me. As each vote for me was given to him, he excommunicated the nun, and he cursed and pounded and beat the ballots with his fist and burned them. He has left the nuns excommunicated for fifteen days now. (*Letters* 1, 22 October 1577: 3)[26]

The following year, Teresa is still fretting about the incident. She writes to Teutonio de Braganza, "It hurts me deeply to witness so much scandal in the city on my account and so many anxious souls, for there were more than fifty-four nuns excommunicated. My only consolation is that I did all I could to prevent the nuns from electing me. And I guarantee you that one of the greatest trials that could come to me on this earth would be to see myself at the Incarnation" (*Letters* 2, 16 January 1578: 9). Teresa is certainly sincere when she says she does not want to assume the priorate, but the incident left her feeling dejected, especially since it led to the next crisis: the abduction and incarceration of John of the Cross and Germán de San Matías.

John of the Cross (1542–1591), whom Teresa had met at Medina del Campo in 1567, became one of her most enthusiastic collaborators and a key figure in the Carmelite reform, although he was not, as some admirers contend, cofounder of the Discalced Carmelites.[27] When they met, Teresa was fifty-two and he was only twenty-five, but she immediately recognized in him a mature and sensitive spirit. She writes in *Foundations* that he "pleased me very much" (*CWST* 3, 3:17) and noted that he "always lived a life of great perfection and religious observance" (*CWST* 3, 13:1). He had just been ordained and planned to join the Carthusian order because he was drawn to its tradition of silent contemplation. However, Teresa spoke to him about her reformist projects and he wound up joining the Discalced Carmelites. Teresa undertook to train him in the Discalced charism and concluded that "he was so good that I, at least, could have learned much more from him than he from me" (*CWST* 3, *Foundations* 13:5). It was the beginning of a lifelong friendship. Fray Juan, as she called him, helped to establish the first Discalced friary in Duruelos and went on to serve the reform by founding convents and *colegios* (schools). Today he is known as one of Spain's greatest mystic poets. He was beatified in 1675 and canonized in 1726. In 1926 he was named a doctor of the church.

At Teresa's urging, the Dominican visitator Pedro Fernández assigned Fray Juan and Fray Germán as confessors to Encarnación when certain nuns expressed dissatisfaction with their Calced confessors. The prior of Ávila, Alonso Valdemoro, removed Fray Juan and Fray Germán on the grounds that Encarnación was not officially a Discalced convent, but Ormaneto ordered the two friars restored. Now Gutiérrez, probably still reeling from the balloting incident, moved against them again. On the night Maldonado granted his unwilling absolution to the Encarnación nuns, friars from the Toledo monastery kidnapped Fray Juan and Fray Germán. The former was imprisoned in the Toledo friary and the latter in San Pablo de la Moraleja.

Rescuing Fray Juan

Teresa immediately went to battle to rescue her captured lieutenants. Awakened during the night with news of this catastrophe, Teresa gathered her wits and the next day wrote an impassioned letter to King Philip II, imploring him to intervene on behalf of the two Discalced friars. The structure of this letter reveals not only Teresa's self-assertiveness but also her political shrewdness. Teresa begins by flattering the king; he is the champion of the Virgin and the Carmelites; they have nowhere to turn but to him: "I strongly believe that our Lady has chosen you to protect and help her Order. So, I cannot fail to have recourse to you regarding her affairs" (*Letters* 1, 4 December 1577: 1). By depicting herself as only the intermediary, Teresa makes her plea more compelling. She is not asking a favor for herself or even for her friends, but for the Virgin.[28] She recognizes that she is being overly bold ("I beg you to pardon me for so much boldness"), but as foundress it is her place to protect her order, even if this means overstepping the bounds of social decorum (*Letters* 1, 4 December 1577: 1).

Teresa then enlightens the king about the circumstances leading up to the abduction. She begins by painting a wretched picture of Encarnación under Calced direction. The Calced confessors who were in charge proved to be "a great hindrance to the recollection and religious observance of the nuns." Under their direction, Encarnación had become lax and the sisters were miserable. In order to free themselves of these friars, the nuns had attempted to have Teresa return as prioress, but she declined, believing she would be of no help as long as the Calced remained (*Letters* 1, 4 December 1577: 2). (She does not mention that Tostado had taken a strong stand against the nuns' position or that Gutiérrez had excommunicated the nuns who supported her.) In order to give the nuns some relief, she explains, she placed Fray Juan and Fray Germán at Encarnación. (She does not mention that Fernández officially made the appointment.)

The contrast she establishes between the Calced confessors and these two is striking. About Fray Juan she says, "He is so great a servant of our Lord that the nuns are truly edified, and this city is amazed by the remarkable amount of good he has done there, and so they consider him a saint; and in my opinion he is one and has been one all of his life" (*Letters* 1, 4 December 1577: 3). To bolster her argument she appeals to authority. Ormaneto, the nuncio, was aware of "the harm that the friars of the cloth were doing" and "gave orders under pain of excommunication that the [Discalced] confessors be restored to their house," since they had been driven out by the Calced. Teresa recounts that Ormaneto also ordered "that no friar of the cloth under pain of excommunication go to the Incarnation for business purposes, to say Mass, or hear confessions, but only the Discalced friars and secular clergy" (*Letters* 1, 4 December 1577: 4). However, once Ormaneto died, the Calced returned. Now, Hernando Maldonado, prior of the Toledo Calced Carmelites and a man capable of "making martyrs," has stolen away Fray Juan and Fray Germán and is holding Fray Juan prisoner in his own monastery (*Letters* 1, 4 December 1577: 5). "The whole city is scandalized," writes Teresa, since Maldonado has acted not only immorally but also illegally. She builds tension by stressing how dangerous the Calced captors are: "I would consider the confessors better off if they were held by the Moors, who perhaps would show more compassion" (*Letters* 1, 4 December 1577: 6). In the case of Fray Juan, he is so frail she fears for his life.

Although Teresa's letters often seem jumbled or spontaneous, this plea to the king appears to have been written in a state of composure. Teresa was certainly frantic about the fate of her friars, but she must have forced herself to sit down and construct a persuasive argument. She presents her points in a logical order: (1) Philip has a religious duty to serve the Virgin. (2) The Calced are enemies of the Virgin because they abuse her daughters. (3) The Discalced confessors serve the Virgin by edifying her daughters, and one of them is truly a saint. (4) The Discalced serve with papal approval, while the Calced were officially banned from the convent. (5) Now the Calced have returned illegally to criminally capture the Discalced confessors, creating a scandal in one of the king's own cities. These arguments lead to an obvious conclusion. The king has the moral, religious, legal, and political duty to act on behalf of the Discalced friars.

Teresa ends by reiterating that all she is asking of the king is that he serve God by helping the Carmelites. He, as the supreme human power in the realm, and the Lord are their only hope. She prays that he live many years, since he is so needed on earth to champion God's honor. By portraying Philip II as a guardian of Christendom, she elevates him, in keeping with the notion of divine right, to an almost supernatural level. She makes him, like herself, an instrument of God's will. The implication in her protests of unworthiness is that she dares to address him only because she, as God's general, must do everything possible to realize her holy mission. Although she is only a lowly nun, God has conferred on her the authority to do whatever is necessary to accomplish the task with which He has charged her. Thus, she as foundress and Philip as king are partners in a celestial enterprise. What we will never know is how Philip reacted to this letter. He did not answer, and he did not order the Calced friars to release John of the Cross. However, Fray Germán escaped from prison in March 1578 and Fray Juan escaped later that year, in August.

The king may not have even read this letter. In fact, argues Slade, Teresa may not have expected him to: "Teresa knew enough about court procedures and Philip's disinclination to take personal appeals to have made the rhetorical wager that he would never see the letters. She also knew that upon arriving at court, the letters would have been opened and read by the secretaries, priests, or aristocrats, precisely the kind of influential people to whom she needed to make her case" ("Teresa of Avila and Philip II" 233). Whether Philip actually read the letter or not was less important than simply getting her message to influential people at court.

Several scholars have remarked on the tone of "confident familiarity" in Teresa's letters to the king.[29] For Slade, what appears to be familiarity is actually "an impression of prior sympathetic communication" or "an illusion of collegiality" that enables Teresa to plead her case more effectively—either to the king himself or to his advisors ("Teresa of Avila and Philip II" 234). By emphasizing the divinity of kingship and through her characteristic self-abasement, Teresa casts Philip "as a forgiving, loving Christ and herself as a wayward but repentant sinner" ("Teresa of Avila and Philip II" 234). At the same time she elevates herself to the level of coprotector of the faith, reminding Philip not only of his commitment to the reform but also of his indebtedness to her. The Calced abuse has become a public scandal right in the king's own back yard. As Slade points out, expressions such as "the *city* is amazed," "the *people* look on [John] as a saint," "the *whole place is thoroughly scandalized*," and "the matter is a cause of *public scandal*" suggest that "in addition to inciting social unrest, the seizure of these priests is an affront to Philip's personal honor" because the abuses are taking place near Philip's court ("Teresa of Avila and Philip II" 239). It is this disgraceful situation that Teresa is struggling to contain. She not only casts Philip as the order's protector, she casts herself as his, thereby suggesting that the government is duty-bound to act on John's behalf.

During the following months Teresa wages an intense campaign against the Calced, informing her friends in high places of her enemies' perfidy. For example, to Teutonio Braganza, the recently named archbishop of Évora, she writes, "Great effort and many plans have gone into discrediting us, especially Padre Gracián and me, the ones against whom they strike. I tell you that they have spread so many calumnies against this man and sent so many accusations to the king, very serious ones (and about these monasteries of discalced nuns), that you would be shocked if you knew about them and that they could invent so much evil" (*Letters* 2, 16 January 1578: 6). Without itemizing the accusations, Teresa paints a vivid picture for one of the wealthiest and most powerful men in Spain. Don Teutonio was a firm ally of Teresa and had her *Way of Perfection* printed at his expense in 1583, the year following her death.

After Tostado received orders to desist from visiting in Andalusia and Castile, Gracián received royal permission to resume his duties. The reformers had extensive contacts at court. Gracián, whose father and two brothers served the king, was particularly well placed. However, because there had been so many complaints from the Calced, both the pope and the nuncio were opposed to his resumption of power, which meant that his lone support came from Philip. He "was now in desperate straits," writes Smet. "He was relying only on the strength of the royal mandate" (2:87). As soon as the Calced friars of Andalusia got wind of Gracián's return, they mounted an attack against him, arguing that if he had ever had an apostolic commission, the nuncio had relieved him of it. On 23

July 1578 Sega confirmed his earlier stance, issuing a brief that formally revoked Gracián's commission and ordered him to hand over under pain of excommunication all documents concerning his visitations and reforms. The harshness of Sega's position led Teresa to weigh her options carefully. Teresa's talent for Realpolitik allowed her to constantly adjust her tactics, and she intuited that a demonstration of humility on the part of the Discalced might sway Sega. However, it was difficult to get Gracián to cooperate. Concerned for Gracián's safety, Teresa writes to Roque de Huerta in August: "I think this is the day he [Gracián] must speak to the King, for he arrived at El Escorial yesterday. Watch carefully that if he is placed under the authority of the nuncio his safety will be guaranteed. For I see that many things are being done that have no legal backing. It is necessary to insist on the matter of our becoming a separate province" (*Letters* 2, 9? August 1578: 1). She led suit by making an act of obeisance to Sega and begging him not to place the Discalced under Calced provincials.

The constant harassment was taking its toll on Gracián. He had passed incognito through Ávila after leaving El Escorial, and, even though the king had sided with him against the nuncio, Teresa found him depressed. A few days later she wrote to him expressing her sorrow at seeing him in such a state: "My heart was in anguish not knowing what to do at seeing you so afflicted, and rightly so, on being in such danger in everything and constrained to go about hiding like a criminal" (*Letters* 2, 14 August 1578: 1). She spurs him on with advice on tactics. First, she tells him, he should avoid controversy: "It seems to me you ought to recall the light that Paul saw—for it was confirmed by what Ángela saw—and withdraw as much as you can from this fire, as long as you don't anger the King, no matter what Mariano tells you" (*Letters* 2, 14 August 1578: 5).[30] Gracián was in a bind because Sega had forbidden that he make any further visitations while the king had given him permission to do so. Mariano wants Gracián to take a stance in his own defense, but Teresa advises him to avoid fanning the flames. She counsels him to assume a position of humility with Sega in order to avoid provoking Sega's anger while at the same time defending his own rights: "If you should speak to the nuncio, defend your position if he is willing to listen and explain that you will always be happy to obey him" (*Letters* 2, 14 August 1578: 7). She advises him not to appear afraid and to explain that he only attempted to resume his visitations because Tostado was threatening to destroy the reform. As a woman, Teresa feels compelled to intersperse her advice with expressions of humility, yet she displays impressive leadership and confidence in counseling Gracián and other men on political strategy.

In addition to directing Gracián and her other lieutenants, Teresa had to go on the offensive herself. At the end of August she composed a document, to be circulated among influential people in Madrid, in which she defended Gracián and attacked Filippo Sega's brief of July 23. Although hastily prepared—time was of the essence—the document sets forth an orderly, reasoned argument against Sega that rests on a point of law: Ormaneto had a papal commission to manage the visitations, while Sega does not or at least has shown no evidence of it. Teresa begins by pointing out that Gracián undertook his visitations in Andalusia at Ormaneto's command and that legal scholars she has consulted in Alcalá, Madrid, and Toledo (important centers of learning) opine that his authority continued even after Ormaneto's death. Furthermore, Diego de Covarrubias y Leiva, president of the Royal Council, shares this view. When Sega arrived and revoked Gracián's authority, explains Teresa, Gracián, uncertain about how to proceed, went to the archbishop, who "scolded him and told him he had the courage of a fly" for not challenging Sega (*Letters* 2, End of August 1578: 2). It was the archbishop's idea that Gracián appeal directly to the king. The crux of Teresa's argument involves the illegitimacy of Sega's order: "Some learned men and even the *presentado* Romero, whom I asked about this here, said that since the nuncio had not presented his faculties for issuing orders in this case, Padre Gracián was not obliged to stop, and they gave many other reasons for this" (*Letters* 2, End of August 1578: 3).[31] In other words, Sega had withdrawn Gracián's visitation rights without license to do so.

Teresa cites authorities and witnesses who claim that Sega himself admitted in their presence that he had no authority over Gracián. Furthermore, she argues, the president of the Royal Council ordered Gracián to continue his work because "it was the will of God and of the King" (*Letters* 2, End of August 1578: 5). As proof of Gracián's authority, "the council furnished him with many writs so that everywhere he could call for help from the secular arm" (*Letters* 2, End of August 1578: 5). Caught between Sega and the king, explains Teresa, Gracián had to yield to Philip, who is, after all, protector of the order. Teresa's last point is that Sega has had ulterior motives from the beginning: "It is definitely known that the nuncio was seeking to have Tostado do the visitation. . . . And we know for certain that Tostado was determined to close down all our houses" (*Letters* 2, End of August 1578: 7). She ends as she would a formal testimony: "This is the whole truth, and there are other things as well" (*Letters* 2, End of August 1578: 9). Teresa's clear, tough argumentation shows that she was indeed capable of the kind of reasoned exposition early feminist critics sometimes characterized as a "masculine" style of rhetoric.[32]

In spite of Teresa's promise of obedience, Sega's hostility intensified. At the end of September Teresa wrote to Gracián, urging him once again to send two Discalced friars to Rome to represent the still unofficial Discalced province. The following month, Gracián's commission reached the end of its term, which had originally been established in 1576. On October 9 the Discalced Carmelites held an emergency meeting at Almodóvar, and Antonio de Jesús Heredia was elected provincial of the unauthorized province. Sega thought that Gracián had manipulated the election and moved aggressively to undo the results. He declared the procedure invalid and forbade Antonio, under pain of excommunication, to assume his duties. Furthermore, he brought all Discalced nunneries and friaries under the jurisdiction of the Calced provincials of Castile and Andalusia. Antonio, Gracián, Mariano, and other Discalced friars were placed under arrest in different monasteries. Teresa, who had been opposed to calling this second Almodóvar meeting, wrote to Roque: "Oh unfortunate friars, called by their superior to a chapter that became the sole reason for their imprisonment. Padre Antonio received much in writing against his convoking the chapter at this time. Now I am begging those unfortunate friars to be silent for the love of God and to wait and not do anything precipitous in this regard. There is no doubt that they have given the nuncio good reason for being angry. In the very beginning he was forewarned by the other Carmelites" (*Letters* 2, 24 October 1578: 6). Teresa saw that, with their impetuousness, her lieutenants were playing right into the hands of their enemies, yet she was incapable of controlling them.

As troubles mounted, Teresa appealed to old friends for help. She wrote, for example, to her former confessor, Pedro Hernández, who was then living in Madrid and who she thought might inform the nuncio about the misdeeds of the Calced: "The devil cannot bear the genuine way in which these [Discalced] friars and nuns serve our Lord. I tell you, you would be consoled to witness the perfection of their life. There are now nine houses of discalced friars and many good subjects in them. Since they have not been joined into a separate province, the disturbances and trials they undergo from those of the cloth are so many as to be indescribable. . . . Of me they say I am a restless vagabond and that the monasteries I have founded were without permission of the pope or general. . . . Many other things, unrepeatable, do those blessed friars say about me" (*Letters* 2, 4 October 1578: 2–4).[33] Teresa begs Hernández to "undeceive" Sega about the Discalced, since, as her former confessor, he knows her soul and understands her noble intentions. The same day she sends another letter to a Jesuit friend through Roque, begging for the same favor. Over the following months she wrote to other influential people, among them the duchess of Alba, in an effort to secure their support.

Teresa's long-term goal was the creation of a separate Discalced province because she believed her friars and nuns would not be free from persecution until they were out from under the yoke of the Calced. As a woman, she could not go to Rome to argue her case herself, but she prepared a detailed memo for her messengers in which she laid out her plan for the governance of nuns.[34] Fearing the Calced had poisoned Rubeo's mind against the reform (unbeknownst to her, Rubeo had died on September 4), she instructs as follows: First, Rubeo should "become persuaded not to accept as true what they have told him about Teresa of Jesus, for she has done noth-

ing but be a very obedient daughter" (*Letters* 2, Mid-October 1578: 2).
Second, he should put the nunneries under Discalced friars of the primitive rule and not friars of the mitigated rule, who in the past have done
great harm. She specifies that the nuns desire to be under the jurisdiction
of the general of the order and should be governed by Gracián or, if the
general objects, by Antonio de Jesús or John of the Cross. Third, the superior who governs the monasteries should not be bound more rigidly than
those of other orders with regard to their right to expand or found houses.
This last provision was necessary in order to ensure the growth of the reform. When Teresa learned of Rubeo's death later that month, she reversed
her decision to send representatives to Rome, deciding to wait for a more
propitious moment. With regard to Rubeo, she tells Gracián, "I greatly
grieved over the news written to me about our Father General. I feel deep
sorrow, and the first day I cried and cried without being able to do otherwise. I so regret the trials we caused him, for he certainly didn't deserve
them, and if we could have gone to see him, everything would have proceeded smoothly" (*Letters* 2, 15 October 1578: 1). There can be no doubt
that Teresa's expressions of grief were sincere. In spite of their quarrels,
Rubeo had helped her immensely at the beginning of the reform, and her
words suggest she hoped she could still count on his support. She would
always believe her problems with Rubeo were due to a misunderstanding.

As might be expected, Teresa's efforts infuriated her enemies. The ax
fell hardest on the Seville convent, where two nuns—Beatriz de la Madre
de Dios and a lay sister, Margarita de la Concepción, her confidante—
brought serious accusations of carnal indecency against Teresa, Gracián,
and María de San José.[35] The two women had reported visions and reve-
lations to their confessor, Garciálvarez, who demanded that they make
protracted general confessions. Alarmed, María de San José dismissed the
confessor, who appealed to the Calced Carmelites. This played right into
Sega's hands. The Calced "took the opportunity to spread salacious rumors about their enemies, alleging that Gracián kissed and embraced the
nuns and danced naked before them, that he spent the night in the convent, and that he was involved in illicit relationships with María and Teresa" (Weber, *María de San José* 4). Beatriz de la Madre de Dios, who was
apparently rather unbalanced, also alleged that Teresa paraded around
town in secular clothes and that she urged nuns to confess to each other.
Sega placed the nuns under the Calced provincial, Diego de Cárdenas, who
quickly deposed María de San José and confined her to her cell for six
months, appointing Beatriz, her accuser, as prioress. Next, Beatriz, Margarita, and their dismissed confessor denounced María and Teresa to the
Inquisition. María de San José writes that the charges were full of lies and
"the most abominable and filthy words that can be imagined. Of the best
of them, all that can be said is that they are unmentionable. But so you can
see the Devil's malice, I shall mention one or two: They had to put that old

woman [Teresa] into the hands of white men and black men so that she could have her fill of wickedness; and she would carry young women from place to place, under pretense of founding convents, so that they could be just as wicked" (*Recreation* 155). The inquisitors interrogated the inhabitants of the Seville Carmel, who confirmed the allegations.

January 31 was a day of intensive letter-writing for Teresa, who must have spent hours preparing two long missives—one for her old friend Hernando de Pantoja, prior of Las Cuevas Monastery in Seville, and the other for the nuns of the Seville Carmel. In the letter to Pantoja, she lays the responsibility for the nuns' testimony on the inquisitors, whose protracted and hostile questioning she believes wore down the nuns: "My fear is that the interrogators completely confused the nuns. This must have happened without it being realized, for in the process things were deduced from the nuns' remarks that are completely false, for I was there at the time the supposed events occurred, and nothing of the sort took place. But I am not surprised that they managed to confuse the nuns, for in one case the interrogation lasted six hours" (*Letters* 2, 31 January 1579: 5). The Inquisition did not pursue the charges of carnality, procurement, and violation of the sacrament of confession. Later, the witnesses against Teresa, María, and Gracián recanted. But at the time, Teresa did not know what the outcome of this catastrophe would be.

A good general knows when to rebuke and when to console. Although Teresa could be tough, she believed that in most cases nuns were best governed with a gentle hand. On the same day she wrote to Pantoja, she also wrote to the nuns of the Seville Carmel, not to scold them but to comfort them. She depicts them not as wrongdoers but as victims of two instigators and some overzealous interrogators. Her letter expresses compassion for the sense of abandonment she knows they must feel without the guidance of Gracián, who, because has been relieved of his duties by Sega, will no longer provide them with spiritual direction. She begins: "The grace of the Holy Spirit be with your charities, my daughters and sisters. You should know that I have never loved you as much as I do now, nor have you ever been so obliged to serve the Lord, for he has given you the great favor of being able to taste something of his cross and share in the terrible abandonment he endured on it" (*Letters* 2, 31 January 1579: 1).[36] Her words of encouragement are meant to fortify their spirits.

At the same time, she encourages them to show kindness toward the malefactors. Even María de San José must treat Beatriz, now prioress, with the respect due her office: "Courage, courage, my daughters. Remember that God does not give anyone more trials than can be suffered and that His Majesty is with the afflicted. . . . Prayer, prayer, my sisters, and now let humility shine forth—and obedience in such a way that no one, especially the former prioress, practices it more toward the appointed vicaress"

(*Letters* 2, 31 January 1979: 2). However, Teresa did not so easily forget the havoc Beatriz had wrought. In a letter to Gracián written the following spring she mentions "this miserable vicaress [who] has been known for spreading serious calumnies" (*Letters* 2, April? 1579: 2). The Spanish is even more graphic than Kavanaugh's English translation. The term Teresa uses is *negra vicaria* (black [evil] vicaress).

By May, Ángel de Salazar had rectified the situation by deposing Beatriz and replacing her with Isabel de San Jerónimo, one of Garciálvarez's cousins, and the archbishop had forbidden Garciálvarez from saying Mass for the Carmelite nuns. On 3 May 1579 Teresa writes to Isabel and María de San José, with an invitation to share her letter with the community. She thanks and praises both women for their service and asks about many of the nuns individually. The motherly, encouraging, upbeat tone of this missive indicates that the crisis at the Seville Carmel had passed. Still, Teresa cannot sign off without a sardonic dig at the principal malefactor: "My regards to Sister Beatriz de la Madre de Dios and tell her that I rejoiced that she is now without a trial, for in a letter I received from her, she told me what a great trial that office was for her" (3 May 1579: 23). Obviously, Teresa is delighted that Beatriz has been pushed off of the prioral chair. Curiously, Teresa never speaks ill of Garciálvarez, the real culprit in the affair.

In the meantime, Sega was continuing his investigation of Gracián. On 20 December 1578 he absolved Gracián from the censures made against him by the investigative body, but he deprived him of the office of reformer and imposed several punishments: Gracián was confined to the monastery of Alcalá, sentenced to flagellations and fasts, forbidden to correspond with anyone except family or to meddle in Carmelite affairs. His confinement was short-lived, however. On 1 April 1579 Sega removed the Discalced Carmelites from the authority of the Calced, and the persecutions stopped. By the beginning of 1580, Gracián was back in Seville, where, on February 19, he was elected prior. The following month Ángel de Salazar appointed him visitator for the Discalced friaries and nunneries beyond the Sierra Morena in Andalusia, and on June 29 Salazar reinstated María de San José as prioress of Seville.

Smet argues that Sega had never wanted to keep the Discalced subjected to the Calced; his only objective was to rein in Gracián and other reformers who had gotten out of control. Once he had accomplished that goal, he was content to allow the Discalced to govern themselves (Smet 2: 93). However, the reality is more complicated. Intricate negotiations went into the extrication of the Discalced from Calced authority. Teresa, convinced that only the creation of a separate province could guarantee freedom for the Discalced, was still angling for representation in Rome. Two Discalced friars, Juan de Jesús Roca and Diego de la Trinidad, were finally preparing to make the trip. On 2 May 1579 Teresa wrote to Pedro Juan de Casademonte, a Madrid businessman, about arrangements for financing their journey. Additional money had yet to be raised, however.

The pecuniary problem was solved when the wealthy Francisco de Bracamonte, who needed a dispensation from Rome in order to marry his cousin Ana, offered to pay the expenses of Roca and his companion. In exchange, Roca, an expert in canon law, would bring Bracamonte's petition before the pope. Early in 1579, Roca went to see Teresa in Ávila "in great secret . . . disguised as a Portuguese priest" (Efrén de la Madre de Dios and Steggink 820).[37] Roca's extreme caution testifies to the danger of his mission during this period of persecution. Around that time, Teresa wrote to Niccolò (hereafter Nicolás) Doria, her business manager and a clever negotiator who managed the affairs of the Discalced friars while Gracián and Mariano were in prison.[38] In her letter she asks him whether to found a house in Rome then or to wait for a more opportune moment. A wrong move, she worries, could result in "a war terrible for everyone" (10 February 1579: 1).[39] But Teresa was already at war, and Doria was her intelligence officer, ensconced in the nuncio's bureaucracy where he could keep an eye on things.

During the months of March and April, Teresa, with the help of Roque de Huerta, launched a veritable letter-writing blitz in order to ensure the success of the mission.[40] Although few of these letters are extant, in her missive to Roque she charges him with their distribution. With regard to Gracián, Mariano, and the other friars being brought to trial, Teresa writes that if justice is not done, "there is no better time than now for us to suffer without fault" (*Letters* 2, 12 March 1579: 2). However, she is doing more than offering the friars' suffering up to God. She mentions that she has arranged to have a large number of documents in favor of the Discalced sent to Diego de Montoya, a canon lawyer in Rome who is arguing on their behalf, although, she says, their defense really depends not on Montoya but on the king, to whom she has written through Roque. By April Gracián has been freed, but the separate province still has not been established. The caution with which Teresa writes to her newly released friend—referring to Roca as "the traveler" rather than by name—shows that she is still apprehensive about the outcome of the negotiations in Rome and is leaving as little as possible to chance:

> The traveler has everything ready now, and the more I deal with him, the more hope I have that he will do everything very well. We had an argument here because I wanted a copy made of the letter to the king so as to send it with the first shipment of mail to the canonist Montoya along with a parcel of letters I am now sending to his mother for delivery to him. And I am writing him that this letter will be brought to him now, or if not, that two fathers will bring it who are going to Rome to render

obedience to our Father Vicar General. And it seems to me that in a matter so serious it is wise to proceed along two different paths. (*Letters* 2, Mid-April 1579: 4)[41]

Teresa was maneuvering both offensively and defensively. She was actively preparing her troops and allies for the battle for independence in Rome, but she was also cautioning her men to appear cooperative and obedient.

Finally, in May the two friars left, Roca disguised as a captain and both men using false names (Efrén de la Madre de Dios and Steggink 821–22). Once in Rome, they proceeded with utmost caution, working behind closed doors with Montoya and the king's ambassador. In the meantime, back in Spain the king's counselors were working zealously in support of the reform, putting more and more pressure on Sega. Efrén de la Madre de Dios and Otger Steggink write, "The nuncio Sega missed seeing by several days that while he thought he had won the battle, even managing to get the Court to receive Tostado, in reality he had been trapped by the subtle political maneuvering of the king" (823). Finally, under pressure from Philip II, Sega proposed the creation of a separate Discalced Carmelite province on 15 July 1579. Days later, Teresa wrote to Teutonio de Braganza mentioning "how well our affairs are coming along" (*Letters* 2, 22 July 1579: 2).[42] The next day she sent an urgent letter to Gracián, telling him, "I am very glad to see how our Lord is guiding these affairs" (*Letters* 2, 23 July 1579: 2). Three days later she wrote to Roque expressing her joy at the upward turn of events in Spain and her hope that negotiations in Rome would go as well.

They did, but not right away. The tortuous struggle went on for a year, until, on 22 June 1580, the papal brief *Pia consideratione* allowed the Discalced friars and nuns to establish a separate province. Teresa did not hear the news until August 1. On August 6 she wrote to María de San José: "You should know that five days ago our brother Fray Jerónimo Gracián received a letter from Fray Juan de Jesús in Rome. . . . In the letter Fray Juan tells Padre Gracián that the brief concerning the matter of our negotiations has been given to the king's ambassador in Rome to send to the king and that the brief was being brought in the same mail delivery as his own letter. And so we are certain that it is now in the hands of the king" (*Letters* 2, 6 August 1580: 6). It perhaps stung her that Roca communicated this momentous news to Gracián rather than to her, but she had had enough experience with male ecclesiastics to know that they often sidestepped women, even women in positions of authority. On August 8 she wrote to her old friend Gaspar Daza matter-of-factly: "When I arrived in Ávila, they told me that the documents from Rome had arrived and were in accord with our proposal" (*Letters* 2, 8 August 1580: 3). The following year, Philip II gave instructions for the brief dividing the Calced and Discalced into separate provinces.

Teresa had struggled long and hard, using correspondence as her ammunition, and in the end she had won. However, her letters contain few celebratory remarks. By the time victory came, she was old and ill, and her success was marred by the death of her beloved brother Lorenzo on June 26. Anyhow, there was no need to gloat. Teresa had always known they would win. After all, she was God's general, and with God on her side, how could she lose?

Chapter 4

Correspondence and Correspondents

Of Saint Teresa's approximately 450 extant letters, nearly half were directed to four recipients: to Gracián, 95 (21.1%); to María de San José, 62 (13.7%); to Lorenzo de Cepeda and to María Bautista, 18 each (8% total). By examining Teresa's sustained communication with these four correspondents, representing 42.8 percent of her epistolary writing, we gain insight into the workings of her personality, relationships, and world.

Letters to Gracián

At the time Saint Teresa met Fray Jerónimo de la Madre de Dios Gracián in Beas, where she had gone to make a foundation, she was in need of friars to promote the male branch of the reform.[1] It was the spring of 1575, and Gracián had professed as a Discalced Carmelite friar only two years earlier, on 25 April 1573. Nevertheless, he was already serving as Carmelite visitator in Andalusia *in solidum* with Francisco Vargas.[2] He was thirty; Teresa was sixty. She was immediately taken with him. She was impressed by his profound spirituality, his charismatic personality, his gentleness, and his solid ideas on governance. They spoke at length on matters concerning the order and found they shared the notion that kindness and sensitivity were more effective tools for guiding souls than severity. With the exception of John of the Cross, Teresa had not found many able friars for her projects, and Fray Jerónimo seemed an ideal collaborator.

Teresa often refers to Gracián in hyperbolic terms from 1575 to 1578, perhaps the most difficult years in early Discalced Carmelite history. Soon after the meeting she writes to her good friend, Isabel de Santo Domingo: "Our *padre* Gracián has been here for over twenty days. I tell you that though I have spoken with him a great deal, I have not yet come to fully grasp the worth of this man. He is without fault in my eyes. . . . I have never seen perfection with so much gentleness" (*Letters* 1, 12 May 1575: 2).[3] She writes to Rubeo, the Carmelite general, that "Gracián is like an angel" (*Letters* 1, 18 June 1575: 2) and also tells Bishop Álvaro de Mendoza about his good qualities (*Letters* 1, 11 May 1575: 2). Her affection is evident in a letter to Gracián, in which she refers to him by his code name "Paul": "I hope in God that everything will go well, for the Lord is turning Paul into an enchanter" (*Letters* 1, 7 December 1576: 4). Mary Luti, who has studied the relationship between the two, concludes that Teresa was, quite simply, "enthralled" (35).

Some historians and biographers have depicted Teresa as positively giddy upon meeting Gracián, detecting an erotic subtext in her lavish praise of him.[4] We cannot know whether such a conjecture is justified, but there can be no doubt but that Teresa was immediately taken with Gracián. She writes in *Foundations* that "it seemed from the way he pleased me that those who had praised him had hardly known him at all" (*CWST* 3, 24:1). Her interest in him was both spiritual and practical. He was a deeply devout man, filled with zeal for her project, and his approach to convent administration was similar to her own. For some scholars, Teresa's friendship with Gracián was the most important in her life. In his overview of Teresa's correspondence with her younger disciple, Alfonso Ruiz concludes: "Although we had no other evidence, [her letters alone] would be enough to show us that the love that united these two people was so profound and unusual that instances of such affection can hardly be found."[5] Ruiz adds, "Gracián displaces, when he appears on the scene, all the other friends who had won a place in the Saint's always loving heart, outstripping the competition" (107–8, translation mine). Shirley du Boulay seconds: "It was in Beas that she met the man who was to be, for the rest of her life, her closest friend. . . . It was in this relationship that Teresa was most herself—foundress and woman, mystic and mother, lover and beloved" (188). A surprising and seemingly impetuous decision by Teresa, made not long after meeting Gracián, would seem to validate this assessment.

In her *Spiritual Testimonies* Teresa describes how, shortly after meeting Gracián, she decided to make a vow of obedience to him. He in turn determined to consult her on all matters concerning the order. This vow, she explains, required considerable inner struggle, as it involved a degree of relinquishment of authority. However, her decision was confirmed by a vision in which God, acting as a matchmaker, joined her hand to Gracián's in a kind of spiritual marriage (*CWST* 1, *Spiritual Testimonies* 36:2). Rather than enslaving her, this union made her freer because it enabled her to better serve God. Teresa uses marriage imagery again in a letter to Gracián written in 1577. Referring to herself by the code name of Ángela and to Gracián by the code name of Paul, she writes that he should "be at ease, for the matchmaker was so qualified and made the knot so tight that it will be taken away only when life ends. And after death the knot will be even tighter, for the foolish striving for perfection will not be so excessive and the remembrance of you will rather help her praise the Lord" (*Letters* 1, 9 January 1577). Some critics have intimated romantic overtones in her use of the image of the marriage knot in particular. Luti notes that although "Teresa aspired to objectivity," she is "fairly transparent about the strength of [her] attraction" (36). Marcelle Auclair suggests that because of her affection for Gracián, Teresa felt "something very much akin to feminine jealousy" for María de San José, the prioress of the Seville Carmel, with whom Gracián also had a warm friendship (260).

It is easy to see how biographers could have reached this conclusion. Teresa comments in her *Spiritual Testimonies* that her vow to Gracián makes her feel disloyal to previous confessors, making her sound a bit like an unfaithful wife suffering pangs of conscience.[6] Yet, judging from the *Spiritual Testimonies*, it is more likely that Teresa considered Gracián a kind of divine gift to her, an answer to her prayer for an understanding confessor who would provide coherent spiritual direction. Casting her spiritual and emotional bond with Gracián as a marriage allowed Teresa both to legitimize it and to endow it with a permanence that, after her difficult experiences with incompetent spiritual directors, she craved.

Gracián returned her affection, but the constant gossip to which he later became subject may have made him feel the need to clarify the chaste nature of their relationship: "This great love I bore Madre Teresa of Jesus, and she for me, is a very different bond from what is usually had in the world, for *that* love is dangerous, vexatious and causes thoughts and temptations that afflict and slacken the spirit, disturb the sensuality. But this love that I had for Madre Teresa of Jesus and she for me produced in me purity, the spirit and love of God, and in her consolation and relief from her trials" (*Anastasio* 319). Likewise, Teresa felt the need to rationalize what must have seemed like a strange liaison: "It will seem inappropriate that he should have informed me of so many personal matters about his soul," she writes in *Foundations*. "At times he had reason for so doing because he thought that on account of my age and from what he had heard about me I had some experience" (*CWST* 3, 23:11).[7] She and Gracián were right to be wary because in 1578, María de San José, Teresa, and Gracián were all denounced to the Inquisition for immoral behavior.

If Teresa's intense devotion to the much younger Gracián has intrigued modern scholars, it is, at least in part, because it seems so out of character. From the time Teresa founded the first Discalced Carmelite convent in 1562, she demonstrated astonishing toughness and determination. How could a woman with Teresa's smarts and political acumen be taken with a young man such as Gracián, whose imprudence had already aroused suspicion among both the church and Carmelite hierarchy? In hindsight, it seems inconceivable that Teresa would submit to the dominance of this reckless young friar, no matter how enthralled she was with his spiritual gifts. She admits in her *Book of Foundations* that she had severe reservations about following his directive to found in Seville: "Since I saw that a foundation in Seville was the resolve of my major superior, I immediately submitted, although . . . I had some very serious reasons against [it]" (*CWST* 3, 24:4). Why, then, did she go along with this badly conceived scheme?

Researchers have tended to attribute her decision to her vow of obedience to Gracián, based on his own account. In his *Peregrinación de Anastasio*, Gracián describes how he tested Teresa's humility, submitting her to mortifications and sanctions to the point that she made no move without him. William Walsh wrote in his 1943 biography that Teresa submitted to Gracián's orders with "all the generosity and confidence of a pure and childlike soul" (444) and that "her obedience to Gracián, as the superior assigned to her by the Lord God, was so complete that test it as he would, he could never find a flaw in it" (445). Likewise, Peers saw Teresa's decision to go to Seville simply as an act of obedience to Gracián (*Studies in Spanish Mysticism* 123). Auclair suggests that the vow of obedience was an example of feminine wiliness: "Mother Teresa bent P. Jerónimo Gracián de la Madre de Dios to her will by the means all women employ, be they saints or sinners, geniuses or fools, to bring men under their domination: she vowed obedience to him" (262). And once the vow was made, declares Auclair, Teresa had no choice but to go to Seville (268).

In more recent years, scholars have offered a more multitextured view of this relationship. Luti, writing nearly five decades after Walsh, insists that although Teresa was aware of Gracián's faults, she overlooked them because she saw his participation as crucial to the success of the reform (39). For Luti, the "marriage" between Gracián and Teresa was a real marriage—albeit a rocky one—that is, an indissoluble union necessary to ensure the movement. Efrén de la Madre de Dios and Steggink argue that Teresa had to obey Gracián in his role as God's surrogate because it was God's will that the reform move forward (607). Medwick notes that since Gracián was the apostolic visitator to the province and thereby her official superior, she really had no choice (185). None of these scholars suggests that Teresa obeyed Gracián slavishly, but all of them see the vow of obedience as the instrument that placed her in an inferior position and allowed him to prod her to Seville against her better judgment.

Yet, it is possible that Teresa's submission to Gracián's authority has been overstated. In a spiritual context, submission to God is always unconditional, but submission to human beings is always conditional. As described in Genesis, disobedience to God is the essence of sin. In the New Testament, Jesus's obedience to God is the source of salvation. Thus, obedience in a religious context is positive and liberating. A vow of obedience to a spiritual director does not imply blind submission to another's will, but submission to God though the authority he has delegated.[8] Teresa's stipulation in her *Spiritual Testimonies* that her vow of obedience would apply only "to serious matters so as to avoid scruples" and only "so long as there was nothing in opposition to God or my superiors" displays a clear understanding of the limited nature of the vow of obedience (*CWST* 1, 36:7). She was not swearing blind allegiance to Gracián, but merely promising to accept his direction in spiritual matters and, even then, only with respect to those issues she deemed important enough to discuss with him. She was clearly aware of the dangers of scrupulosity (unwarranted and compulsive fear of sin) and of her responsibility to determine whether his commands were legitimate.

It is significant that Teresa had had Jesuit confessors. She had probably made the *Spiritual Exercises* and so would have been familiar with the kind of collaborative arrangement between priest and directee intrinsic to Jesuit spiritual practice.[9] The vehemence with which Teresa condemns the confessors who discounted her mystical experiences by attributing them to the devil and the warmth with which she praises the Jesuits suggest she appreciated a priest-directee arrangement in which her views were taken seriously. Recently, critics have begun to reevaluate Teresa's relationships with her male associates. Weber suggests that even though Teresa wrote in obedience to spiritual directors, she worked with them collaboratively, for the most part retaining control of her words ("Three Lives of the *Vida*" 110). Judging from her letters, she clearly had a collaborative relationship with Gracián. If she agreed to make a vow of obedience to him, it was because she believed the relationship would enrich her spiritually without obliterating her will.

Although Teresa obeyed Gracián's command to found in Seville on the grounds that she owed him obedience, she could have done otherwise. Since the order was made in defiance of Rubeo's directive and she had stipulated that she would obey Gracián's commands only so long as they did not contradict her superiors, she could have refused. She knew Rubeo had forbidden new foundations in Andalusia. The year before she had written to María Bautista, prioress of Valladolid, who thought Beas was in Andalusia: "You should know that Beas is not in Andalusia, but five miles this side, for I know that I cannot make foundations in Andalusia" (*Letters* 1, End of September 1574: 3). In *Foundations* she notes that if she had been aware that Beas was in Andalusia, she would never have founded there (*CWST* 3, 24:4). Teresa also knew that if she objected to the foundation, Gracián would not insist. She wrote to Bishop Mendoza: "I truly believe that he would not have placed me under any obligation, but his desire for this was so great that if I hadn't complied, I would have been left with a disturbing scruple that I wasn't being obedient, something I always desire to be" (*Letters* 1, 11 May 1575: 3). It is perfectly possible that Teresa decided to honor Gracián's order because it coincided with her own desire to expand the reform. Although she was chary of Andalusia, three Discalced friaries had already been founded in the south, and Teresa was happy with them, judging from her letter to Gracián of 20 September 1576, quoted in Chapter 3. Furthermore, she had already founded in Beas, which she belatedly learned was under the ecclesiastical jurisdiction of Andalusia, without incident. Perhaps, in spite of misgivings, she was now ready to take the next step.

In spite of her devotion to Gracián, Teresa was not blind to his flaws. Pedra comments that she was astute enough to see that in terms of his apostolic responsibilities, he had his "ups and downs" (45). Although Teresa always treated him with tact and respect, she assumed many roles—mother, collaborator, teacher, spiritual director, and defender—that placed her on equal footing with him, or even in a position of superiority. Like several other nuns who enjoyed close relationships with priests, she often addresses him as "my son" in her letters, reversing the customary roles of spiritual "father" and "daughter."[10]

In many missives Teresa assumes the position of a hovering mother, showing keen concern for Gracián's health. She frequently warns him against overtaxing himself. In one letter she warns him not to work "like a Jesuit"—an order known for its rigor: "It's necessary that you realize that you are not made of iron, and that many in the Society have ruined themselves through overwork" (*Letters* 1, 9 January 1577: 2). She advises him to rest sufficiently: "It seems to me that you are allowing yourself very little [respite], for if you are going to Matins and getting up early, I don't know how you are getting enough sleep" (*Letters* 1, October 1577?: 1).[11] Later she writes again, "I tell you, *mi padre*, that it would be good for you to get your sleep. Realize that you have a great deal of work, and the tiredness is not felt until the head gets into such a condition that there is no remedy, and you already know how important your health is. . . . When it is time to sleep, set aside your projects, however necessary" (*Letters* 1, December 1577?: 1). This concern for Gracián's health lasted until the end of her life.

In April 1579, Gracián had just been released from his confinement in Alcalá, where he had been seriously ill. Teresa writes to him, scolding him for not keeping her informed of his condition. "What you have been going through adds greatly to my pain. God forgive you for the days you made me go through with your fevers and blood spitting. And they tell me you have been suffering like this for some time. I don't know what it is that you did not let me know" (*Letters* 2, April 1579: 2). In the fall of 1579, Gracián was pushing himself to the limit—teaching, preaching, and involving himself in the affairs of the order in spite of Sega's prohibition on such activity. Teresa writes to him, "For the love of God, cut down on your workload. If you do not attend to this in time, you will see that later you will not be able to find a remedy" (*Letters* 2, 4 October 1579: 2). Teresa clearly had no qualms about assuming dominance in her relationship with Gracián in matters concerning his physical well-being. Her own experience with health problems and the debilitating effects of overwork put her in a position to counsel (perhaps he would have said nag!) him on such issues.

But it was not only on such neutral or "nonprofessional" issues as health that Teresa assumed authority. Her letters reveal that she clearly did not conform to the traditional "script" that proscribed women from instructing men in spiritual matters. When Teresa worries Gracián is so overtired he is neglecting his prayers, she writes: "[Paul] shouldn't get into the habit of abandoning so great a treasure. . . . For the blessings the Lord gives in prayer are most remarkable, and I'm not surprised that the devil would like to take them away" (*Letters* 1, December 1577?: 1). When she thinks he is yielding to melancholy, what we now call depression, and scrupulosity, she warns him against these obstacles to healthy spirituality: "My Paul is very foolish to have so many scruples. . . . If while having so good a life you become this pessimistic, what would you have done had you had to suffer as Fray John (of the Cross) does?" (*Letters* 2, August 1578: 3). Teresa's letters show that she was as much a spiritual director to Gracián as he was to her.

When the Calced persecutions begin, Teresa reminds Gracián that suffering is a virtue: "I tell you, *padre*, God loves you very much and you are doing well in your imitation of him. Rejoice since he is giving you what you ask of him which is trials" (*Letters* 1, November 1576: 1). As the harassment intensifies, she advises patience, for "God orders these things so his servants suffer" (*Letters* 2, 15 October 1578: 7). And suffering, she reminds him repeatedly, facilitates spiritual progress. Joan Cammarata has shown parallels between Teresa's letters of consolation and the traditional *epistola consolatoria*, of which Saint Jerome and Saint Augustine provide examples, as do Juan Luis Vives and Antonio de Torquemada. Teresa's consolatory letters share with these prototypes the insistence on *contemptus mundi*—literally "contempt of the world," but more broadly the recognition of the fleeting nature of those things society values (honor, wealth, prestige, power). These letters seek to console sufferers by encouraging resignation through the realization that human pain is transitory and will be cured by God. Suffering is a gift that brings us closer to God, enabling us to experience what he experienced on the cross, and the rewards for sharing Christ's suffering are eternal.[12] While it is certainly possible that Teresa had these models in mind, the notion of *contemptus mundi* was fundamental to monastic withdrawal and deeply ingrained in Teresa's psyche. It would therefore have been natural for her to console Gracián and others by referring to this theme.

However, Teresa is concerned that Gracián does not have the stamina for such suffering. During this period she frets constantly about Gracián's spiritual and physical health. She writes him encouraging letters assuring him that his "trials" are all part of God's plan. By the end of the month, rumors are spreading that Gracián intends to leave the order.[13] Teresa writes to dissuade him: "I am not surprised that anyone who loves you wants to see you free of those dangers and looks for means toward this, although it would not be a good thing to abandon the blessed Virgin in times of such need" (*Letters* 2, October 1578: 1).[14] As the situation improves the following year, Teresa worries that Gracián has come to take pleasure in the role of Christian martyr and will act to provoke new misfortunes: "I am amused to learn that you are again wanting trials. Leave us alone for a while, for the love of God, for you don't suffer them alone. Let's rest for a few days" (*Letters* 2, 21 April 1579: 7). The irony of Teresa's comment reveals sharp psychological insight. She feared Gracián was reveling in his victimhood and that his risky behavior would cause problems not only for him but for them all.

Although she was aware of Gracián's character flaws, Teresa nevertheless valued his spiritual direction, and when political circumstances kept them apart, she suffered. In September 1576, Teresa, captive in Toledo, went through a period of severe spiritual alienation. In a cryptic, highly coded letter, she explains to Gracián, then in Almodóvar, that "Joseph" (code name for God) has provided "Ángela" (Teresa) with a new confessor, who, although satisfactory, is inferior to Paul (Gracián), for "after having Paul, her soul was unable to find comfort or happiness with anyone." (*Letters* 1, 5 September 1576: 4). After Sega granted Gracián his freedom early in 1579, Teresa wrote to him again: "God be blessed . . . that the separation will soon end and poor Ángela will be able to confer about her soul. For since your absence she has not been able to confer with anyone about anything that might bring her relief" (*Letters* 2, 21 April 1579: 2). Teresa was neither in awe of nor submissive to Gracián, but she appreciated his guidance and garnered spiritual sustenance from their friendship. At times she consoled him, and at times she allowed herself to be consoled by him. In this sense, Teresa and Gracián were spiritual partners.

Gracián held the title of visitator, with the authority that title conferred, but Teresa held the title of foundress, which also conferred authority. With respect to the female convents, her sex alone was enough to grant stature. Gracián routinely consulted her about visiting convents and, in fact, she composed *On Making the Visitation* to guide him in this task. The tone of her letters on the subject is confident and commanding: "You should be careful, *padre mío*, in this matter, and believe that I understand women's nature better than you" (*Letters* 1, October 1575?: 2). Teresa insists repeatedly on the ability of women to understand and guide other women. Gracián apparently accepted her authority in this area, since he had her write *The Interior Castle* primarily for the enlightenment of other nuns.

Just as Gracián consulted Teresa on convent visitation, she consulted him on convent governance. Money is a frequent theme in her letters to him; she mentions dowries and legacies repeatedly: "Now a postulant, very capable and talented, has received the habit here. Her patrimony is valued at twenty thousand ducats. But we don't think she will leave much to the house in comparison with what she could, for she is very attached to her blood sisters" (*Letters* 2, 7 July 1579: 2). Often Teresa consulted him on issues concerning particular nuns. In one case, a story was circulating about a pregnant nun in Paterna. Teresa patently dismisses the allegation: "I think a charge like that is the greatest stupidity" (*Letters* 1, 13 December 1576: 4). Nevertheless, she inquires of Gracián, "on what grounds the accusation was made against the nun who is a virgin and bearing a child" (*Letters* 1, 13 December 1576: 4). In another letter she complains of an "insufferable" girl, the daughter of a wealthy lawyer, whose whining and hypochondria finally forced Teresa to transfer her from Alba de Tormes to another convent (*Letters* 2, 7 July 1579, 18 July 1579). Sometimes she reprimands Gracián for countering her policies: "I was annoyed that you would go to the extreme of accepting another blood sister in a community where there were already two" (*Letters* 2, 14 May 1582: 1).[15] These and many other letters show that Teresa and Gracián regularly made decisions collaboratively but that she assumed the decisive role in what might be considered "domestic" matters.

Although we have no examples of Gracián's letters to Teresa, a 1576 document containing an exchange between the two—Gracián wrote down his comments in the left-hand column with room on the right for Teresa to answer—illustrates the kind of give-and-take in which they must have often engaged. The questions and answers do not correspond perfectly, but the document reveals an interesting interpersonal dynamic. Teresa, using the code name Laurencia, has apparently asked about a well-to-do candidate she offered to admit without a dowry in spite of pressures to make the woman pay. Gracián agrees with Teresa that it is acceptable to forgo the dowry in the spirit of poverty. If anyone gives her an argument, writes Gracián, "Let Laurencia point out that she has a superior who will decide and that she can no longer do anything about the matter" (*Letters* 1, August 1576: 1). However, since Teresa made the arrangement without consulting him, he ponders (a bit peevishly) "whether it would be fitting to give Laurencia orders so that from here on she not give her word about receiving any nun without informing Eliseo [code for Gracián]" (*Letters* 1, August 1576: 2). Teresa responds with what seems like exaggerated humility: "Your paternity has no need to give me an order, for I consider the order already given and will carry it out . . . even were you not the superior, I would not receive anyone without telling you about it, if you were close by, or even, I believe, far away" (*Letters* 1, August 1576: 2). Although Gracián appears to have the upper hand, Teresa's hedge—"if you were close by, or even, I believe, far away"—strategically compromises her promise of obedience and gives her leeway to make her own decisions.

Although she exercised power within the convents, as a woman working for reform within a larger organization Teresa was often relatively powerless. She constantly had to navigate among higher-ups anxious to silence or restrain her. As we saw in Chapter 3, one way in which Teresa tried to exercise influence was through Gracián. However, Teresa soon realized that she could not control her spiritual son. When Ormaneto charged Gracián with continuing his visitations in Andalusia, Teresa, demonstrating a keen understanding of human psychology, urged him to exercise prudence: "All of them are determined to obey your paternity and help you in suppressing any sinful abuses, as long as there are no extreme solutions taken in regard to other matters" (*Letters* 1, 27 September 1575: 1). Fifteen years of grappling with powerful men had taught her the wisdom of avoiding direct confrontation.

However, just as Teresa's vow of obedience to Gracián left room for maneuvering, so did his pledge to consult her in matters concerning the order. As we saw in Chapter 3, when he began his visitation of the Casa Grande on 21 November 1575, the friars raised a ruckus, bolting the door and holding him inside. According to his own description of these events in *Peregrinacón de Anastasio*, Gracián thought they were going to kill him. Instead of heeding Teresa's advice to avoid "extreme solutions," he threatened them with excommunication and did, in fact, excommunicate them, causing Teresa to complain bitterly about his conduct to her friend María Bautista.[16] Not only did Gracián disregard her advice, but he backed Rubeo's decision to confine her in Toledo. She complains to María Bautista: "Father Visitator has not allowed me to leave here because for now he has more authority over me than our most Reverend Father General. I don't know where it will all end up" (*Letters* 1, 30 December 1575). Teresa's resentment of Gracián is manifest in the letters of this period. His high-handedness has exacerbated conflicts within the order and placed constraints on her movement. If Teresa was momentarily enthralled with Gracián when she met him in Beas, by the end of 1575 she was thoroughly aggravated with him.

In fall of the following year, Gracián continued expending what Teresa considered an inordinate amount of energy on some of the smaller Andalusian monasteries, which were not reforming fast enough to suit him. She scolds: "Do not think, *mi padre*, that you can make things perfect with one stroke. . . . Hardly will you have left when they will return to their former ways, and by doing this are exposing yourself to a thousand dangers" (*Letters* 1, 20 September 1576: 1). Teresa is annoyed because Gracián is dragging his heels on a much more urgent matter: the creation of a separate Discalced province. Acutely aware that time is of the essence because the nuncio is mortally ill, she urges Gracián to send two Discalced friars to Rome to petition for the partition of the order: "Your paternity should make every effort that they not delay in going. . . . Don't take this as a secondary matter" (*Letters* 1, 20 September 1576: 9).[17] Furthermore, she is irked that he has failed to make known a brief from the nuncio appointing him apostolic visitator of the Calced Carmelites in Andalusia, a document that would have established his authority over them: "Why you did not send the brief, certainly if there were reason for doubt, it would have been better to think of this beforehand" (*Letters* 1, 21 October 1576: 2). During the following two years, Teresa writes to Gracián repeatedly about the need to send Discalced friars to Rome. After the chapter meeting in Almodóvar, her insistence intensifies. On 29 September 1578 she writes that even one representative would be a help, although two would be better. The following month she writes once more: "Everyone is amazed that we don't have anyone in Rome to carry out our business for us, and so those others do whatever they want" (*Letters* 2, 15 October 1578: 1).[18] As her correspondence makes clear, her efforts to influence Gracián's behavior were largely unsuccessful. His lack of common sense undoubtedly infuriated her, for she reprimanded him time and again.

And yet, in her letters to friends she usually defended and praised him. Even though she had already had a taste of Gracián's impetuousness, she writes to her sister Juana, "You ought also to know that they have given Padre Gracián authority over all the Discalced friars and nuns down here and up there as well; no better thing could have happened for us. He is the ideal person" (*Letters* 1, 12 August 1575: 4). A few days later she berates María Bautista, who had apparently criticized Gracián's recklessness in Andalusia, "If you find faults in him, it must be because you have not spoken much with him and do not know him well. I tell you he is a saint, not at all impetuous but very cautious" (*Letters* 1, 28 August 1575: 9). At the time, Gracián was threatening to excommunicate the rebellious Calced Andalusian friars. His hotheadedness had already exacerbated the situation in the south, and Teresa had tried repeatedly to restrain him. Yet, like a fond mother, she shields him from criticism. In her letters to María de San José she waxes lyrical about his virtues, urging the prioress to care for and even coddle him.

Teresa's protectiveness is perhaps understandable given the persecution Gracián was enduring. On 23 July 1578 Sega issued a brief revoking Gracián's authority. Gracián went into hiding at the home of a friend in order to avoid receiving official notification. Teresa, uncertain of his whereabouts, composed a letter, deliberately vague, which she sent to Mancera with instructions to the subprior to forward it to Peñaranda, "and not to let anyone know . . . but to keep the matter to himself" (*Letters* 2, 9 August 1578: 1).[19] The cryptic nature of this letter makes it difficult to decipher: "If by chance you did not go where you told me you were going, I am sending another messenger to Valladolid and informing Mother Prioress of how she should respond. Roque is very insistent that nothing different be said, for that would be our ruin" (*Letters* 2, 9 August 1578: 1). Teresa appears to be creating a "script" to enable anyone who might be interrogated by Sega's men to protect Gracián. She warns Gracián to be wary of kidnappers, even when going to Mass. She clearly has the abduction of John of the Cross fresh in her mind. She instructs Gracián to speak with "Joannes," possibly code name for Juan de la Roca, before making any move. Although the letter is enigmatic, the core message is clear: danger lurks everywhere.

Halfway through her writing, Teresa is interrupted: "I was at this point when the Reverend Padre Rioja arrived at the door with the notary to give notification of [Sega's] brief" (*Letters* 2, 9 August 1578: 8).[20] The ferocity of the document shocks her: "God forgive me, for I am still unable to believe that the nuncio ordered such a thing, I mean in that style" (*Letters* 2, 9 August 1578: 8). Immediately, Teresa tries to calm and soothe Gracián, assuring him that he has done nothing wrong: "Since you proceeded so justly in everything and since you waited almost a year without making any visitations . . . I don't know how one can speak like this" (*Letters* 2, 9 August 1578: 8). Rather than fault Gracián, Teresa blames the nuncio for proceeding illegally: "All the learned men say that even though the nuncio gives you orders, you are not obliged to obey since he does not show the patent letters that support his authority" (*Letters* 2, 9 August 1578: 9). She lays out a plan to send her trusted traveling companion, Julián de Ávila, to the nuncio with a promise of obedience to "win his favor" and beseech him not to put them under jurisdiction of the Calced (*Letters* 2, 9 August 1578: 10).[21] In the meantime, Gracián must stay out of Sega's way: "The saintly Paul remains at home with me" (*Letters* 2, 9 August 1578: 12). She concludes with assurances that there is nothing to fear, as God is on their side.

This letter is so vivid that one can imagine Teresa biting her knuckles as she wrote it. One can see her jumping up to receive Rioja, trembling with rage at Sega's words, taking a breath and sitting back down to comfort Gracián. It reveals, perhaps more than any other in the epistolary collection, the depth of her feelings for Gracián. Teresa reassures him as though he were a frightened child; she bolsters his confidence, calling him a saint twice. She reassures him of her loyalty, evoking her vow of obedience to him. But Teresa's positive tone belies her fear. Like many a worried mother, she presents a façade of self-assuredness to her child while struggling to conceal her own anxiety. Her letters of the following weeks show her agonizing over Gracián's safety. She writes to Roque de Huerta, who is acting as her intermediary: "My worry now, the greatest I've had, is whether our *padre* has fallen into the nuncio's hands. I would much rather see him in the hands of God and amid the dangers of travel to Rome, even if worse, and among those friars chosen to go" (*Letters* 2, 19? August 1578: 1). Teresa's desperation is almost audible here. The confidence she expressed previously in her ability to sway Sega is completely gone.

Not all Teresa's letters are so intense. Teresa had a sharp sense of humor, and although she was careful to observe the rules of etiquette in her correspondence to Gracián, addressing him respectfully as Your Reverence, Your Paternity, or less formally, My Father or even My Son, she was comfortable enough in their relationship to tease him. An expert rider (women in those days rode mules), she chides Gracián about his propensity to fall from his mount: "It would be good if they tied you to the saddle so that you couldn't fall. I don't know what kind of donkey that is" (*Letters* 1, October 1575?: 5). Having met his mother, she writes to him about her, "She has a simplicity and openness that put me in seventh heaven. In these she greatly surpasses her son" (*Letters* 1, 20 September 1576: 2). Even in her last letters, written when she was old and ill, she maintains her wit. When, late in 1581, one of Teresa's friends from Malagón gives her some coins for Gracián, she writes to him: "I am doing all I can not to keep them for myself. The ways things are going, it won't be long before I'm tempted to steal them" (*Letters* 2, 29 November 1581: 3). Many of Teresa's letters to Gracián are full of playful banter. Others attest to her willingness to break the rules for him, as when she orders that he be given his meals in the convent parlor or supports his efforts to have his underage sister, Isabel, admitted to the order.

During her last years Teresa continued to write to Gracián, sharing news about her foundations, inquiring about his health and reporting on her own, or scolding him for some gaffe. But now a new theme begins to emerge: his neglect. She often reproaches him for not writing, revealing just how much his silence hurts her: "You should tell that gentleman [Gracián himself], that although he is by nature careless, he should not be so with [Ángela]. Where love is present, it cannot be asleep so long a time" (*Letters* 2, 4 October 1579: 1). She feels increasingly abandoned by him. In her last letter to Gracián, written a month before she died, she reprimands him for going to Andalusia instead of helping her with business in Castile. Teresa is now mortally ill but still struggling with the details of convent administration, and Gracián's departure has left her overburdened. "The reasons for you to go didn't seem to me to be sufficient," she scolds him. "I don't know why, but I so felt your absence at such a time, that I lost the desire to write to you" (*Letters* 2, 1 September 1582: 2). After filling him in on developments in various houses, she goes on: "I don't know for what purpose you have to stay so long in Seville, for they told me you will not be returning until the time of the chapter—which greatly increased my pain" (*Letters* 2, 1 September 1582: 6). In spite of her distress, she offers him advice on a myriad of matters. For as long as she knew him, Teresa was concerned for Gracián: his welfare, his work, his psyche, and his soul.

Like most human relationships, the bond between Teresa and Gracián was variegated and fluctuating. Teresa neither trusted Gracián like an innocent child nor was able to judge him with complete objectivity. What role he played in her spiritual development is unclear, since Teresa already had a developed notion of her own spirituality before she met him. Still, she valued his guidance and never found another confessor she trusted as much. Although she viewed her relationship with Gracián as a spiritual marriage, Teresa's role was more that of mother—bossy and scolding, yet loving and indulgent—than that of an obedient wife.

Letters to María de San José (Salazar)

Teresa hoped that one day María de San José, one of her most trusted friends, would succeed her as foundress. Teresa had met her at the palace of Luisa de la Cerda, where as a child María had entered into service. The thirteen-year-old María was fascinated with the famous holy woman who reputedly had visions and levitated. Educated by Doña Luisa, María knew French and Latin and was an excellent poet; in one of her letters Teresa jokingly refers to her as a *letrera* (roughly, "brain") (*Letters* 2, 28 March 1578: 4). After Teresa founded a convent on Doña Luisa's estate in Malagón, María took vows and in 1572 became prioress. She accompanied Teresa to Beas, where both women met Gracián, and when Teresa founded in Seville, she named her prioress.

María's friendship with Gracián caused her endless problems. Both were attractive and of about the same age—he was born in 1545 and she in 1548—which made them easy prey for wagging tongues. In their war of calumnies, the Calced accused them of immoral behavior, causing María to temporarily lose her position as prioress of the Seville Carmel. Scandal was to pursue Gracián and María even after the Discalced were free of Calced domination; he was actually accused of fathering a child with her.[22] Two years after Teresa's death in 1582, Gracián sent María to Lisbon as prioress of a new foundation. When Nicolás Doria rose to power within the order, his antagonism toward Gracián produced severe repercussions for María. Doria thought that Gracián indulged prioresses and encouraged them to resent priestly authority, and so he modified Teresa's Constitutions in order to limit the power of prioresses and bring them under clerical control. With the support of Gracián and John of the Cross, María de San José and Ana de Jesús, prioress of the Madrid Carmel, audaciously went over Doria's head and appealed directly to the pope, who sided with the women.[23] Enraged, Doria had María imprisoned in her convent and deprived of communion and the right to participate in convent affairs. In the ensuing battle, Gracián was incarcerated and removed from the order, although he was later readmitted. After Doria died, María was sent to a remote convent in Cuerva, where the nuns were instructed to treat her coldly. Alone and dejected, she died in 1603 at the age of fifty-five.

Teresa considered both Gracián and María her "spiritual children," but her epistolary writing reveals different relationships with each. In her letters to María, Teresa usually refers to Gracián as "our *padre*," or, occasionally, "my Paul," while in her letters to him, she usually refers to María as "the Prioress." In spite of this businesslike moniker, Teresa was deeply fond of María. On her way to Toledo, she writes about how much she misses her and the other Seville nuns (*Letters* 1, 18 June 1576: 1). Later, from Toledo, she writes, "I have such a desire to see you that it would seem I have nothing else to think about" (*Letters* 1, 7 September 1576: 4). Teresa mentions repeatedly how much she enjoys receiving her letters (*Letters* 1, 2 July 1576: 4; 9 September 1576: 1) and admonishes her to look after her health, for "it is better to cater to yourself than to be sick" (*Letters* 1, 11 July 1576: 6). After a misunderstanding with María she writes, "I am not surprised by your affection for me, for I have always felt the same way toward you. . . . There is no longer any reason to speak of what happened in the past" (*Letters* 1, 13 October 1576: 3). Yet tension often existed between the two.

In spite of her warm words for María, Teresa frequently complains of her "aloofness" and lack of "sympathy and love" (*Letters* 1, 2 July 1576: 2). Teresa sometimes acts like a jealous stepmother who sees her adopted daughter as a more beautiful, educated rival. At times she comes across as a nagging mother, always finding fault. On one occasion she complains about María's handwriting: "Whenever you try to improve your handwriting it gets worse" (*Letters* 1, 2 July 1576: 3). Her favorite form of denigration is the backhanded compliment, as when she praises one of María's letters to Mariano as "very good, if it were not for that Latin." While Teresa appreciated María's intelligence and administrative talents, her disparaging references to her as a *letrera* and Latinist suggest uneasiness with female erudition. "God deliver all my daughters from presuming to be Latinists," she writes (*Letters* 1, 19 November 1576: 2). Although Teresa promoted female literacy by stipulating in the Constitutions that nuns must learn to read, she was wary of excessive learning in women.[24] She once wrote of a certain aspirant: "As long as she knows how to recite the psalms and is attentive to all the rest, nothing else is required" (*Letters* 2, 17 April 1578: 3).[25] Perhaps Teresa attributed to María's erudition an overconfidence that led to conflicts with confessors.

Many of Teresa's barbs are veiled in humor. In the letter quoted above about María's use of Latin with Mariano, Teresa also teases the prioress about feigning ignorance with *her*: "I was amused that you spelled out the date. Please God you didn't do so to avoid humbling yourself by putting it down in numbers" (*Letters* 1, 19 November 1576: 1). The implication is that María "dumbed down" her letter to Teresa by not writing Arabic numerals although she knew how to do so. On another occasion Teresa calls María "a fox," given to ruses (*Letters* 1, 9 January 1577: 2). Although in the context of the letter these ruses apply to white lies María tells to shield Teresa from bad news, the implication is that María is a wily creature. In the same letter Teresa teasingly accuses María of sanctimoniousness for adopting the policy of extreme sartorial austerity proposed by Garciálva-rez, the Seville confessor: "You ought to know that some adversity is being prepared for Padre Garciálvarez, for they say that he is educating you in pride; tell him this" (*Letters* 1, 9 January 1577: 9). Later, when María is going through a tortuous period due to the calumnies of two of her nuns, Teresa calls her "very wretched," but does so affectionately; the message here is that although María is no saint, she has done nothing to merit the abuse she is suffering (*Letters* 2, 3 May 1579: 2).[26]

Since we do not have María de San José's letters to Teresa, it is impos-sible to know to what extent the prioress teased her right back. Judging from María's other writing, it is clear that she had a sharp sense of humor, ample self-confidence, and a stinging wit.[27] Undoubtedly the two women engaged in banter that sometimes included potentially hurtful jabs. How-ever, we must be careful not to read too much into this joking. Although Teresa and María were often at odds, they were close friends. Most of their repartee probably reflects easy familiarity rather than true hostility. Still, as we shall see below, in the last years of the 1570s a serious rift de-veloped between them.

Teresa's correspondence with María begins in May 1576, just after Rubeo turns against the reform and Calced persecutions intensify. As opposition to Gracián grows, Teresa becomes increasingly protective of him. Indeed, Gracián is a predominant subject in Teresa's letters to María. Teresa frequently makes excuses for Gracián's carelessness, alleging he is "too busy" to think things through: "When you ask our *padre* for his opinion on a matter, you need to inform him about everything without hurrying; otherwise, because he's so busy, the importance of the mat-ter will escape him" (*Letters* 1, 7 September 1576: 15). Teresa constantly frets over Gracián's well-being. When discord with the Calced increases after the Almodóvar chapter, Teresa writes to María, begging her to "re-member to tell our *padre* to be careful" (*Letters* 1, 20 September 1576). When Gracián fails to write, Teresa makes excuses for him. She pleads with María to keep her informed because "our *padre* . . . won't have time" (*Letters* 1, 26 September 1576: 4). When María dallies with her letters, Teresa scolds: "I don't know how it is you let the muleteer leave without sending a letter, especially since our *padre* is down there. . . . For goodness sake, don't do this any more. . . . Our *padre*'s letters are short, and when he doesn't have time to write, you should be sure to do so" (*Letters* 1, 5 October 1576: 1). She writes to María constantly about Gracián's "trials" and orders her to do everything possible to alleviate them. Teresa casts María in the role of protective older sister whose job it is to watch over her brother and report back to her.

Although Teresa loved María, she adored Gracián. He was the favorite. No matter how aggravated Teresa became with his bungling and bullying, she constantly reminds María how fortunate she is to have him near. She extols his spiritual guidance and his sermons. She acts as though having Gracián in Seville should be enough to alleviate all María's ailments. When María falls ill, Teresa writes, "I don't know how you can be sick since you have our *padre* there" (*Letters* 1, 13 December 1576). In spite of the tongue-in-cheek irony of the remark, Teresa's weakness for Gracián is clear. When rumors circulate that Gracián's life is in danger, Teresa orders María to give him meals at the convent, even if she must borrow money to cover expenses. However, she warns María of the need for discretion: "I am writing him with much insistence that he not allow anyone to eat in the monastery parlor—see that you don't start something—except for himself since he is in such need, and if this can be done without it becoming known" (*Letters* 1, 15 June 1576: 2). Teresa insists that María feed him meat, even though the nuns must do without (*Letters* 1, 31 October 1576: 5). Although often terse with María when instructing her on convent administration, she lavishes her with praise for pampering Gracián: "I am so obliged because of the care you take to provide our *padre* with every comfort, as he tells me; thus my love for you has even grown greater" (*Letters* 1, 7 December 1576: 1). Teresa is aware that by ordering María to feed Gracián, she is putting them all at risk: "I wouldn't want it to be known . . . where he is eating, for that would open the door to what cannot be allowed for another superior" (*Letters* 1, 11 November 1576: 6). Not only could such behavior be considered a violation of the cloister, it could become a precedent for other priests and stoke the Calced campaign of calumny. Thus, Teresa tries to regulate Gracián's visits: "Outside of meal times he [should] not go there often, lest this be noticed" (*Letters* 1, 19 November 1576: 5). Through these letters to María de San José we come to understand the magnitude of Teresa's devotion to Gracián and her dependence on María to protect him in her stead. A not-so-unusual mother-son, mother-daughter dynamic plays itself out in the epistolary writing. With Gracián, Teresa is the adoring mother who is willing to overlook her son's shortcomings even though he exasperates her; with María she is less forgiving.

Although Teresa constantly wrote to María about Gracián, she did not write to Gracián about María with the same obsessiveness. Often when she does mention "the Prioress" it is to encourage Gracián to eat at the convent or allow himself to be cared for. This is not so surprising, given that Gracián was the one who was out in the world, threatened by hostile forces. In spite of Teresa's sometimes bossy tone, there is no clear evidence that María resented this constant prodding. She herself was apparently quite devoted to Gracián, referring to him affectionately in her *Book for the Hour of Recreation* (56) and throughout *Ramillete de mirra*. For his part, Gracián refers to María in his *Peregrinación de Anastasio* as "one of the women with the greatest purity, holiness, spirit, prudence and discretion that I have ever known after Mother Teresa" (244). María de San José mentions repeatedly in *Ramillete de mirra* that she and Gracián corresponded until she was ordered to have no further contact with him. Unfortunately, no extant letters from Gracián to María or from her to him remain. If they did, they would certainly help to further illuminate the relationship between the two.[28]

Teresa's friendship with María suffered a serious blow in 1578 when Teresa refused to support the prioress's demand that Beatriz de la Madre de Dios and Margarita de la Concepción provide her with a written statement about their visions.[29] Weber believes that Teresa thought that María was making too much of the women's experiences, which she, Teresa, saw as the result of a "humoral" or psychological disorder that could be treated with a change of diet (" 'Difficult' Daughter" 8). Teresa apparently won Gracián over to her way of thinking, for she writes to María that she is "delighted that our *padre* gave orders that the two nuns . . . eat meat" (*Letters* 2, 4 June 1578: 9). However, the nuns' confessor, Garciálvarez, rejected Teresa's explanation and demanded exhaustive general confessions of the women. María, believing he was aggravating the situation, sought to have him removed. Garciálvarez had already caused problems earlier by siding with a disgruntled nun named María del Corro, who in 1575 accused Teresa and María de San José to the Inquisition, so the prioress's concern is understandable. Since Article 41 of the Constitutions stipulated that "all the Sisters should give the prioress a monthly account of how they have done in prayer," María apparently felt justified in dealing with the matter herself. The result was an impasse, explains Weber: "Garciálvarez believed that María was trespassing into priestly territory during the monthly 'accounts of prayer,' and María believed that she had the authority to restrict Garciálvarez's access to the nuns" (" 'Difficult' Daughter" 9). When María sought Teresa's support to dismiss the confessor, Teresa declined, embracing instead a position of "charismatic non-alarmism" through which she sought to defuse the crisis (" 'Difficult' Daughter" 9).

The reform was already at risk, with John of the Cross in prison and Sega threatening to excommunicate Gracián, and Teresa may have been loath to provoke further dissention. Besides, the Inquisition persecuted *alumbrados* energetically in Seville, and it is possible that Teresa feared that the nuns' written statements might contain compromising material and fall into the wrong hands (Weber, " 'Difficult' Daughter" 9). From a personal standpoint, Teresa may have been growing irritated by María's emergent independence. Teresa's brother Lorenzo had lent money to buy the Seville convent, which María had still not paid back. Yet having decided the house was unhealthy, she was now making plans to buy a new one—without even consulting Teresa! "If you have so much money," Teresa writes her, "don't forget what you owe my brother" (*Letters* 1, 10 December 1577: 11). Such high-handedness was clearly getting on Teresa's nerves. The debt would be a source of friction between the two women until Lorenzo died in 1580.

Teresa bristled not only at María's lack of fiscal responsibility but also at her lack of tact. A master of diplomacy herself, Teresa writes to María repeatedly advising her to use discretion with priests, including Mariano, Heredia (*Letters* 1, 2 July 1576: 3), and Doria (*Letters* 2, 24 June 1579). She even counsels María on the importance of using the correct form of address with dignitaries (*Letters* 1, 7 September 1576: 4). In the midst of the conflict with Garciálvarez, Teresa writes to María to smooth things over. She praises Garciálvarez as the one she "trusts most" (*Letters* 2, 4 June 1578: 14) and details the good things he says about María (*Letters* 2, 4 June 1578: 16). Although Teresa was a fighter, she knew that charm and diplomacy were often effective tactical tools, especially for a woman. She urges María to "suffer and be silent," reminding her of their indebtedness to Garciálvarez (*Letters* 2, September? 1578). But María considered the priest a pawn of the devil who "was upsetting everything and bringing the house down around my ears" (*Recreation* 153), and instead of following Teresa's advice, she forged ahead with her plan to dismiss him. He struck back by appealing to the Calced, under whose jurisdiction the Discalced now found themselves. The provincial, Diego de Cárdenas, interrogated the nuns, whose accusations against Teresa and María went to the Inquisition.[30] Although the inquisitors did not pursue the charges, Garciálvarez replaced María with his cousin, Isabel de San Jerónimo.

During this period of intense trials, Teresa does not abandon her spiritual daughter. On the contrary, her letters from spring 1579 exude affection. After Isabel assumes the priorate, Teresa writes jointly to her and María: "The love I had for you has doubled to the extreme, even though it was great; and for you [María] especially, since it was you who suffered the most" (*Letters* 2, 3 May 1579: 2). Weber suggests that this is Teresa's way of asking for forgiveness (" 'Difficult' Daughter" 15). Interestingly, these expressions of fondness continue even after the crisis has passed. When María vacillates about whether or not to resume her position, Teresa writes her an encouraging, upbeat letter: "My daughter, set aside those foolish notions . . . that lead you to refuse to be prioress again" (*Letters* 2, 24 June 1579: 3). After María has been reinstated, Teresa sends her another effusive letter from Valladolid: "Although my love for you was great, it has now increased so much that it amazes me. And so I experience desires to see you and embrace you warmly" (*Letters* 2, 22 July 1579: 1). This affection for María de San José is manifest even in Teresa's letters to Gracián. Rather than "the Prioress," she now calls her by name. She writes from Valladolid: "Sister María de San José is . . . loved by everyone; she is a little saint" (*Letters* 2, 18 July 1579: 4), and then, "Sister María de San José is . . . an angel" (*Letters* 2, 25 July 1579: 4). Was Teresa still feeling guilty about abandoning her spiritual daughter in a time of need? Was she feeling old, lonely, and nostalgic? We shall never know. However, the prickliness of earlier correspondence had not disappeared altogether. It reasserted itself from time to time. In a letter written at the end of December 1579, Teresa makes reference to an unpleasant communication (now lost) she had sent to María and to which María responded with kindness and humility—perhaps trying to unruffle feathers. The friendship between Teresa and María de San José required work on both their parts.

Money was a constant source of conflict. Teresa nagged María incessantly about settling accounts with Lorenzo. A year after making the Seville foundation, she writes, "Let's try to repay quickly the money advanced by my brother" (*Letters* 1, 2 July 1576: 2). Not only this debt, but also the general financial health of the Seville Carmel worried Teresa. Fearing that María will be forced to pay a tax on the property, Teresa suggests she accept a nun and her sister with dowries large enough to cover it, even though one of the girls is only fourteen years old (*Letters* 1, 18 June 1576: 3). On another occasion she agrees to consider a postulant with a scar—even though she is finicky about physical flaws—because the convent needs the money (*Letters* 1, 7 September 1576: 6). However, she later concludes that "if whatever the facial mark they say she has is unsightly she should not be accepted" (*Letters* 1, 9 September 1576: 6). She notes that another girl "will bring a little over 400 ducats in addition to her trousseau," and, best of all, will make the money available right away. She laments that a particular aspirant has died before she could enter the convent with her dowry (*Letters* 1, 9 September 1576: 4). On another occasion she warns María: "Don't accept the daughter of the Portuguese—or whatever he is—if he doesn't first deposit with a third person what he must give you" (*Letters* 1, 26 September 1576: 2). And she praises María for having her nuns earn money by making and selling stockings (*Letters* 1, 7 September 1576: 6).

Finally, on 13 October 1576 Teresa writes to María de San José that the matter of the excise has been settled. However, Lorenzo has bought an estate at La Serna, near Ávila, for fourteen thousand ducats and therefore needs for María to pay him back. Nearly three years later she is still begging for the money: "When you can, begin repaying my brother; know that he has his needs, for he has many expenses" (*Letters* 2, 22 July 1579: 6). It irritates Teresa that María seems to be wasting money on interest when she is in a position to pay off her debt. She writes her again: "Although you don't do so all at once, you can pay something" (*Letters* 2, End of December 1579: 7, 10). She returns to the same subject on February 8–9 of the following year, asking María not only to pay back Lorenzo but also to make a contribution to the two Discalced friars who are going to Rome. The obsessiveness with which she pounds this theme belies any image theologians and artists have created of a beatific Teresa, habitually so lost in ecstasy that she is oblivious to the economic realities of running a convent or an estate.

Many of Teresa's letters to María involve the governance of convents, and these will be taken up in Chapter 5. Teresa makes recommendations on disciplining nuns, caring for the sick, furnishing chapels, and dealing with Jesuits. She discusses the advisability of accepting one aspirant over another—the financial contributions a woman might make, her political connections, her spiritual gifts, and her talents. Once she asks María to consider a lay sister that Gracián has recommended (*Letters* 1,13 October 1576: 9). Often she inquires about the health and spiritual growth of individual nuns. She comments on the progress of Teresita, her young niece, and thanks María for the excellent training she is giving her (*Letters* 1,9 September 1576: 11). She makes frequent mention of gifts María has sent her and of the cost of postage.

Perhaps María, a smart and competent prioress, sometimes became annoyed at Teresa's persistent intervention. It is evident that she did not always follow Teresa's advice. However, she assimilated her lessons and adopted her philosophy of governance, which stressed *suavidad* (gentleness) over rigor. Years later, when she wrote her own book of advice to prioresses, she reiterated the need for patience, kindness, and understanding when governing women. For her part, Teresa recognized in María a brilliant administrator capable of carrying on her work. In one of her last letters she wrote: "If my opinion were followed, they would elect you foundress after my death. And even if I were living, I would be eagerly in favor, for you know much more than I do, and are better; that is the truth. I have the advantage over you of having a little experience. But not much attention should be paid to me anymore, for you would be startled to see how old I am and how incapable of anything" (*Letters* 2,17 March 1582: 1). A little more than six months later, Teresa died. Sadly, María never became her successor.

Letters to María Bautista (Ocampo)

Like María de San José, María Bautista (Ocampo) was one of Teresa's closest friends, but while the former was a cultured woman raised in the palace of one of Spain's most powerful families, the latter was an orphaned relative educated under Teresa's auspices. This may help to explain why Teresa treated María de San José with a degree of deference even when scolding her, while she sometimes lashed out at María Bautista without restraint, even though she clearly loved her. María Ocampo was born in 1548, the same year as Gracián, and was the daughter of Teresa's cousin Diego de Cepeda. Orphaned at five years old, she went to live with an aunt and uncle in La Puebla Montabán, in Toledo, where Teresa met her when she made a pilgrimage to the shrine of Guadalupe. Later, Teresa brought her to Encarnación Convent to be educated. When Teresa decided to found the first Discalced Carmel in Ávila, María contributed a thousand ducats from her inheritance. She entered San José in 1563. In 1567 she accompanied Teresa to found in Medina del Campo and eventually entered the Carmel at Valladolid, where, in 1571, she became prioress.

Because María Bautista was kin and a close friend, Teresa treated her with great trust and intimacy. Many of Teresa's letters to María are filled with teasing reprimands, the kind reserved for confidants. "If the prioress of Medina had not informed me that you are well," she writes, "I would have been feeling sorry for you, thinking that you must be ill since you haven't written for so long" (*Letters* 1, End of June 1574: 1). Although she shared information about health problems with all her friends, with María Bautista she was particularly expansive on the subject. All during 1574, when Teresa was seriously ailing, she wrote to María Bautista about her health. One friendly, lighthearted letter, full of news and gossip, nevertheless reveals that she was suffering from "the torment of melancholy," what we now call depression (*Letters* 1, 14 May 1574: 1). Teresa tells of "a terrible cold along with many other ailments" and mentions some medicine she is sending for a Dominican prioress because "I am distressed about her illness, since I have suffered so much from it in these recent years; that pain is without mercy" (*Letters* 1, End of June 1574: 2). She laments that she is so old and tired that "it would frighten you to see me" (*Letters* 1, 16 July 1574: 2). Later she writes, "Perhaps it would make you sadder to see me, I'm so old and worn out" (*Letters* 1, 11 September 1574: 4). She inquires constantly about María's health as well: "Take care of your health (now you see how important that is and how it saddens me that you are ill)" (*Letters* 1, 11 September 1574: 2). María often sent Teresa gifts of food with medicinal properties. In one letter Teresa scolds her gently for sending *scorzonera*, a medicinal herb that Teresa cannot abide because she finds it too sweet (*Letters* 1, End of June 1574: 3). In another she thanks her for sending nuts to settle her stomach (*Letters* 1, 16 July 1574: 3). These letters portray a friendship between two women who were sincerely concerned about each other.

It was to María Bautista that Teresa revealed her most private fears. "Look, my daughter, when I am without such a serious illness as I have had here, I become very frightened if I feel the least stirring of attraction toward something. This is for you alone, because those who do not understand me will have to be guided by their own spirit. And indeed, if there is anyone with whom I can allow this stirring, it is with the one to whom I am writing" (*Letters* 1, End of June 1574: 2). Sometimes Teresa expresses thoughts that only María can understand; without having access to María's letters, it is impossible for the modern reader to reconstruct the context. However, we *can* sense the tremendous fondness Teresa had for María and how comfortable she felt opening up to her.

Many of Teresa's letters to María Bautista, like those to María de San José, concern the everyday running of convents—financial matters, postulants, convent politics—discussed in detail in Chapter 5. Teresa shares with María Bautista the tribulations of making foundations; she details a future trip to Beas and complains of the cold in Segovia. But what stands out in the plethora of minutiae that fill these letters is the pain of separation. "Knowing of your own disappointment seems to console me for having to leave without seeing you," she writes as she sets out from Segovia for southern Spain. A short stop in Valladolid, she laments, would be too tiring. "One does nothing but visit and one even gives up sleep so as to continue talking—and idle words are never lacking—for great is the desire to be with you." Besides, "many things I would like to speak to you about cannot be discussed by letter" (*Letters* 1, End of September 1574: 1). Reading this, one can almost feel Teresa's yearning to sit by the fire with her old friend and gossip.

Yet, it is often with one's closest friends that one loses control. While Teresa was usually (although not always) fairly diplomatic when asserting her authority over men, with women she could be extremely harsh. In letters to her spiritual daughters, Teresa presents herself as an authority figure whose will is not to be challenged. Some of her letters to María Bautista reveal a usually concealed facet of her personality: her fiery temper. An efficient, decisive administrator, María Bautista sometimes made decisions without consulting Teresa. Something of a micromanager, Teresa became irked when María manifested too much independence or when her choices seemed to promote her own convent. As foundress, Teresa had a global view of the reform and all the female Carmels, which, she believed, gave her the authority to make certain macromanagement decisions, including which postulants to accept where.

From mid-1574 Teresa's letters to María Bautista make frequent mention of Casilda de Padilla, a young girl from a noble family who wanted to enter the order against her family's wishes.[31] On 28 August 1575 Teresa writes to her friend about two postulants; one of them was probably Casilda, whom María intends to admit to her convent.[32] Teresa is furious that María has precipitated Casilda's case while delaying that of the other candidate, who was proposed by Teresa's Jesuit friend Francisco de Olea. Now the second girl has changed her mind, putting Teresa in an embarrassing position vis-à-vis Olea. At the time, the situation in Seville was turning thorny. Teresa was so tired, pressured, or infuriated when she wrote this letter that parts of it are garbled. She omits words and uses vague terms to refer to people (*la monja*, "the nun"; *la suya*, "yours"— that is, your nun, presumably Casilda). What is perfectly clear, however, is her rage at María's making a decision without consulting her.

Teresa starts out by sweet-talking her correspondent: "It is a strange thing how almost all letters tire me . . . except yours, and answering them even more so. But to receive and answer yours is refreshing" (28 August 1575: 2).[33] She inquires about María's health and chats about her brother Lorenzo, who has recently arrived from America. Given this airy opening, the prioress must have been astounded by what follows: "Although your Reverence is so proud of yours [your novice, Casilda], I am telling you that, if the nun you talk so much about [Casilda] were really destined for your convent, you'd have no choice but to take her, because what has already been done is more important than [what *you* think]. So don't suppose you're so smart. Just tend to your own house. You'd have done a lot of damage if you'd tried to stop her" (28 August 1575: 5). Casilda was commonly held to be destined for sainthood, and Teresa is annoyed that María Bautista, having "bagged the prize," seems more interested in the prestige of the Valladolid Carmel than in the good of the order. "That you think you know everything is just dreadful, and then you say that you are humble, when all you care about is your own little house without considering what is essential for all of them" (28 August 1575: 7). Each Carmel had a residency limit, and the admission of the new sister caused María Bautista to go over her maximum. Teresa fears that María's actions could now leave other convents short of nuns.

Furthermore, she is furious that María failed to seek her advice on the matter. "If I had understood the situation in the first place, I would not have admitted her, but there's no help for it now" (28 August: 1575: 6). Since Teresa maintained the right to determine which postulants would be accepted in her convents, in her mind María had overstepped her authority. Not only had María failed to act on Olea's recommendation, but she had also ignored Teresa's views: "This [Casilda] is not the postulant I wanted to send you." Now Teresa is in a bind with Olea, and all because "you are inflexible!" (28 August 1575: 7). She lashes out at María: "No prioress has ever taken such a stance with me, nor anyone who is not prioress. I tell you that by acting in such a way you will lose my friendship. You should know that I don't like it one bit that all you [Valladolid nuns] think there is no one capable of seeing things as your Reverence can. . . . As if it weren't enough that your Reverence is so rebellious, you have to teach the other nuns to be that way, too. For all you know, this girl [Olea's relative] could actually be more saintly than anyone else. I don't know how . . . you became so vain" (28 August 1575:7–8).[34] Did María tremble as she read this letter? Did she cry? Did she stomp off in a rage? Or did she burst out laughing? We can never know the answer to these questions; we can only imagine that Teresa's words provoked a strong response.

But Teresa had not yet finished. She goes on to reprimand María Bautista in the harshest terms for speaking ill of Gracián.[35] The gruffness of her words suggests that Teresa was under tremendous strain. Writing from Seville, she had just recently learned of the unfavorable decision of the Piacenza chapter. Everything was going wrong. Feuding between Calced and Discalced was intensifying, calumnies were mounting against her, and Rubeo was angry with her. If Teresa lashes out at María Bautista, it is perhaps because she is trying to assert her control over a domain that seems to be slipping away. At the end of the letter she regains her composure and softens her tone. Perhaps she is afraid of alienating María Bautista, one of her oldest friends. Once again adopting a posture of humility, Teresa quips, "One of the things that make me happy to be here and willing to remain longer is that nobody has any idea of that farce about my sanctity which I was subjected to up there" (28 August 1575: 12). If Teresa sometimes treats María Bautista like an errant child whom she, as spiritual mother, must reprimand, it is because they enjoyed a familiarity that permitted Teresa to let down her guard and express her frustration.

By the time Casilda finally professed on 13 January 1577, Teresa had calmed down. She writes to María Bautista in December 1576 and then again on 26 January 1577 about a question that had arisen regarding the girl's dowry, but after giving her advice, Teresa leaves the negotiations in María's hands: "Do not pay attention to what I have said other than to draw light about what would be more fitting. I would not want to impose . . . on you, for you have enough trials" (*Letters* 1, Middle of December 1576: 5). The following month, she writes again to congratulate María on the profession, concluding with what Kavanaugh calls "affectionate irony" (*Letters* 1:484n8): "May he be blessed who does it all, for you are very wretched" (*Letters* 1, 26 January 1577: 5).

Four months pass between Teresa's angry letter to María Bautista and her next communication—or at least no extant missives exist dated between late August and late December 1575. In the interim María has sent Teresa two letters filled with recommendations concerning Teresa's nephews' use of the title *Don* and other family matters. Teresa comments sardonically: "You make me laugh. . . . As usual you have advice to give" (*Letters* 1, 30 December 1575: 1). Still, her anger has subsided. Myriad crises have exhausted her, and she seeks comfort in the warmth of an old friendship. Even though she once chided María Bautista for criticizing Gracián, she now divulges her frustration with him for continuing to provoke the Calced friars and her fear that he will get himself killed. She chafes over Rubeo's order that she retire to a convent in Castile and expresses her longing to join María Bautista in Valladolid. She mulls over Lorenzo's illness and reveals that that he is considering becoming a friar, although the project "has gone nowhere nor will it" (*Letters* 1, 30 December 1575: 13). In María Bautista she has a kindred spirit with whom she can unburden herself.

When she writes again in February, her frustration over being unable to settle in Valladolid with María Bautista and her anger with Gracián for siding with Rubeo on her detainment in Toledo are patent: "With regard to my going to Valladolid, were they in their right minds when they thought I could make the choice rather than go where I was sent. . . . I don't believe [Gracián] ever had the intention that I go there permanently; but yes, that was my desire" (*Letters* 1, 19 February 1576: 2). By April things have gone from bad to worse. Teresa writes to María Bautista that her brother Lorenzo, who has gone into debt helping the Seville nuns, is being pursued by the law for failure to pay an unjust excise tax: "Now he is in hiding on our account, and it was lucky that he wasn't put in prison here, which is like hell; and everything here is done without justice, for they want us to pay what we do not owe" (*Letters* 1, 29 April 1576: 3). In addition, María del Corro has launched an attack of calumnies against the convent and has denounced Teresa and others to the Inquisition: "Nonsense . . . was what she said of us, that we tied the hands and feet of the nuns and flogged them—would to God that all the accusations had been of that sort" (29 April 1576: 6).[36] The most serious charges involve disrespect for the sacraments, in particular the accusation that the prioress heard nuns' confessions, which is why the allegation of flogging seems minor to Teresa. The letters of 1575 through 1577 chronicle the terrible trials of this dark period and a friendship solid enough to withstand both explosions and tears.

By the end of 1576 María Bautista was ill and depressed. Teresa was battling the Andalusian Calced and the Carmelite hierarchy through the mails, long distance from Toledo, but she found the time to write her old friend a long newsy letter that covers topics as diverse as the departure of Juan of Austria for Flanders disguised as the valet of a Fleming and the inadvisability of accepting a blind postulant into the convent. With feigned gruffness she scolds María Bautista, "If you would believe what I tell you once in a while, we could avoid a lot of trouble. Did I not insist the other day in a letter that you not have yourself bled anymore! I don't know what nonsense has got into you, even though the doctor does give his consent." And then, in a more serious tone, "Your illness has been very distressing to me since the affliction is in your head" (*Letters* 1, 2 November 1576: 1). At the end of the letter she adds, "Continue with your cure, for love of God, and try to eat well, and don't remain alone thinking about nothing. . . . I would like to be there, for there's much I would talk about for your entertainment" (*Letters* 1, 2 November 1576: 8). Teresa is especially concerned about María's spiritual state: "Concerning what you say about your interior life, the greater the disturbance the less attention you should pay to it, for it clearly proceeds from a weak imagination, and bad humor; and since the devil sees this, he adds his bit" (*Letters* 1, 2 November 1576: 8).[37] Although Teresa was temperamental, this letter reveals how tender she could be with those she cared about.

The following years were turbulent for María Bautista, as they were for other Discalced religious. When Sega issued his 1578 brief ordering the Discalced nuns and friars to submit to the provincials of Castile and Andalusia, María Bautista wrote to Teresa describing the trauma of being notified.[38] As it becomes increasingly evident that the Discalced need representation in Rome in order to establish a separate province, Teresa writes to María Bautista asking her to contribute money toward the expenses of the two friars who will make the trip and the fees for the canon lawyer Montoya. Gracián's sister María de San José Dantisco (not to be confused with María de San José Salazar) has entered the Valladolid convent, and the king, out of gratitude for services rendered by the girl's uncles and grandfather, has given five hundred ducats as a dowry, of which Teresa requests at least three hundred, in addition to money for Gracián's mother's living expenses.

Teresa directs her letter not to María Bautista alone but to all the Valladolid nuns, apparently because she thought the prioress too protective of her own convent's resources and wanted to appeal to a broader base. Teresa proceeds like the expert fundraiser she is. First, she invokes the nuns' sense of duty and sisterhood: "I want you to keep in mind that from the time that house was founded, I have never asked you . . . to accept a nun without a dowry or anything else of consequence, which has not been the case with other communities. . . . I am worried that what is so important for the service of God might fail for lack of money" (*Letters* 2, 31 May 1579: 1). Teresa describes the extensive efforts that have been made to seek funding elsewhere and the urgency of the enterprise. She then gets right to the point, demonstrating considerable sophistication about the money-lending process: "Padre Nicolao writes from Madrid that he has found a person who out of deference to him will advance two hundred ducats in view of Sister María de San José's dowry on condition that your house send him a promissory letter. . . . I ask you out of charity that as soon as this letter arrives you call for a notary so as to testify that sister has made her profession. Thus the action will be completely valid, for without this nothing can be done. Send it to me at once along with your promissory letter. The two statements should not be sent together, but kept on separate pages" (31 May 1579: 3).[39] Although not all the communities can contribute, she explains, the Valladolid Carmel has an obligation because of the windfall produced by María de San José's dowry. "This is why we all wear the same habit, that we might help one another, for what belongs to one belongs to all" (*Letters* 2, 31 May 1579: 4). The concluding words confirm the notion that Teresa appeals to the sisters because she does not trust María Bautista to sacrifice the convent's newfound riches for the good of the order: "I ask Mother Prioress not to oppose what the sisters want to do, for I am very confident that they are no less daughters of the order than the sisters in our other houses who are doing what they can" (*Letters* 2, 31 May 1579: 10). Through this cajoling Teresa attempts to shame the Valladolid nuns into supporting her and to pit them against the prioress if she fails to go along.

Her tactic worked. The nuns authorized the expenditure immediately. On June 9 Teresa writes to María Bautista thanking her for her support: "I assure you that even if the money had been given for my own use, I could not be more grateful. You have all shown your generosity and in a gracious way. . . . I am asking God to give you back much more than you have given. Read this part to the sisters" (*Letters* 2, 9 June 1579: 2). By then Sega had withdrawn the power of the Calced over the Discalced, and Ángel de Salazar had ordered her to continue with her foundations. In her letter she promises to visit the nuns soon and begs that no fuss be made for her arrival, but in this they did not obey. The following month she writes to Gracián from Valladolid recounting the elaborate reception she has received.

The letters from the last three years of Teresa's life suggest that her relationship with María Bautista had once again become strained. Teresa's insistence on assigning nuns to convents using her own criteria undermined the authority of prioresses and caused resentment. Early in 1582 Teresa, weak and ill, was on her way to Burgos with several nuns, among them Catalina de la Asunción, who had professed at Valladolid. Teresa writes to the girl's mother boasting of how she wrested Asunción away from María Bautista: "I don't think I accomplished a small feat by bringing Asunción with me, considering the resistance to this" (*Letters* 2, 16 January 1582: 4). María Bautista must have still been fuming later in the year when Teresa returned. In a letter from Valladolid to Mother Tomasina Bautista, prioress in Burgos, Teresa reveals how unhappy she is at María Bautista's convent and how anxious she is to be gone (*Letters* 2, 27 August 1582). Around the same time, Doña Beatriz de Castilla y Mendoza, mother-in-law of Teresa's nephew Francisco, threatened a lawsuit over the provisions of Lorenzo de Cepeda's will. As executrix of her brother's estate, Teresa struggled to defend his wishes. However, María Bautista sided with Doña Beatriz in the dispute, a distasteful development to which Teresa makes oblique reference in a letter to Gracián written on 1 September 1582.

Teresa's relationship with María Bautista, like her other relationships, was complex and contradictory. Many of Teresa's letters to María Bautista reveal great affection, but like blood sisters, these two strong-willed women were often engaged in battles of one-upmanship.

Letters to Lorenzo de Cepeda

Throughout her career Teresa saw her younger brother Lorenzo as a collaborator and supporter. She shared her plans for the reform with him and turned to him for money when she founded her first Discalced Carmelite convent in 1562 and later when she founded in Seville in 1575. As a young man of nineteen, he had sailed for the New World. Along with his brothers Hernando, Jerónimo, Antonio, and perhaps Rodrigo,[40] in 1546 he took part in the battle of Añaquito, in which Gonzalo Pizarro led antiroyalist forces against the viceroy.[41] Antonio died in combat and Lorenzo was wounded, but he went on to recover and marry a wealthy young noblewoman named Juana Fuertes Espinosa. Industrious and well connected, he launched a successful career in finance and politics. He accumulated considerable capital from business investments, held public office, and eventually became mayor of Quito. When his wife died in 1567, he decided to return to Spain with his children, but did not actually arrive until 1575. By then, Teresa was in Seville, struggling with the Andalusian Carmelites.

Naomi Miller and Naomi Yavneh point out that although the patriarchal structures of early modern Europe gave male members of a family power over females, they could also afford protection, and men sometimes used their social and financial positions to advance their sisters' projects (9). Brothers of nuns were sometimes avid defenders of their sisters' spiritual integrity. Susan D. Laningham explores the bonds between the Cistercian nun María Vela y Cueto and her brothers Diego and Lorenzo, the latter of whom tried to have María canonized.[42] Although the relationship between Teresa and Lorenzo was not unique, it differed from most examples of sibling alliance in that Teresa, not her brother, functioned as head of the family. Since her brothers had gone to America, Teresa served as executrix of her father's estate when Don Alonso de Cepeda died in 1543, and she was the one who had to deal with the resulting squabbles and lawsuits. In 1553, when her younger sister Juana married, it was Teresa who negotiated the nuptial agreement. However, even though Teresa was the de facto *pater familias*, she always addressed Lorenzo with utmost respect.

Throughout Teresa's career, Lorenzo was one of her most reliable supporters. Teresa kept him abreast of her plans for the reform from the beginning. In her first extant letter to him, she lays out the project: "There will be no more than fifteen nuns in [the monastery], who will practice very strict enclosure, never going out or allowing themselves to be seen without veils covering their faces. Their life will be one of prayer and mortification" (23 December 1561: 1). In a later letter written in 1570 she modifies this plan, stipulating that the number of nuns should not exceed thirteen: "Since according to our constitutions we do not beg for alms, but we eat what is brought to the turn for us, which is more than sufficient, our number must be small" (17 January 1570: 18). Teresa was a pragmatic administrator who modified the rules as necessity demanded. The convent she was writing about in the 1570 letter was in a remote area where it would be difficult to provide food, and so she reduced the maximum number of nuns. The care she took to keep Lorenzo informed of these details suggests he took an avid interest in the affairs of the reform, which is evinced by his ample financial support.

As Teresa was supervising the transformation of the house purchased by her brother-in-law Juan de Ovalle into the first Discalced convent, she ran into a deficit from which Lorenzo rescued her. In her *Life*, Teresa specifies the problems she encountered making this first foundation, but downplays her struggle to finance it. Instead, she describes the shortfall as a minor difficulty, quickly resolved by supernatural forces: "Once when in need, for I didn't know what to do or how to pay some workmen, St. Joseph, my true father and lord, appeared to me and revealed to me that I would not be lacking, that I should hire them. And so I did, without so much as a penny, and the Lord in ways that amazed those who heard about it provided for me" (*CWST* 1, *Life* 33:12). Writing with spiritual directors and inquisitorial censors in mind, Teresa strives to show God's approval of her project and avoids elaborating on the pecuniary crisis.

However, Teresa not only prayed to heaven but sought financial backing here on earth. She appealed to Lorenzo, who sent a substantial donation. The daughter of a merchant, Teresa shows herself in her thank-you letter to be a shrewd marketer who understood the value of making her collaborators feel appreciated. She assures Lorenzo that his donation was urgently needed and put to good use. She aggrandizes him while disparaging herself: "The amount of money . . . would have been enough to keep a poor worthless nun like myself who goes about in patches—which I now consider an honor, glory to God—out of need for some years" (*Letters* 1, 23 December 1561: 1). By belittling herself as a "worthless nun," she subtly assures him of the righteousness of her cause: she is not seeking wealth, laurels, or power. Yet, by describing her tattered garments as a badge of honor, she emphasizes the divine merit of her mission and suggests celestial rewards for her collaborators.

Lorenzo's collaboration in the Seville project was complicated because the money he provided to María de San José was a loan, not a gift. María's delay in repaying Lorenzo caused him considerable grief because he had made generous donations to charity and was now in need himself. Teresa, watching out for her brother's interests, badgered María to settle accounts. At the end of 1576 she assures Lorenzo: "Now she tells me she has the money she owes you" (*Letters* 1, November 1576: 1). However, as we saw above, three years later Teresa was still prodding María to pay. At the beginning of 1580 Teresa wrote to Lorenzo, telling him that she had spoken with María, and "almost four hundred ducats will soon be delivered" (*Letters* 2, 9–10 February 1580: 3). However, Lorenzo succumbed to influenza and died months later.

Teresa's letters to her brother show she was concerned with family as well as convent business. When Teresa wrote to Lorenzo in 1561, Juan de Ovalle was threatening a lawsuit on behalf of his wife, Teresa's younger sister Juana, to obtain a larger share of her father's estate. Teresa knew that this might prove disastrous for the family of María de Guzmán, her older widowed half-sister. Alonso de Cepeda had unwittingly caused the conflict by dividing his estate unevenly between the children of his first and second marriages. To help resolve the problem, Lorenzo agreed to give Juan a sum of money. Teresa's letter to Lorenzo reveals her fiscal astuteness: "He is by nature good, but in his case it would be unwise to trust in that. When you send him the 1,000 pesos, you should ask him for a written promise to be given to me; and the day that he reintroduces the lawsuit, 500 ducats will go to Doña María" (*Letters* 1, 23 December 1561: 7). Teresa knew better than to trust her brother-in-law's word. She insisted on a written agreement, with specific sanctions should Ovalle fail to comply.

A related matter involved the profits from family property in Gotarrendura: "Martín de Guzmán received 300,000 maravedis from them and it was only right that this amount went to Juan de Ovalle. Along with the 1,000 pesos you sent, he is taken care of" (*Letters* 1, 23 December 1561). Comments such as these reveal both insightfulness and a sense of justice. Later on, when Lorenzo sends more money from the Americas, Teresa writes to Juana expressing her disapproval of some of her husband's investment plans (*Letters* 1, December 1569: 4). Given Ovalle's greed, hotheadedness, and lack of common sense, Teresa believed she had to protect the interests of her younger sister. In 1570 Ovalle went to Seville to claim some silver Lorenzo had sent him. Part of the money was to provide an income for Juana and one hundred pesos were to go to Teresa, whose letter to her brother reveals that she had overseen the operation herself: "I did no small thing in managing these affairs," she writes. "I have become so adept at bargaining and managing business affairs for these houses of God and of the order that I am abreast of everything" (*Letters* 1, 17 January 1570: 5). Although Teresa cultivated humility, she was aware of her own strengths, and managing money was one of them. For her, there was no contradiction between business and devotion to God. The success of the reform depended in part on her ability to manage financial affairs, and since Lorenzo was one of her principal supporters, family business and God's business were entwined.

Lorenzo helped Teresa with more than finances. Sometimes she entrusted him with important missions, such as the transference of confidential papers. While she was detained in Toledo, she wrote to her brother, then living in Ávila, to send her some documents from the San José convent. Ormaneto, who was trying to defend Teresa against Rubeo, had requested the original patent letters authorizing her foundations. Describing the chest where they are hidden, Teresa instructs Lorenzo to gather these patents with great secrecy and to have the subprioress prepare a list of the nuns, their ages, and their years in the convent, which had also been requested by Ormaneto. "There is no reason for the nuns to know about this," she warns (*Letters* 1, 2 January 1577: 7). She also asks for "the writing on prayer"—possibly her *Spiritual Testimonies*—which is in the same small chest, again urging secrecy: "Don't let anyone open the chest unless it's you yourself. . . . Were I to learn that you [told] someone [what the papers contain], I would never let you read anything again" (*Letters* 1, 2 January 1577: 5). This letter reveals that Teresa saw her brother as an aide capable of dealing with highly sensitive, even secret matters pertinent to the reform. On another occasion Lorenzo apparently attempted to retrieve Teresa's *Life* from the Inquisition after the princess of Eboli had denounced it as a "book of visions." Teresa kept him abreast of the investigation, writing early in 1577: "There is good news about my papers [the manuscript of *Life*]. The Grand Inquisitor himself read them . . . and told Doña Luisa that they contained nothing the Inquisition would have to deal with, and there were good things in them rather than bad" (*Letters* 1, 27–28 February 1577: 8).[43] Just as María Vela y Cueto's brother protected and promoted her, Lorenzo defended Teresa.

Much of what she shares with Lorenzo is gossip and chitchat. She communicates news about family and friends, especially about their sisters Juana and María. She inquires about Lorenzo's household, including his servants. The family dramas that unfold in these letters reveal how much pain Teresa's relatives sometimes caused her and how far she was from achieving the perfect detachment she knew to be essential to spiritual health. Two particularly poignant letters deal with Pedro de Ahumada, her emotionally disturbed sibling, who returned with Lorenzo from the New World and took up residence with him at his estate, La Serna. Bitter and ill, Pedro resented his parasitic existence and took out his frustration on those around him. Soon he left La Serna and took off on his own. It is clear that Teresa disliked Pedro—she called him "crazy"—yet begs Lorenzo to help him. In her first letter to Lorenzo on the subject, she admits to feeling little pity for Pedro but believes God is using him to tempt her and Lorenzo "to see the extent of our charity." Clearly struggling with her lack of compassion, she writes: "I make up for it by thinking immediately of what I ought to do to please God" (*Letters* 2, 10 April 1580: 1). She begs Lorenzo, who is ill himself, not to take Pedro back to La Serna, yet she worries that the unfortunate man, whom she describes as "a drifter," will not be able to survive without help. She beseeches Lorenzo to provide for him, if not out of love, then out of Christian duty.

Lorenzo evidently wrote back to her proposing that Pedro go to live in a Discalced friary. However, she rejects this suggestion, not only because the friars do not take seculars but also because Pedro is so finicky about food: "Even now if the meat in an inn is not tender and well cooked, he can't eat it; he will go along only on pastry" (*Letters* 2, 15 April 1580: 7). Teresa's comments about Pedro reveal the complexities of the Cepeda-Ahumada family dynamic. If Teresa loved Lorenzo, she felt real aversion toward Pedro. Still, she believed it was the family's responsibility to protect him and urged Lorenzo to do what he could for him. Teresa's letters to Gracián and others written after Lorenzo's death evince her efforts to find a home for Pedro. At one point she considered placing him with Lorenzo's son Francisco, but Pedro's tendency to meddle made the arrangement impossible.

As in Teresa's letters to Carmelite friends, health is a recurring topic in her missives to Lorenzo. She frequently inquires about his physical state and gives detailed accounts of her own. "I am very sorry about your ailment," she writes from Toledo. "The cold will soon begin to bother you. I am better than I have been in years" (*Letters* 1, 24 July 1576: 2). A knowledgeable herbalist, Teresa often suggests remedies for Lorenzo's diverse ailments: "Tell [your servant] to throw some of the enclosed pastilles around your room or close to the brazier, for they are very healthy and pure. . . . However mortified you want to be, you can use them. They are excellent for rheumatism and headaches" (*Letters* 1, 17 January 1577: 15). Several weeks later she writes him, "Take great care not to give up sleep and to eat enough at your collation" (*Letters* 1, 27–28 February 1577: 7). Until the end of Lorenzo's life Teresa fretted over his health and offered him medical advice.

However, she was more concerned about his interior health, for the most significant bond between Teresa and Lorenzo was spiritual. Teresa became her brother's spiritual director after he returned to Spain, following a centuries-old tradition of nuns offering guidance to their order's supporters. Since nuns were revered for their ties to the divine, relatives and friends naturally expected them to provide spiritual direction (Lehfeldt 41). For Teresa, the relationship with God entailed an active commitment to help others. Thus, in her letters she urges her brother to serve God actively and assures him that his contributions to the reform will bring rewards: "May it please [God] that you always advance in his service. Since there is no measure to his remunerations, we should never stop trying to serve the Lord. Each day we will advance at least a little further, and with fervor." (*Letters* 1, 23 December 1561: 5). In the same letter she mentions sending him relics, since she knows that in the initial phases of prayer, relics, images, and readings can be beneficial.

Teresa also encourages Lorenzo to prioritize, placing greater importance on the perfection of his soul than on other obligations; for example, he should engage in acts of charity, even if this means disregarding his children's immediate future: "You should not have your boys marry soon, so that you can do more for your own soul. If you begin to get entangled in other expenses, you won't have enough for everything. And, after all, this is the recompense you deserve for all the trouble you went through to earn it: to spend as much as you can in the service of the One . . . who will give you his kingdom" (*Letters* 1, November 1576: 1). Although Teresa may seem to be self-interestedly angling for increased donations, in view of her conviction that actively serving God is a means of spiritual self-realization, her advice to Lorenzo represents an effort to guide his actions into conformity with God's will.

The importance Teresa attached to her role as Lorenzo's spiritual director is obvious from her tenacity in performing her directorial duties, even during the bleakest days of the reform. From Toledo she guides him through the stages of prayer, referring him to her *Way of Perfection*, of which he apparently had a copy for his personal use (*Letters* 1, 2 January 1577: 8). She scolds him jokingly for making spiritual decisions on his own—in one case, he made a vow to strive for greater perfection—after he had promised her obedience: "How could you make a vow without telling me?" she writes, "That's a nice kind of obedience!" (*Letters* 1, 2 January 1577: 9). Teresa's gentle reprimand stems from her dread of excessive rigor, which, as she explains in *Foundations*, can damage one's health or trigger spurious mystical experiences. Lorenzo was struggling with prayer, but Teresa knew his anxiety was necessary to the spiritual process and that it would eventually dissolve into detachment. She writes to him: "I have already passed through this kind of prayer, and the soul afterward usually finds rest. . . . It is a touch of love that is given to the soul" (*Letters* 1, 17 January 1577: 6). In this letter Teresa synthesizes many of her teachings on prayer, personalizing them to fit Lorenzo's particular situation.

One of Lorenzo's concerns was the erotic arousal that accompanied his intense spiritual feelings.[44] It is a testimony to Lorenzo's closeness with Teresa that he shares his concern over this sensitive issue with her. Georges Bataille asserts that sexual pleasure often occurs with mystical experience, since the powerful emotions at the root of intense spirituality find expression in every possible way (225). Teresa says as much in her response to Lorenzo: "As for the lascivious feelings that you tell me about, don't pay any attention to them. For although I have never experienced this—for God in his goodness has always delivered me from those passions—I think it must happen because the delight of the soul is so great that it arouses these natural feelings; they will die away with the help of God if you pay no attention to them" (17 January 1577: 7). Although Teresa is coy regarding her own experience in this area—in spite of the highly sensual descriptions of mystical union in *Life*—she makes it clear that such reactions are not abnormal or harmful if they are properly handled.

Teresa was also interested in Lorenzo's children, and her comments about them exude warmth and affection. Although the Discalced Carmelite Constitutions stipulated that postulants had to be at least seventeen years old, she allowed her niece Teresita to live with the nuns at San José de Ávila from the age of nine.[45] Teresa's fondness for Lorenzo's little girl is manifest in many of her letters. "Tell Teresa not to fear that I love anyone as much as I do her," she writes to her brother. "I long to see her" (*Letters* 1, 2 January 1577: 13). Throughout her epistolary writing Teresa mentions Teresita, often giving accounts of the child's progress to family and friends. After Teresita takes vows at fifteen, her proud aunt writes to Lorenzo's younger son, also named Lorenzo, now in Quito: "I find my consolation in Sister Teresa de Jesús (Teresita). She is now a woman and always growing in virtue. . . . God truly speaks in her. . . . He is guiding her" (*Letters* 2, 15 December 1581: 3). However, Teresa's relationship with her niece was marred when, in the dispute over Lorenzo's will, Teresita sided with María Bautista against her aunt.

Teresa was also interested in her nephews. She frequently asks about them in her letters to Lorenzo and sometimes mentions sending some little gift. For example, in one missive she refers to some Christmas carols for Francisco (*Letters* 1, 2 January 1577: 23). She was particularly concerned that the boys not put on airs, as did the children of many Spaniards who returned home rich from the Americas. In particular, she was sensitive to the use of titles. She had asked Lorenzo not to use the title *Don* and tells María Bautista: "The title Don is given in the Indies to all those who have vassals. But when my nephews arrived here, I asked their father not to call them by that title" (*Letters* 1, 29 April 1576: 8). Teresa is distressed because, in spite of her urging, her brother-in-law Juan de Ovalle insists on calling the boys *Don*, and now they have become accustomed to it and refuse to give it up. However, when the boys become adults, Teresa herself always addresses them as *Don* in her letters.

Scholars have argued that Teresa's rejection of worldly honor—which she elaborates in *The Way of Perfection*—was probably due to her Jewish ancestry. As we saw in Chapter 1, at considerable cost the family had acquired patents of nobility to erase the stigma of their ethnicity. Perhaps because their nobility was "purchased," Teresa felt uncomfortable with titles and rejected their use in her convents. It is significant that in all of her writing Teresa never mentions her Jewish background or the patents, except in her 1561 letter to Lorenzo—that is, within the confidentiality of the family. Yet, Teresa understood the importance Spanish society attached to honor. She knew that in Spain's new mercantile society, property and wealth were essential to honor. For this reason, she urges Lorenzo not to sell his land, since by keeping it, "you are providing your children with something more than property, which is honor" (*Letters* 1, 2 January 1577: 9). Such comments show that although she advocated detachment from the world, Teresa was a pragmatist.

Teresa was keenly interested in the boys' education. While her brother is still in America, she writes to him about Ávila's excellent schools: "The Jesuits have a school where they teach grammar and hear the confessions of the students once a week and make their students so virtuous that it is something to praise God for" (*Letters* 1, 17 January 1570: 8). The year following Lorenzo's return to Spain, Teresa laments that he still has not seen to his sons' education and warns him that she is ready to take matters into her own hands: "I gave a great fear that if you do not start now to take much care about the education of these boys, they will soon be mixing with some of the haughty crowd in Ávila. It's necessary that you make them go at once to the Society, for I am writing about it to the rector as you will see" (*Letters* 1, 9 July 1576: 1). Lorenzo did, in fact, put his sons in the Jesuit *colegio* of San Gil in Ávila.

Later, Teresa attempted to take an active part in the marriage arrangements for her elder nephew, Francisco. (Lorenzo had already returned to America, where he married at nineteen and successfully managed his father's Quito estate.) A few days before her brother died, Teresa wrote to him to suggest a Segovian girl as a potential wife for Francisco. The union did not materialize, but later that year Francisco married Orofrisia de Mendoza y Castilla, an aristocratic girl of fourteen, without informing his aunt. If Teresa was miffed, she does not show it. She writes to her nephew Lorenzo that the bride's "noble background is unsurpassable in Spain," and adds, "They gave him four thousand ducats" (*Letters* 2, 27 December 1580: 5–7). When she writes to Lorenzo again the following year, she mentions that Francisco's wife is "tied on all sides to the most illustrious families in Spain" (*Letters* 2, 15 December 1581: 1). Teresa's enthusiasm for this marriage reveals her to be extremely worldly. As for Lorenzo's marriage, Teresa seems satisfied, if not ebullient: "[God] has given you a wife with whom you can live in great peace. This is most fortunate, for it gives me great joy to think that you have a wife like this" (*Letters* 2, 15 December 1581: 2). In reality, the equanimity expressed in these letters masks serious worries about her nephews, for both drew her into thorny situations.

Soon after her brother died, Francisco found himself in need of money, which made marriage to a wealthy society girl extremely attractive. As it turned out, Doña Orofrisia was not able to solve his financial problems. Furthermore, Francisco's mother-in-law, Doña Beatriz de Castilla y Mendoza, complicated Teresa's life by contesting Lorenzo's will, which stipulated that should Francisco die without an heir, Teresita would inherit his estate and use it to build a chapel at the Ávila Carmel. Teresa writes to Doña Beatriz in December 1581, trying to placate her and settle the matter without a lawsuit, but the dispute dragged on into the following year, when Teresa herself died. Teresa did manage to reach an agreement with Francisco, but he was a poor administrator and only fell more deeply into debt. He returned to America in 1591 in hopes of improving his fortune, but things went badly. Eventually, he settled in a Franciscan monastery in a little town in Ecuador, where he did, in fact, die without an heir. Teresita, who had taken Doña Beatriz's side, later regretted her stance. When Teresa died, relatives tried to persuade Teresita to leave the convent and claim her inheritance, but instead she elected to profess.

Teresa's other nephew, Lorenzo, also caused his share of headaches. Before returning to America, he fathered an illegitimate child in Ávila. In her 1580 letter to him, Teresa mentions obliquely her hopes that he will cease his reckless behavior and reform. When she writes to him the following year, she must broach the subject more directly because the little girl must be provided for. Teresa's sister Juana has agreed to raise her, but Teresa is adamant that Lorenzo take financial responsibility for her education. Expressing great affection for the child, Teresa attempts to stir Lorenzo's sense of duty: "Even though what you did is very distressing to me because of its being an offense against God, when I see how much this little girl resembles you, I can't help but welcome and love her. . . . May God make her His servant, for she is not at fault, and so don't be negligent in taking care to see she is brought up well" (*Letters* 2, 15 December 1581: 4–5). Teresa also wants Lorenzo to finance Teresita's profession. Her epistolary writing shows that, until the end of her life, Teresa functioned as the virtual matriarch of the Cepeda y Ahumada clan, attending to family affairs, making certain family members took care of one another, disciplining wayward children, and troubleshooting potential crises.

Teresa's letters to Lorenzo throw light on a sibling relationship in which the woman was the leader, teacher, and spiritual guide. Teresa looked out for Lorenzo's financial well-being, struggling to keep Juan de Ovalle and María de San José from taking advantage of him. She guided him on the purchase and sale of property, on his children's education, and on dealing with Pedro, their mentally disturbed brother. As his spiritual director, she guided Lorenzo through the roughest patches of his spiritual journey. After he died, she strove to defend the integrity of his will, to guide his children, and to provide for his illegitimate grandchild. In spite of the patriarchal nature of early modern Spanish society, this is one case in which the woman held the authority.

Chapter 5

Letter-Writing
as Self-Representation

Teresa constantly had to vie with men who sought to limit her mobility, recast the reform according to their own visions, or destroy it altogether. Letter-writing enabled her to both claim and exert authority. Lisa Vollendorf argues that for early modern women, writing itself was an assertive act (*Lives* 60). Every letter Teresa wrote was an act of self-representation that served to affirm and solidify the authority she needed to achieve her end. Even a thank-you note to an aspirant's mother affirmed her position as foundress. Through correspondence Teresa cast herself in different roles that enabled her to more effectively exercise her influence.

In order to project an image of herself that inspired compliance without appearing arrogant or aggressive, Teresa portrayed herself in her letters, as she often did in her books, as an instrument of God's will. She represented the reform as God's project rather than as her own. As God's tool, she claimed for herself the right to proceed as he instructed her, and she expected others to respect her leadership. In her very earliest extant letter to Lorenzo, Teresa makes it clear that the success of San José was guaranteed because "God wants it to be done and will provide" (*Letters* 1, 23 December 1561: 3). Teresa asserts her agency in God's plan throughout her epistolary writing, and she encourages her collaborators' dedication by casting them as co-agents.

In order to boost their flagging spirits, Teresa often reminds her followers of the sanctity of their mission. This was especially necessary after she founded in Seville on 29 May 1575. When she learns that Gracián is begging for food to avoid eating in Calced monasteries, she cheers him on: "I tell you that if God hadn't given me understanding that all the good we do comes from his hand and how little we ourselves can do, it wouldn't be unusual for me to experience a bit of vainglory over all that you are doing" (*Letters* 1, End of November 1576: 1). Two years later, during the heat of the Calced persecutions, she writes to Gracián: "We have no cause for fear, my Father: we must praise God, who is leading us by the way He himself went" (*Letters* 2, 9 August 1578: 21). In 1579, when the unreformed friars circulate calumnious rumors about the Discalced nuns in

Seville, Teresa writes to Hernando de Pantoja, a Carthusian prior who had befriended her in Seville, begging him for continued support and assuring him of the holiness of his work: "I have the greatest confidence that His Majesty will come to the defense of His servant friars and nuns. . . . I beg your Paternity, for the love of Our Lord, not to abandon them. . . . But His Majesty, who knows [these nuns], will help them and will give your Paternity the charity to do the same" (*Letters* 2, 31 January 1579: 7). The same day, Teresa sends words of encouragement to the Discalced nuns of Seville, assuring them of God's protection: "God, in his goodness, will soon fix everything, so try to keep up your spirits" (*Letters* 2, 31 January 1579: 4).[1] During the most desperate times, Teresa reassures her collaborators that their troubles "are from God and that His Majesty looks after our affairs more than we do" (*Letters* 2, 12 March 1579: 1). Their trials, she promises, are part of God's plan for the triumph of the reform.

Foundress

Teresa launched the Carmelite reform with a clear objective: to foster the relationship between souls and God. María Carrión has elucidated the parallel between a nun's physical withdrawal into the convent and the inward spiritual movement of the soul seeking God (133).[2] For Teresa, the cloister liberated women by removing them from the commotion of secular life and enabling them to devote themselves wholly to prayer. Interiority provided nuns with protection not only from the temptations of the material world but also against social norms that reduced women to mere custodians of their husbands' or fathers' reputations. In contrast with the "delusion and loss" that characterize the outside world, the cloister offered enlightenment. Teresa synthesizes this idea in a letter to Isabel de Jimena, a Segovian woman who wished to give up her wealth and take vows: "Despite dangers so dangerous as youth, wealth, and freedom, the Holy Spirit gives you light to want to leave them aside. And the things that usually frighten souls, such as penance, enclosure, and poverty, enabled you to understand their value and also the delusion and loss that would have been yours had you followed after the former dangers" (*Letters* 1, End of 1570: 1). In *Way of Perfection* Teresa extols convent life because it fosters detachment and creates a prayer community in which nuns find a nurturing spiritual environment.

The affective spirituality derived from the *devotio moderna* and other late medieval religious movements assumes a "magisterium of Jesus," effectively rejecting formal Scholastic theology (Sánchez Lora 192–99). Although this "new spirituality" was promoted by men (Erasmus, Juan de Valdés, Osuna, Juan Luis Vives), it also found great favor among women, who discovered in it a vehicle for their own spiritual longing. The unmitigated rule validated women's spirituality by emphasizing affective experience rather than academic theology as it was taught in the universities (from which women were barred). In Discalced convents women were allowed to live in poverty in imitation of Christ, just as men did in the reformed male orders. Although conservative theologians were suspicious of mental prayer, especially when practiced by women, "Teresa not only believed that mental prayer was safe for women, she was also convinced that the Church urgently needed women's prayers" to battle the incursion of Protestantism into previously Catholic areas (Weber, "Spiritual Administration" 124).[3] In an age in which a woman was defined by her attachment to a man, Teresa's position constitutes not only a defense of women's ability to pursue higher forms of prayer and contemplation, but also a rejection of the patriarchal social structure. Male authors, from poets to moralists, described women in terms of their bodies, focusing on their beauty or chastity. Teresa, on the other hand, insisted on woman's spiritual dimension; for her, the soul was "an extremely rich palace, built entirely of gold and precious stones," inhabited by a "great King," God (*CWST* 2, *WPV* 28:9). She urges her nuns not to imagine that they're "hollow inside" (that is, just an outer encasement) but to remember their "inner richness and beauty" (*CWST* 2, *WPV* 28:10). Each woman must cultivate her own soul in her own way and at her own pace. Each must find her own "way of perfection."

Administrator

In order to ensure that Discalced convents met her standards, Teresa reserved for herself the right to make administrative decisions about their operation. She derived authority for her role from the very fact that she was a woman, claiming insight into female psychology and convent life that men lacked. Although much of Teresa's writing seems disconcertingly misogynistic, she transforms her womanly shortcomings into assets by pointing out that since God loves the weak and lowly, he often graces women with spiritual favors.[4] The favors she herself has received, along with her experience as a woman and a nun, give her, she believes, the authority to guide, command, and reprimand her collaborators. Men, she suggests, simply cannot deal with women as effectively as she can, which is why she tells Gracián in no uncertain terms: "I understand women's nature better than you" (*Letters* 1, October 1575?: 3). Gracián agreed with her. He requested that she write *The Interior Castle* for the spiritual guidance of nuns, and it was for him that she wrote the instructional manual, *On Making the Visitation*, which instructed visitators how to deal effectively with prioresses and their charges.

Teresa took a personal interest in every aspect of convent administration. Her letters show that she constantly advised her prioresses about the minutiae of effective management. This even involved the proper use of titles. Although Teresa was adamant that titles not be used in her convents and berates Gracián for addressing her as reverend ("Oh what distress these envelopes that address me as reverend cause me" [*Letters* 2, End of February 1581: 3]), she routinely addressed male ecclesiastics by that title. Teresa understood that, in society, knowing the correct form of address was crucial, especially because the success of the reform depended on the support of powerful people. That is why she instructs María de San José to verify the correct title for Antonio Figueredo, the chief mail carrier: "You can find out down there whether you must use the title *magnífico* or something else" (*Letters* 1, 7 September 1576: 4). Such attention to detail suggests that years of struggle with authorities had taught Teresa extreme caution; the slightest affront to a powerful person could produce dire consequences for the reform.

One important aspect of convent administration was the selection of novices. Whenever possible, Teresa herself screened potential postulants and even wrote to many of them about their prospects. For example, in one instance she sent a letter to two aspirants advising them to get their father's consent before attempting to take the veil (*Letters* 1, Mid-March 1574). Because she believed she understood women better than men did, Teresa was not shy about contradicting male ecclesiastics when it came to judging prospective nuns. When Nicolás Doria sends her a potential novice, also recommended by Ambrosio Mariano, Teresa writes to Mariano that "the person proposed by Señor Nicolao will not be accepted, even if you are . . . satisfied with her" (*Letters* 1, 21 October 1576: 5).[5] She rejects Mariano's assessment of the candidate on the grounds that men are not so skilled at judging women: "I was amused by your saying that just by seeing her you will be able to recognize the kind of person she is. We women are not so easy to get to know. After many years of hearing confessions, confessors themselves are amazed at how little they have understood. And it is because women cannot express their faults clearly, and the confessors judge by what they are told" (*Letters* 1, 21 October 1576: 7). That is, because women are inarticulate ("cannot express their faults clearly"), priests misunderstand them. Teresa claims the advantage over priests (in this case, Mariano), not by asserting her intellectual superiority, but by resorting to common beliefs regarding women's inarticulateness.[6]

One of Teresa's greatest challenges as an administrator was financing her convents. Funding the reform was a monumental task. Teresa had to purchase and furnish houses, some of which required extensive repairs, and see to their upkeep. She also had to feed and clothe her nuns. Although she was adamant that no postulant would be turned away for lack of a dowry and no postulant accepted simply for her fortune, it is clear from her letters that she did consider dowries as a source of income. In fact, dowries are a recurring theme in Teresa's letters. In her 1561 missive to Lorenzo, she exults: "With God's favor I have received two dowries" (*Letters* 1, 23 December 1561: 3). Later she writes to María Bautista: "They have spoken to me of two nuns with very good dowries who would like to enter here. They would bring more than two thousand ducats each; this could go to pay for the house, which cost four thousand, and to pay the six hundred to the canons, and still more" (*Letters* 1, 11 September 1574: 6).[7] To María de San José, who is worried about paying the annuity on the Seville convent, Teresa mentions two sisters who are prospective postulants: "A dowry of 300 ducats will be given for the one who has entered . . . and the other sister will give the same amount, with which you would be able to pay the annuity for this year." At first, she is tempted to overlook the age of the younger girl: "If there is no other solution, you could accept her. The trouble is that she is only fourteen years old; for this reason I say she shouldn't be accepted unless nothing else can be done" (*Letters* 1, 18 June 1576: 3).[8] However, she reverses herself at the end of the letter, advising María to refuse the underage girl.

Later that year, she writes María again, itemizing the amount that each new postulant will bring. In spite of her conviction that no woman should be rejected for lack of money, she comments that "it would be a difficult thing to accept someone now who has nothing for a dowry" (*Letters* 1, 7 September 1576: 8). Although these letters make Teresa sound calculating, she did often take in women with little money. In 1568 she writes to Doña Luisa about a gifted nun: "She has no more than 200 ducats, but the nuns are so much alone and the needs of a monastery in its beginnings so great that I said they should take her" (*Letters* 1, 27 May 1568: 12). And she tells Lorenzo, who was preparing to return to Spain from America, "I took in a nun who had nothing for a dowry, not even a bed, and I offered this to God that you and your children will arrive in good health." But then, as if to offset this loss, she adds, "In Medina someone entered with a dowry of 8,000 ducats, and another entered here [Toledo] with 9,000" (*Letters* 1, 17 January 1570: 17–18). Throughout the epistolary collection we see Teresa struggling to maintain a balance between practicality and principle.

Teresa looked to her family for financial support—not only to her brother Lorenzo but also to her sister Juana. She writes to Juana quite frankly from Encarnación, where Ángel de Salazar had placed her as prioress: "I need some *reales*" (*Letters* 1, 4 February 1572). At the time the convent was in dire straights due to previous mismanagement. Teresa begs her sister not only for money but also for food: "Send [some] turkeys, since you have so many" (*Letters* 1, February–March 1572: 2). Two and a half years later, while Teresa is still at Encarnación, she asks María Bautista if she knows anyone "who would give us a loan on good collateral worth more than a thousand" (*Letters* 1, 11 September 1574: 3) or if she knows "anyone there who could lend me some *reales*?" adding, "I don't want them as a donation but only until I am paid what my brother gave me"

(*Letters* 1, 11 September 1574: 5). Encarnación was still under Calced rule, which meant that nuns were allowed private property. However, even though many of them came from wealthy families, the common holdings were pitiable. To save money, Teresa avoided using convent provisions for her own sustenance, which is why she had to turn to relatives. Thanks to her management skills, she eventually succeeded in turning the financial situation of Encarnación around.

Teresa oversaw every detail of convent finances. The following sales agreement for some dovecotes is typical: "This day, Quasimodo Sunday, 1564, Juan de San Cristóbal and Teresa of Jesus entered into agreement on the sale of a group of dovecotes for 100 ducats free of tithes or duties. The amount will be paid in this manner: 10,000 maravedís now and 10,000 by Pentecost Sunday; the remainder will be paid by St. John's feast of this year" (*Letters* 1, 9 April 1564: 1–2). In a letter to Lorenzo she notes that no one ever demands an accounting of her or intervenes in the finances of the reform, suggesting that she manages the assets of the five existing monasteries single-handedly (*Letters* 1, 17 January 1570: 20). Although she complains jokingly that this makes a lot of work for her, she seems to prefer the arrangement, as it gives her complete freedom to make financial decisions.[9] After the reform begins to gain momentum, Teresa's pecuniary dealings become more complicated. For example, at Malagón she must find a benefice for the current chaplain in order to replace him with a Carmelite, which means convincing Doña Luisa to make the necessary payments (*Letters* 1, 27 May 1568: 7).[10] After the purchase of a house in Seville, she at first celebrates the excellent deal she got—"All say that what we paid was nothing and are certain that today it would cost 20,000 ducats to build" (*Letters* 1, 9 May 1575: 3)—only to find herself embroiled in a conflict over an excise tax due to a notary's error (*Letters* 1, May 1576). Teresa insisted that precise financial records be kept in the convents. She specifies in the Constitutions that "at least two of the key-bearers should know how to write and keep accounts" (34) and that the treasurer must record income and expenses (*CWST* 3, 38). Finance is so vital to Teresa's work that money is a topic in at least seventy-five of her extant letters.

Teresa also attended to the legal issues involved in her foundations. In a letter to Alonso Ramírez, brother of the founding benefactor for the Toledo Carmel, she discusses the difficulty of obtaining licenses for the convent (*Letters* 1, 19 February 1569: 3). She also writes to María de Mendoza, who helped with the foundation in Valladolid, about her efforts to get a license (*Letters* 1, End of March 1569: 4). To Pedro de la Banda, whose house Teresa purchased for the foundation in Salamanca and who continued to make demands on her well after the sales contract was signed, she declares: "From what everyone says, I am not obligated to all of this [that you request] until the license arrives" (*Letters* 1, 8 October 1573). Complications with licenses arose frequently, a situation Teresa attributes, in the letter to Ramírez mentioned above, to the devil's dissatisfaction with the success of the reform.

In a note to Isabel de Santo Domingo, prioress of the Pastrana Carmel, Teresa complains that her plans to found in Caravaca have been delayed because the license turned out to be invalid (*Letters* 1, 12 May 1575: 4). The following month she writes to Rubeo about another, similar problem: "The license . . . contained so many unsuitable requirements that I did not want to proceed with [the foundation]" (*Letters* 1, 18 June 1575: 2). She grumbles to Doña Isabel Osorio, a prospective postulant, about the intricacies of obtaining a license for a house without an income (*Letters* 2, 3–4 December 1579: 5). The year before her death, Teresa writes directly to Gaspar de Quiroga, archbishop of Toledo, requesting a license to found in Madrid (*Letters* 2, 16 June 1581: 1). When she is detained in Toledo and denied the right to found more convents, she defends herself by arguing that she has always acted within the constraints of legality: "I never went anywhere to make a foundation . . . without a written order or license from the prelate" (*Letters* 1, January–February 1576: 15). Her letters to Gracián are filled with advice on permits. For example, she writes to him repeatedly about obtaining a license for the friary at San Alejo, near Valladolid (*Letters* 2, 18 July 1579: 3; 17 February 1581: 13). The frequent mention of licenses and related documents in the epistolary collection illustrates the importance Teresa attached to the *business* of founding convents. Although she sometimes bemoans her excessive administrative commitments, she usually preferred to see to these obligations herself.

Upon occasion she had to delegate power, but even then she maintained a supervisory role. In November 1575, when she founded in Caravaca, for the first time in her career she handed over authority to another nun, Ana de San Alberto. However, she sent Ana detailed instructions on how to proceed: "Have a lawyer look at the contract in which [the sponsors] agree to provide an income for the monastery. And show him the certified patent that you have from our most reverend Father in virtue of which, in addition to the power of attorney given you by me, you may accept the monastery without any onus or financial obligation or anything else, for that is how it is given in the contract" (*Letters* 1, 24 November 1575). As the daughter of a merchant, Teresa undoubtedly learned about the importance of contracts and procedures as a young girl. Her familiarity with legal terms ("certified patent," "power of attorney," "without any onus or financial obligation") attests to ample practical experience.

Growing up in a litigious *converso* family probably also taught her the value of keeping accurate records. Each convent had a chronicler who had to keep a precise and complete convent history. After the 1576 inquisitional investigation of the Seville Carmel, Teresa writes to María de San José: "Tell Sister [Isabel de] San Francisco to be a good historian of all that happens" (*Letters* 1, 15 June 1576: 3). Above all, the chronicles had to be factual: "If Sister San Francisco is going to be the historian, she should not exaggerate, but state very simply what has taken place" (*Letters* 2, 3 May 1579: 16). It is thanks in part to these detailed accounts that today's scholars are able to reconstruct fairly comprehensive convent histories.

"Mother General"

As chief administrative officer of all the Discalced female convents, Teresa had a role akin to that of father general: she made decisions that affected the entire order (although at the time the unmitigated branch did not constitute a separate entity). To ensure the smooth operation of her convents, Teresa invested prioresses with great authority. Although prioresses were officially elected by the community, Teresa actually handpicked each one herself. The importance she attached to finding competent prioresses is evident in a playful letter she wrote to María de San José toward the end of her career: "However wretched you are, I would like to have some more like you, for I wouldn't know what to do if I had to make a foundation now. I don't find any prospective prioresses" (*Letters* 2, End of December 1579: 13). Although Discalced Carmelite convents were egalitarian for their day, prioresses were definitely in charge, and Teresa was in charge of the prioresses. She wrote to them constantly, guiding them in their administrative duties, inquiring about their health and needs, and offering direction in particular situations. Teresa's letters to prioresses provide insight not only into her talents as an administrator but also into daily life in Carmelite convents.

Teresa insisted on influencing the selection of postulants and sometimes, as we saw in her letters to María Bautista (Chapter 4), this could lead to conflicts with prioresses. However, because she had an overview of all the convents and wanted to preserve approximately the same number of nuns in each, she insisted on maintaining the upper hand. As we saw above, money was one factor in determining the selection of postulants. Physical appearance and talents were also factors. For example, Teresa writes to María de San José: "I had refused that postulant because they told me she had I don't know what kind of scar" (*Letters* 1, 7 September 1576: 6). However, practical considerations (the girl's dowry) cause her to reassess the situation: "In our present need one could consider if it may not be fitting to give her a try" (*Letters* 1, 7 September 1576: 6). In the end, though, she decides against admitting her. Although it may seem surprising that Teresa attached such importance to looks, early modern thought equated physical beauty with moral excellence and scars with moral imperfection (Cirlot 280). Concern with appearance is also evident in Teresa's frustration with Gracián's younger sister Isabel, whom Teresa had accepted at the age of eight as an underage postulant. Although Teresa was fond of the child, she found her stiff laugh annoying. She tells María de San José: "I don't know how to correct the way she holds her mouth, for she keeps it very tight and has a laugh that is extremely cold, and she always goes around laughing. Sometimes I make her open her mouth, at other times close it, and at other times tell her not to laugh. She says it's not her fault but her mouth's, and she's right" (*Letters* 1, 9 January 1577: 6). In comparison, Teresa finds her niece Teresita lovely: "Whoever has seen the charm of Teresa, physical and otherwise, must notice the difference more." She adds, "I'm only telling you this in secret. Don't say anything to anyone" (*Letters* 1, 9 January 1577: 6). Although she is embarrassed by her own pettiness, Teresa is a perfectionist who cannot overlook Isabel's flaw.

In early modern Europe, convents were sites of artistic and musical activity, and postulants with special talents were sometimes admitted without a dowry.[11] Music played an important part in Teresa's houses; she herself played the tambourine and loved to sing. Although she reputedly had a mediocre voice, Teresa appreciated talent in others. Twice she writes to María de San José about a woman with a beautiful voice who, regrettably, failed to take vows (*Letters* 1, 7 September 1576: 10; 9 September 1576: 4). She mentions in a letter to Gracián that his little sister Isabel often sets aside her needlework and sings: "Mother Foundress / Is coming to recreation. / Let's all dance and sing / And clap our hands in jubilation" (*Letters* 1, End of December 1576: 1). On one occasion she sends Lorenzo a little song for John of the Cross that she had received from the Encarnación nuns and asks that her nephew Francisco sing it (*Letters* 1, Christmas Season 1576–1577). In her next letter to her brother she speaks of some verses composed by one of the nuns at San José, adding, "During these Christmas festivities we did a lot of this in recreation" (*Letters* 1, 2 January 1577: 22). She asks him to send one of his carols, for "the sisters sing everything" (*Letters* 1, 2 January 1577: 23). Frequent references to songs and singing show that life in Discalced Carmelite convents was not all austerity and mortification. Teresa herself wrote poems to sing or recite at professions and other festivities. The Constitutions allowed prioresses to give nuns an hour of recreation each day, and although games were forbidden, the women were encouraged to relax and entertain each other, provided they did not engage in gossip or offensive behavior (*CWST* 3, 27). Judging from Teresa's letters, singing was a favorite pastime.

Teresa saw a close connection between music and spiritual experience. In both *Spiritual Testimonies* (*CWST* 1, 12:1) and *The Interior Castle* (*CWST* 2, VI, 11:8) she mentions how, when the novice Isabel de Jesús (Jimena) sang for her one Easter, she went into a trance. She notes in one of her letters that her own compositions could produce the same effect: "I once composed [a song] while in deep prayer, and it seemed I entered into even greater quiet" (*Letters* 1, 2 January 1577: 23). Chanting constituted an integral part of Carmelite life, and one of the duties of the prioress was to "take care of the choir so that the recitation and chanting [can] be done well" (*CWST* 3, Constitutions 35). Chanting was so important that Teresa stipulated just how it was to be done: "The chant should never be sung with musical notation but should be done in a monotone and with uniform voices" (*CWST* 3, Constitutions 3). She also specifies that the sisters should to take care not to miss this exercise (*CWST* 3, Constitutions 4). However, in the case that chanting could not be done properly, Teresa preferred that her nuns forgo it. She writes to María de San José that the Paterna community should refrain from chanting, since there are so few nuns there: "In no way do I think they should sing anything until their number increases, for this would bring discredit on all" (*Letters* 1, 26 November 1576: 2). Teresa apparently thought that the scrawny choir would produce a sound unworthy of the psalms the nuns chanted; she feared that the exercise would prove counterproductive both for the convent's reputation and the nuns' spiritual well-being.

Teresa was also concerned about clothing. The Constitutions state: "The habit should be made of coarse cloth or black, rough wool, and only as much wool as is necessary should be used. The sleeves should be narrow, no wider at the opening than at the shoulder. Circular, without pleats, and no larger in the back than in the front, the habit should extend to the feet. . . . Let sandals made from hemp be worn and, for the sake of modesty, stockings of rough wool or of cloth made from rough tow" (*CWST* 3, 12).[12] Teresa often wrote to prioresses on the matter of habits and undertunics. For example, she told María de San José: "Since you are wearing tunics of worsted wool, you can wear underskirts made of the same material without any imperfection. I much prefer this to fine wool" (*Letters* 1, 9 September 1576: 13).[13] Soft fabric should always be avoided: "The material they use for the underskirts here [in Toledo] is like what you used for [my niece] Teresa, although coarser, the coarser the better" (*Letters* 1, 22 September 1576: 1). She mentions in another letter to María that Ana de San Alberto, prioress of Caravaca, has sent her "a habit made of coarse wool," which is "the most suited to our purposes that I've worn— very light." She also notes with approval that the nuns themselves "made the material for the undertunics" (*Letters* 1, 19 November 1576: 4). She points out that in Toledo "no one . . . wears, or has worn, worsted cloth except me, for even now with all the freezing cold, I have not been able to do otherwise" (*Letters* 1, 9 January 1577: 9).

Teresa's letters show that even though she was strict about dress, she was also flexible and willing to modify the rules according to circumstance (climate, health of the nuns, etc.). When Garciálvarez begins dictating more austere dress for the Seville nuns, Teresa writes to María de San José insisting that she take into consideration the Andalusian climate when determining what fabrics to use: "Because of the heat down there you couldn't wear anything but underskirts of light material, but not the same for the habit" (*Letters* 1, 9 January 1577: 9). Furthermore, "To wear the tunic in summer is foolish. If you want to please me, take it off when this letter arrives, however great a means of mortification it is" (*Letters* 2, 1 February 1580: 2). Teresa was adamant that all the nuns in a single convent should dress the same, unless an exception had to be made for health reasons. She writes to Ana de San Alberto: "Regarding the cloth underskirts . . . if you are unable to buy others for everyone at once, dispose of the cloth ones little by little until they are all gone. Sell them for as much as you can" (*Letters* 1, 2 July 1577: 11). When the Constitutions are revised in 1581, Teresa instructs Gracián, who will represent her at the chapter in Alcalá, on changes she wants made concerning dress: "In regard to the 'stockings of rough wool or cloth made from rough tow' that nothing be specified or said more than that they should wear stockings so that the nuns won't be having scruples. And where it says 'the toques should be made of fine tow,' say 'linen'" (*Letters* 2, 21 February 1581: 5). Teresa wanted the nuns to be able to adapt to the seasons or other circumstances without having to feel guilty about it. Gracián did in fact effect these changes.

As we have seen, health is a recurrent theme in Teresa's epistolary writing. Teresa not only gives her friends, male and female, detailed accounts of her own health but inquires constantly about theirs. When she writes to prioresses, she often asks about the health of particular nuns, sometimes recommending remedies for ailments. Ensuring nuns' health was one of her primary concerns, for, as she writes to María de San José, "with good health one can put up with anything" (*Letters* 2, 6 January 1581: 6). When she suspects that María Bautista is not taking care of herself, she scolds, "You should be pampering yourself, for your health is important to us" (*Letters* 1, 16 July 1574: 3). When Brianda de San José, the Malagón prioress, gets up from her sickbed to attend to business, Teresa writes to her: "I'm amazed that they order you to get up in weather like this. For goodness' sake don't do so—it would be enough to kill you—until the weather gets better; but not now, for it's even dangerous for those who are big and healthy" (*Letters* 1, 18 December 1576).

Teresa had an extraordinarily modern understanding of the effects of stress on health. When Isabel de San Jerónimo, a mentally unbalanced nun at the Seville Carmel, became delusional and difficult to control, Teresa was concerned not only about her but also about the effects of her behavior on María de San José, who suffered from a heart condition. She writes to María: "I was very disturbed by this heart trouble you have, for it is very painful; and I am not surprised, with all the terrible trials you have suffered" (*Letters* 2, 4 June 1578: 4). But Teresa does more than commiserate; she assumes the authority of a doctor: "Take note of what I am going to say. Try to see her [Isabel de San Jerónimo] as little as possible, for with your kind of heart trouble it would be so harmful for you that you could end up in a bad condition—and note that this is an order" (*Letters* 2, 4 June 1578: 5). Even when writing to church authorities Teresa takes it upon herself to instruct on the evils of stress. For example, she warns Don Teutonio de Braganza that the distress resulting from his political troubles might affect his health (*Letters* 1, 3 July 1574: 2). Throughout her epistolary writing Teresa comments on the effects of stress on her own health, making it clear that her knowledge of the relationship between mind and body derives from her own experience.

Teresa's insight led her to attach great importance to diet. The Constitutions say little about food but that "meat must never be eaten except as the rule prescribes" (*CWST* 3, 11). In a letter to Lorenzo cited earlier she notes that "according to our Constitutions we do not beg for alms, but we eat what is brought to the turn for us, which is more than sufficient" (*Letters* 1, 17 January 1570: 18). Upon founding the Discalced Carmelites Teresa abrogated the mitigated rule, according to which nuns could eat meat three times a week, in favor of the original rule of Saint Albert, which allowed meat only in the case of illness. Yet this insistence on austerity did not constitute an endorsement of food deprivation. In a letter to María de San José, Teresa expresses her concern about a community in Paterna, where the nuns suffer from hunger (*Letters* 1, 26 November 1576: 2). Elsewhere she tells María, "Try to borrow money for food. . . . Don't go hungry, for that grieves me very much" (*Letters* 1, 28 June 1577: 9). Teresa worries about the friars as well. As we have seen, she was particularly concerned about Gracián, who, during the Calced persecutions, was often forced to live in miserable conditions and suffered illness as a consequence. She often writes to him instructing him to eat properly or expressing her sorrow that Calced persecutions have forced him to go hungry (*Letters* 2, 14 August 1578: 9). In her letters on this subject Teresa comes across as a devoted mother, concerned for the well-being of both her daughters and her sons.

Teresa made exceptions to the dietary rules when circumstances demanded. Although she had originally envisioned sponsor-free convents in which nuns would live on charity and refrain from eating meat, pragmatism led her to alter that plan and accept the patronage of Doña Luisa de la Cerda for the Malagón Carmel, founded in 1568. Since fish was hard to obtain in that area, Teresa allowed meat. As she explains to the father of two prospective postulants to another convent: "If it seems too rigorous to abstain from meat, the foundation could be made like the one made on Palm Sunday in Malagón. It could easily be done since there are bulls that enable us to do so. We approved their having an income in Malagón and eating meat, since there was no possibility of doing otherwise in that place" (*Letters* 1, 28 June 1568: 9).[14] It is noteworthy that when writing to Lorenzo, who favors the original plan to found in poverty, Teresa stresses austerity, but when writing to the girls' father, who is apparently concerned for his daughters' comfort, she insists reassuringly that the girls would have some leeway. Flexibility and expediency are the hallmarks of Teresa's administrative style, and she knew how to present a situation in the most favorable light to her multiple correspondents.

Whenever a nun showed signs of infirmity, Teresa immediately examined her diet and sleeping habits. She regularly prescribed meat for ailing nuns and friars. She writes to her friend Domingo Báñez about Ana de Encarnación, prioress of Salamanca, who had been ill, "Don't consent for the prioress [Ana] to stop eating meat, and tell her to take care of her health" (*Letters* 1, 28 July 1578: 6). Similarly, she wrote to Gracián to make certain his sickly secretary, Fray Bartolomé de Jesús, ate meat (*Letters* 2, 17 February 1581: 2). And when the subprioress of Soria fell ill, Teresa wrote to the prioress: "If she always needs to eat meat, it doesn't matter that she does so, even during Lent, for one does not break the rule when a necessity is present; nor should one be strict in this matter" (*Letters* 2, 28 December 1581: 5). However, it would be a mistake to conclude that Teresa was lax. Unless there was a reason for disregarding dietary policy, she expected her nuns to conform. When, toward the end of her career, the confessor at San José wanted to change the Constitutions to permit meat in the diet, Teresa wrote to Gracián complaining about it (*Letters* 2, 27 February 1581: 2).

In her concern for mental health, Teresa was ahead of her time. The church's mistrust of female ecstatic experience often led male clerics to attribute it to hysteria, and Teresa's comments on women's volatility suggest she had assimilated the dominant opinion. She was reluctant to assert the veracity of her own mystical experiences and repeatedly invited *letrados* to assess them. Likewise, she evaluated with caution reports by women of their supernatural experience. The medical literature of the period relates spurious supernatural experience to mental illness, especially melancholia (depression), as well as to the heretical practice of illuminism and even demonic possession. Michel Foucault has shown to what extent the sixteenth century associated deviant religious experience, especially demonic possession, with madness and with the body.[15] Doctors of the period associated mental illness with sin; melancholy could result from excessive self-contemplation and solitude, leading to moral vulnerability, which could indeed invite the machinations of the devil. Like her contemporaries in the medical field (Cristóbal Acosta, Tomás Murillo y Velarde), Teresa saw melancholy as a medical condition resulting from humoral imbalances and aggravated by particular lifestyles, such as excessive prayer, unmitigated seclusion, or sleep or food deprivation (Soufas 41).

Melancholia as a sign of spiritual depravity was more likely to be associated with women than men.[16] In men, melancholia, meaning "black bile" (the body fluid that was thought to cause a melancholic disposition when it occurred in excess), was often associated with genius. Aristotle wrote that "all men who have become outstanding in philosophy, statesmanship, poetry or the arts are melancholic" (*Problems*, Qtd. Schiesari 7). This attitude continued into the Renaissance, when "depression became translated into a virtue for the atrabilious man of letters" and, in fact, a mark of brilliance or spiritual superiority (Schiesari 7). A sign of inspiration, it was viewed as "an eloquent form of mental disturbance," a kind of gift that transformed frustration into heroic suffering and creativity—a notion that preserved and affirmed the masculine ego (Schiesari 8). However, this grandiose view of melancholia did not extend to women, whose emotional suffering was seen as "everyday," a natural part of the feminine makeup. Rather than contributing to great works of art, female melancholia was thought to generate inarticulateness. Women melancholics could "no longer find a place in the symbolic order's prime system, language" (Schiesari 15). Either they were ignored or else their "babbling" was attributed to demonic intervention.

Although Teresa does not describe melancholia in women as creative genius, she does not ignore or automatically demonize it. Teresa shows herself to be sensitive to the signs of melancholia and other mental illness in *Foundations*, in which she describes specific treatments for afflicted nuns. To the extent that she realized that mind, spirit, and body were connected, Teresa reflected the medical thought of her time. She believed a weak mind could render a person susceptible to the devil's ploys, but rather than ostracize mentally weak nuns, she preferred to regulate their food and activities and to reintegrate them into the community. Teresa did not accuse of sinfulness those nuns who claimed supernatural experience, but she did consider the possibility that they might be suffering from mental or physical illness, and she believed that this condition could be ameliorated with modifications in diet and routine.

The cases of Isabel de San Jerónimo and Beatriz de la Madre de Dios will serve as examples. Both women became delusional and excessively prayerful, and Beatriz along with her friend Margarita began to spend inordinate amounts of time in confession with Garciálvarez. Teresa suspected mental instability and thought that a change of diet would help. She wrote to Gracián about Isabel: "It will be necessary to make San Jerónimo eat meat for a few days and give up prayer, and tell her not to speak to anyone but you, or that she write to me, for her imagination is weak and she meditates on what she thinks she sees or hears" (*Letters* 1, 23 October 1576: 9). Two years later, when Beatriz manifested the same symptoms and claimed to see visions, Teresa writes to María de San José expressing her satisfaction that Gracián had ordered "the two nuns who are so deep into prayer [to] eat meat" (*Letters* 2, 4 June 1578: 9). In *Foundations* Teresa recommends that melancholic or hysterical nuns be kept busy with domestic tasks. Likewise, she advises María de San José to "make little" of the claims of the women, to keep them occupied, and to discourage them from spending time writing down their visions, which will only serve to inflate their importance in the nuns' minds (*Letters* 2, 4 June 1578: 9). However, when all else fails, Teresa is not opposed to corporal punishment: "Perhaps a thrashing will get [Isabel] to stop screaming" (*Letters* 2, 4 June 1578: 6). In spite of her illness, Isabel became provisional prioress of the Seville Carmel because of the stature conferred by her age after María de San José was forced to step down.[17] In 1579 Teresa wrote to Isabel and María with advice on how to deal with Beatriz. Teresa advises against isolation and in favor of activity because "her being alone and with only her thoughts can do her much harm" (*Letters* 2, 3 May 1579: 12). In spite of the damage Beatriz did by making false accusations against Teresa and María, Teresa ordered that she be treated kindly, and Beatriz eventually recovered.

Teresa was wary of excessive mortifications, including fasting, which could trigger harmful psychological reactions such as spurious visions. The Constitutions say relatively little about fasting, except that "a fast is observed from the feast of the Exaltation of the Cross, which is in September until Easter, with the exception of Sundays" (*CWST* 3, *Constitutions* 11). Teresa mentions her own fasting in several of her letters and sometimes praises that of others, as when she extols to María de San José the fasting of the Caravaca nuns (*Letters* 1, 19 November 1576: 4). Nevertheless, she was wary of fasting by nuns who were frail or unbalanced, and she gives specific instructions to Gracián that Beatriz "should fast only sparingly" (*Letters* 1, 23 October 1576: 10). Later, when Beatriz goes to Paterna, Teresa writes to María de San José to tell the prioress there "to make [Beatriz] eat meat after Lent is over and not let her fast" (*Letters* 1, 1–2 March 1577: 6).

By Teresa's day fasting had become a fetish among religious women seeking to intensify their spiritual experience. Carolyn Walker Bynum points out that the fasting requirements of the medieval church were actually quite moderate, but by the twelfth and thirteenth centuries food asceticism had begun to grow, especially among women, even as moralists warned that it could lead to self-delusion (*Holy Feast* 46–47, *Fragmentation* 139–43).[18] Rudolph Bell cites the example of Catherine Benincasa, who practiced extreme fasting in defiance of her confessors' orders to eat (*Holy Anorexia* 22–53). Bynum cites the case of Angela di Foligno, who desired to give up eating entirely, only to realize that extreme fasting was a temptation of the devil and, in fact, pathological (*Fragmentation* 142). These examples show that for centuries church authorities had understood the dangers of fasting and had considered them to be particularly severe in women. By prohibiting Beatriz from fasting, Teresa sought to reduce her vulnerability to demonic deception.

Perhaps because she was often ill, Teresa became something of an expert on home remedies for both physical and mental ailments. She constantly asserts her authority in this area, offering her nuns advice about the medicinal properties of plants and minerals. "Be careful not to drink sarsaparilla water," she warns María de San José, "even though it may be good against hysteria" (*Letters* 1, 7 September 1576: 12). The following month she writes again, telling her to avoid sarsaparilla water and to treat her fever with something other than purgatives (*Letters* 1, 13 October 1576: 1). The dangers of sarsaparilla water come up again in reference the illness of the prioress at Malagón (*Letters* 1, 31 October 1576: 4). Teresa recommends a certain syrup to María Bautista to combat melancholy and fever and another to increase energy (*Letters* 1, 4 May 1574: 1; 29 April 1576: 7). She warns María de San José that the prioress of Malagón, who has a fever, should forgo sweets because "they would kill her" (*Letters* 1, 26 January 1577: 6). She also asks María to send her some courbaril resin, which was mixed with rose-colored sugar to make pastilles for rheumatism (*Letters* 1, 26 January 1577: 10). She praises the medicinal properties of "orange-flower water" (*Letters* 1, 1–2 March 1577: 2) and begs María to send her some in any form: "If you can find any, send some crystallized orange blossoms, dry, and sprinkled with sugar. . . . Otherwise send the sweets. But I prefer the orange blossoms, whatever the price, even if only a small quantity" (*Letters* 1, 9 April 1577: 5). Teresa's letters constitute a small encyclopedia of homeopathic cures popular during her time.

Since the convent building had to provide an environment conducive to both prayer and good health, Teresa paid close attention to the physical premises and location of her houses. The Constitutions state, "The house, with the exception of the church, should never be adorned, nor should there be anything finely wrought, but the wood should be rough. Let the house be small and the rooms humble: something that fulfills rather than exceeds the need. It should be as strong as possible. The wall should be high, and there should be a field where hermitages can be constructed so that the Sisters may be able to withdraw for prayer as our holy Fathers did" (*CWST* 3, 32). Teresa writes in *Foundations* about the difficulty of finding the right houses for her convents, financing them, obtaining patents, and dealing with landlords, sellers, and tenants reluctant to move. In Medina del Campo she found a dilapidated house with crumbling walls and an entrance way so dirty and decrepit that "it was necessary to clear away the dirt, since overhead was nothing but a rustic roof of bare tile." However, thanks to the landlady's butler, who offered her "many tapestries . . . and a blue damask bedhanging," she managed to make the place livable (*CWST* 3, *Foundations* 3:8–9). In Salamanca the former occupants of the house, university students, had left it "a mess," requiring her to put in a great deal of physical labor (*CWST* 3, *Foundations* 19:4). Often Teresa cleaned and made repairs with her own hands. We can only imagine this saintly woman down on her knees scrubbing!

Teresa's letters permit us to observe firsthand her efforts to obtain suitable buildings in a salubrious area. For example, she writes to Gracián about the Malagón Carmel, complaining that the house is seriously in need of renovation. Since "the setup of the house is bad," she has sent a messenger to Doña Luisa de la Cerda, the sponsor, to ask for help. If Doña Luisa does not come through, Teresa will transfer the nuns to Paracuellos, which seems to her "a very healthy place to live" (*Letters* 1, 15 June 1576: 5, 7). Later she writes to Gracián about the house in Salamanca, which is also in disrepair, and suggests she may place a new postulant with a dowry there to help with the expenses (*Letters* 2, 10–11 March 1578: 4). However, the house proves inadequate, and Teresa writes to María Bautista that she had procured permission from the bishop to buy another (*Letters* 2, 9 June 1579: 3). Not only is the original house "very unhealthy," but the nuns "are undergoing much difficulty from the one who sold it to them, which has led to daily confrontations and a generally stressful situation" (*Letters* 2, 24 June 1579: 8). When she first founds in Seville, Teresa fears the nuns will be uncomfortable in the Andalusian heat. When it turns out otherwise, she writes to María de San José that she is "greatly consoled to know that the house is cool" (*Letters* 1, 9 September 1576: 12). Letters such as these reveal Teresa's hands-on approach to property management. She was constantly buying, unloading, and renovating property, and when renovations had to be made, she traveled around Spain to supervise operations.

Experience had taught Teresa that it was better to maintain control of the foundation process herself. She had left the initial acquisition of the Seville house to Gracián and the permits to Mariano with disastrous results. Yet, Teresa could not be everywhere, and with her busy schedule, poor health, and inferior status as a woman, she often had to count on men to do the groundwork. When she decided to found in Burgos, she asked Canon Jerónimo Reinoso to scout around for a house. Worried that he has made an inappropriate choice, she writes him: "[The Canon Salinas] says that [the house] is located in a place where there is a lot of noise from the street and surrounded by all sides by vulgar people. If you have leased it, I have nothing more to say. . . . But if you have not, wait and don't take it until you see if we can find another house in a neighborhood more suitable to our way of life" (*Letters* 2, 24 April 1581: 1). Teresa was no less concerned with neighborhood than modern buyers who intone "location, location, location!"

Since the process of withdrawal into the soul was to be reflected by withdrawal into the convent building, Teresa was naturally concerned with the interiors of her houses. She counted on her prioresses to maintain their convents clean and orderly and to respect the rules on simplicity. On one occasion she congratulates María de San José on keeping her house "very neat" (*Letters* 1, 2 July 1576: 6). In a letter to Gracián she writes, "For the love of God, make sure that the beds are clean, as well as the table napkins, no matter how much you spend, for it is a terrible thing if cleanliness is not provided. In fact, I would like to see this prescribed in the Constitutions, and I don't think that doing that would even be enough" (*Letters* 2, End of February 1981: 2). The care she devoted to furnishings and decoration is astonishing, considering other demands on her time. She herself decided to grace the entrance of San José de Ávila with statues of Saint Joseph and the Virgin (*CWST* 1, *Life* 32:11). Teresa's many extant thank-you notes attest to the multitude of gifts she accepted from donors for the adornment of other convents. She writes twice to Doña Inés Nieto, wife of the secretary of the duke of Alba, thanking her for a statue of Our Lady for one of the monasteries (*Letters* 1, 28 December 1574: 3; 19 June 1575: 1). Later in 1575 she mentions the statue again: "The more I look at the statue the more beautiful it seems; the crown is lovely" (*Letters* 1, 31 October 1575: 3).[19] When she leaves Seville for Toledo, she writes playfully to Diego Ortiz, who had promised to send her a statue of Saint Joseph for her new domicile: "It's no small thing for me to have to give up so soon the statue of Our Lady. I will feel extremely lonely without it. So, in charity, you can provide a remedy for me by sending the one you are going to give me for Christmas" (*Letters* 1, 16 December 1576: 3).[20] While the Alcalá chapter was taking place, Doña Ana Enríquez sent Teresa a statue for the foundation she was making in Palencia. In spite of how busy she was, Teresa took the time to thank her: "You have honored us greatly with the statue you donated, which stands alone on the main altar, and it is so well done and large that there is no need for others" (*Letters* 2, 4 March 1581: 4).

Teresa could be quite precise about interiors. Her brother Lorenzo had left money for a chapel at the San José convent, and after his death Teresa took care that his wishes be respected. She writes to the nuns in Ávila that the main vault should be built "according to the drawing that was made for this and that you all saw," and that the iron grille should be "not the most costly, but well fashioned and pleasing to the eye" (*Letters* 2, 7 October 1580: 7). These comments supplement others Teresa makes in *Foundations* about the physical plants of convents. She was concerned, for example, about water supplies; she not only comments on the well in Medina del Campo (*CWST* 3, *Foundations* 1:4) but even reputedly helped design a well for the convent at Villanueva de la Jara.[21] With regard to the layout of the convent in Soria, she suggested to the prioress, Catalina de Cristo, that the kitchen and refectory be moved downstairs to make things easier for the cooking staff (*Letters* 2, 15 May 1581: 6; 15–17 September 1582: 1). She actually sent Lorenzo to observe a stove designed by María de San José so she could have it copied (*Letters* 2, 15 April 1578: 9), and when the project fizzled she wrote to María, "Concerning the stove, we want you to know we spent almost one hundred *reales*, and it was worthless—so much so that we broke it apart. It used up more wood than any benefit that was coming from it" (*Letters* 2, 3 April 1580: 11). From relics and statuary to kitchen furnishings and wells, Teresa attended to every detail.

Within Teresa's administrative structure, prioresses oversaw not only the day-to-day running of the convents but also their charges' spiritual development. One of Teresa's innovations was "a system of governance based on an expanded spiritual magisterium for prioresses working in close collaboration with prelates who shared their vision" (Weber, "Spiritual Administration" 126). For Teresa, the spiritual journey was not a solitary endeavor. As Gillian Ahlgren writes, "Soulful self-knowledge is not possible in a vacuum. The only way to start exploring the essential depths of our personhood is through prayer, and this includes prayerful conversations with others" (*Entering* 34). Thus, the soul "necessitates strong companions . . . for perhaps humans cannot sustain the realization of the God-human potential without tender, ongoing support mediated by other humans" (Ahlgren, *Entering* 74). Teresa writes extensively in her books about her own efforts to find competent spiritual directors, explaining that once she found one, "prayer began to take shape as an edifice that now had a foundation" (*CWST* 1, *Life* 24:2). Teresa herself gave spiritual direction to men as well as women, including her brother Lorenzo, the archbishop of Evora Teutonio de Braganza, the Jesuit rector Gaspar de Salazar, and, of course, Gracián.

Sensitive to the strictures against women teaching theology, Teresa was careful to avoid presenting herself as a *letrada*. She responded to a letter from Gonzalo Dávila, rector of the Jesuit community in Ávila, who had jokingly reproached her for her presumptuousness: "It is a long time since I have been as mortified about anything as I was on receiving your message today, for I'm not so humble that I want to be taken for proud. . . . You really know how to mortify me and make me realize my true nature, since you think I presume to know how to teach. God deliver me from such a thing! . . . One of my great faults is to judge others' experience by my own with regard to prayer, so please don't take into account anything I say. God will certainly have given you other talents than the ones he gave to a poor little woman like me" (*Letters* 2, June 1578: 1, 3). Although Teresa reverts here to her accustomed rhetoric of humility, portraying herself as a *mujercilla* favored by God only because of His special concern for the lowly, she not only continued to offer spiritual direction herself but empowered her prioresses to do so.

Fundamental to the process of spiritual development is "discernment of spirits," through which an individual learns to discriminate between thoughts and sentiments inspired by God and those stimulated by the enemy of human nature—that is, between authentic and specious spiritual favors.[22] Teresa's letters to María de San José regarding Beatriz de la Madre de Dios and Isabel de San Jerónimo illustrate the care she took in this matter: "In regard to Beatriz, her prayer is good, but insofar as possible avoid paying attention to these things in conversation or in any other way" (*Letters* 1, 1–2 March 1577: 5). Teresa avoids outright condemnation of Beatriz, giving her credit for "good prayer," but rejects her claim to authentic mystical experience. She counsels María to thwart Beatriz's potential exploitation of her supposed ecstasies for attention, and she makes it clear that as Beatriz's superior, it is up to María to control the situation: "You know that this depends very much on the prioress. San Jerónimo did not speak of that here, because the prioress immediately interrupted and scolded her, and so she kept quiet" (*Letters* 1, 1–2 March 1577: 5).

Teresa cites the case of Isabel de San Jerónimo as an example of how to deal with nuns who might be vulnerable to the devil's tricks because of mental instability. Before Isabel de San Jerónimo went to Seville, she had been in a convent in Castile, where the prioress had clamped down on her eccentric behavior, a modus operandi for dealing with overwrought nuns that Teresa recommends.[23] While Teresa was in Seville, Isabel "never carried on in this way," evidently because Teresa knew how to control her, but Teresa worries that Isabel may regress now that she has gone to Paterna, where the prioress may not know how to manage her (*Letters* 1, 1–2 March 1577: 5). Although Teresa now finds herself in Toledo, she attempts to control the situation from afar by writing directly to Isabel, always taking care never to overstep María: "Our *padre* [Gracián] would like me to write to her in a severe manner with respect to this. Read the enclosed letter that I am writing her, and if it seems all right to you, send it to her" (*Letters* 1, 1–2 March 1577: 6). Teresa's main concern is that Isabel could fall prey to an incompetent confessor.[24]

Confessors were on her mind because María was still dealing with Garciálvarez, who had been encouraging Beatriz's eccentric behavior. In Teresa's view, the best way to manage meddling confessors was to avoid them. She cites the Beas Carmel as an example of a convent where the prioress's excellent spiritual direction minimizes the role of the confessor: "The prioress in Beas writes me that the nuns speak only of their sins with their confessor and that they are all finished within a half hour. She tells me it should be like this everywhere, that they are all very much at peace, and that they have a great love for their prioress in whom they confide." (*Letters* 1, 1–2 March 1577: 6). When prioresses have questions about spiritual direction, suggests Teresa, they should go to her, rather than to priests, for advice: "Since I have some experience in this matter, you could ask them why they don't write to me but go and ask someone who perhaps doesn't have as much as I do" (*Letters* 1, 1–2 March 1577: 6). Weber remarks that it is easy to see how Teresa's "broad interpretation of the prioress's role as informal spiritual director could lead to an infringement on a priest's authority as confessor and discerner of spirits" ("Dear Daughter" 255). In Weber's opinion, it is not surprising that Teresa was denounced to the Inquisition for hearing confessions, but, rather, that she was never prosecuted. Teresa's self-confidence derived from her own mystical experiences, which had been authenticated after careful examination by learned men. Edward Howells notes that when Teresa appeals to her "experience," she "does not mean sensations or emotions but a field of knowledge, which in mystical union is the field of supernatural or immediate knowledge of God" (Qtd. Ahlgren, *Entering* 80). This, in addition to administrative expertise and a good grasp of feminine psychology, enabled her to advise prioresses.

Legislator

One of Teresa's great but rarely mentioned talents was the ability to craft legislation. Teresa ensured that her convents would offer women a lifestyle conducive to spiritual growth by setting forth a body of operational regulations. The brief granting her permission to found San José in Ávila gave her "the power to make licit and respectable statutes and ordinances in conformity with canon law" as well as to make modifications as the need arose (Kavanaugh, *CWST* 3:311). This first set of laws, now lost, was somewhat fluid, as Teresa was experimenting to see which practices would foment the greatest perfection (Kavanaugh, *CWST* 3:312). She probably drafted these Constitutions, which Rubeo approved when he visited Ávila in 1567, soon after making her first foundation. Later versions show that Teresa made changes as time went on, leading Kavanaugh to comment that she saw the document as an evolving text (*CWST* 3:313). The Constitutions provided a daily schedule for convent life, descriptions of the responsibilities of each position (prioress, subprioress, etc.), and penal regulations required by existing convent codes. They "were designed to preserve the ascetic ideal of the reform while protecting the right of all nuns to aspire to contemplation" (Weber, "Spiritual Administration" 126). Teresa sought to maintain a balance between solitude and community, work and prayer, discipline and spiritual freedom.

When the brief *Pia consideratione*, issued on 22 June 1580, separated the Discalced Carmelites into a discrete province, it was only through correspondence that Teresa was able to assert her authority as legislator of the reform. In February 1581 Gracián was preparing for the chapter meeting in Alcalá, at which the Constitutions for the newly independent order would be revised. As a woman, Teresa could not attend the meeting herself, even though she was the one who had composed earlier versions of the Constitutions. Anxious to maintain the integrity of the rule, she wrote to Gracián repeatedly to make sure he would incorporate her ideas. Gracián responded with a request for suggestions, which she circulated among the nuns, agreeing to send their comments back to him after first reviewing them herself (*Letters* 2, 17 February 1581: 7).

One of Teresa's main concerns was maintaining rule rather than rigor. On the one hand, she reaffirmed the requisite of enclosure, which she had adopted even before it was endorsed by the Council of Trent, as well as the imperative of the veil: "There is no reason why confessors should see [the nuns] with faces unveiled, or the friars of any order, and much less our own Discalced friars" (*Letters* 2, Mid-February? 1581: 3). On the other hand, she stipulated that no restrictions should be added that might make the nuns unhappy; the Constitutions should not seem "stricter than they are" and the nuns should not be subjected to "more than what they promised" (*Letters* 2, Mid-February? 1581: 2). Teresa had always striven for balance, but an inclination toward extreme asceticism was emerging among some friars.

To reduce the influence of stern and controlling priests, Teresa gave prioresses authority to choose confessors for their convents. She insisted that the 1581 Constitutions spell out the right of a prioress, in consultation with the provincial, to appoint a convent chaplain, who could also serve as the ordinary confessor. In addition, prioresses were to have the authority to engage other confessors or preachers from within or outside of the order. Having suffered at the hands of incompetent confessors herself, Teresa wanted to make certain her nuns worked with knowledgeable and experienced priests. She had already moved to control the conduct and selection of confessors in *On Making the Visitation* (1576), in which she stipulates that the prioress must remain vigilant with regard to the conduct of confessors and that no confessor must ever be a vicar (a superior with authority over a convent): "It is very important to inquire about procedures concerning the confessor, and not from one or two nuns but from all of them, and about how much power he is given. Since he is not the vicar, nor must there ever be one, for this office was taken away so that he might not have such power, it is important that communication with him be only very moderate, and the less there is the better" (*CWST* 3, *Visitation*, 39). As February wore on, Teresa apparently grew increasingly concerned about the chapter. She wrote another letter, either to Gracián or the commissary (the addressee is not clear, and the original has been lost), setting down eight points she considered essential to the new Constitutions.[25] Although that document is not extant, Teresa articulates her thoughts on confessors in a letter to Gracián:

> I consider it very important that vicars not also be confessors to the nuns, and this should always be so. It is imperative for these houses that the nuns have the friars as confessors, as you say and I myself see. . . . I have seen clearly that if the vicar likes some nun, the prioress cannot prevent him from talking to her as much as he wants, for he is the superior. This can result in a thousand woes. For this reason, and for many others, it is also necessary that they not be subject to the priors. It will happen that someone who doesn't know much will give orders that are disturbing to all the nuns. . . . The greatest good that can be done for these nuns is that no talking with the confessor take place other than what is necessary for the confession of sins. . . . Our entire existence depends on our keeping

out these wicked devotees, these destroyers of the brides of Christ. It is necessary always to think of the worst that can happen in order to remove this occasion of sin, for the devil enters without our realizing it. (*Letters* 2, February 1581: 1–3)

The forcefulness of Teresa's language attests to the importance she attaches to this matter. She argues that the nuns have derived great benefit from Gracián's direction but that she cannot count on other confessors being as effective. She begs Gracián to ensure her provisos on confessors are included in the new Constitutions, a request to which he acceded.

Although Gracián agreed with Teresa ("as you say and I myself see"), he apparently thought she was making too much of the issue. She protests: "I don't know why you say we should be silent in regard to the friars being our confessors. . . . Nor do I understand why you must not speak about matters concerning us" (*Letters* 2, February 1581: 4). Perhaps Teresa feared that once in Alcalá, Gracián would lose his focus and fail to advance her agenda. She reminds him that he *must* defend the nuns' interests: "You really owe this to these nuns, for you cost them many tears" (*Letters* 2, February 1581:4). Although she was still the foundress, Teresa now found herself dependent on a volatile, capricious man. As in other letters, she resorts to the kind of smooth persuasion she hopes will secure his allegiance. She expresses her great confidence in him and assures him that she has often sung "the benefit we derive from your visitations" (*Letters* 2, February 1581: 4). However, Teresa's adulation betrays uncertainty; Gracián's impulsiveness has caused her problems before.

A few days later she writes to him again, this time with the recommendations she has received from the different Carmels. The most important one—the only one she mentions specifically—is from Isabel de Santo Domingo: "The prioress of Segovia has reminded me of the freedom we have to invite preachers from outside the order. I had omitted this, thinking it was already a given" (*Letters* 2, 21 February 1581: 3). The authority of prioresses to invite outside preachers strengthened their position within the convent, enabled them to ensure proper spiritual guidance for their nuns, and gave them the means to offset the negative influence of unsatisfactory confessors. However, Teresa was aware that this aspect of female prioral autonomy was susceptible to opposition from future generations of male clerics: "*Mi padre*, we must not [only] consider those who are living at present, but at a later time some persons could come along who in being made superiors will oppose such freedom and many other things" (*Letters* 2, 21 February 1581: 3). Teresa believed that reinforcing the authority of prioresses through the Constitutions would help safeguard the future of the order. Priests could undermine the rule either through excessive severity or through negligence. In Ávila, for example, dietary restrictions had already been relaxed, much to Teresa's chagrin. In order to prevent future erosion of the rule, she itemized for Gracián her requirements on austerity and other matters and instructed him to have them enshrined in the Constitutions, which she wanted printed: "I would like to have these Constitutions put into print, for different renderings of them are going about. There are prioresses who when copying them—and without thinking they are doing anything wrong—add or delete whatever they like. A strict, unmistakable precept should be set down against deleting or adding to the Constitutions" (*Letters* 2, 21 February 1581: 8). Perhaps Teresa had a premonition of things to come.

Although Gracián did, in fact, promote her agenda at the chapter, Kavanaugh notes that when writing about the sources of the Constitutions, he lists Rubeo, the visitator Pedro Fernández, and himself without even mentioning Teresa (*CWST* 3:317). For Kavanaugh the reason is clear: "Seemingly it was not feasible in the mind of these men to include a woman among the legislators" (*CWST* 3:317). From the very beginning, in fact, at least some Discalced friars resisted Teresa's authority. Antonio de Heredia, cofounder with John of the Cross of the first Discalced friary, wrote that he made decisions independently of Teresa: "I was governed not by Mother Teresa but by the Constitutions of the Order and by the reform laid down by a general chapter in Venice in 1524" (Qtd. Moriones, *Teresian Carmel* ch. 6). Whatever Gracián's motivations may have been for omitting Teresa from the register of sources, the fact is that for future generations of male clerics, Teresa's legacy of strong female administrators became increasingly problematic.

In 1585, three years after Teresa's death, Nicolás Doria was elected second Discalced provincial and initiated proceedings to modify the Constitutions. At the core of Doria's objections was the existing policy of monastic governance, in particular, the autonomy the Constitutions granted prioresses in the selection of confessors and preachers and the management of the spiritual, financial, and disciplinary affairs of their communities. He also opposed the relatively relaxed relationship that existed between male and female religious, which made it possible for prelates and prioresses to work collaboratively, as well as for alliances to develop between prioresses and male members of the aristocracy.[26] Doria's intention was to impose increased rigor in the female communities in order to return them to a lifestyle more in consonance with the primitive rule. Unlike Teresa, who insisted that rules existed to protect the spiritual integrity of the convents, Doria seemed to see them as an end in themselves. Moriones writes that Doria's goal "consisted of bringing the order to the highest degree of perfection, giving it a legislative structure and a system of government that closed all doors to any risk of laxity" (*El P. Doria* 12).[27] Doria's personal animosity toward Gracián, whom he saw as an ally of the prioresses, exacerbated the situation. Doria subjected Gracián to rigorous punishments, depriving him of his duties and putting him through tortuous legal procedures. Finally, he ruled that Gracián be exiled to Mexico, although thanks to the intervention of the cardinal, the order was never carried out.

In 1584 María de San José left Seville to found the Discalced convent of San Alberto in Lisbon, where she, along with Gracián, organized the resistance against Doria. In 1587 Gracián wrote to the nuns in Lisbon, suggesting they send a petition signed by all of them to the forthcoming chapter urging that the Constitutions not be changed. And this time, he did not forget to mention Teresa but instead bolstered his own authority by invoking her name:

> The conservation of the Order, with which Mother Teresa de Jesús charged me, has me thinking night and day about what would be best for these female monasteries. . . . Since Mother Teresa de Jesús, with so much common sense, spirit, good counsel and holiness ordered these Constitutions, and past chapters and other prelates such as apostolic commissaries, provincials and generals of the order have approved them, and experience has shown how well they have worked, ask the [upcoming] chapter participants that they by no means attempt to alter, remove, change or add anything. (*Cartas*, 19 February 1587)[28]

Infuriated, Doria charged Gracián with moral laxity. María de San José began a writing campaign on Gracián's behalf. (Unfortunately, these letters have been lost.) As a result, Doria forbade any further communication between them.

In 1590 María and another Discalced prioress, Ana de Jesús, went over Doria's head and appealed to Pope Sixtus V to preserve the 1581 Constitutions in what came to be known as "the nuns' revolt." The pope acceded to their request, issuing the brief *Salvatoris*, which confirmed the Constitutions and required papal approval for any modifications. However, Doria did not give up easily. He used his court connections to appeal to Philip II to block approval of the brief. Sixtus V died later that year, and the next pope, Gregory XIV, imposed a compromise that, without completely discarding the 1581 Constitutions, still gave Doria most of what he wanted. Now Doria had the upper hand, and he immediately retaliated against the rebels and their supporters. He deprived John of the Cross of his office as definitor and *concilario*, exiling him to the monastery of Peñuela and then attempting to expel him from the order. (John died in 1591, before the expulsion could be carried out.) Doria did expel Gracián (who was later reinstated) and sentenced Ana de Jesús to three years' imprisonment. María de San José was deprived of voice and vote (that is, forbidden from taking part in convent politics) and placed under house arrest for nine months. Thus, the outcome that Teresa feared did indeed come to pass.

Educator

Discalced convents offered women not only opportunities for spiritual development but also an education. Since the Middle Ages, male and female monasteries had been centers of learning, but with the advent of universities in the thirteenth century, academic instruction shifted from the cloister to the classroom.[29] Since women were excluded from these centers of higher learning, female education declined. In the sixteenth century not all religious houses provided instruction. One important feature of Discalced convents was the promotion of female literacy.

In spite of Teresa's repeated claims to ignorance, she was well read in the vernacular. She mentions in *Life* and elsewhere the influence in her own spiritual journey of works such as the *Confessions* of Saint Augustine and the *Vita Christi* of Ludolph of Saxony, which she read in Spanish translation. The Valdés Index of 1559 prohibited many devotional books popular among nuns, as well as fourteen editions of the Bible and nine of the New Testament. Teresa protests the ban indirectly when she writes, "If our nature were not so weak and our devotion so lukewarm there wouldn't be any need . . . for other books" (*CWST* 2, *WPV* 21:3). The implication is that since women are indeed imperfect, they do need books. The index affected Teresa personally, and in fact caused her great distress: "When they forbade the reading of many books in the vernacular, I felt that prohibition very much because reading some of them was an enjoyment for me, and I could no longer do so since only the Latin editions were allowed. The Lord said to me: 'Don't be sad, for I shall give you a living book'" (*CWST* 1, *Life* 26:5). Although Teresa's rich spiritual experience constituted a "living book," much of the knowledge that provided the foundation for that experience derived from books whose messages would continue to nourish her spirit. A letter from Teresa to Luis de Granada reveals just how important she considered his books for her own and her nuns' edification (*Letters* 1, May 1575). Because she wanted to make books accessible to her nuns, she required them to learn to read, and article 40 of the Constitutions charges prioresses with having them taught. Article 8 stipulates: "The prioress should see to it that good books are available, especially *The Life of Christ* . . . the *Flos Sanctorum*, *The Imitation of Christ*, *The Oratory of Religious*, and those books written by Fray Luis de Granada and Father Fray Pedro de Alcántara." In fact, some books by these authors had been banned.

Teresa mentions books throughout her letters. She tells Doña Luisa de la Cerda that she "once read in a book that the reward for trials is the love of God" (*Letters* 1, 7 November 1571: 2). Similarly, she offers Gracián spiritual advice based on "a book [she] once read" (*Letters* 1, December 1577: 1). At meals nuns customarily ate in silence while one nun read from some inspirational tome. In a letter to María de San José Teresa refers to this practice, mentioning a story from Sunio's *Vitae Sanctorem* (1578), which the nuns were reading (*Letters* 2, 4 June 1578: 6). Teresa cherished books as gifts. She writes to Don Antonio Gaytán thanking him for an inspirational book he sent her (*Letters* 1, End of 1574: 1) and to Gracián thanking him for some books he has sent the nuns (*Letters* 2, 1 December 1581: 4). In a letter to Tomasina Bautista, prioress of the Burgos Carmel, she mentions a shipment of books she is expecting (*Letters* 2, 27 August 1582: 5). Although Teresa does not routinely quote patristic authorities in her letters, she does occasionally mention one of them, as, for example, when she cites Saint Augustine in her missive to Isabel de San Jerónimo and María de San José (*Letters* 2, 3 May 1579: 7). Teresa's repeated reference to books shows that they continued to influence her long after the publication of the index.

Although all nuns were required to learn to read, white-veiled nuns, who performed menial tasks, usually did not learn how to write. Black-veiled or choir nuns, who were responsible for praying the Office and held important administrative positions, received a more thorough education, learning to read and write. Some used their writing skills to produce literature—hagiographies, chronicles, spiritual treatises, poetry, and plays. Many wrote *Vidas*, nearly always at the command of their confessors. These were not autobiographies in the modern sense, but spiritual memoirs that included prayers, descriptions of visions and locutions, and commentaries. Isabelle Poutrin remarks that late sixteenth-century religious houses became "autobiography workshops," where nuns turned out *Vidas* at a prodigious rate (131–34). Arenal and Schlau argue that Carmelite convents developed into true intellectual communities, where women's lives were recorded and thereby validated ("Leyendo yo").

Teresa's letters to her brother (Chapter 4) illustrate the importance she attached to the education of her nephews, but she was also concerned about girls' education. In a letter dated 27 May 1568 to Doña Luisa de la Cerda, she mentions plans to establish a school for girls, a project that unfortunately never came to fruition. However, she did encourage John of the Cross and others to found Discalced Carmelite men's colleges, a project she mentions frequently in her letters to Gracián from 1578 on. Although women were forbidden to teach, Teresa's letters show that she was an important educational force within the reform.

Disciplinarian

Teresa states in the Constitutions that "it is the duty of the Mother prioress to take great care in everything about the observance of the rule and Constitutions, to look after the integrity and enclosure of the house, [and] to observe how the offices are carried out," but she insists that "these things should be done with a mother's love" (*CWST* 3, 34). The kind of rigor Doria and his successors tried to impose went against the grain of Teresa's policies, which discourage harsh discipline (*CWST* 3, *Foundations* 18:6) and extreme mortifications (*CWST* 3, *Foundations* 18:8–12). For Teresa, rules did not exist for their own sake but to mold the spirit and guide it toward God. In a letter on governance to María Bautista she insists on the principle of *suavidad*, gentleness, which she believed to be more effective than severity: "Everything is done with love. I don't know whether this is because I have no reason for acting otherwise, or because I have come to understand that things are better dealt with this way" (*Letters* 2, 1579–1581?). Moriones points out that the "gentleness and discretion with which Saint Teresa was able to calm the fervor of her disciples . . . was interpreted by some as laxity," but those who attempted to impose iron-clad obedience actually betrayed Teresa's intentions because they "became so rigorous that they lost all sense of compassion" (*El P. Doria* 92).

In a perfect convent, according to Teresa's model, joyful nuns or friars would obey out of love, not out of fear. Teresa chided those who carried rules to an extreme or insisted on excessive austerity. The "discalcedness" of the order's name was a symbol of poverty and simplicity, not a literal description—a notion she makes clear in a letter to Mariano: "I have to laugh that Padre Fray Juan de Jesús says I want you all to go barefoot, for I am the one who always opposed this" (*Letters* 1, 12 December 1576: 5). She insists that friars eat well and perform manual labor. "I am fond of strictness in the practice of virtue," she says, "but not of austerity. . . . I am not very penitential" (*Letters* 1, 12 December 1576: 8). Although the order embraced material minimalism, Teresa believed that a sound body was conducive to a healthy spirit.

For Teresa, governing with *suavidad* also meant disciplining with *suavidad*. This was a matter not only of Christian charity but also of administrative expediency. Teresa knew that rough treatment bred resentment. Nuns treated fairly and gently by their prioress would be more malleable. Teresa's 1579 letter to Isabel de San Jerónimo and María de San José, written after Isabel took over as prioress of the Seville Carmel, offers a lucid exposition of Teresa's ideas on discipline.[30] In it Teresa reiterates many of the principles she has stated elsewhere, for example, in *Foundations*. The impetus for this advice-filled letter is the turmoil caused by the false accusations of Beatriz de la Madre de Dios and Margarita de la Concepción against María de San José. Now that the ruckus is over, Teresa counsels her and the new prioress on how to deal with the wrongdoers. Here Teresa asserts her authority by casting herself in the role of wise and experienced prioress, whose counsel younger prioresses should heed. She depicts Beatriz not as a criminal but as a mentally unstable woman in need of patience and compassion. As a child Beatriz had been accused by some maids of wanting to kill her aunt and as a result had been treated harshly by her mother, which may have led to her psychological problems (*CWST* 3, *Foundations* 26:3–4).[31] Teresa uses Beatriz as an example of the trouble an unbalanced nun can cause, with the subtle suggestion that such women not be admitted to convents. However, when they are, they must be dealt with firmly but kindly.

Teresa makes it clear that she sees Beatriz, not Margarita, as the instigator. She reminds Isabel and María that she had alerted them early on about the menace posed by Beatriz's condition, "so that you would be on your guard." She points out that "I was never satisfied with her spirit" and even "spoke of the matter with Padre Maestro Gracián." Thus, Teresa was not surprised when the scandal erupted (*Letters* 2, 3 May 1579: 7). The message is that prioresses must be vigilant and reject potentially disruptive postulants; in other words, such problems must be nipped in the bud. In spite of her not-so-subtle "I told you so," Teresa does not reprimand Isabel and María but instead expresses great affection for them. She guides them with *suavidad*, just as she advises them to guide Beatriz and Margarita. Teresa is exhausted, she writes, for the uproar has worn her out. Now she seeks reconciliation in the convent, and the best way to achieve it is through gentleness.

In spite of her policy of *suavidad*, Teresa was not about to let the troublemakers revert to their old behavior. She was especially concerned about Beatriz, whose mental condition made her susceptible to negative influences. In order to keep Beatriz in check, Teresa instructs that she not be allowed to speak to anyone without another nun present, "someone very astute," and that she be kept away from Margarita altogether (*Letters* 2, 3 May 1579: 12). Aware of Garciálvarez's role in the indictment, Teresa orders that Beatriz should confess only to a Discalced friar of her own choosing.[32] She should not be kept in absolute isolation, however, and she should be kept busy, as "her being alone and with only her thoughts can do her much harm" (*Letters* 2, 3 May 1579: 12). "Keep careful watch," Teresa advises, "especially at night," since that is the time when the imagination is often most active (*Letters* 2, 3 May 1579: 14).

Teresa understands that Isabel and María must certainly be indignant with Beatriz and Margarita, but she advises them to avoid discussing the incident. Otherwise, they will play into the hands of the devil, who "is working to discredit these monasteries" (*Letters* 2, 3 May 1579: 15). Although Teresa's repeated reference to the devil may strike modern readers as antiquated, her observations reveal a sharp understanding of psychology and group dynamics. She knows that constant rumination on the affair will make it difficult for Isabel and María to forgive and move on; by sharing their thoughts with one another, they will fan the flames of resentment, which inevitably will spread to the rest of the convent. Wisely, Teresa instructs them to be patient and to pray. Eventually, Beatriz and Margarita may have a falling out, and, when they do, they will no longer be a menace to the convent. In the meantime, she says, Isabel and María can relieve their frustration by writing down their thoughts. This letter reveals how clearly Teresa understood the human tendency to embellish events in memory and imagination. She knew that if the nuns indulged this tendency, discord would intensify. In order for the Seville nuns to recover from their ordeal, they would have to stop fussing over their hurt. To this end, she sought to impose silence on both the troublemakers and their victims, as well as on other members of the community. But Teresa also knew that these women would need a release for their frustration and their nervous energy, and for this she prescribed work or journaling.

Rather than attributing Beatriz's bad behavior to malice, Teresa attributes it to "an unstable imagination," which made her "a ready prey for the wiles of the devil [who] knows very well how to profit by one's natural condition and poor judgment." Her sensitivity to the signs of melancholy prompts her to counsel Isabel and María not to judge Beatriz harshly, for in her weakened mental state she cannot be held entirely responsible for her actions: "She has neither the mind nor the talent for inventing such things" (*Letters* 2, 3 May 1579: 7). Furthermore, without God's guidance, we are all capable of foolish behavior: "If God were to withdraw his hand from us, what evils might we not commit?" (*Letters* 2, 3 May 1579: 7). By classifying Beatriz's behavior as a health rather than as a disciplinary issue, Teresa hopes to avoid reprisals and restore peace to the Seville Carmel. She points to God's hand in the upheaval Beatriz has caused: "Perhaps all this was necessary for her humility. If God should grant us the favor that she come to her senses about what she has done and retract it, we will have all gained through suffering, and it could be the same for her, for God knows how to draw good from evil" (*Letters* 2, 3 May 1579: 8). Teresa recommends that the two prioresses "not manifest toward [Beatriz and Margarita] any kind of dislike" and that they ensure that the other nuns show them "sisterly kindness" (*Letters* 2, 3 May 1579: 10). Through gentle treatment, Teresa wishes to remove any justification for continued hostility on Beatriz's part and perhaps even hopes to shame Beatriz into cooperating with the new prioress.

Second guessing Isabel and María, Teresa strives to prevent them from making further mistakes that might aggravate the situation. Astutely, she urges them neither to send Beatriz and Margarita away nor to mention Beatriz's scheming to her mother, also a nun at the Seville convent, for those courses of action would only serve to stir up more animosity: the outcast nuns could complain that they were poorly treated, and Beatriz's mother would feel obligated to defend her daughter, thereby factionizing the convent population. Furthermore, were the errant nuns expelled to another convent, they would have more cause and opportunity to disparage María de San José, whereas if they stay in Seville, they can be more easily controlled: "I fear that now again the devil will stir up in them other temptations—that you wish them harm and treat them badly—and it would make me very angry if you gave them any occasion for so thinking" (*Let-*

ters 2, 3 May 1579: 11). Another factor Teresa took into consideration was Jesuit support for Beatriz and Margarita, which made it advisable to avoid exacerbating the situation.

Although Teresa could be warm and encouraging, she could also be autocratic. As foundress and chief administrator, she believed her subordinates' vow of obedience bound them to abide by her decisions. Consequently, she was strict with her prioresses and could be cross with them when they failed to comply with her demands. When dealing with prioresses, Teresa was never shy about asserting her authority as foundress and de facto *madre* of all of her convents. We saw in Chapter 4 how she lashed out at María Bautista for accepting Casilda de Padilla as a novice against her (Teresa's) wishes. Her insistence on maintaining control is manifest throughout her correspondence; her letter of 30 May 1582 to Ana de Jesús will serve as an example.

Ana, who had professed in Salamanca ten years before, was a close friend of Teresa's and became prioress of the Beas Carmel in 1575. In 1581, a little less than a year before her death, Teresa authorized Ana to establish a convent in Granada with John of the Cross, a task they completed in January 1582. In a letter to Gracián, Teresa specified which nuns would join Ana in Granada: "Three . . . are going from Beas with Ana de Jesús, who is to be prioress. Then there are two more from Seville and two lay sisters from Villanueva" (*Letters* 2, 29 November 1581: 9). However, Teresa knew Ana would not happy about these directives, and she had already started to get herself worked up about Ana's possible response: "Ana de Jesús will be annoyed, since she likes to run everything herself" (*Letters* 2, 19 November 1581: 10). In fact, Ana took more women with her than Teresa had stipulated, and, as a result, she and her nuns felt cramped in the home of Doña Ana de Peñalosa, where they were to reside until they could procure their own house. Ana wound up sending the two lay sisters back to Villanueva de la Jara as well as making other decisions on her own regarding the foundation in Granada.

Indignant, Teresa writes her a scathing letter.[33] She starts out by criticizing Ana for keeping information from her and from the provincial (Gracián): "I find it amusing that you make such a fuss complaining about the Provincial, when you've neglected to send him any news since that one letter in which you told him you'd made a foundation, and you did the same thing to me" (30 May 1582: 1). Teresa is miffed because Ana has gone ahead and bought a house without consulting her, thereby undermining her authority: "You were so intent on not obeying that I've suffered quite a bit of distress over it, both because it will look wrong to the rest of the Order and because other prioresses might take the same liberties, since you've set such a bad example" (30 May 1582: 3). She goes on to scold Ana for abusing the hospitality of her hosts and for sending some sisters back to Villanueva, instead of to Beas, where they came from. She complains that "it was wrong from the beginning . . . and the whole mess is causing a scandal" (30 May 1582: 5). Ana's excuse was that the archbishop would try to suppress the convent if she failed to stand her ground, but Teresa calls her bluff; she knows that the license had already been granted and that the archbishop cannot revoke it: "I laughed at the way you tried to frighten us by saying the Archbishop would try to suppress the monastery. He can no longer do anything about it. I don't know why you think he's so powerful. He'll drop dead before he manages to do anything about this. But if your house is going to instill disobedience in the Order, it would be better for it not to exist, since what matters is not having lots of monasteries, but the holiness of the women in those that we have" (30 May 1582: 6).

Teresa's rage is obvious not only from her words but also from the confused structure of the letter. Many of Teresa's letters lack logical transitions, but this one is especially fragmented, with Teresa jumping from the Granada foundation to problems in Valladolid, where nuns were indignant that some of their former sisters had been returned to them and blamed Gracián for allowing it, to the situation in Beas, where some nuns had become overly attached to Ana de Jesús and followed her to Granada. As usual, Teresa defends Gracián, arguing that Ana had no right to send any of her nuns anywhere at all, since by Gracián's command they were members of the Beas community: "Your Reverence alone is to blame. . . . You paid no more attention to him than if he had no position at all" (30 May 1582: 7). However, she then directs Ana to send the Beas nuns back, asserting her authority as foundress, "for in matters related to the Discalced nuns I have the same power as our Father Provincial. In virtue of this I declare and command that with the exception of the Mother Prioress, Ana de Jesús, all nuns who came from Beas shall return there as soon as arrangements can be made to send them" (30 May 1582: 10). Teresa's fury seems to grow as she writes. The authoritative—or authoritarian—style of this paragraph reveals Teresa's determination to impose her will and not be trifled with. Formulas such as "I declare and command" (*digo y mando*) and the abrupt change from "your Reverence" to the third person ("the Mother Prioress, Ana de Jesús") turn this letter into a kind of decree.

Still, Teresa's position is not so difficult to understand. In the last years before her death, she saw several of the houses she had founded dissolve into laxity. In some—Malagón, San José de Ávila, Alba de Tormes—negligence and disputes among sisters distanced the communities from the original Discalced ideals. The actions of the Beas nuns revealed a personal attachment to Ana de Jesús that Teresa viewed with alarm. At the end of her letter she changes her tone to one of entreaty:

God's will is that His brides should be free from all attachments, except to Him. I do not want your house to develop as the Beas house did: I have never forgotten a letter those nuns wrote me after your Reverence had ceased serving as prioress: even a Calced nun wouldn't have written such a thing. That is the way rivalries and other misfortunes begin. You don't even realize it at the beginning. So for this one time, please don't honor any opinion except for mine. Later, when you are settled, you can reevaluate the situation and decide if they can [are detached enough to] return [to Granada]. . . . Oh, true spirit of obedience! How can one see a nun standing in the place of God and not feel repugnance about loving her!" (30 May 1582: 11–13).

Nuns must be strong enough to suppress such attachments: "Your Reverence and the other nuns must behave like men, not silly women [*mujercillas*]" (30 May 1582: 13). Teresa is distressed about a number of other things she mentions in this letter, among them Ana's insistence on being addressed by her title, the custom of the Beas nuns of going out of the convent to tend the church rather than respecting the cloister, and Ana's failure to write to Gracián.

While this letter makes Teresa appear to be a stickler for the rules, it is important to remember that she was consistent in her resolve to govern with *suavidad* (gentleness). Teresa's exasperation with some of her followers—particularly Mariano, María Bautista, and Ana de Jesús—stemmed not from a mindless attachment to a set of laws but from the fear that their independence would lead to outright disobedience, which would undermine their personal relationship with God as well as the integrity of the order.[34] She used letters to guide—and, sometimes, to yank—straying disciples back into line.

Politician and Diplomat

Throughout this study we have seen how Teresa directed—largely through letters—the battle for the survival of the reform. However, she also had to deal with countless other conflicts. Her letters show that she was constantly putting out fires, some large and some small, several of them involving the Jesuits. We will examine one particular incident as an example. In 1578 a Jesuit priest, Gaspar de Salazar, attempted to transfer out of the Society of Jesus into the Discalced Carmelites, creating a knotty political and diplomatic dilemma for Teresa.

Teresa was greatly indebted to the Jesuits. When she first began to experience mystical favors, her confessors and spiritual directors reacted skeptically. Men such as Gaspar Daza insisted that Teresa's experiences might be demonically inspired and even argued that she should undergo exorcism.[35] It was not until the Jesuits established a *colegio*, or school, in

Ávila in 1554, that Teresa found a confessor who took her mystical experiences seriously. Diego de Cetina was only twenty-four and had been a priest for one year, but he listened to Teresa and bolstered her confidence. Teresa writes about him: "He left me consoled and encouraged, and the Lord helped me and him to understand my situation and how I should be guided" (*CWST* 1, *Life* 23:18). When Cetina was transferred out of Ávila, another Jesuit, Juan de Prádanos, replaced him as Teresa's confessor. Prádanos was only about twenty-seven and also newly ordained, but, like his predecessor, he encouraged Teresa and taught her new ways to pray, perhaps introducing her to the *Spiritual Exercises*.[36] After Prádanos became ill, Teresa received a new Jesuit confessor, Baltasar Álvarez, a somewhat insecure young priest who constantly put her to the test, yet was cautiously supportive. In 1557 Francisco de Borja, the former grand duke of Gandía and future general of the Society of Jesus, went to Ávila, where Teresa met him. Borja determined that Teresa's "experience was from the spirit of God and . . . it seemed to him that it would no longer be good to resist" (*CWST* 1, *Foundations* 24:3). Borja was an extremely influential man, and his endorsement legitimized Teresa's experiences, enabling her to advance spiritually and eventually to launch the reform.

In an account of her life made for the inquisitor of Seville, Teresa mentions nine Jesuit confessors, apparently forgetting Cetina and Prádanos, who would have made eleven (*CWST* 3, *Spiritual Testimonies* 58:3). The repeated mention of Jesuit friends and advisors throughout her epistolary writing make it clear that Teresa maintained a close relationship with the Society during much of her life. She mentions Jesuits in her letters to prioresses and others, and clearly thought Jesuit support was vital. During the period of persecutions against the reform she writes to Gracián that her foundations "gain a great deal from being attached to the Society of Jesus. . . . These fathers have been my main help and I would never fail to recognize this" (*Letters* 1, October 1575: 3). And when problems arise in Seville, Teresa suggests to María de San José that she have Garciálvarez speak to the Jesuits and ask someone from the Society to hear the nuns' confessions (*Letters* 1, 5 October 1575: 5, 6). It is not surprising, then, that even when sticky situations crop up involving the Society, Teresa tries to maintain their goodwill.

Yet the relationship was actually rocky from the very beginning. When Teresa was attacked by the town council for founding San José in Ávila, it was a Dominican, not a Jesuit, who spoke on her behalf (even though later Álvarez claimed to have supported her). As we saw in the discussion of Teresa's letters to María Bautista in Chapter 4, Jesuits sometimes suggested postulants for Teresa's foundations, exerting undue pressure on her and putting her at odds with prioresses. Jesuits repeatedly intervened in Carmelite matters. As we saw above, they interceded for Beatriz de la Madre de Dios and Margarita de la Concepción in Seville, one reason Teresa mentions for handling the two women so delicately (*Letters* 2, 3 May 1579: 11). When, in 1578, Gaspar de Salazar decided to leave the Jesuit order and join the Carmelites because of a revelation he claimed to receive from God, it ignited a very touchy situation. Salazar was a friend of Teresa's, and Juan Suárez, the Jesuit provincial, accused her of encouraging the switch. Now he wants her to write to Salazar and persuade him to remain in the Society.

Teresa has just broken her arm, yet she writes several lengthy letters on this matter. To begin with, she flatly denies the accusation: "His Majesty knows—and the truth of this will come to light—that I have never wanted this, still less urged him to take such a step" (*Letters* 2,10 February 1578: 2). She insists that she did not even know about Father Gaspar's intention, that she heard about it from a third party, and that the news left her so "disturbed and distressed" that it damaged her health (*Letters* 2,10 February 1578: 2). She takes a skeptical stance with respect to the revelation, arguing that "I would not have been so shallow as to think that for so slight a reason a great change like the one mentioned should be undertaken" (*Letters* 2,10 February 1578: 3). She encourages Suárez to investigate, and while she acknowledges her friendship with Salazar, she downplays her influence on him: "I will never deny the great friendship that exists between Father Salazar and me or the favor he shows me. Yet I am certain that in what he has done for me he has been moved more by the service it renders our Lord and our Blessed Mother than by any friendship" (*Letters* 2,10 February 1578: 5). She goes on to tell Suárez that if she once needed friars, now she has over two hundred and therefore has no motive for luring Salazar away. She closes by swearing her friendship to the Jesuits: "In my dealings with the Society I hold their concerns close to my heart and would lay down my life for them" (*Letters* 2,10 February 1578: 6). Over the years Teresa had self-fashioned herself as an authority figure, and Suárez's assumption that she had the influence to convince Salazar to return to the Jesuits is a tribute to the success of that endeavor. However, for Teresa personal power was not an end in itself but a tool for advancing the reform. She needed the Jesuits to secure the success of her project; she was not interested in becoming their rival or engaging in turf battles with them. She assures Suárez that they are all comrades in the battle to win souls for God; Salazar has no need to change orders to serve the Lord.

Although her letter to Suárez is diffident and restrained, her irritation with him is evident in another letter, written four days later, to Gonzalo Dávila, the Jesuit rector in Ávila. Teresa assures Dávila that Suárez has been misinformed concerning her intentions. She bristles: "I read Father Provincial's letter more than twice, and I find in it such a lack of openness and so much certitude about what never entered my mind that you should not find the distress it caused me surprising" (*Letters* 2,14 February 1578: 1). She insists that she has no authority to write to Salazar to dissuade him from making the move, as the Jesuit provincial has asked. She argues that it would make more sense for Suárez, who is Salazar's superior, to write to him himself. At the time this incident occurs, John of the Cross is in prison in Toledo and Teresa has her hands full. The pressure Suárez is putting on her strikes her as overly harsh: "I do not think I deserve to receive trials from the Society, even if I were to have had a part in this matter" (*Letters* 2, 14 February 1578: 6). Suárez wants Gracián to instruct all the Carmelite monasteries to refuse Salazar, which has only increased Teresa's irritation.

Two weeks later she writes to Gracián telling him that Carillo (her code name for Salazar) is not taking the Jesuit demands seriously; he has "laughed" at her letter asking him to rethink his decision and told her she is like a "mouse afraid of the cats" (*Letters* 2, 2 March 1578: 4). She complains that the Jesuits "are being difficult" and appears to have no intention of acceding to their demands. She tells Gracián that Salazar is so determined that no one can block him and affirms she is prepared to receive him if he moves ahead with his plan (*Letters* 2, 2 March 1578: 5–6). Dávila apparently accepted Teresa's decision, because during the summer of 1578 he wrote to her requesting spiritual guidance, which she gladly gave. Perhaps in an effort to mend fences, Teresa wrote to the duchess of Alba on 6 May 1580, asking her to intercede on behalf of the Jesuits, who were being threatened with expulsion from their house in Pamplona. But in spite of her efforts, the relationship between Teresa and the Society continued to erode.

Another incident occurred in 1581, when Casilda de Padilla, the promising young novice whom María Bautista had accepted at Valladolid, left the Carmelites to become a Franciscan. The situation could easily have put Teresa at odds with the Society. Her Jesuit friend Olea had not wanted Casilda there in the first place; he had supported another postulant, whom María Bautista had passed over in order to take Padilla. Now Casilda, under the direction of a Jesuit confessor, had left the Carmel to become abbess at the Franciscan convent of Santa Gadea. Teresa writes cautiously to Gracián: "Despite everything, I don't think it would be fitting for us to change our attitude toward members of the Society. For many reasons this would not be good for us to do, and one reason is that most of the nuns who come here do so through them" (*Letters* 2, 17 September 1581: 5). Still, it is clear that Teresa is beginning to feel uncomfortable about her dependence on the Jesuits for postulants: "But it will be a great thing to have our own fathers, for then we can detach ourselves little by little from the others" (*Letters* 2, 17 September 1581: 5). Teresa's reluctance to offend the Society reflects not only her long association with it and a sincere affection for many Jesuit priests, but also her concern over a serious rift that was developing over a foundation she was planning to make in Burgos that the Society opposed.

Teresa's benefactress in Burgos, Doña Catalina de Tolosa, had previously befriended and assisted the Jesuits, who were enraged that she was now offering financial support to the Carmelites. The nuns were anxious to find a residence because the archbishop refused to approve the foundation until they had one. At the time, they were living in a house previously occupied by Jesuits, and in April 1581, Teresa wrote to Jerónimo Reinoso, one of the canons helping with the foundation, to ask him either to secure this house for the nuns or else to look for another. Teresa preferred the first option, not only because the house was already outfitted with a chapel but also because it was in the downtown area, in full view of the populace that would support it with alms. However, in her letter she is extremely careful to avoid aggravating her shaky relationship with the Society. "If those fathers mind, then I wouldn't want it," she tells Reinoso (*Letters* 2, Mid-April 1581: 2). Her refusal to take the house without the Jesuits' consent shows how diplomatic she was trying to be about moving in on what they considered their territory. She displays equal sensitivity in a letter to Gracián in which she describes another potentially tricky situation. A rich Flemish family had left a portion of its fortune to the Jesuits, but their daughter now wished to enter San José in Ávila and have part of the inheritance transferred from the Jesuits to the Discalced Carmelites. Teresa, trying to avoid an escalation of tempers, writes to Gracián that she has advised the woman not to haggle about this (*Letters* 2, 26 October 1581).

By the following March the nuns have moved into the Hospital de la Concepción. Teresa writes to Alonso de Martínez, another of the canons helping with the foundation, describing her continuing dispute with the Jesuits, who have decided to give her the cold shoulder: "These fathers are defending themselves vigorously. . . . Now, as soon as we left the house of Catalina de Tolosa, they went to see her. And they sent me word that I should not tire myself in trying to get them to come to see us, for unless their general in Rome gives them orders to do so, they will not come to see us until we have a monastery. They don't want to give the impression that their order and ours is all one order—look at that for an idea! . . . The day will appear when others will come with a different attitude" (*Letters* 2, 1 March 1582: 3). The last sentence tempers Teresa's expression of outrage; she does not blame the whole order for the stupidity of a few, and she is certain that future Jesuits will adopt a more kindly attitude toward her nuns and friars.

Even after the foundation was finally made, the Jesuits continued to show hostility. Teresa writes to Canon Reinoso in May that "a manifest enmity is beginning to take shape" and blames "those fathers" for spreading rumors about the Carmelites. The reason for everything, she insists, can be attributed to "these despicable interests"—that is, pecuniary concerns. She is convinced that the devil has had a hand in the conflict, since he thrives on rivalries (*Letters* 2, 20 May 1582: 3). Worse yet, the Jesuits are trying to turn Doña Catalina against her: "Now they told Catalina de Tolosa that they didn't want her to have anything to do with the Discalced nuns lest she be contaminated by our manner of prayer" (*Letters* 2, 20 May 1582: 3). Yet, despite this appalling behavior, Teresa still refuses to condemn the entire order. She writes to Doña Catalina in August that in spite of their snubs, "what they did wasn't sufficient reason for giving up all communication with them" (*Letters* 2, 3 August 1582: 2). The following month she writes to Catalina de Cristo, prioress of the Soria Carmel, encouraging her to work with the Jesuits: "I am happy that you are doing what you can with them, for this is necessary, and the good or the bad . . ." (*Letters* 2, 15–17 September 1582: 6). The letter is damaged and this section is incomplete, but it is evident that Teresa still believes the alliance between Jesuits and Carmelites is salvageable. She has gathered all her diplomatic skills to mend the rift with the Society, reinforcing bonds with Jesuits in Soria, Ávila, Palencia, and elsewhere, since those in Burgos continue to rebuff her.

The letters we have examined in this chapter illustrate the tremendous range of issues in which Teresa exerted sway. By asserting her authority as foundress, she was able to influence every aspect of Carmelite life: prayer, governance, discipline, dress, physical plant, food, money, and much more. An administrative genius, she was able to juggle many activities at once, attending to legalities and fundraising at the same time she was sharing remedies for stomachaches. Unfortunately, her position of authority caused blame to fall on her when something went wrong. When the Calced Carmelites became embittered with Gracián, they persecuted Teresa as well. When Beatriz de la Madre de Dios brought false accusations against María de San José, she extended her charges to include Teresa too. And when the Jesuits took umbrage at Doña Catalina's perceived betrayal, they held Teresa personally responsible. These letters give an idea of the delicate balance between authority and diplomacy that Teresa constantly had to maintain.

Chapter 6

Forging Sainthood:
Teresa's Letters as Relics

O f the thousands of letters that Saint Teresa wrote, only about 230 authenticated autographs remain, some of which are not entirely in Teresa's hand (Rodríguez Martínez and Egido 51). Illness and exhaustion frequently prevented her from writing her own letters. She used several amanuenses, among them her nurse and companion Ana de San Bartolomé.[1] However, even when Teresa dictated letters to others, she sometimes added post data and marginal notes. The Valladolid collection contains examples of letters begun by amanuenses but continued by Teresa, who was apparently so anxious to express herself in writing that she yanked the page away from her secretary. The remaining of the approximately 450 extant letters are duplicates, some made to ensure delivery of at least one copy, some made to preserve Teresa's words for posterity.

Of the thousands of letters that have been lost, some were destroyed and others were passed from hand to hand until they disappeared. Rodríguez Martínez and Egido cite the odyssey of Teresa's letters to Gracián as an example. When Teresa died, Fray Jerónimo had a pile of her letters "four fingers high." Due to the internecine disputes among Discalced Carmelites, he wound up traveling from Spain to Italy and North Africa, and then on to Flanders and Brussels. He gave the letters to his sister, prioress of the Consuegra Carmel, for safekeeping. She passed them on to another brother, Tomás Gracián, with the expectation that they would be used in Teresa's beatification process. Before the letters were dispersed and lost, seventeenth-century friars had the chance to copy many of them (Rodríguez Martínez and Egido 52). The scattering of Teresa's letters continued throughout the centuries and still goes on today. Egido laments that convents often gave away Teresa's letters as gifts to benefactors without taking into consideration their historical importance. Even now, holders sometimes store them or pass them on to relatives rather than turning them over to institutions that would preserve them. As a result, letters disintegrate and are lost forever.[2]

Preserving Teresa's Epistolary Legacy

Fortunately, some early Discalced Carmelites did have the foresight to safeguard these irreplaceable documents. The largest collection of extant autographs is housed at the Discalced Carmelite convent in Valladolid. The collection consists of forty letters to María de San José, as well as one to Doña María de Mendoza, the original sponsor of the Valladolid foundation. María de San José took the letters Teresa had written her to Lisbon, and through a circuitous route they came into the possession of Francisco Sobrino, who would later become archbishop of Valladolid. He deposited them in the Discalced Carmelite convent, where two of his sisters, María de San Alberto and Cecilia del Nacimiento, were nuns.[3] The importance Sobrino attached to these treasures is evinced by the preface to the collection:

> Todas las cartas aunque no contienen nada de particular importancia de doctrina ni su storia por solo ser todas firmadas de la Me Sta Teresa y haberse escritas de su propia mano y letra sino son dos o tres que son de mano agena, y por la veneración que se debe a todas sus cosas se recogieron aquí en este libro y en estas hojas hasta la foja 119—el qual libro porque quede en lugar y reuerencia que se deue, le entrego oy a la Me Priora y convento de nuestra Señora de la Concepción de las descalças Carmelitas de esta ciudad como a casa suya para que en el se guarde con la veneración que se deue a tan santa madre y fundadora—en Valladolid a seis dias del mes de agosto de mill y seiscientos y catorce años.
>
> Fray CI F^r Fran^{co} Sobrino

> [All the letters, even though they contain nothing of any particular doctrinal or historical importance [are valuable], if only because they were signed by our Mother Saint Teresa and were written by her own hand, and in her own handwriting, except for two or three that were written by someone else, and because of the veneration that we owe everything of hers, we gathered them up into this book and in these pages up until folio 119. So that this book will remain in a place where it will be treated with the reverence owed it, I hand it over to the prioress and nuns of Our Lady of the Immaculate Conception, of the Discalced Carmelites of this city, as to her own house, so that it will be kept here in this convent with the veneration that we owe such a holy mother and foundress—Valladolid, the sixth day of the month of August, of 1614.
>
> Friar Francisco Sobrino]

A table of contents follows the preface with a note that although some of the letters "don't seem to contain anything special, even so, there is always some teaching in the words of this holy mother."[4] The prioress María de

San Alberto copied the letters, editing, annotating, and arranging them in chronological order. Although many were given away to friends and donors, in recent years efforts have been made to protect those that remain. Photocopies have been made for use by researchers, and the originals have been bound and preserved using modern methods of conservation. Today the Valladolid nuns at Rondilla de Santa Teresa cherish the collection and consider it the convent's greatest treasure. Smaller collections of letters are housed at Discalced convents in Seville, Alcalá de Henares, and Madrid. The rest are dispersed in convents, museums, libraries, universities, and private holdings.

Although Sobrino and his sisters recognized the value of even Teresa's most banal correspondence, most early seventeenth-century Carmelites attached little importance to letters that dealt with the everyday affairs of the reform. Instead, they searched Teresa's epistolary writing for nuggets of spiritual wisdom that would justify her veneration as a saint. The gossipy, news-laden letters that paint such a vivid picture of Teresa's multifaceted personality and career were of little interest to them. Rodríguez Martínez and Egido have called attention to the tendency of early editors to manipulate the text according to their own preconceptions, needs, and interests (54). The accuracy and objectivity for which modern historians strive were alien to those men.

Today the Biblioteca Nacional in Madrid houses several collections of early copies of Teresa's letters as well as some original autographs, including a letter to Gracián and another to Álvaro de Mendoza, both quite deteriorated. Mss. 12.763 primarily contains copies of doctrinal letters dating from around 1640, reproduced from autographs. The accuracy of these texts has made them an invaluable resource for researchers and editors. Mss. 12.764, on the other hand, has been dismissed by modern investigators such as Rodíguez Martínez and Egido as a hodgepodge of mutilated and apocryphal documents of little historical interest (55). This curious collection of folios, dated 1654, contains letters compiled by two Discalced Carmelite friars, Pedro de la Anunciación and Diego de la Presentación, to serve as the text for the first printed version of Teresa's *Epistolario*, edited by Juan de Palafox y Mendoza, archbishop of Osma, in 1656. The first section is meticulously inscribed, with margins of one and a quarter inches on the left and quarter-inch margins on the right, and is preceded by a detailed index. The handwriting of the amanuensis is clear and even. However, even a superficial perusal reveals that several of the letters are counterfeit.

Reconstructing Teresa

In spite of its apocryphal elements, Mss. 12.764 is worthy of interest. It exposes the concerted effort that seventeenth-century Spanish ecclesiastics made to reconstruct Teresa, transforming her into an obedient, submissive virgin who could serve as an emblem of female sanctity. To understand why this was necessary, it will be useful to examine sixteenth- and seventeenth-century attitudes toward women and holiness.

During Teresa's lifetime, mental prayer and claims to mysticism met with harsh resistance, in particular from Dominican theologians suspicious of ecstatics. These detractors, who held that doctrinal instruction should be reserved for university-trained *letrados*, found Teresa's writings transgressive. Their view was that "for the general population, spirituality should be limited to the practice of vocal prayer, traditional ceremonies, listening to sermons about the pursuit of the Christian virtues, and obeying one's confessors" (Carrera 79). Restrictions on female education meant that women's spiritual experience was usually affective rather than intellectual. Teresa's validation of female spirituality through her writing and foundations alarmed conservative theologians. In 1578 the papal nuncio Filippo Sega famously called her "a restless, gadabout, disobedient, and contumacious woman" (Qtd. Peers, *CW* 3:150).[5] In 1589, the energetic inquisitor Alonso de la Fuente initiated a crusade to have Teresa's books banned on the grounds that they contained heretical elements. De la Fuente even suggested they might really be creations of the devil rather than of Teresa because "they exceed the capacity of women" (Qtd. Weber, *Rhetoric* 160). In five successive memorials to the Inquisition written between 1589 and 1591 he repeats the allegation, noting: "That learned men should come to learn from a woman and recognize her as a leader in matters of prayer and spiritual doctrine . . . is an argument for the novelty [i.e., heterodoxy] of this doctrine, in which woman was wise, and the men who subjected themselves to her were foolish" (Qtd. Weber, *Rhetoric* 160). Francisco de Pisa, professor of Holy Scripture in Toledo, held a more positive opinion of Teresa but still believed that her books should be withdrawn from circulation and not reprinted or translated into other languages, since there were other books from which "one can safely and profitably learn of the spiritual path, without having a woman come along and teach" (Qtd. Weber, *Rhetoric* 162). Some *letrados* defended Teresa, including an anonymous theologian who not only praised her teaching but even suggested that women might be more spiritually receptive than men (Weber, *Rhetoric* 162). Still, the Inquisition had investigated Teresa five times for unorthodoxy, and when Teresa's canonization procedures were initiated early in the seventeenth century, some theologians were still arguing that her mystical doctrine was diabolical in origin and that her writings should be outlawed.

Because the post-Tridentine church remained suspicious of "spirituals"—those who cultivated interiority and mental prayer instead of academic theology—female canonization could be highly problematic. Unsurprisingly, canonizations of men outnumbered those of women four to one. Ahlgren has examined the problems presented by Teresa's candidacy for sainthood, "particularly her lack of conformity to women's religious roles and her continuing function as a teacher of mystical doctrine" (*Politics of Sanctity* 149). Those who defended her sanctity had to find a way to make Teresa acceptable to a church loath to recognize women as spiritual teachers. One tactic her champions used was to describe her as a *mujer varonil* (manly woman) whose intelligence, energy, character, and sincerity distanced her from others of her sex. They were aided in their efforts by Teresa's propensity to use military metaphors, urging her nuns to be "warriors" and "strong men" in defense of the reform.

In the early modern period certain attributes such as dependability, loyalty, and foresight were considered "masculine," even though some moralists argued that unusual women might possess them.[6] Teresa's supporters bestowed authority on her by citing her singularity as proof of divine favor.[7] Only through God's miraculous intervention, they argued, could a woman achieve what Teresa did. In particular, they had to portray Teresa's pedagogical insight, writing skill, and doctrinal expertise as God-produced anomalies. Seventeenth-century images of Teresa with pen in hand (Villamena, Hieronymus Wierix, Velázquez,[8] Rubens, Obidos) usually include doves and angels to show that Teresa's writing was guided by the Holy Spirit. This depiction of Teresa came to have emblematic value for the institutional church.

From 1523 until 1588 no saint had been canonized, partly in response to Protestant depictions of Catholics as superstitious and idolatrous and partly due to uncertainty on the part of several Catholic reformers about the intercessory power of saints. By the end of the sixteenth century, however, clerics concerned about the incursions made by Protestants into previously Catholic areas sought new canonizations as a means of galvanizing the faithful. Holy persons such as Teresa, Isidro Labrador, and Ignatius of Loyola were likely candidates because they had a popular following. They also had value to the institutional church, "which needed strong Tridentine models for the laity, role models who respected the church hierarchy, adhered to the sacramental system, and, in short, epitomized what it meant to be a 'good Roman Catholic' " (Ahlgren, *Politics of Sanctity* 146). However, the active, mobile life that Teresa had led and the kind of spirituality she had practiced made her a difficult candidate for canonization. It was necessary to reconstruct her, to transform her into a model of feminine virtue characterized by humility and obedience. Teresa's popular following would not have been enough to ensure her canonization. Other factors had to come into play. Her candidacy succeeded, argues Ahlgren, due to the persistent pressure on the pope from the Spanish king and nobility, the convincing depiction of Teresa as a role model for women, and the church's endorsement of mysticism as an element of Counter-Reformation identity ("Negotiating Sanctity" 380). However, even after Teresa was canonized in 1622—only forty years after her death—male clerics continued to feel the need to reconstruct her image.[9]

Pierre Delooz contends that all saints are reconstructions; their lives are remodeled in conformity with a collective image of sanctity.[10] Thus, saints have to be studied as a manifestation of social perceptions not of the period in which they lived but of the period that elevated them as models of holiness. Peter Burke notes that saints are cultural indicators: "Like other heroes, they reflect the values of the culture which sees them in a heroic light" (45). Burke distinguishes five categories of individuals that were most likely to be canonized in the late sixteenth and seventeenth centuries: (1) founder of an order, (2) missionary, (3) agent of charitable activity, (4) pastor or good shepherd, (5) mystic.[11] Of these, Teresa falls into the first and last group. She also falls into another category greatly appreciated in the late Middle Ages: that of martyr.

Although modern readers may not see her in this light, Christopher Wilson has shown that both in Europe and colonial America, the Transverberation, the scene from Teresa's life that artists most often depicted, was seen as an image of martyrdom.[12] Among those who depicted the Transverberation were Collaert and Galle (1613), Peter Paul Rubens (1614), Anton Wierix (before 1624),[13] and Josefa de Óbidos (1672). A banner depicting the Transverberation adorned the interior of Saint Peter's Basilica in Rome on the day of Teresa's canonization. The most famous representation of the Transverberation is probably the statue created by Gianlorenzo Bernini (1647–1652), now in Santa Maria de la Vittoria in Rome. Wilson shows that images of the Transverberation proliferated in the New World as Carmelites sought a unifying icon to give cohesiveness to their order. Teresa was not celebrated for her intellectual achievements; in fact, notes Burke, no theologians or teachers—no counterparts of Saint Thomas of Aquinas—were canonized during this period (51). Theological insight and pedagogical talent were not valued enough to warrant canonization even in men, let alone in a woman.

During the late sixteenth and early seventeenth centuries, a plethora of biographies of Teresa became available, among them Fray Luis de León's concise *De la muerte, vida, virtudes y Milagros de la Santa Madre Teresa de Jesús*;[14] Diego de Yepes's *Vida, virtudes y milagros de la Bienaventurada Virgen Teresa de Jesús* (1587); Francisco de Ribera's *La vida de la madre Teresa de Jesús, fundadora de las Descalzas y Descalzos* (1590); and Jerónimo Gracián's *Declaración en que se trata de la perfecta vida y virtudes heroicas de la Santa Madre Teresa de Jesús* (1611). As most of the titles suggest, the purpose of these books was to celebrate Teresa's virtues and miracles, not to offer a realistic portrait of a reformist nun. More influential than books were the iconographic drawings and paintings highlighting scenes from Teresa's life. These created a vivid image in the public's mind of Teresa's supernatural powers. The triumph of print culture meant that such images could reach a wide audience. By the sixteenth century, female saints increasingly came to dominate the Catholic imagination. Frances E. Dolan asserts that "For post-Reformation Catholics, the saint's life became a feminized genre" (176). In Protestant England, saints' lives circulated in manuscript and print and were propagated through engraved images. These lives served to unite and inspire Catholics but also contributed to Protestant propaganda, which characterized Catholicism as a carnivalesque, topsy-turvy, feminized religion in which women were worshipped and prayed to.

Much of the Teresian iconography of the seventeenth century was inspired by the twenty-five engravings of the *Vita B. Virginis a Iesu*, created in Antwerp in 1613 by Adriaen Collaert and Cornelis Galle.[15] The latter was a member of the circle of Christopher Plantin, a shrewd businessman who ran the largest printing firm in Western Europe and managed to maintain Catholic affiliations while at the same time serving Calvinists (Eisenstein 178). These engravings illustrate the principal events in Teresa's life as described in her writings, highlighting the supernatural and miraculous. The Collaert and Galle prints depict Teresa's three-day paroxysm; Teresa casting out demons; Teresa in the company of the Virgin, Saint Peter, and Saint Paul; Teresa reviving her dead nephew; Teresa being encouraged to found convents by the Virgin and Saint Joseph; Teresa being crowned by God after founding San José in Ávila; Teresa levitating; and Teresa being led out of the darkness in Salamanca by a pair of angels. These images penetrate Teresa's visions, depicting the miracle with the same realism as the living person, thereby making the viewer witness to the supernatural event. Like much medieval and early modern art, they blur the line between the worldly and otherworldly. The prints spread immediately throughout Catholic areas and inspired Teresian iconographers well into the eighteenth century. In 1614, the year of Teresa's beatification, Francisco Villamena depicted for the first time Teresa writing by inspiration of the Holy Spirit (Moura Soubral 50–54).

Plays and poems written in honor of Teresa's beatification or canonization stressed her obedience to God's call, her "miraculous" foundations, her stature as one of God's chosen, and even her great beauty. In her *Quintillas a santa Teresa de Jesús en su beatificación*, Cristobalina Fernández de Alarcón (1576?–1646), following Petrarchan models, recreates Teresa as a traditional Renaissance *dama* with blond ringlets surrounding her "celestial face." Like the male poets of her day, Fernández de Alarcón describes beauty in formulaic metaphors: Teresa's countenance is "carmín de Tiro"[16] (Phonecian red) and "alabastro y cristal" (alabaster and crystal); her eyes are sapphires and her lips, coral. Fernández depicts the Transverberation to provoke *admiratio*: a seraphim with flaming sword descends from heaven: "Y puesto ante la doncella, / mirando el extremo de ella, /

dudara cualquier sentido / si él la excede en lo encendido / o ella le excede en ser bella" (And standing before the maiden, / gazing at her magnificence / any witness would wonder / if he exceeds her in radiance / or she exceeds him in beauty). The *Quintillas* end with the suggestion that Teresa has been "marked" by God like Saint Francis of Assisi (who received stigmata) and an allusion to mystical marriage. Although religious authorities cast Teresa's heroic virtue as "manliness," Fernández stresses Teresa's femininity, defined as physical beauty, a sign of God's favor.

Lope de Vega depicts Teresa as a charming *dama* in his hagiographical play *Santa Teresa de Jesús*, probably written for Teresa's canonization in 1622.[17] Like all hagiographic literature, Lope's play is not meant to create a realistic portrait of the subject but to inspire awe and devotion.[18] Lope may have drawn from early graphic depictions of Teresa's life, such as the Collaert and Galle engravings. There is no evidence he actually read her books. Although Teresa often depicted herself as a miserable sinner who, by God's mercy, enjoyed many spiritual favors, Lope was not interested in exploring his subject's insecurities. His task was to celebrate Teresa as a Spanish saint at a time when the church hierarchy in Rome was anxious to express its gratitude to Spain for defending the faith against Protestantism and when, at home, national morale was low.

Lope's play consists principally of a series of tableaux depicting several of the scenes that appear in the Collaert and Galle engravings: the Transverberation, the paroxysm, the first foundation, Teresa's miraculous resurrection of her dead nephew, her first Discalced friary, and her mystical marriage to Jesus. Lope handles Teresa's role as reformer with discretion. Rather than a shrewd, energetic politician, Lope's Teresa is the recipient of divine grace and a miracle worker. When God inspires her to found a male monastery, angels in work clothes appear to complete the construction. If the letters and books reveal a Teresa constantly scrounging for money to buy supplies, pay laborers, placate landlords, and furnish chapels, Lope's saint has no such concerns. When her brother-in-law Juan del Valle offers her money, Teresa refuses because angels require no payment.[19] Through scenes such as these Lope conveys iconographically the divine nature of Teresa's mission.

The explosion of depictions of Teresa in the arts during the early decades of the seventeenth century stemmed largely from political circumstances. Teresa had an enthusiastic following among the people, and different groups attempted to harness her following to advance their own agendas. As early at 1617, during the reign of Philip III, the Discalced Carmelites petitioned the Spanish Cortes, or parliament, to make Teresa co-patron of Spain, along with the existing patron, Saint James (Santiago) of Compostela, arguing that her teachings were an important tool for evangelization and empire-building. Thus, Carmelites seeking to increase the prestige of the order linked Teresa to Spain's expansionist program. Philip II's constant wars had left Spain bankrupt. By the beginning of the 1600s the country was suffering from widespread inflation and other economic troubles. During this time of collective disillusionment and angst, many Spaniards craved an emblem of national unity to rally around. However, although the king initially supported the movement to make Teresa copatron of Spain, immediate opposition on the part of many influential political and religious leaders compelled Philip III to reverse his position on the grounds that Teresa had not yet been canonized.

In 1627, five years after Teresa's canonization, her supporters made another attempt to have her named copatron of Spain, and now the pope himself issued a brief validating the copatronage. However, this time opposition was even more adamant than before. Francisco Quevedo, one of Spain's most energetic and ferocious political writers, attacked the plan in prose and in verse. For Quevedo, the idea of promoting Teresa to copatron seriously discredited Saint James, Spain's heroic patron who, according to legend, evangelized the Iberian Peninsula before returning to Jerusalem to be martyred. Brother of John the Evangelist and one of the twelve apostles, James was thought to be able to offer special protection to Spain because of his closeness to Jesus. He was revered as the quintessential warrior saint and was believed to appear routinely to Spanish troops in order to lead them to victory. "¡Santiago y cierre España!" (Saint James and close ranks!) was Spain's traditional battle cry.

Quevedo had just been made a knight of the Order of Santiago, known as the *santiaguistas*. Originally founded to provide protection from Moorish bandits for pilgrims traveling to and from the tomb of Saint James at Compostela, the Order of Santiago was a military-religious order whose knights took a vow of evangelization and were known for their strong defense of Christianity against the Moors. By Quevedo's time, membership had become a coveted honor, and the poet was a resolute defender of the order's champion. Saint James was, in Quevedo's words, "gran patrón de España / y no pastoril espíritu de caña" (the great patron saint of Spain, / and not a shepherd-like spirit with a flimsy staff) (*Contra el Patronato de Santa Teresa de Jesús* 449). He was a hero, an apostle, and Spain's natural protector. Teresa was simply not in his league.

Although some critics have accused Quevedo of sexism, Katie Mac-Lean, who has studied the case in depth, argues that Teresa's merits were not really the question. Quevedo praises the newly canonized saint as a mystic and reformer but believed that during this time of flagging national spirit, Spain needed strong emblems evocative of its glorious past to boost its sense of national identity. In the Spanish mind, Santiago was the celestial commander of Spanish armies, both in Europe and across the sea. MacLean explains:

For Quevedo and other conservatives, the apostle's position could not remain undamaged if he were to share his title with another. The diminishing of Santiago the Apostle had potentially serious consequences for the Spanish Crown if one believed in this celestial pact between the apostle and his *alférez*, the king. One of the advantages for the Crown and the nation is purely that of status. Few European nations could claim the presence of one of Christ's apostles on their soil, nor could they claim that an apostle originally Christianized them. This raised Spain's profile as a Christian realm with respect to its neighbours. The Spanish secular and ecclesiastical hierarchies also felt privileged by this and by the reconquest, and assumed the role of defenders of the faith as the Protestant Reformation took hold in northern Europe. By preserving the pre-eminence of Santiago as the only patron saint of Spain, Quevedo hoped to preserve Spain's unique tie to Christ and to the primitive Church. (904–5).

For Quevedo and his fellow conservatives, Saint James the Warrior was inextricably entwined with the Spanish national character. The apostle embodied the country's bellicose spirit, manifest in its struggle against Protestant and Muslim heretics, and its missionary zeal, manifest in its conquest and evangelization of the New World. His patronage was a validation of "Spain's view of itself as the nation most qualified to extend Christianity's universal apostolate" (MacLean 905). He emblemized Spain's "militant Catholicism" and its "expansionist state policy" (906). For old-school conservatives, argues MacLean, Spain's heroic traditions were rapidly being undermined by a new class of upstarts—*letrados*, or university-educated men, who won power not with the sword but with the pen. These men occupied important positions in the royal and municipal bureaucracies, and many conservatives blamed them for Spain's deteriorating state. Ironically, Teresa, who always insisted on her own lack of learning, was sometimes depicted writing diligently at her desk, which caused *santiaguistas* to associate her with these audacious new upstarts and strengthened their resolve against her. The "newness" of Spain's new woman saint may have disturbed them more than her femaleness. In a sense, it was a class issue. Teresa represented the rising class of ink-stained bureaucrats that had replaced the warrior-nobles of Spain's glorious past, personified for centuries by the charging Saint James.

In the end, Teresa was no match for the defenders of Saint James, and the case for copatronage was dropped. The episode had actually been a war between competing constructs. No certifiable historical evidence exists that Saint James actually evangelized Spain. Just as the sanitized image of Teresa accomplishing the reform without a struggle served the friars promoting her cause, so did the image of the combatant-saint serve conservatives longing to return Spain to its former loftiness. But even though the patronage movement failed, diverse factions would continue to reconstruct Teresa according to their own needs and purposes.

After Teresa's canonization, her image continued to evolve. Over the years male Discalced Carmelites grew increasingly uncomfortable about having a woman as their founder. As we saw in Chapter 5, following Teresa's death the matriarchal administrative structure she had constructed during her lifetime was methodically dismantled by men like Doria. The Carmelite leadership began to look for a canonizable patriarchal figure to replace the matriarch. Gracián, Teresa's closest male associate, had been expelled from the order in 1592 and, in spite of his reinstatement, was not considered a serviceable candidate. However, by the mid-seventeenth century John of the Cross had grown in stature to the point that he was being promoted as the originator of the Carmelite reform. Christopher Wilson has studied how the religious iconography of the seventeenth and eighteenth centuries reconstructed Teresa and John. He notes that in spite of John's relatively small role in restructuring the order, in art and hagiography he "was given the status of co-reformer, a male counterpart to Teresa, as if he were her spiritual twin—and, at times, an authoritative presence looming over her" ("Masculinity Restored" 4). Wilson argues that "the attempt to pump up his persona was also closely tied to the long process of posthumously reshaping Teresa in conformity with expected parameters of gender" ("Masculinity Restored" 5). While the Collaert and Galle engravings depict Teresa as a central figure, as the seventeenth century wears on, John grows in stature. Although John is known to have been physically small, in images of the two of them together he eventually becomes as large as Teresa, occupying a position of equality or superiority. For example, in one Collaert and Galle engraving, Teresa, towering over John of the Cross and Antonio de Jesús, sends them off to Duruelo to found the first Discalced Carmelite friary; here she is clearly portrayed as the founder of an order with both male and female branches. Another series by Arnold van Westerhout, dated 1716, does not show Teresa in a position of leadership; instead, she is shown visiting the Duruelo monastery, where John stands elevated above her at the entrance, and she, "[as] if awed by his spiritual stature . . . tilts her head to the side in a gesture that conveys deference and admiration" (Wilson, "Masculinity Restored" 14). Over the decades Teresa was thus reconstructed and transformed into a subservient, docile woman who acted under the guidance of the more authoritative John.

Letters as Instruments of Reconstruction

Teresa's letters played a significant role in the reconstruction process, and it is in this respect that Mss. 12.764 is of interest. The document begins with the following note from the copyist to Diego de la Presentación, Discalced Carmelite general:

Iesus María
R.P.N.G.

Deviendose al religiosissimo çelo de VR P^e Nuestro hijo verdadero de Santa Teresa de Jesús nuestra gran Madre el auer solicitado para aumento a sus glorias, consuelo desus hijos e hijas y fruto vniuersal de todos los fieles, por sus mandatos y ordenes se buscasen en todas las Provincias de España copias fidedignas de cartas originales de N.G. M^e para darlas a la publicidad y que no quedasen ocultas doctrinas tan divinas y celestiales: y auiendo yo obedecido a V.R.P.N. en reconocerlas dichas copias y disponerlas para el logro de sus intentos favorecido en ocupacion tan propria demi afecto a la Santa y reconocido siempre ala verdad de mi insuficiencia vuelvo a ponerlas dela manera que mejor ha parecido convenir para que passando VRPR por ellas los ojos suplan mis defectos y consiga con la corrección dellos el fin de su cuydado, Dios Nuestro Señor mas gloria, La Santa mayor afecto y estimacion todos sus hijos e hijas mayor confianza, los fieles todos de la Iglesia mayor luz y consuelo y yo, oxala, el auer sauido obedecer según mi deseo. Los de VRPN propicie el cielo y premie la Santa.

Humilde siervo e hijo de VR
†
Fr Juan de Jesús Marya

[Jesus and Mary
Our Reverend Father General:

Owing to the great religious zeal of Your Reverend Father,[20] true son of Saint Teresa of Jesus, our exalted Mother, you have solicited for her greater glory, the consolation of her sons and daughters, and the universal edification of the faithful, by your command and order, that a search for accurate copies of the original letters of Our Glorious Mother be carried out in all the provinces of Spain, in order that they be made public and that such divine and heavenly doctrine not remain hidden. And I have obeyed Your Reverend Father by examining and preparing them so that your objectives can be achieved, assisted in this special task by my own affection for the Saint. Always aware of my own shortcomings, I am arranging them in the way that seems best to me. As Your Reverend Father reviews them, your eyes will correct my errors, and by correcting them, be satisfied with the end result, and bring to Our Lord God greater glory, awaken greater affection and esteem for the Saint, and inspire greater trust in her sons and daughters, greater light and consolation in the faithful of the Church, and as for me, I hope I have been able to comply as I have wished. May Heaven grant Your Reverend Father your wish and reward the Saint.

Humble servant and son of Your Reverend Father

†

Friar Juan de Jesús María][21]

This brief note sheds considerable light on the purpose of the collection, which is clearly to turn Teresa's letters into objects of devotion through their publication and distribution by Palafox. Friar Juan does not mention Teresa's shrewd political maneuvering, her energetic negotiating, her governing and legislative talents, or her keen psychological insight, all of which her authentic letters reveal. Instead, for the compilers of Mss. 12.764, Teresa's letters were important for their doctrinal content, which would serve as a guiding light for the faithful. This doctrinal content was not the result of reading, study, or intellectual insight, but was of "divine and heavenly" origin. In 1654, when Diego de la Presentación undertook the compilation, Teresa had been canonized only thirty-two years earlier. He perhaps thought the letters would serve to solidify Teresa's saintly image, thereby bringing prestige and cohesion to the order. But since the vast majority of the letters actually dealt with business, political, and administrative matters, the compilers felt compelled not only to make a careful selection in order to weed out the mundanities but also to supplement the epistolary collection with letters that, in their opinion, Teresa should have written but did not.

The collection contains seventy letters, including not only those supposedly written by Teresa but also some addressed to her—among them one from the rector of the Jesuit monastery in Ávila and another from the Carmelite provincial. Words in Latin are neatly printed, and corrections in red ink and written in another hand have been stripped in, suggesting that a great deal of care was taken in the preparation of the text. The second part of Mss. 12.764 consists of more letters, written in different hands, the result of the early practice of binding more than one manuscript together. This second "book" was less meticulously prepared than the first corpus of letters and, in fact, seems to have been assembled rather willy-nilly.

The preface, "Al Lector"(To the Reader), reveals how diligently the principal compiler, Diego de la Visitación, sought to substantiate the authority of these documents as texts for spiritual guidance:

Breve material ofrezen los afectos de hijo a la piedad ardiente, a la estimación justa y devota de los escritos de Santa Teresa de Jesús, nuestra gran Madre. Cartas son suyas que ha solicitado religioso zelo del bien de las almas, pocas (triunfo lamentable de el tiempo, si ya no ha sido de algún descuydo culpable) y buenas, pero tan llenas de Espiritu diuino y de su discreción mas que humana, que podre adultarlas lo que de vna de el Maximo Jerónimo escrita al Santo Varon Pamachio, dixo del Desiderio Erasmo. *Hæc Epistola.* (dice) *tamet sí breuis est, tamei multum haber et eruditionis, et eloquentia, vtpote scripta a viro omnium et fortissimo, et eloquentissimo.* Breves palabras ofrezco al lector en estas cartas de la gran Teresa mi madre: *fames multum habent et eruditionis et eloquentia,* pero tan proprias de su eloquencia, de su dirección y espiritu, y tan para nuestra enseñanza q ellas mismas publican ser la Santa su misma autora. *Vtpote a muliere omnium eloquentissima* migajas son como caydas de la mera abundantissima de la celestial doctrina de sus libros con q alimenta su espiritu a todos sus hijos de la Iglesia. Dixe como caydas, por q no los escribio la Santa de proposito, ni para q saliessen a luz sino muy a caso entre domesticos cuydados para sus manuales y ordinarias correspondencias. Pero migajas tan estimables que llenan y dan tal satisfaccion al alma, que ellas solas pueden acreditar de muy diuino el caudal de su eloquencia y de su sabiduria, pues satisfacer y artar con lo menos que uno ofreze siempre fue credito soberano de grandeza indicio de excellencia abundancia manifiesto.

Doy fee de ser las copias que presento sacada fidelissimamente de otras que conserva oy en sus archivos nuestra sagrada religion y de las que con cuidado y con precepto de los Superiores de ella se han podido en todas las Provincias de España descubrir. Y si bien que ni vna palabra se aya puesto en ellas aduertidamente, como lo aseguro, que no sea de la santa, es preciso el advertir que de algunas copias ha sido reservar de la emprenta muchos párrafos que por contener materias domesticas y de confianza no gustara la santa entregarlos a la publicidad. Las que en muchas de ellas toca la Santa se percipen mal, por ser respuestas de otras cartas que no vemos (achaq que en muchas debieron [¿?] tienen notado los curiosos. Pero las doctrinas que encierran son de tanta importancia que a quenta de ella sufre el discurso lo que hecha menos para toda su satisfaccion.

Tambien es justo advertir lo primero, que en muchas cartas de nuestra santa no se halla puesto el lugar donde las escrivia, aunq en algunas se colige de el contexto y que aunque casi siempre pone el dia dela fecha rara vez señala el ano y que si lo esta en algunas, es de letra agena y de mujer y poco constantemente, porque en muchas esta borrado y emendado, en muchas, variando los anos. Por todo lo quel y por ver que en muchas se contradize a la verdad, y en otras todo es andar aluzinando no se ha podido ajustar el orden de las cartas con el tiempo que se escribieron. A la verdad el intento que se pretende en quien leyere sus doctrinas que es el bien del Alma no empeña mucho a este cuidado.

Lo segundo q si en las cartas se hallaren algunas doctrinas y sentimientos opuestos se pondere que como santa y prudente supo mudar de opinion, haciendola la experiencia, el tiempo, y conocimiento de las materias alterar lo establecido para darlo verdadera firmeza y <u>Autoridad</u> con el acierto con q se veran reformadas por ella misma muchas resoluciones de la santa que en el asiento y govierno de su reforma en la direccion de sus hijos y hijas y para su mayor perfeccion y consuelo auia determinado en los principios q despues ajustandose a las circunstancias y ocurrienzias de los trampos altero [¿?] y sera bien tenerlo entendido los que alegan sentimientos y dictamenes primeros de la santa. Los quales ella misma (emos es mas e vera despues) modera y muy prudentemente.

Lo tercero q las cartas de nsa gloriosa Madre suelen tener por sello vnas calabera, atrabesados dos huesos: otras, un nombre de Jesús, pequeños ambos sellos y aun pareze q los de la calabera son diferentes unos de otros. La cortesía de sus cartas es de dos dedos al principio en donde esta la Cruz y escrito Jesús. A los lados es poco mas de un dedo. Pocas abreviaturas, letra corrida, nota familiar muy discreta y apacible y todas llenas de sabiduria del Cielo. Desnudas las ofrezco de otras glosas, doctrinas, realces y primores por no ofender mi insuficiencia. Las de la Santa contentándome con mostrar las decencia q es justo a palabras tan venerables y dexando su ilustración a maior capacitado.

Últimamente advierto q no permitiendo darse a la emprenta algunas cartas, por ser como se ha dicho domesticas correspondencias. No he querido priuar las almas de muchos documentos, auisos y doctrinas del Cielo que en ellas he podido entresacar y se ponen en el remate del libro juntando a ellas otros q ha dado la misma santa desde el Cielo a varias personas de su religión y algunos versos q en la tierra <u>entre las llamas de amor</u> supo componer y cantarle a Dios esta criatura de todas maneras sabia y celestial.

[Filial affection can add little of substance to the ardent piety and the moral and spiritual value of these writings of Saint Teresa of Jesus, our great Mother. These letters are hers, compiled with religious zeal for the well-being of souls. Few are left (due to the terrible ravages of time, or else to lamentable carelessness), but these are so good, full of divine Spirit, and her more than human discretion, that I can say of them what the great Jerome said to that holy man Pammachius[22] of Desiderio Erasmus:[23] Although an epistle may be brief, he says, it can have much erudition and eloquence, inasmuch as it is written by a strong, masculine, eloquent man. I offer only a few words to the reader about these letters of the great Teresa, my mother: there is great hunger for erudition and eloquence, but these are so typical of her style of eloquence, of her guidance and spirit, and so useful for our instruction, that they themselves attest to having been written by the Saint, their true author. Even though she was a woman, she was entirely eloquent. These are like crumbs fallen from her heavenly doctrine, just like the books with which she nourishes the spirit of her sons of the Church. I said "like crumbs fallen" because the Saint didn't write them for the purpose of instruction, or to make them public, but just included [these crumbs] in passing among [her writings on] domestic matters in her regular correspondence. But they are such worthwhile "crumbs" that they fill you up and give such satisfaction to the soul, that all by themselves they can serve as proof of the great value of her eloquence and wisdom, for to satisfy and fill up with even the little things that one has to offer is a sign of the highest greatness and excellence.

I swear that the copies I present here were faithfully made from others that are presently held in the archives of our holy order and which, by the command of our Superiors, were carefully gathered from all the Provinces of Spain, which we combed in order to find them. And although not a word has been included in them deliberately, as I can assure you, that wasn't written by the Saint, I must clarify that from some copies it was necessary to hold back from the presses many paragraphs that, because they contain information on domestic and private affairs, the Saint would not want to be made public. Many of them are unclear with regard to what pertains to the Saint, since they are answers to other letters to which we do not have access (a problem that other inquisitive investigators have noted). However, the doctrine they include is of such importance that the material that has been left out will not be missed.

It's also right to mention, first of all, that in many of our Saint's letters there is no mention of where they were written, although in some you can guess from the context, and that, although she almost always puts the day and the month on her letters, she rarely indicates the year, and if it is included in some, it is in someone else's handwriting, a woman's, and quite inconsistently. In some it is rubbed out and in others it has been corrected by changing the year. Because of all of this, and because in some letters [the date] isn't accurate, and in others it's just a guess, we haven't been able to put the letters in chronological order. The truth is that for the readers' purpose, which is to glean her doctrine for the good of their souls, it doesn't really matter.

The second thing is that if in these letters you find doctrines and perceptions that contradict each other, you should ponder the fact that Saint Teresa, so holy and prudent, was capable of changing her mind, based on her experience, the circumstance, or the knowledge that things change. This gives her real steadfastness and <u>Authority</u>, for you have the knowledge that the Saint revised many resolutions she made concerning the direction and administration of her reform for the guidance of her sons and daughters, and for their greater perfection and consolation, altering determinations she made at the beginning and adjusting them according to circumstances, events, and the whims of chance. It would be good for those who attribute certain early sentiments and opinions to the Saint to keep this in mind, for she herself (as we will see later) reasonably and prudently sometimes modified her view.

The third thing [to keep in mind is] that the letters of our glorious Mother usually bear the seal of a skull, sometimes with crossbones, or else the name of Jesus—both seals are small.[24] And it seems that even the ones with the skull are not all the same. The margin of her letters is two fingers wide at the beginning, where there is a cross and the word "Jesus."[25] At the sides the margin is a little more than a finger wide. With few abbreviations and fluid hand, producing a familiar feeling, very discreet and easygoing, these letters are all full of heavenly wisdom. I offer them free of any additional explanation, doctrine, enhancement or embellishment, so that my own imperfection won't offend. I am satisfied just to show those of the Saint, with the graciousness due such venerable words, and to leave the clarification to someone more able than I.

Finally, I'd like to point out that some letters have been withheld from press, since they are, as I said before, domestic correspondence. I have not wanted to deprive souls of many documents, pieces of advice, and celestial doctrines that I have derived from these [suppressed] letters, and so these [fragments] appear at the end of the book along with others that the Saint gave from Heaven to several persons of her order, and some verses this in all ways wise and celestial creature composed and sang to God while she was <u>inflamed with God</u>, while still on earth.]

The compiler takes considerable care to establish the authenticity and worth of Teresa's epistolary writing. He compares her with Saint Jerome, whose highly regarded letters were among Teresa's favorite readings.[26] He elevates her to the level of male writers by stressing her "manly" eloquence, possible because of the divine origin of her doctrine, and dignifies the discussion of her letters with quotes from Latin. Throughout the preface he reaffirms the legitimacy of his product by explaining the compilation process and the selection criteria. By recognizing openly that the collection is not complete, since he has eliminated paragraphs pertaining to "domestic and private" material that "the saint wouldn't want made public," he enhances his image of honesty while showing respect for Teresa. At the same time, he emphasizes that these letters are to be viewed as relics for veneration rather than as accurate historical documents.

While the doctored letters prepared under the direction of the Carmelite general undoubtedly served to bolster the image of the order by casting Teresa as a supernatural guide, the motives of Palafox in publishing them may also relate to his own political dilemma and developing ascetic tendencies. Palafox had been bishop of Puebla and general visitator of Mexico. Soon after his arrival in New Spain, he clashed with the Franciscans, Dominicans, and Augustinians over their administrative and financial abuses. He was rewarded for his reformist efforts by being appointed bishop of Mexico and de facto viceroy, supplanting the current viceroy, Diego López Pacheco Cabrera y Bobadilla, marquis de Villena, who had been charged with mismanaging money and sympathizing with the Portuguese. Palafox became an avid protector of Mexico's Indians, protesting against forced conversions and arguing that persuasion was the only legitimate way of bringing the native peoples to the faith. This stance brought him into conflict with clerics favoring harsher measures.

Palafox's most trying ordeals stemmed from his clashes with the Jesuits, whose privileges and exemptions he believed undercut his episcopal authority. He appealed to the pope, but after a long struggle the Jesuits managed to have him relieved of his duties and sent back to Spain, where he was named bishop of Osma. Feeling he had failed as a reformer, Palafox turned to asceticism and reflection; he devoted his final years to writing pastoral letters and spiritual works. The publication of Teresa's letters with his own copious notes was part of this project, which Palafox may have seen not only as a means of providing his flock with spiritual guidance but also as a sort of personal vindication.[27] The prologue to the letters contains a biographical note by an unnamed source praising the bishop for his many accomplishments and berating those who have brought libelous accusations against him.

Palafox's first volume of 65 letters was published in 1658; the second volume of 107 letters was published in 1674, fifteen years after Palafox's death. The collection begins with a letter from Palafox to Diego de la Visitación, dated 15 February 1656, that bolsters Fray Diego's defense of Teresa's intercessory powers; in fact, Palafox even attributes to Teresa's writing the miraculous conversion of a diehard Protestant. Like Fray Diego, Palafox argues that God illuminated this "very prudent virgin" with heavenly doctrine, but rather than laud Teresa's great eloquence, he praises her simplicity, arguing that true spiritual wisdom is not found in theological treatises but in everyday correspondence, which allows the soul to pour forth its interior in "vivid colors."[28] (This may be an oblique jab at some of Palafox's highly intellectual Jesuit detractors.) Fray Diego emphasizes that while Teresa's letters contain many doctrinal gems, she never meant them for public consumption; Palafox, on the other hand, suggests that the very purpose of such letters is to guide believers: "What else are the informal letters of saints, but veiled counsel, offered with gentleness to the faithful?" Thus, Teresa becomes a collaborator in the project, proffering "veiled counsel" not just to her correspondents, but to all Catholics. Her eloquence stems not from her style, but from the heavenly inspired doctrine she offers, which ignites and inspires followers.

The value of the letters, argues Palafox, is that they teach the faithful to conduct themselves in a spiritual manner in everyday situations. While her treatises offer guidance on perfecting our interior lives, says Palafox, the letters apply these lessons to social intercourse. Palafox justifies Teresa's role as teacher in the usual ways. First, although she has performed "heroic acts" that merit imitation, she guides the faithful in a womanly way: with gentleness. What "I admire," says Palafox, is the "grace, sweetness, and solace" with which she guides souls. She is a seductress who, while winning hearts for God, garners admirers for herself: "No one who reads the Saint's writings fails to seek God, and no one seeking God through her writing fails to become devoted to and enamored of the Saint." But unlike the loveliness of ordinary women, Teresa's perfection does not inspire others to desire her, but to emulate her. Teresa has a miraculous power to inspire imitators, argues Palafox, which is why every Carmelite nun is an exact replica of her. However, he adds that the core of her strength is not her womanliness, but her manliness. Like Teresa's supporters for canonization, Palafox confers authority on Teresa by stressing her "virility": "Without a doubt, Saint Teresa, although by nature a woman, in her valor, spirit, zeal, greatness of heart, courage, and superior conceiving, thinking, problem solving, execution of projects, and getting things done was a great man." Her letters are so full of learning that they seem to come "from a magnanimous, great and manly heart rather than from a humble, discalced nun." Palafox, like many of his contemporaries, was uncomfortable with Teresa's sexual identity and felt compelled to transgender her.

And like them, he sought to demonstrate that Teresa was imbued by divine grace with superhuman qualities that removed her from the natural order. Palafox writes that she was such an inspired teacher that when Alonso Velázquez, his predecessor as bishop of Osma, asked her for instruction on how to pray, she wrote him a detailed letter, a kind of *abecedario espiritual* (spiritual ABCs) that laid out step-by-step directions. The angels in heaven rejoiced, says Palafox, to see "the disciple teaching the teacher, the daughter teaching the father, the nun teaching the bishop." This was a special grace God bestowed on Teresa because of her humility, devotion, and other virtues, he explains. In fact, adds Palafox, Teresa's writing is so powerful that "just by reading the Saint's works, one of the most learned heretics of Germany, who was never moved by the most obvious truth or by the pens of the wisest Catholic thinkers, just by reading the works of this divine teacher, which he took into his hands for the purpose of impugning them, was, quite the opposite [from what he expected], so enlightened, vanquished, convinced, and overwhelmed by them, that, even though he had publicly burned her books and abjured her errors, became a son of the Church." He was not converted by the writings of the great Augustine, Ambrose, or Jerome, exclaims Palafox, but by those of "a humble maiden"—a description likening Teresa to the Virgin. If Teresa's treatises are so potent, Palafox goes on, then these spiritual letters will be even more so, which is why he has undertaken their publication.

Rather than being organized chronologically, the letters are arranged

"hierarchally," that is, according to the importance of the recipient, starting with King Philip II. The purpose of this presentation may be to stress
that Teresa was spiritual guide to kings and other great men, which would
have enhanced her position as a supernatural phenomenon. Many of the
letters are clearly misdated, since they refer to events that took place at
times different from the date supplied by Fray Diego. The collection ends
with a series of *Avisos* (Counsels) that, according to Palafox, Teresa offered to her followers posthumously, from heaven.

This is not the place for a detailed analysis of this problematic collection. One particularly vivid example will illustrate how the epistolary
served seventeenth-century supporters of Teresa in their efforts to recast
her as a replica of the obedient and submissive Virgin Mother. Letter
8, addressed to "the Illustrious Señor Don Alonso Velázquez, Bishop of
Osma," is as noteworthy for Palafox's commentaries as for the content.
Velázquez was a church luminary of the late sixteenth century. Teresa met
him in Toledo when he was canon at the cathedral, and, in spite of his
many other obligations, he became her confessor. She tells Gracián in a
letter that God himself guided her toward Velázquez because he was a
learned man and able to direct her competently (*Letters* 1, 5 September
1576: 1). In 1578 Velázquez was named bishop of Osma. He was helpful to
Teresa in her struggles against the Calced and when she founded in Soria
(*CWST* 3, *Foundations* 30:2–3).[29] Teresa's final *Spiritual Testimony*, in
which she gives an account of the present state of her soul, was written for
him in 1581. In 1583 he became bishop of Compostela and died four years
later, in 1587. Only one authenticated extant letter, dated 21 March 1581,
from Teresa to Velázquez exists—a businesslike account, only three short
paragraphs long, of the progress of the Soria Carmel.

The tone of the authenticated letter is professional and matter-of-
fact. Teresa first excuses herself for not writing more, explaining that she
has been busy attending to the new foundation. She mentions a "further
complication" about a house—she had decided against purchasing some
properties she had originally wanted—and expresses regret that she will
have to stay in Palencia over the summer. Referring to the Soria project,
she says she is glad he is not in the midst of "the trials that accompany
these things, which are always terrible," but she does not elaborate (*Letters* 2, 21 March, 1581: 2). Teresa concludes by assuring Velázquez that
she is fine and that affairs of the reform—meaning the chapter meeting in
Alcalá—are going well. Naturally, the fact that Teresa wrote a succinct,
to-the-point business letter to Velázquez does not preclude the existence
of other letters, now lost. Around the time Teresa wrote her last *Spiritual
Testimony*, Velázquez was involved in a dispute with the city council of
Osma over his activities in Soria, and he had lost his sight in one eye.[30]
He and Teresa spent ample time talking about spiritual matters and ex-
changed written communications. In his troubled state he may well have

asked her for advice. However, the instructive letter included in the Pala-fox edition does not appear in the recent editions of Teresa's letters and is surely apocryphal.

The letter to Velázquez that appears in the Palafox edition revolves around two main themes: obedience and revelation. The letter portrays Teresa as a diffident woman whose only source of spiritual knowledge is divine revelation: she dares to write to the bishop only because he has commanded her to, and the information she imparts to him has been re-vealed to her directly by God. Certainly, Teresa did write her major works out of obedience, and indeed took her vow of obedience very seriously.[31] She praises the virtue of obedience in many of her books and letters. How-ever, as we have seen throughout this study, while Teresa often employed the rhetoric of humility when writing to influential men, she was not shy about articulating opinions, complaints, and proposals concerning the re-form. Precisely because she claimed authority based on her personal expe-rience, she displayed considerable confidence when dealing with superiors.

The authenticated letter to Velázquez begins with the same salutation Teresa uses for other dignitaries: "The grace of the holy spirit be with your lordship." After this routine greeting, she states her business. In contrast, letter 8 begins, "Most very reverend father of my soul," an uncharacter-istic salutation, since in no other missive does Teresa address a prelate as "father of my soul." What follows is a declaration of obedience: "One of the greatest mercies for which I am indebted to our Lord, is for giving me the desire to be obedient; for in this virtue I feel great contentment and consolation, as the thing I commend most to our Lord. . . . You ordered me [to write to you]. . . . I have done it, disregarding my insignificance and only taking into account your command, and with this faith I trust in your goodness, and that you will receive what I try to convey, and will receive my goodwill, since it is born of obedience" (letter 8: 1–2). Palafox's comments on the passage suggest that it was included for the very pur-pose of highlighting Teresa's obedience. He points out that she acts "*out of obedience, of which she is greatly enamored*" and that she "is right to be [enamored], since this virtue is the repose and calm of the spirit in which it rests." He clarifies that "those who obey, and write under discipline, write correctly. Pity those of us who command, if we act any way we please, and not as one who obeys the rules that have come down to us!" (letter 8, note 5, italics Palafox's). As a woman, Teresa was an appropriate model of obedience. Although Teresa departs from the natural order of things by becoming the "disciple teaching the teacher, the daughter teaching the father, the nun teaching the bishop," Palafox argues that she was loath to do so; if she wrote to Velázquez, it was only because obedience trumps all other virtues. It seems likely that Palafox saw Teresa's epistolary writing as a vehicle for his own teaching. He holds Teresa up as an example not only for women but for all—perhaps especially for his arrogant, abusive, insubordinate Jesuit detractors. For Palafox, whether or not the letter was authentic was probably insignificant. What counted was the image of the obedient handmaiden of God into which Teresa had been recast since her canonization.

The rest of the letter is a synthesis of Teresa's spiritual teaching as articulated in *Life*, *Way of Perfection*, and *Interior Castle*, which she offers to Velázquez as a revelation she received from God. Having told God of the bishop's excellent qualities, "it was shown to me . . . that what you are lacking is prayer with a lighted lamp, which is the light of faith" (letter 8: 3). Palafox comments that these words are proof of supernatural communication: "She says that what she writes comes from God, that is what 'it was shown to me' means: it was given to me to understand . . . because she prayed to God about it, and in prayer is where God communicates with souls, that is, she had a revelation about it. And so, in my opinion, this letter is as much of God as it is of the Saint" (letter 8, note 6). Teresa then explains the process of recollection, once again stressing the virtue of obedience: we must be "like worms in the earth . . . humble, and subject to the Creator . . . worms of the earth, because even though birds of the sky peck at them, they don't raise themselves up from the earth, or give up the obedience and submissiveness they owe their Creator" (letter 8: 13, 15). The lesson, according to Palafox, is that "all of us prelates should learn that zeal, charity, and desire to honor God are not enough, without prayer" (letter 8: 10). However, he is concerned that the letter might give the impression that Velázquez was lax about prayer, and so adds that "the saintly prelate certainly did pray, although perhaps he lacked sufficient perseverance in the practice of prayer" (letter 8, note 17).

It would be unfair to apply today's notions of scholarship to seventeenth-century collections of Teresa's letters. Just as icons of saints were meant to motivate the faithful rather than to offer a true likeness of the subject, the epistolary collection was meant to inspire rather than to inform. Accuracy was not a central issue. These same relaxed criteria apply to BN Mss. 19.347, prepared under the direction of Pedro de la Anunciación for the second volume of letters undertaken by Palafox and published in 1674, fifteen years after his death.

Palafox's first volume met with such success that four editions followed in eight years despite invectives issued by cynical Jesuits against its hyperbolically baroque notes and hierarchical (rather than chronological) arrangement of the letters. It was not until the following century that, guided by the spirit of the Enlightenment, Carmelite investigators under the direction of the general, Pablo de la Concepción, undertook a more accurate compilation of Teresa's epistolary writing. Guided by scientific principles and trained in paleography, this new generation of investigators sought to put together an authentic corpus of letters. With limited resources Fray Manuel de Santa María traveled throughout Castile to collect and categorize Teresa's correspondence. Rodríguez Martínez and Egido note that even though the new collection contains a few apocryphal missives, it is largely accurate and has served as the basis of modern editions (55–56). In spite of this excellent piece of scholarship, printed editions of Teresa's epistolary writing from the late eighteenth century reflect the criteria used for the Palafox edition rather than the more erudite approach.

The nineteenth century saw a new surge of interest in Teresa's letters, particularly in France. Ateliers Catholiques, a publishing house established by Abbot Jacques-Paul Migne (1800–1875) to turn out affordable religious books, produced a new edition of Saint Teresa's complete works, including the letters arranged in rough chronological order. These constituted the second volume of a three-volume set (Paris, 1840). A few years later another more complete edition was published by Father Marcel Bouix (Paris, 1861), with an invective "against Palafox and everything Spanish" (Rodríguez Martínez and Egido 57). At almost the same time, Vicente de la Fuente published a collection of Teresa's letters in his second volume of *Escritos de Santa Teresa* (Madrid, 1861). Although De la Fuente brought to light some new letters, his edition suffers from many inaccuracies.

It was not until the twentieth century that the text and order of Teresa's letters were fixed, thanks in large part to the efforts of Silverio de Santa Teresa, whose "gigantic" effort represents a "decisive step" in Teresian scholarship (Rodríguez Martínez and Egido 58). Published by Monte Carmelo from 1922 to 1924, this edition provided accurate texts of letters arranged chronologically, critical and historical notes, fragments, and apocryphal missives. It served as the basis for early twentieth-century translations into English, German, French, Dutch, and Italian. The 1959 edition of Teresa's *Epistolario*, compiled by Efrén de la Madre de Dios and Otger Steggink and published by Biblioteca de Autores Cristianos, improved on Father Silverio's work by refining the accuracy of the texts and chronology. It also includes fragments and apocryphals, as well as some letters addressed to Teresa. The 1977 edition contains 441 of Teresa's letters, as well as two new letters included in the appendix, fragments, apocryphals, and memoranda. Having located four new autographs and conducted additional paleographic research, the editors have adjusted the texts of some letters and omitted materials addressed to Teresa. In 1979 Father Tomás Álvarez published an edition of Teresa's epistolary writing with useful introductions.

The 1984 edition by Luis Rodríguez Martínez and Teófanes Egido is the most accurate edition to date. Building on the work of Silverio de Santa Teresa, Efrén de la Madre de Dios and Otger Steggink, and Tomás Álvarez, the editors reexamined autographs to resolve certain discrepancies, included twelve new letters, modernized spellings, and updated the chronology. Their information-filled introduction outlines Teresa's major epistolary themes, describes some of the characteristics of her style, and provides historical and biographical facts on her correspondents.

For years, English speakers depended on the translation of Teresa's letters by E. A. Peers, the only one readily available. Although for the most part accurate, this edition distorted Teresa's writing somewhat by omitting her salutations and polishing her occasionally messy style. The new translation by Kieran Kavanaugh, published in two volumes (2001, 2007) by the Institute of Carmelite Studies, provides a more precise rendering of the text as well as useful synopses at the beginning of each letter and ample biographical notes.

Conclusion

For generations, clerics and critics have found Teresa's down-to-earth epistolary style somewhat embarrassing. The dynamic, multifaceted woman revealed in the epistolary writing is poles apart from the idealized figure promoted by Teresa's seventeenth-century apologists. Not only early compilers such as Diego de la Presentación but even modern editors such as Silverio de Santa Teresa have shuddered at the exposure the letters give to the flesh-and-blood woman Teresa de Jesús, who laughed, cried, and got ill, frustrated, and angry, just like everyone else. Teresa's political maneuvers, her administrative acumen, and her interest in food, decoration, medicine, money, and domestic issues made them uncomfortable. For these men, the practical, straight-thinking Teresa revealed in the letters was at odds with the image of the perfect and pure Catholic saint. Silverio actually apologized for daring to reveal the "domestic and intimate aspect" of Teresa's life.[1] As we saw in Chapter 1, certain early twentieth-century critics such as Américo Castro objected to Teresa's chattiness, her earthiness, and her inelegance. They found her concern for the everyday and her use of conversational language distasteful, and they thought her disregard for epistolary style vulgar. But for today's cultural historian, these down-to-earth qualities are precisely what make the letters fascinating.

The letters portray a woman of keen intelligence with an enormous capacity for work and normal human emotions. Yet this more realistic representation in no way diminishes Teresa's relevance or exemplarity. On the contrary, modern readers will find in this more comprehensive image of Teresa a model to admire and emulate. For people of faith, Teresa continues to serve as an example of devotion that transcends external, perfunctory expressions of religion and leads to a profound understanding of the bond between God and the human soul. This grasp of the spiritual core of every individual and the notion that one serves God by serving others were the forces that galvanized Teresa to launch the reform. She was convinced that by giving others the opportunity to devote themselves entirely to prayer, she was doing God's will. The image of this real and very complex woman who was both deeply spiritual and politically savvy has inspired myriad modern admirers of all faiths, from Catholics and Protestants to Jews and Buddhists.

However, one does not have to be a believer to appreciate Teresa, for she definitely speaks to our secular world. At a time when women are emerging as leaders in all fields, Teresa stands out as a precursor. She is an example of a woman who triumphed in a highly patriarchal society, navigating the treacherous waters of misogyny and cultural intolerance. Teresa bucked obstacles as daunting as those faced by any modern female politician, scientist, academic, or CEO to become a powerful administrator, legislator, and spiritual leader. She moved beyond her own immediate sphere of influence—the convent—to negotiate with prelates and nobles. Her letters not only tell the story of the Carmelite reform but also show how one woman stood firm and even kept her sense of humor in the face of terrible adversity. In one sense, Teresa had an advantage over modern women. At a time when women's inferiority was generally taken for granted, in spiritual matters women were often considered privileged, since Scripture teaches that God favors the weak. Women's spiritual sensitivity was taken as evidence that "the last shall be first," an argument that Teresa used to bolster her authority. Today's women have countless opportunities that sixteenth-century women did not have, but they cannot claim privileged sacred knowledge to help shield them from the "old boys' club," as Teresa did.

Teresa's letters allow us to know her in a deeply personal way. They reveal her warmth and profound spirituality, and they expose her vulnerability as well—how easily she was hurt by a perceived snub, how furiously she reacted when her advice was ignored. More than anything, they show the great joy she took in founding and administering convents. Through letters she guided her spiritual daughters; she attended to their lodgings, their material needs, their health, their daily routine. She was also concerned about her spiritual sons, in particular Gracián, whom she shepherded through endless political trials. And on top of everything, she was the de facto *pater familias* of the Cepeda-Ahumada clan, whose bickering, lawsuits, and financial problems gave her no rest.

In addition to providing an ample portrait of Teresa, her epistolary writing paints a vivid picture of many aspects of sixteenth-century Spanish life. Her letters offer insight into the importance of epistolary protocol and sensitivity to social hierarchy; her insistence on the proper use of titles, even as she forbade them in her convents, shows how cognizant she was of worldly matters.

Teresa's *Epistolario* shows how women's letter-writing differed from models used by male professionals, bureaucrats, and literate artisans. They present examples of women's writing from a period when few women wrote, and they show how important the post could be to an order that stressed female education. Teresa's letters demonstrate that by sharing news and offering each other moral support, the reformed Carmelite sisters, like the Jesuits, achieved a "union of hearts" that helped them survive. The letters portray in stunning detail the struggles of the incipient reform. The numerous references to patents, permits, and licenses suggest that founding a convent could be a bureaucratic and legal nightmare. The extreme attention that Teresa paid to every aspect of finance—the purchase, renovation, and furnishing of houses, and taxes, fees, and dowries—expose the complicated business of founding and running convents. Teresa's letters to the officials of the order and the church illustrate just how adept she was at political maneuvering, even when the authorities tried to manacle her.

The epistolary writing depicts the minutiae of convent life in early modern Spain. It provides cultural historians with a wealth of information on the values, thoughts, and activities of a significant segment of the Spanish female population in the sixteenth century. Teresa's letters show the wide range of responsibilities assumed by prioresses in her convents and suggest that women religious excelled as chroniclers, accountants, nurses, and educators. Mention of nuns singing, celebrating, reading, cooking, preparing cures, writing, sewing, and even raising money by selling their products helps us to understand the vibrancy of the conventual experience. The importance Teresa placed on money and physical appearance tells us much about the values of the mercantile society in which she lived.

We are only beginning to mine the rich treasury of early modern epistolary writing. Much work remains to be done, especially in the area of women's letters. The convents of Spain and Latin America have performed a tremendous service by preserving thousands of documents, including letters, of early modern nuns. The letters of secular women, sometimes stowed and forgotten in private collections, are often harder to come by. However, for today's scholars the search for letters, those precious windows to the past, is a wonderfully worthwhile endeavor.

Appendix

Seven Letters with Original Translations

The original letters are reprinted from Epistolario, edited by Luis Rodríguez Martínez and Teófanes Egido (Madrid: Espiritualidad, 1984).

I

A D. Lorenzo de Cepeda. Quito
Ávila, 23 de diciembre de 1561

1. Jesús. Señor: Sea el Espíritu Santo siempre con vuestra merced, amen, y páguele el cuidado que ha tenido de socorrer a todos y con tanta diligencia. Espero en la majestad de Dios que ha de ganar vuestra merced mucho delante de Él; porque es así cierto que a todos los que vuestra merced envía dineros, les vino a tan buen tiempo, que para mí ha sido harta consolación.

2. Y creo que fue movimiento de Dios el que vuestra merced ha tenido para enviarme a mí tantos; porque para una monjuela como yo, que ya tengo por honra, gloria a Dios, andar remendada, bastaban los que habían traído Juan Pedro de Espinosa y Varrona (creo que se llama el otro mercader), para salir de necesidad por algunos años.

3. Mas como ya tengo escrito a vuestra merced bien largo, por muchas razones y causas de que yo no he podido huir por ser inspiraciones de Dios, de suerte que no son para en carta, sólo digo que personas santas y letradas les parece estoy obligada a no ser cobarde, sino poner lo que pudiere en esta obra, que es hacer un monasterio adonde ha de haber solas quince, sin poder crecer el número, con grandísimo encerramiento, así de nunca salir como de no ver si no han velo delante del rostro, fundada en oración y en mortificación, como a vuestra merced más largo tengo escrito y escribiré con Antonio Morán cuando se vaya.

4. Y favoréceme esa señora doña Guiomar que escribe a vuestra merced. Es mujer de Francisco Dávila, de Salobralejo, si vuestra merced se acuerda. Ha nueve años que murió su marido, que tenía un cuento de renta; ella por sí tiene un mayorazgo sin el de su marido, y aunque quedó de veinte y cinco años, no se ha casado, sino dándose mucho a Dios. Es espiritual harto.

5. Ha más de cuatro que tenemos más estrecha amistad que puedo tener con hermana; y aunque me ayuda harto, porque da mucha parte de la renta, por ahora está sin dinero, y cuanto toca a hacer y comprar la casa hágolo

yo; que con el favor de Dios hanme dado dos dotes antes que sea y téngola comprada (aunque secretamente, y para labrar cosas que había menester yo no tendría remedio), y es así que sólo confiando—pues Dios quiere que lo haga. El me proveerá—concierto los oficiales.

6. Ello parecía cosa de desatino. Viene Su Majestad y mueve a vuestra merced para que lo provea; y lo que más me ha espantado, que los cuarenta pesos que añadió vuestra merced me hacían grandísima falta, y San José (que se ha de llamar así), creo hizo no la hubiese, y sé que la pagará a vuestra merced. En fin, aunque pobre y chica, mas lindas vistas y campo. Con esto se acaba.

7. Han ido por las bulas a Roma, porque aunque es de mi misma orden, damos la obediencia al obispo. Espero en el Señor será para mucha gloria suya si lo deja acabar, que sin falta pienso será, porque van almas que bastan a dar grandísimo ejemplo, que son muy escogidas, así de humildad como de penitencia y oración. Vuestras señorías lo encomienden a Dios, que cuando Antonio Morán vaya, con su favor estará ya acabado.

8. Él vino aquí, con quien me he consolado mucho (que me pareció hombre de suerte y de verdad y bien entendido), y de saber tan particularmente de vuestras señorías, que cierto una de las grandes que el Señor me ha hecho es que les haya dado a entender lo que es el mundo y se hayan querido sosegar, y que entiendo yo que llevan camino del cielo, que es lo que más deseaba saber, que siempre hasta ahora estaba en sobresalto. Gloria sea al que todo lo hace. Plega a él vuestra merced vaya siempre adelante en su servicio, que pues no hay tasa en galardonar, no ha de haber parar en procurar servir al Señor, sino cada día un poquito siquiera ir más adelante y con hervor; que parezca, como es así, que siempre estamos en guerra y que hasta haber victoria no ha de haber descuido.

9. Todos los que con vuestra merced ha enviado dineros han sido hombres de verdad, aunque Antonio Morán se ha aventajado, así en traer más vendido el oro y sin costa—como vuestra merced verá—como en haber venido con harto poca salud desde Madrid aquí a traerlo (aunque hoy está mejor, que era un accidente) y veo que tiene de veras voluntad a vuestra merced. Trajo también los dineros de Varrona, y todo con mucho cuidado.

10. Rodríguez también vino acá y lo hizo harto bien. Con él escribiré a vuestra merced, que por ventura se irá primero.

11. Mostróme Antonio Morán la carta que vuestra merced la había escrito. Crea que tanto cuidado no sólo creo es de su virtud sino que se lo ponía Dios.

12. Ayer me envió mi hermana doña María esa carta; cuando le lleven esotros dineros enviará otra. A harto buen tiempo le vino el socorro. Es muy buena cristiana y queda con hartos trabajos, y si Juan de Ovalle le pusiese pleito sería destruir sus hijos. Y cierto no es tanto lo que él tiene entendido como le parece, aunque harto mal se vendió todo y lo destruyó. Más también Martín de Guzmán llevaba sus intentos (Dios le tenga en el cielo) y se lo dio

la justicia, aunque no bien. Y tornar ahora a pedir lo que mi padre—que haya gloria—vendió, no me queda paciencia.

13. Y lo demás, como digo, sería matar a doña María mi hermana; y Dios me libre de interés que ha de ser haciendo mal tanto a sus deudos; aunque por acá está de tal suerte, que por maravilla hay padre para hijo ni hermano para hermano. Así no me espanto de Juan de Ovalle, antes lo ha hecho bien, que por amor de mí por ahora se ha dejado de ello. Tiene buena condición, mas en este caso no es bien fiar de ella, sino que cuando vuestra merced le enviare los mil pesos, vengan a condición y con escritura, y ésta a mí. Vuestra merced mande a pedir que el día que tornare al pleito, sean quinientos ducados de doña María.

14. Las casas de Gotarrendura aún no están vendidas sino recibidos trescientos mil maravedís Martín de Guzmán de ellas, y esto es justo se le torne. Y con enviar vuestra merced estos mil pesos se remedia Juan de Ovalle y puede vivir aquí (que esto ha hecho) y que se ha venido aquí y tiene ahora necesidad; que para vivir continuo no podrá si de allá no viene esto, sino a tiempos y mal. Es harto bien casado; mas digo a vuestra merced que ha salido doña Juana mujer tan honrada y de tanto valor, que es para alabar a Dios, y un alma de un ángel.

15. Yo salí la más ruin de todas y a quien vuestras señorías no habían de conocer por hermana, según soy. No sé cómo me quieren tanto. Esto digo con toda verdad. Ha pasado hartos trabajos y llevádolos harto bien. Si sin poner a vuestra merced en necesidad puede enviar esto, hágalo con brevedad, aunque sea poco a poco.

16. Los dineros que vuestra merced mandó, se han dado como verá por las cartas. Toribia era muerta y su marido. A sus hijos, que los tiene pobres, ha hecho harto bien.

Las misas están dichas (de ellas creo antes que viniesen los dineros), por lo que vuestra merced manda y de personas las mejores que yo he hallado, que son harto buenas. Hízome devoción el intento porque vuestra merced las decía.

17. Yo me hallo en casa de la señora doña Guiomar en todos estos negocios, que me ha consolado por estar más con los que me dicen de vuestra merced. Y digo más a mi placer, que salió una hija suya de esta señora—que es monja en nuestra casa—y mandóme el provincial venir por compañera adonde me hallo harto con más libertad para todo lo que quiero que en casa de mi hermana. Es adonde hay todo trato de Dios y mucho recogimiento. Estaré hasta que me manden otra cosa, aunque para tratar en el negocio dicho, estaría mejor estar por acá.

18. Ahora vengamos a hablar en mi querida hermana la señora doña Juana, que aunque a la postre, no lo está en mi voluntad, que es así cierto, que en el grado que a vuestra merced, la encomiendo a Dios. Beso a su merced mil veces las manos por tanta merced como me hace. No sé con qué lo servir, sino con que al nuestro niño se encomiende mucho a Dios, y así se

hace, que el santo fray Pedro de Alcántara lo tiene mucho a su cargo (que es un fraile descalzo de quien he escrito a vuestra merced) y los teatinos y otras personas a quienes oirá Dios. Plega a Su Majestad lo haga mejor que a los padres, que aunque son buenos, quiero para él más. Siempre me escriba vuestra merced del contento y conformidad que tiene, que me consuela mucho.

19. He dicho que le enviaré cuando vaya Antonio Morán un traslado de la ejecutoria—que dicen que no puede estar mejor—y esto haré con todo cuidado. Y si de esta vez se perdiere en el camino, hasta que llegue la enviaré, que por un desatino no se ha enviado (que porque toca a tercera persona, que no la ha querido dar, no lo digo); y unas reliquias que tengo, también se enviarán, que es de poca costa la guarnición.

20. Por lo que a mí envía mi hermano, le beso mil veces las manos; que si fuera en el tiempo que yo traía oro, hubiera harta envidia a la imagen, que es muy linda en extremo. Dios nos guarde a su merced muchos años y a vuestra merced lo mismo, y les dé buenos años, porque es mañana la víspera del año de 1562.

21. Por estarme con Antonio Morán, comienzo a escribir tarde, que aun dijera más, y quiérese ir mañana, y así escribiré con el mi Jerónimo de Cepeda; mas como he de escribir tan presto, no se me da nada. Siempre lea vuestra merced mis cartas, que no irá.

22. Harto he puesto en que sea buena la tinta; la letra escribo tan aprisa, y es, como digo, tal hora, que no la puedo tornar a leer.

23. Yo estoy mejor de salud que suelo. Désela Dios a vuestra merced en el cuerpo y en el alma como yo deseo, amén.

24. A los señores Hernando de Ahumada y Pedro de Ahumada por no haber lugar no escribo; harélo presto.

25. Sepa vuestra merced que algunas personas harto buenas que saben nuestro secreto (digo del negocio) han tenido por milagro enviarme vuestra merced tanto dinero a tal tiempo. Espero en Dios que cuando haya menester más, aunque no quiera, le pondrá en el corazón que me socorra.

De vuestra merced muy cierta servidora.

Doña Teresa de Ahumada

Don Lorenzo de Cepeda, Quito
Ávila, 23 December 1561

1. Jesús. Señor: May the Holy Spirit be with your mercy[1] always, amen, and may he repay you for the care with which you have so diligently aided all [of us]. I hope in the majesty of God that your mercy will gain much in his eyes. Certainly, all those to whom you sent money received it at such an opportune time that I was greatly consoled.

2. I believe it was God who stirred your mercy to send me so much, since for a ragged little nun like me—and I take it as a badge of honor to

go around in patches, glory to God!—what Juan Pedro de Espinosa and Varrona[2] (I think that's the name of the other merchant) brought is enough to keep me out of need for some years.

3. I have already written your mercy a long letter about a matter that for many reasons and causes I could not avoid, since it was inspired by God. It is hard to speak of these things in a letter, but I will just say that holy and learned people have told me that I should not be cowardly, but instead should move forward with this project, which consists of founding a female monastery where there would be only fifteen nuns and no more. They would practice strict enclosure, that is, they would never go out or allow themselves to be seen without veils covering their faces. They would devote themselves to prayer and mortification, as I've already written to you in a long letter, and I'll write another for Antonio Morán to take with him when he leaves.

4. That lady Doña Guiomar[3] has been so kind to me. She is also writing to you. She's the wife of Francisco Dávila, from Salobralejo, if your mercy recalls. Her husband died nine years ago and had an annual income of one million maravedís.[4] She herself has an entailed estate in addition to what she inherited from her husband. Although she was widowed at twenty-five years old, she has not remarried but instead has devoted herself totally to God. She's deeply spiritual.

5. We have been fast friends for more than four years, in fact, we're closer than sisters. Although she helps me a lot—she contributes a large portion of her income to the foundation—at the present moment she is without funds, so it is up to me to buy and furnish the house. With God's favor I received two dowries ahead of time and I've purchased the house (although secretly, and without money to make the necessary repairs), so it was only by trusting in God—because God wants me to do this, and will provide for me—that I made an agreement with the workers.

6. It seemed like a crazy thing to do. But then His Majesty comes along and moves your mercy to provide. And what has really amazed me is that the forty extra pesos you added were exactly what I needed. I believe that Saint Joseph (after whom the convent will be named) made your mercy do this, and that he will repay your mercy. Anyway, although poor and tiny, the house has beautiful views and a field. So it all turned out fine.

7. They've gone to Rome for the papal bulls, for although the house belongs to my own religious order, we render obedience to the bishop.[5] I hope in the Lord that this house will bring him much glory, if he allows it to be founded, and I think he will, because the women who are going to occupy it are exemplary souls. They are a select group, commendable for their humility as well as for their penance and prayer. I beg you all to pray to God for this project. By the time Antonio Morán[6] departs, with God's favor everything will be done.[7]

8. [Antonio Morán] came here and was a great consolation to me. He

seems like a good-natured, loyal, and intelligent man. I was particularly happy to hear about all of you, for truly, one of the great gifts the Lord has given me is that he has given all of you understanding of how fickle the world is, and so you have chosen to live quietly and, as I understand, have taken the path that leads to heaven. That's what I most wanted to know, for up until now I was worried about it. Glory to the One who takes care of everything. May it please him that you always advance in his service, for there is no limit to the rewards. We should never stop trying to serve the Lord. Every day we should advance, at least a little, in our commitment. It may seem, in fact it is so, that we are always at war and that until we are victorious we cannot let down our guard.

9. All those with whom your mercy has sent money have been trustworthy men, but Antonio Morán has surpassed them all. He has sold the gold for a higher price and without having to pay a premium, as your mercy will see, and has brought the money here from Madrid despite being in poor health (although today he feels better, it was just a temporary downturn). I see he really has your best interests at heart. He also brought the money from Varrona, and attended to everything with great care.

10. Rodríguez[8] also came here and did everything very well. I will send a letter to you with him, for perhaps he will be the first to leave.

11. Antonio Morán showed me the letter you had written to him. Believe me, all this care comes not only from his virtue but also from God's grace.

12. Yesterday my sister Doña María[9] sent me the enclosed letter. When they bring her the other money, she will write again. Your help came just in time. She is a very good Christian and has been going through a lot. If Juan de Ovalle[10] brought suit against her, it would just destroy her children. And he certainly doesn't have as much of a claim against her as he thinks he does, even though everything was sold at a loss and the whole thing turned into a disaster. But Martín de Guzmán (may God rest his soul) also had a claim, and the judge ruled in his favor, even though he didn't get enough. And now for Ovalle to turn up and claim what my father—God keep him in his glory—sold, it just makes me fume.

13. As for everything else, as I was saying, it would just kill Doña María, my sister. God deliver me from the self-interest that infects relatives. It has reached the point here that it's a miracle when some father cares about his son or a brother cares about his brother. That's why Juan de Ovalle's behavior doesn't surprise me. Actually, he has done the right thing by setting this litigation aside for now out of love for me. Deep down he is a good person, but in this case I wouldn't trust in that. When you send him the one thousand pesos, you should ask him for a promissory note in writing to be given to me. Your mercy should make it clear that the day he reintroduces the lawsuit, five hundred ducats will go to Doña María.

14. The houses in Gotarendura[11] are still not sold, but Martín de

Guzmán received three hundred thousand maravedís from them, and it was only right that this amount go to Ovalle. Along with the one thousand pesos you're sending to Ovalle, he has been taken care of. He will be able to live here (as he has been), for he has come here and now is in need. He would not be able to live here comfortably for long periods without help from over there. His marriage is good, and I'm telling you that Doña Juana is so honorable and virtuous that you want to praise God for it. She has the soul of an angel.

15. I am the worst one in the family. I don't know how you all even recognize me as your sister, I'm so bad. How is it that you love me so much? I say this is all truthfulness. Juana has undergone so many troubles and borne them really well. If your mercy can send her some money without putting yourself in need, please do it soon, even if you send just a little at a time.

16. The money that your mercy sent was distributed as you can see from the letters. Toribia[12] and her husband are both dead, but the money was a great help to her children, who are poor.

The masses have been said as you wished, some of them even before the money arrived, by the best persons I could find, all of them very good. I was moved by the intentions for which you had them said.

17. I am currently staying at the home of Doña Guiomar while we take care of these business affairs. I enjoy being with people who speak to me about you. And something else that makes me happy: One of this lady's daughters, who is a nun at our monastery, had to come and stay with her mother, and our provincial ordered me to be her companion. This is much better for me because I have more freedom for everything I want to do than I would have at my sister's house. All the conversation here is about God, and we live in great recollection. I will remain here until they tell me to do something else, although in order to attend to the business matters mentioned above, I'm better off here than elsewhere.

18. Now let's speak of my dear sister, Doña Juana. Even though I've left her for the last, she is not last in my heart, truly, for I pray to God for her as intensely as I do for you. I kiss your mercy's hands a thousand times for all the kindness you do me. I don't know how to repay you except by praying fervently to God for your child.[13] And the saintly friar Pedro de Alcántara (about whom I wrote to you) has promised to pray for him, too. Also the Jesuits and other persons to whom God listens. May God make him better than his parents, for good as you are, I want even more for him. Continue writing me about your joy and resignation to God's will, for it gives me so much consolation.

19. I mentioned that when Antonio Morán leaves, I will take care to send along the patent of nobility,[14] which they say was drawn up perfectly. And if this time it gets lost en route, I'll keep sending others until one arrives. For

some silly reason it was not sent earlier (it was up to a third party who didn't take care of it, but what's the point of talking about it?). I'm also sending some relics I have. The reliquary boxes aren't worth much.

20. I kiss my brother's hands a thousand times for all he has sent me. If it had come in those days when I still wore gold [jewelry], I'd have been really jealous of the image,[15] because it's so beautiful. May God keep your mercy and his wife for us for many years, and may he give you a happy New Year, for tomorrow is New Year's Eve of 1562.[16]

21. I'm sitting down to write pretty late because I spent so much time with Antonio Morán. I'd say even more, but he wants to leave tomorrow. I'll write again through Jerónimo de Cepeda,[17] and since that will be soon, that's enough for now. Always read my letters yourself.

22. I made an effort to use good ink. The handwriting shows that I wrote quickly. It is, as I said, so late that I cannot take the time to reread it.

23. My health is better than usual. May God give your mercy health in body and soul, as I desire, amen.

24. I'm not writing to Señor Hernando de Ahumada and Señor Pedro de Ahumada[18] because there's no time, but I'll write to them soon.

25. I want your mercy to know that some very good persons who are privy to our secret (I mean the business about the new convent) think it's a miracle that your mercy sent me so much money just at this time. I hope that when there is a need for more, God will put it into your heart to help me again, even though you may not want to.

Your mercy's loyal servant,

Doña Teresa de Ahumada

2

Al P. Jerónimo Gracián, Toledo
Sevilla, octubre de 1575
[Falta el comienzo de la carta.]

1. Si ella quisiese, haría vuestra paternidad harto bien a la casa en dejarla allí; si no, la trae acá, que con las monjas se podría venir hasta Malagón.

2. A usadas que nunca me haga este placer. No hay casa más necesitada de personas de talentos que la de Toledo. Aquella priora acaba presto, mas no creo habrá otra mejor para allí; aunque está harto mala, mas es cuidadosa y aunque es amiga de «los gatos», tiene muchas virtudes.

3. Si vuestra paternidad viere es bien, podrá renunciar y hacer elección aquélla, como que la mata la tierra caliente conocidísimamente. Mas yo no entiendo quién pudiese ir por priora, que todas casi la quieren tanto que no se harían con otra, a lo que creo, aunque nunca faltará alguna tentada, que sí hay.

4. Vuestra paternidad, padre mío, advierta en esto y crea que entiendo mejor los reveses de las mujeres que vuestra paternidad, que en ninguna manera conviene para prioras ni súbditas que vuestra paternidad dé a entender es posible sacar a ninguna de su casa, si no es para fundación. Y es verdad que aun para esto veo hace tanto daño esta esperanza, que muchas veces he deseado se acaben las fundaciones porque acaben de asentar todas.

5. Y créame esta verdad (y si yo me muriere no se le olvide), que a gente encerrada no quiere el demonio más de que sea posible en su opinión una cosa. Hay muchas que decir sobre esto, que aunque yo tengo licencia de nuestro padre general (que se la pedí) para que cuando a alguna hiciese mal la tierra, se pudiese mudar a otra, después he visto tantos inconvenientes, que si no fuese por provecho de la orden, no me parece se sufre, sino que es mejor se mueran unas, que no dañar a todas.

6. No hay ningún monasterio que esté cumplido el número, antes en algunos faltan hartas y en Segovia creo tres o cuatro, que a mi parecer he tenido harta cuenta con esto. En Malagón di no sé cuántas licencias a la priora para tomar monjas—avisándola harto lo mirase mucho—cuando trajimos estotras, porque hay pocas. Quíteselas vuestra paternidad, que más vale acudan a él; y créame, padre mío, ahora que no estoy tentada, que entiendo yo con el cuidado que vuestra paternidad lo mira, que me será consuelo grande quitarme de él. Ahora en el punto que están las cosas podrá haber mejor orden; mas quien ha habido menester a unos y a otros para fundarles del aire, algo debe haber habido menester contentar.

7. Dice Séneca, contentísimo, que ha hallado más en su prelado de lo él ha podido desear; da hartas gracias a Dios. Yo no querría hacer otra cosa. Su Majestad nos le guarde muchos años.

[Y crea vuestra paternidad que ganan tanto en andar asidas a la Compañía, aunque alguna vez se yerre por esto en algo, como el tiempo lo dirá y yo de que a vuestra paternidad vea. Al menos han sido ellos la principal ayuda que he tenido y jamás lo dejaré de conocer. Y no quisiera quitara vuestra paternidad en Valladolid les enviaran algo de la huerta, que también ellos son pobres y a ellas les sobra. Y créame, mi padre, que mostrar gracia en alguna nadería, que no se puede excusar con algunas personas. Sólo esto me ha parecido de las visitas un poco riguroso, aunque, pues lo hizo vuestra paternidad, debía de haber causa.][19]

8. Yo le digo que me da un enojo de estas sus caídas, que sería bien le atasen para que no pudiese caer. Yo no sé qué borrico es ése, ni para qué ha de andar vuestra paternidad diez leguas en un día, que en un[20] albarda es para matar.

9. Con pena estoy si ha caído en ponerse más ropa, que hace ya frío. Plega al Señor no le haya hecho mal. Mire, pues es amigo del provecho de las almas, el daño que vendría a muchas con su poca salud, y por amor de Dios, que mire por ella.

10. Ya está Elías más sin miedo. El rector y Rodrigo Álvarez tienen gran esperanza se ha de hacer todo muy bien.

11. A mí todo el miedo que antes tenía se me ha quitado, que no puedo tenerlo aunque quiero.

12. Ruin salud he traído estos días. Heme purgado y estoy buena, lo que no he estado en cuatro o más meses, que ya no se puede llevar.

Indigna hija de vuestra paternidad

Teresa de Jesús

To Padre Jerónimo Gracián, Toledo
Seville, October 1575
[The beginning of the letter is missing.]

1. If that's what she wants, your paternity would be doing a lot for the house by leaving her there. If not, let her come down here and she can go with the nuns as far as Malagón.[21]

2. Customarily, I wouldn't want anyone to do me this favor. There's no house more in need of talented people than Toledo. Their prioress will soon be at the end of her term of office, but I don't think there's anyone else who will be as good as she for that house. Although she's very ill, she's careful. And even though she's friendly with "the cats,"[22] she has many virtues.

3. If your paternity thinks it's a good idea, she could resign, giving as a reason the notorious hot weather of the region, which is killing her. Then they could have another election. But I don't know who could go there as prioress, since they all love her so much that they might not be able to get used to someone else. That's what I think at least, although there'll always be someone willing to give it a try.

4. Your paternity should be careful about this and trust that I understand women's volatility better than you. You must never let a prioress or one of her nuns think it possible to transfer out of her house except to make a new foundation. And really, I even think their expecting to make new foundations does a lot of harm. I often wish we were done making foundations so that all the nuns could just stay put.

5. And believe me when I tell you this bit of truth (and if I die don't you forget it) that the devil likes nothing better than for cloistered nuns to think they can get out of their convents. There's a lot I could say about this, although I did ask and receive permission from our father general[23] [to make transfers], since sometimes a nun can't adapt to a place[24] and then she can go to another. But since then I've seen so many problems [arising from this practice] that I don't think it should be allowed, except for the good of the order.[25] Even if a few die, it's better than harming all of them.

6. There isn't a single monastery that's completely full, and some are quite short of nuns—in Segovia I think they're short three or four—for I have been

paying close attention to this. In Malagón I gave the prioress permission I don't know how many times to receive nuns—warning her to be very careful about this—for we took some nuns away from there[26] and now only a few are left. Your paternity should revoke that permission, for it's better that they have recourse to you. And believe me, Father, I no longer feel tempted [to make such decisions] because I know the care with which you attend to these things, and I'd be just as happy not to deal with this anymore. As things are going now, we can probably proceed in a more orderly way, but since I had to make these foundations out of thin air and depend on help from other people, I've had to be cooperative.

[And believe me, your paternity, they gain a great deal from their association with the Society of Jesus, even though some mistakes may have been made in this regard as time will tell and I will show. In any case, the Jesuits have been my main source of help, and I would never fail to recognize this.[27] I wouldn't want your paternity to prevent the Valladolid nuns from sending something from their garden [to the Jesuits], since they have more than enough and the fathers are poor. And believe me, Father, graciousness even if it involves just a small gesture should never be overlooked when it comes to certain people. This is the only thing that seemed a little rigorous about the visitations, even though, since you were the one who made them, there must have been a reason.][28]

7. Seneca[29] is delighted and says that his superior is even better than he could have imagined. He is giving thanks to God. I couldn't ask for more. May His Majesty keep him for many years.

8. I tell you, I get really angry hearing about those falls you have. They ought to tie you to the saddle so you don't keep falling. I don't know what kind of a donkey that is or why your paternity has to cover ten leagues a day. With a pack-saddle that's enough to kill you.

9. I am worried about whether you're dressing warmly enough. After all, it's getting colder. Please God that you haven't fallen ill. Since you like to attend to people's souls, think of how many people would suffer if you were to get sick. For the love of God, take care of yourself.

10. Elías[30] isn't so afraid any more. The rector and Rodrigo Álvarez[31] are very hopeful that everything will work out well.

11. As for me, I've lost all the fear I felt before. I couldn't even be afraid if I wanted to.

12. I've been in wretched health lately. I've taken purgatives and I'm okay now, better than I've been in the last four months or so. It got to the point where I couldn't carry on.

Your paternity's unworthy servant

Teresa de Jesús

3

Al P. Jerónimo Gracián. Sevilla
Toledo, 20 de septiembre de 1576

1. Jesús. La gracia del Espíritu Santo sea con vuestra paternidad. No piense, mi padre, perfeccionar las cosas de un golpe. ¿Qué fruto se hace en dos o tres días que están en esas casitas, que no le haga tanto el padre fray Antonio? Porque no han salido, cuando se tornan como estaban, y es ponerse en mil peligros.

2. La señora doña Juana tiene muy creído que vuestra paternidad hace lo que yo le suplico. Plega a Dios que en esto sea así. Ha estado su merced acá tres días, aunque no la gocé todo lo que quisiera, porque tuvo muchas visitas, en especial del canónigo; quedaron grandes amigos. Yo le digo a vuestra paternidad que es de las mejores partes las que Dios la dio, y talento y condición, que he visto pocas semejantes en mi vida, y aun creo ninguna; una llaneza y claridad, por lo que yo soy perdida. Hartas ventajas hace a su hijo en esto. Grandísimamente me consolara de estar adonde la pudiera tratar muchas veces. Tan conocidas estábamos como si toda la vida nos hubiéramos tratado.

3. Mucho, dice, se holgó acá. Quiso Dios que se hallase una posada cerca de una señora viuda que estaba con solas sus mujeres. Estuvo muy a su gusto y aquí junto, que lo tuve a gran dicha. De acá se llevaba aderezado lo que había de comer, que me dio la vida lo que vuestra paternidad me mandó que poseyese para no estar atada a cosa de convento, que me fuera harto trabajo. Con no ser todo nada, se hizo más a mi gusto.

4. En gracia me cae decir vuestra paternidad que le abriese el velo; parece que no me conoce: quisiérale yo abrir las entrañas. Estuvo hasta el postrer día la señora doña Juana su hija con ella, que me pareció harto bonita y me hace gran lástima verla entre aquellas doncellas, porque en hecho de verdad, según decía, tiene más trabajo que acá. De buena gana le diera yo el hábito con el angelito de su hermana, que está que no hay más que ver de bonita y gorda. La señora doña Juana no acaba de espantarse de verla. Periquito, su hermano, que vino acá, en todo su seso no la acababa de conocer. Es toda la recreación que acá tengo. Harto dije a la señora doña Juana ya al postrer día. Parece estaba algo movida, según me dijo Ana de Zurita, que la dijo que había estado aquella noche así y que no estaba muy fuera de ello, que ella se vería más. Dios lo haga. Vuestra paternidad se lo encomiende, que como se le parece en harto, mucho la querría conmigo.

5. Como vio la señora doña Juana el contento y trato de todo, va determinada de procurar con brevedad enviar a la señora María a Valladolid, y aun creo estaba arrepentida de haberlo quitado a la señora doña Adriana. Muy contenta fue, a lo que me parece, y creo no es nada fingidora.

6. Ayer me escribió su merced una carta con mil requiebros, que dice que

no sentía acá su pena y tristeza. Hánmela rompido con otras (que han sido estos dos días sin cuento las que me han venido, que me tienen tonta), que harto me pesó, que se la quería enviar a vuestra paternidad.

7. El día que fue de acá, dice que le había faltado la terciana al señor Lucas Gracián y que está ya bueno. ¡Oh, qué bonita cosa es Tomás de Gracián! Mucho me contenta; también vino acá. Hoy he escrito a su merced cómo iba vuestra paternidad. Bueno estaba.

8. Yo, pensando cuál querría más vuestra paternidad de las dos, hallo que la señora doña Juana tiene marido y otros hijos que querer, y la pobre Lorencia no tiene cosa en la tierra sino este padre. Plega a Dios se le guarde, amén, que yo harto la consuelo. Díceme que José le ha tornado a asegurar y con esto pasa su vida, aunque con trabajos y sin alivio para ellos.

9. Vengamos a lo del capítulo, que vienen contentísimos, y yo lo estoy muy mucho de cuán bien se ha hecho, gloria sea a Dios. ¡A usadas que no queda vuestra paternidad sin alabanzas grandes de esta vez! Todo viene de su mano; y aun quizá hacen mucho las oraciones, como vuestra paternidad dice.

10. Hame contentado en extremo el celar las casas, que es muy buena traza y provechosa. Mucho he puesto con él que ponga mucho en los ejercicios de manos, que importa infinitísimo. Dije que lo escribiría a vuestra paternidad, porque él dice que no se trató en capítulo. Yo le dije que estaba en las constituciones y regla, que a qué iba sino a hacerlo guardar. También me contentó, tanto que no lo creía, el haber expelido de la orden los que echaron, y poderse hacer es una gran cosa.

11. También me contentó mucho la traza que se daba de procurar la provincia por vía de nuestro padre general con cuantas maneras pudiéramos; porque es una guerra intolerable andar con disgusto del prelado. Si se puede hacer a costa de dineros, Dios los dará, y dense a los compañeros, y por amor de Dios vuestra paternidad ponga diligencia en que no se detengan en ir. No lo tome por cosa accesoria, pues es lo principal; y si ese prior de la Peñuela le conoce tanto, él iría bien con el padre Mariano, y cuando no se pudiese acabar nada, hágase con el papa; mas harto mejor sería estotro y es ahora bonísima coyuntura. Y visto lo que se ve en Matusalén, no sé qué aguardamos, que no es tener acá nada y quedarnos al mejor tiempo perdidos.

12. Sepa que un clérigo amigo mío me dijo este día (que trata conmigo cosas de su alma) que tiene por muy cierto que Gilberto ha de morir muy presto—y aun me dijo que este año—y que de otras personas que lo había entendido otras veces, que jamás erraba. Ello es cosa posible, aunque no hay que hacer caso de esto; mas como no es imposible, es bien que vuestra paternidad traiga delante que puede ser, para los negocios que nos cumplen; y así trate las cosas de la visita como cosa que ha de durar poco. Fray Pedro Hernández para todo lo que quiso ejecutar en la Encarnación, hacía por mano de fray Ángel, y él se estaba desde lejos, y no por eso dejaba de ser visitador y de hacer su hecho. Siempre me acuerdo lo que ese provincial hizo

con vuestra reverencia cuando estaban en su casa; que no querría, si fuese posible, se lo desagradeciese.

13. Quéjanse que se rige vuestra paternidad por el padre Evangelista; también es bien que vaya con advertencia, que no somos tan perfectos que no podría ser tener con algunos pasión y con otros afición, y es menester mirarlo todo.

14. La priora de Malagón está algo mejor, gloria a Dios, aunque hay poco que hacer caso de esto, según los médicos dicen. Mucho me espanté que quisiese vuestra paternidad dejar en mí—¡ni hablar!—en la ida yo a Malagón, por muchas causas; lo uno, que no hay para qué, que yo no tengo tanta salud para curar enfermas ni tanta caridad; para la casa, digo la obra, mucho más hago aquí, que las monjas estando allí Antonio Ruiz, no tienen qué hacer; y aunque hubiera gran ocasión, como vuestra paternidad ve, es a mal tiempo.

15. Otra cosa buena. Dice que ni me lo manda ni le parece es bien que vaya, y que haga yo lo que mejor me pareciere. ¡Harto buena perfección fuera pensar yo que había de ser mejor mi parecer que el de vuestra paternidad! Como me dijeron que ni estaba con sentido, ni para hablar, que harto encarecieron, envié a decir que tuviese cuenta con la casa Juana Bautista, que a mi parecer era la mejor; porque se me hace tanto de mal traer las monjas de tan lejos hasta más no poder, que voy deteniendo; y escribí a la priora para que, si estuviese para leer la carta, que aquello era lo que me parecía; mas que si le parecía otra cosa, que ella podría poner la que quisiese, porque esto es de orden.

16. No quiso a Juana Bautista y puso a Beatriz de Jesús y dijo era muy mejor; y quizás lo será, mas a mí no me lo parece. Tampoco quiso fuese Isabel de Jesús maestra de novicias, que están tantas que me tienen con harta pena; y ésta, que lo ha sido, no ha sacado malas novicias, que aunque no es avisada, es buena monja. Tampoco le pareció ni al licenciado, sino Beatriz lo tiene todo y ella está harto fatigada. Si no lo hiciere bien, se podrá dar a otras, y para lo de casa mejor es cualquiera, a mi parecer, que traerla de fuera, mientras Dios guarda la priora. Bien vi yo que vuestra paternidad lo había hecho por darla contento. Mas si me diera alguna tentación de ir, harto recia cosa fuera; porque aun no lo he pensado, me parece, ir a una parte, cuando lo sabe todo el mundo; que por mi querer yo digo a vuestra paternidad que gustara en parte de estar allí algunos días.

17. Ayer estuvo acá doña Luisa y pienso acabaré con ella que dé cuatro mil ducados este año (que no había de dar sino dos mil) y dice el maestro mayor que si esto da, que de esta Navidad en un año labrará adonde puedan estar las monjas, digo que podrán estar en este tiempo. En fin, se parece bien que guía Dios a vuestra paternidad, que harto ha de aprovechar mi quedada aquí; y aun para mi contento, que harto me lo da no me ver con parientes y siendo priora en Ávila.

18. Extraña es mi condición, que como veo que no le hizo a vuestra

paternidad al caso ver que había gana de no estar aquí para dejarme, me
ha dado un contento grandísimo y libertad para mostrar mis deseos y decir
cuando me parece, de ver que no hace caso de mi parecer.

19. A su maestra de Isabel hice que escribiese a vuestra paternidad,
porque si no se le acuerda su nombre suya es esa carta. ¡Oh, qué hermosita se
va haciendo! ¡Cómo engorda y qué bonita es! Dios la haga santa y a vuestra
paternidad me guarde mucho más que a mí.

20. Perdóneme el haberme alargado y tenga paciencia, pues se está allá y
yo acá.

Estoy buena y hoy es víspera de San Mateo.

21. Esto de Roma suplico a vuestra paternidad se dé prisa; no aguarden al
verano, pues es buen tiempo ahora, y crea que conviene.

Indigna sierva y súbdita de vuestra paternidad.

Teresa de Jesús

22. Con esas monjas no se mate vuestra paternidad, pues ha de ser por
poco tiempo, según dice Matusalén, y aun las aves nocturnas así lo tienen,
que dicen que dijo a Peralta que se diese prisa, que de aquí a dos meses
viniese, y aun dicen que será cierto él ser el todo. ¡Oh, si viese yo nuestro
negocio hecho! Y sea enhorabuena y sáquenos Su Majestad de este sobresalto
a todos.

To Father Jerónimo Gracián, Seville
Toledo, 20 September 1576

1. Jesus. The grace of the Holy Spirit be with your paternity. My Father,
don't think that you can work everything out all at once. How much can you
accomplish in two or three days in those little houses that Fray Antonio[32]
couldn't do in all the time he was there? As soon as you're gone, they'll[33] go
back to behaving just as before, and by going there you are exposing yourself
to a thousand dangers.

2. Doña Juana[34] is completely convinced that you do whatever I ask of
you. God grant that in this case she is right. She was here for three days,
although I was not able to enjoy her company as much as I wished because
she had so many other visitors, especially the canon.[35] They've become great
friends. I assure your paternity that God has given her wonderful qualities—
talent and good character like I've rarely ever seen before in my life, perhaps
never. Such simplicity and candor! I'm completely taken with her. In these
traits she greatly surpasses her son. I only wish I lived where I could converse
with her more often. We got along so well that you would have thought we'd
known each other our whole lives.

3. She says she really enjoyed herself here. God willed that she find
lodging with a widowed lady who lives alone with her maidservants. It was
very much to her liking and close by, which she thought was fortunate. They
prepared her meals here and took them to her, and it was really lucky your

paternity told me to keep some money aside so I wouldn't have to depend on the convent, which would have been awful for me. Not that it was such a lot, but this way I had the freedom to do things as I like.

4. I found it amusing that your paternity told me to lift up my veil for her.[36] It seems you don't know me. I would have opened the depths of my soul to her. Her daughter Doña Juana was here with her until the last day. I found her to be really lovely, and I'm sorry to see her among those other young ladies,[37] since, to tell you the truth, judging from what she says, she's having more trouble there than she would have here. I would be happy to give her the habit along with that little angel, her sister,[38] who is just as pretty and plump as can be. Doña Juana was so surprised when she saw her. And Periquito, her brother, smart as he is, he didn't even recognize her when he came. She is my greatest source of pleasure here. The last day Doña Juana was here I told her all about Isabel. It seems she was deeply moved, according to what Ana de Zurita[39] told me. Doña Juana told Doña Ana that she had been thinking about it all night and was close to making a decision, but that she needed a little more time. May God make it happen. Your paternity should pray for this. Since she is so like you, I would love to have her with me.

5. Since Doña Juana saw how happy and well run the convent is, she has decided to try to send Doña María[40] to Valladolid soon, and I think she's sorry for having dissuaded Doña Adriana[41] from going there. From what I could tell, she left here very satisfied, and I don't think she's at all hypocritical.

6. Yesterday she wrote me a very affectionate letter saying that while she was here she didn't feel any distress or sadness. They tore it up, along with some others—it's just that during the last two days so many have come, it's making me crazy—but I was really sad because I wanted to send it to you.

7. The day she left here she told me that Señor Lucas Gracián[42] had finally got over the tertian fever and was feeling well. Oh, what a lovely young man Tomás de Gracián[43] is. I really like him. He was also here. Today I wrote to him and told him you were doing well.

8. I was thinking today about which of us loves your paternity more. It seems to me that Doña Juana has a husband and other children to love, but poor Lorencia[44] has nothing more in the world but this padre. May God watch over him for her, amen, for I am consoling her as much as I can. She tells me that José[45] has reassured her, and that's how she keeps going in spite of unrelenting troubles with no remedy in sight.

9. Now let's talk about the chapter meeting.[46] The representatives have come back very happy, and I am delighted with how well they have done, glory be to God. As usual, you have received great praise. It all comes from God's hand; and also, perhaps, the prayers help as well, as your paternity says.

10. I'm especially happy about the appointment of a zelator[47] for the

houses, which is a good and very beneficial step. I stressed to him[48] the
importance of manual labor. I told him I'd write to your paternity about
it because the chapter did not deal with this subject. I told him that it was
in the Constitutions and the rule, and that he should make sure it was
practiced. I was also delighted beyond words that they had expelled the ones
they did from the order. It is very important to be able to do this.

11. I was also very happy about the steps taken to try to become a
separate province by appealing to our father general,[49] for it is an unbearable
burden to have to deal with the displeasure of the prelate. If our goal can be
accomplished with money, God will provide it. Let the men going to Rome
have it, and for the love of God, make every effort so that they will not delay
in going. Don't take this as a matter of secondary importance, for it's the
key thing. And if that prior of La Peñuela knows him[50] so well, he should
accompany Father Mariano.[51] And if they can't get anywhere with the
negotiations, they should go to the pope. But it would be much better to take
the first route, and now is the most propitious time. In view of what's going
on with Methuselah,[52] I don't know what we're waiting for. It's like having
nothing concrete here, and then suddenly discovering that we are lost.

12. I want you to know that a priest friend of mine, who discusses
matters of his soul with me, told me today that he's sure that Gilberto[53] will
die soon, in fact, within the year, and that his presentiments are never wrong.
This is possible, although one shouldn't put too much stock in such things.
But since it's not impossible, for the sake of our affairs your paternity should
keep in mind that it could happen and consider visitation issues as short
term. Pedro Fernández[54] carried out all his business at Encarnación through
Fray Ángel[55] and just observed from afar, and he was no less the visitator[56]
for all that, nor did he exercise any less authority. I always remember how
that provincial[57] treated you when you were staying at their house. If you can
avoid it, I wouldn't want you to show any ingratitude.

13. I hear complaints that your paternity is being directed by Father
Evangelista.[58] You should be careful about this. We're not so perfect that we
can avoid feeling dislike for some and affection for others.

14. The prioress of Malagón[59] is somewhat better, glory to God,
although that doesn't mean much, according to the doctors. I was stunned
that you wanted to leave the decision to me about going to Malagón, since
it's out of the question for a lot of reasons. First, there would be no sense to
it, since I'm not healthy or charitable enough to care for the sick. And then,
as for the house, I mean the work on it, I accomplish much more here. Since
Antonio Ruiz is there, the nuns have nothing to worry about. And even if
they really needed me, as your paternity can see, this isn't a good time.

15. Another good thing: you say that you're not ordering me to go and
you don't even think it's a good idea for me to go. You're just leaving it to
me to do whatever I want. That would be some sign of perfection, for me
to think my opinion better than yours. When they told me the prioress was

not fully conscious and couldn't even speak, really making the situation sound bad, I sent word that the direction of the house should be taken over by Juana Bautista,[60] who in my opinion is the best choice. It's so much trouble for me to transfer nuns from far away that I avoid doing so whenever possible. I wrote to the prioress so that she would know my opinion, just in case she was well enough to read the letter. But if she thought otherwise, she could choose someone else, in accordance with the rule of the order.

16. She didn't want Juana Bautista and instead chose Beatriz de Jesús,[61] who she said is much better. That may be so, but it doesn't seem that way to me. Nor did she want Isabel de Jesús[62] to be novice mistress. They have so many novices that I'm worried. Isabel has experience and her novices have turned out pretty well. She's not too shrewd, but she's a good nun. The Licenciado[63] wasn't in favor of Isabel either. Instead, Beatriz has wound up with everything, and she is exhausted. If she can't manage, there are others who can pitch in. Anyone from this house would be better, in my opinion, than someone brought in from outside, as long as God preserves the life of the prioress. I have seen that your paternity did everything possible to please her. If I should be tempted to go, it would be really hard. No sooner do I think about going somewhere, than everyone knows it. If it's really up to me, I can tell your paternity that I wouldn't mind spending a few days there.

17. Doña Luisa was here yesterday, and I think I'll get her to give four thousand ducats this year (she had pledged to give only two thousand). The construction manager says that if she gives this amount, that by Christmas of next year the nuns will be able to live there. It seems that God is guiding your paternity, for my stay here will be beneficial, and even brings me happiness, especially since I don't have to put up with relatives or be prioress in Ávila anymore.

18. My character is strange. When I saw that your paternity didn't mind leaving me here, where I had no wish to stay, I felt great joy and freedom to express my thoughts and desires, knowing you don't pay any attention at all to what I think.

19. I told [your sister] Isabel's novice mistress to write to you. In case you don't remember her name, the enclosed letter is for you. Isabel is becoming so pretty. She's getting so plump and cute. May God make her a saint and watch over your paternity more than he watches over me.

20. Forgive me for making this so long, and be patient with me, since you are down there and I'm up here.

I'm well and today is the vigil of the feast of St. Matthew.

21. About the matter of sending men to Rome, I beg your paternity to hurry. Don't wait for summer. The weather is fine now, and we need to move ahead with this.

Your paternity's unworthy servant and subject,

Teresa of Jesus

22. Don't torment yourself over those nuns.[64] According to what Methuselah says, you won't be a visitator down there for long. And the owls[65] think this too, since they say he[66] told Peralta[67] to hurry up and get back within two months, and they also say that he'll take charge of everything. Oh, if only this matter were concluded! What a great thing it would be if His Majesty would deliver us all from all this distress.

4

A la Madre María de San José. Sevilla
Toledo, 1 y 2 de marzo de 1577

1. Jesús. La gracia del Espíritu Santo sea con vuestra reverencia, hija mía. Con tan buenas nuevas y tantos regalos como ahora me envió, razón fuera alargarme mucho, al menos diérame harto contento, sino que, como la escribí ayer, el trabajo de este invierno de cartas ha venido a enflaquecer la cabeza de suerte, que he estado bien mala. Mejor estoy harto, y con todo, casi nunca escribo de mi letra, que dicen es menester para sanar del todo.

2. ¡Oh, lo que me holgué con tan lindas cosas como me envió por el administrador!, que lo que trabaja en esto de Malagón y en cuanto se me ofrece, no lo puede creer. Y no piense que es menester poco para la buena de la obra, que se ofrecen mil cosas con los oficiales. Dile el relicario pequeño. Entrambos están muy lindos, y todavía es mejor el grande, en especial como acá se aderezó, que venía quebrado el viril, como la he escrito. Echóse uno muy bueno. El pie venía torcido y púsose un molde de hierro. Siempre lo había de hacer así. También le di la jarra, que era la más graciosa que he visto, digo la calderica. ¡No piense que por traer jerguilla es tanto el mal que había de beber en cosa tan buena! También le di el pomo como venía. Halo tenido en mucho. Es hombre de autoridad. En fin, desde allá ha ayudado a su casa de Malagón.

3. El agua de azahar no me dejaban dar, porque le da la vida a la priora y aun a mí me hace provecho, y no lo había. A su madre de la portuguesa pida un poco en mi nombre y nos lo envíe; por caridad, que con esta condición lo envíe.

4. ¡Oh, qué alegre estoy de que se haya pagado eso de la casa! Mas hasta que sea profesa esa monja aun no nos habíamos de holgar tanto. Verdad es que, cuando no fuese, lo dará Dios por otra parte. Mucho le pidan se sirva de quitarme esto de la cabeza. Allá le envié una relación de la ocasión que fue, digo de alguna parte, con el correo que se fue hoy.

5. Su manera de oración me contenta mucho. Y el ver que la tiene y que la hace Dios merced, no es falta de humildad, con que entienda que no es suyo, como lo hace, y se da ello a entender cuando la oración es de Dios. Harto le alabo de que vaya tan bien y procuraré dar las albricias que pide. Ruegue a Dios sea yo tal que me oiga.

6. En la de Beatriz bueno es; mas lo más que pudiere dé de mano a esas cosas en pláticas y en todo. Sepa que va mucho en las prioras.

7. No trató aquí San Jerónimo de eso, porque luego la atajó la priora y riñó, y así calló; y ya ve que cuando estuve yo allá tampoco pasaba mucho adelante. No sé si hicimos mal en que saliese de entre nosotras. Plega a Dios que suceda en bien.

8. Mire, si hallaran el papel que la priora las otras, qué cosa fuera. Dios le perdone a quien la manda escribir. Nuestro padre quisiera la escribiera con rigor en ese caso. Lea esa carta que la escribo, y si le pareciere, envíesela.

9. Hácelo en extremo bien en no consentir que hablen con nadie. De Beas me escribe la priora que solos los pecados tratan con uno, y se confiesan todas en media hora (y me dice que así habían de hacer en todos cabos) y andan consoladísimas y con gran amor con la priora, como lo tratan con ella.

10. Podrá vuestra reverencia decir que, pues en este caso tengo alguna experiencia, que para qué han de buscar los que quizá no tienen tanta, sino escribirme, y en esa tierra conviene más que en ninguna. Y a San Francisco haga que dé carne a ésa en saliendo cuaresma, y no la deje ayunar.

11. Quisiera saber qué es esto que dice que le hace Dios tanta fuerza, que no se declara. Mire el trabajo andar ahora con esos llantos delante de las otras, y que la vean escribir a cada paso.

12. Procure eso que escribió, y enviármelo, y quítela la esperanza de que ha de tratar con nadie sino con nuestro padre, que la han destruido. Entienda que ahí se entiende aun menos de lo que vuestra reverencia piensa este lenguaje (aunque siendo en confesión con el padre Acosta, no puede venir daño); mas yo sé bien que a ella menos que a nadie conviene. Bien está eso que se manda en Paterna de darles alguna anchura, aunque valiera más no haber comenzado, sino lo que había de ser; que en estas cosas de reforma, si con voces alcanzan algo, luego les parece así lo han de alcanzar todo. Muy bien hizo en avisarles anduviesen en comunidad.

13. No he dado las cartas ni relicario a la señora doña Luisa (porque no estaba aquí y vino antier) hasta que aplaquen las visitas. Encomiende a Dios a doña Guiomar y a ella, que tienen hartos trabajos.

14. Como no escribo de una vez ésta, no sé si me he de olvidar de responder algo.

15. Estos cerrojos llevan, que como ellos están acá en las rejas del coro y no me parece son menester más pulidos (aunque yo veo que ella no se contentará) mas pase como acá que no se tienen por más groseras, y mejor es cerrojillos que otra cosa, que yo no entiendo qué cerraduras pide.

16. Los crucifijos se están haciendo. Creo costarán a ducado.

17. Todas se le encomiendan, y Isabel se holgó mucho con los brinquiños y jerga. Dios se lo pague, que yo harto vestida estoy. ¿Piensa que no me pesa de no tener qué la enviar? Sí, por cierto. Mas es cosa extraña la esterilidad de este lugar, si no es de membrillos en su tiempo, y harto mejores lo hay allá.

18. Con las especias se holgaron mucho, y con la catamaca. No me dejaron enviarlo, que harto lo quisiera, porque tienen gran necesidad muchas.

19. Ahí van esas respuestas, que envié a mi hermano y preguntar esa pregunta y concertaron responder en San José y que allá lo juzgasen las monjas los que ahí van; y el obispo hallóse presente y mandó que me lo enviasen que lo juzgase yo, cuando aun para leerlo no estaba la negra cabeza. Muéstrelo al padre prior y a Nicolao; mas hales de decir lo que pasa, y que no lean la sentencia hasta que vean las respuestas; y si pudiere, tórnelo a enviar para que gustara nuestro padre (que así hicieron en Ávila para que se lo enviase), aunque no sea éste camino del arriero.

20. Esa carta le envío que me escribió mi hermano (y de esas mercedes que le hace Dios son muchas las que me escribe, ésa hallé a mano); porque creo se holgará, pues le quiere bien. Rómpala luego y quédese con Dios, que no acabaría con ella y háceme mal. Su Majestad me la haga santa.

21. Ahora me dan una carta de nuestro padre escrita desde Málaga, de quince días fecha; mañana los hace. Bueno está, gloria a Dios.

Son hoy dos de marzo.

22. A todos me encomiende, y envíeme a decir de la salud de fray Bartolomé.

Sierva de vuestra reverencia

Teresa de Jesús

23. Agradézcame ir ésta de mi letra, que ni aun para San José no lo he hecho.

24. Ayer escribí a vuestra reverencia y a nuestro padre por la vía del correo. Por eso no lo hago ahora.

To Mother María de San José, Sevilla
Toledo, 1–2 March 1577

1. Jesus. May the grace of the Holy Spirit be with your reverence, my daughter. With all the good news and all the gifts you sent me, I should write you a long letter; at least, I'd really like to. But I wrote to you yesterday, and the hard work of letter-writing this winter has weakened my head to the point that I was really ill.[68] I'm much better now, but even so, I almost never write in my own hand, for they say I shouldn't if I want to recover completely.

2. Oh, I just loved the beautiful things you sent me through the overseer.[69] You wouldn't believe how much work he does for the convent in Malagón. Whatever I need, he provides. And don't think it's a small thing to keep the construction going smoothly; there are a thousand things to attend to with the workmen. I gave him the small reliquary. Both of them are very lovely, but the larger one is better because of the way they fixed it up here. As I wrote to you earlier, it arrived with the glass broken. The new one they put in is very nice. The base was twisted, so we had a new one made, cast

in iron. We should have done this in the first place. I also gave him the jar, I mean the little pot, which is just the cutest one I've ever seen. Don't think that just because I have to wear a habit of finer material that I have to drink from such a fancy vessel![70] I also gave him the little jar of pomade[71] just as it was. He really appreciated it. He's an upright man. Well, from down there in Seville you've helped the house in Malagón.

3. They wouldn't let me give away the water scented with orange blossoms because it's good for the prioress's health, and it helps me, too,[72] and we'd been out of it. Ask the mother of the Portuguese nun[73] for some more in my name and send it to us. Do it out of charity, that's the condition.

4. I'm just thrilled you paid off the debt on the house. But until that nun is professed we shouldn't rejoice too much. But the truth is that even if she doesn't profess, God will provide another way. Please pray to him to take away my headaches. Today by mail carrier I sent you an account of what brought them on, at least in part.[74]

5. I'm delighted with your way of praying. And recognizing that you have this gift and that God shows you favor is not a lack of humility, provided you understand that it comes from him, not yourself. That's how we know that the prayer is really from God. I praise him that things are going so well for you, and I'll try to rejoice as you ask me to. Pray to God that I can be the kind of person that he will hear.

6. With regard to Beatriz,[75] her prayer is fine, but, as much as possible, in conversation and elsewhere avoid paying too much attention to these things. You know all this depends a lot on the prioresses.

7. San Jerónimo didn't make such a fuss here[76] because the prioress immediately cut her off and scolded her, and so she kept quiet. And you know, she never carried on very much while I was there, either. I don't know if we did the wrong thing by letting her go away.[77] I hope to God that everything will turn out all right.

8. Just think what would have happened if someone other than the prioress had found that page![78] May God pardon the one who told her to write everything down. Our *padre*[79] would like me to write her a firm letter about this. Read the enclosed letter that I wrote her, and if seems alright to you, send it to her.

9. You're doing the right thing by not letting them talk to anyone. The Beas prioress[80] writes to me that the nuns speak only of their sins with the confessor, and they're all done in half an hour. (She says it should be done like that everywhere.) And the nuns are greatly consoled (by these confessions) and have great love for their prioress, in whom they confide.

10. You could ask them why they don't write to me, since I have experience in these matters, instead of going and asking someone who doesn't have as much as I do. And for a matter like this it would be especially appropriate. And make sure that San Francisco eats meat as soon as Lent is over; don't let her fast.

11. I'd like to know what she means when she says that God uses great force over her. She doesn't explain. It's a real nuisance that she goes around weeping in front of the others, and that they see her writing all the time.

12. Try to get a hold of what she wrote and send it to me. And put to rest any hope she may have of discussing this with anyone but our *padre*, because talking with confessors is just what got her into this mess. Be aware that there this language[81] is understood less than you think (although if it is used with Father Acosta[82] in confession, no harm can come from it). But well I know that it is less fitting for her than for anyone. It's a good thing that the Paterna nuns are allowed certain leeway, although it would have been better if from the start they had required only what is obligatory.[83] In these matters of reform, if they succeed once in getting what they want by shouting, they think that they can get whatever else they want in the same way. You did the right thing by telling them to live in community.

13. I have not given the letters or the reliquary to Doña Luisa[84] because she was away and returned only the day before yesterday. I am waiting for all the visits to die down. Pray for her and for Doña Guiomar,[85] since both of them have plenty of troubles.

14. Since I'm not writing this letter all at once, I don't know whether I've forgotten to answer any of your questions.

15. These bolts I'm sending are like the ones that are in the grille in the choir, and I don't think they need to be any shinier (although I suppose you won't be satisfied with them). But use them anyhow, as they do here, for these nuns don't consider themselves any less elegant than you, and a little bolt should do just fine, although I don't know what kind of locks you want.

16. The crucifixes are being made. I think they'll cost a ducat.

17. All the nuns send their regards, and Isabel[86] was delighted with the candy and cloth. May God reward you. I myself have plenty of clothes. Do you think it doesn't make me sad to have nothing to send you? Of course, it does. But the barrenness of this area is so extraordinary, nothing grows here except quinces, when they are in season, and even then, the ones you get there are much better.

18. Everyone was delighted with the spices and the catamaca.[87] They didn't allow me to send any of it away, and I would really have liked to because a lot of nuns need it.

19. Enclosed are the answers to the question I asked my brother.[88] The respondents decided to submit their answers to the nuns of San José, who were to judge them. Then the bishop, who was present, commanded that they be sent to me for judgment, just when my head was in such a terrible state that I could hardly read them. Show them to the Father Prior and to Nicolao.[89] Explain to them what this is all about, and tell them not to read the judgment until they've read the responses. And if you can, send them back so that our padre can enjoy them (for that's why they sent them to me from Ávila), even though this might not be on the muleteer's route.

20. I'm sending you this letter that my brother sent me (about the favors God grants him; he writes me a lot of letters about this, but this one was near at hand), because I think you'll like it, since you're so fond of him. Tear it up afterward, and God be with you, for I'll never finish this and writing is bad for me. May His Majesty make you a saint.

21. Now they've just given me a letter our *padre* wrote from Málaga fifteen days ago, I mean, from tomorrow. He is well, glory to God.

Today is March 2.

22. Remember me to everyone, and let me know about Fray Bartolomé's health.[90]

Your reverence's servant,
Teresa de Jesús

23. Be grateful I wrote this out myself, because even to the nuns at San José de Ávila, I haven't written in my own hand.

24. Yesterday I wrote to you and to our *padre* through the mail carrier. That's why I'm not doing it now.

5

Al rey D. Felipe II. Madrid
Ávila, 4 de diciembre de 1577

1. Jesús. La gracia del Espíritu Santo sea siempre con vuestra majestad, amén. Yo tengo muy creído que ha querido Nuestra Señora valerse de vuestra majestad y tomarle por amparo para el remedio de su orden, y así no puedo dejar de acudir a vuestra majestad con las cosas de ella. Por amor de Nuestro Señor suplico a vuestra majestad perdone tanto atrevimiento.

2. Bien creo tiene vuestra majestad noticia de cómo estas monjas de la Encarnación han procurado llevarme allá, pensando habría algún remedio para librarse de los frailes, que cierto les son gran estorbo para el recogimiento y religión que pretenden, y de la falta de ella que ha habido allí en aquella casa tienen toda la culpa. Ellas están en esto muy engañadas, porque mientras estuviesen sujetas a que ellos las confiesen y visiten no es de ningún provecho mi ida allá—al menos, que dure—y así lo dije siempre al visitador dominico, y él lo tenía bien entendido.

3. Para algún remedio, mientras esto Dios hacía, puse allí en una casa un fraile descalzo, tan gran siervo de Nuestro Señor que las tiene bien edificadas, con otro compañero, y espantada esta ciudad del grandísimo provecho que allí ha hecho, y así le tienen por un santo, y en mi opinión lo es y ha sido toda la vida.

4. Informado de esto el nuncio pasado, y del daño que hacían los «del paño» por larga información que se le llevó de los de la ciudad, envió un mandamiento con descomunión para que los tornasen allí (que los calzados los habían echado con hartos denuestos y escándalo de la ciudad) y que so

pena de descomunión no fuese allá ninguno «del paño» a negociar, ni a decir misa, ni a confesar, sino los descalzos y clérigos. Con esto ha estado bien la casa hasta que murió el nuncio, que han tornado los calzados y así torna la inquietud, sin haber mostrado por donde lo pueden hacer.

5. Y ahora, un fraile que vino a absolver a las monjas, las ha hecho tantas molestias y tan sin orden ni justicia, que están bien afligidas y no libres de las penas que antes tenían, según me han dicho. Y sobre todo hales quitado éste los confesores (que dicen le han hecho vicario provincial, y debe ser porque tiene más partes para hacer mártires que otros) y tiénelos presos en su monasterio, y descerrajaron las celdas, y tomáronles en lo que tenían los papeles.

6. Está todo el lugar bien escandalizado cómo no siendo prelado, ni mostrando por donde hace esto (que ellos están sujetos al comisario apostólico), se atreven tanto, estando este lugar tan cerca de adonde está vuestra majestad, que ni parece temen que haya justicia ni Dios.

7. A mí me tiene muy lastimada verlos en sus manos, que ha días que lo desean, y tuviera por mejor que estuvieran entre moros, porque quizá tuvieran más piedad. Y este fraile tan siervo de Dios está tan flaco de lo mucho que ha padecido, que temo su vida.

8. Por amor de Nuestro Señor suplico a vuestra majestad mande que con brevedad le rescaten, y que se dé orden cómo no padezcan tanto con los «del paño» estos pobres descalzos todos, que ellos no hacen sino callar y padecer, y ganan mucho; mas dase escándalo al pueblo.

9. Que este mismo que está aquí tuvo este verano preso en Toledo a fray Antonio de Jesús, que es un bendito viejo, el primero de todos, sin ninguna causa, y así andan diciendo los han de perder, porque lo tiene mandado el Tostado.

10. Sea Dios bendito, que los que habían de ser medio para quitar que fuese ofendido, les sean para tantos pecados, y cada día lo harán peor. Si vuestra majestad no manda poner remedio, no sé en qué se ha de parar, porque ningún otro tenemos en la tierra.

11. Plega a Nuestro Señor nos dure muchos años. Yo espero en Él nos hará esta merced, pues se ve tan solo de quien mire por su honra. Continuamente se lo suplicamos todas estas siervas de vuestra majestad y yo.

Fecha en Ávila, en este convento de San José, a 4 de diciembre de setenta y siete.

Indigna sierva y súbdita de vuestra majestad.

Teresa de Jesús, carmelita

To the King Don Philip II
Avila, 4 December 1577

1. Jesus. The grace of the Holy Spirit be with your majesty, amen. I strongly believe that Our Lady has chosen you to protect and help her order,[91] which is why I cannot fail to have recourse to you regarding her

affairs. For the love of our Lord, I beg you to forgive me for so much boldness.

2. I am sure your majesty has received news of how the nuns at the Encarnación tried to bring me there,[92] thinking to find some means of freeing themselves from the friars, who are certainly an obstacle to the recollection and religious observance that the sisters desire.[93] And they [the friars] are entirely at fault for the lack of adherence to the rule that has troubled that house. The nuns are very much misguided in their wish that I go there, for I would be of no help as long as they are subject to the [Calced] friars as confessors and visitators. This is what I always told the Dominican visitator,[94] and he understood very well.

3. During the time God allowed this situation to exist, I tried to provide a remedy by placing a Discalced friar in a house next to them, along with a companion friar.[95] He is so great a servant of our Lord that the nuns are truly edified, and this city is amazed by the remarkable amount of good he has done there. In fact, everyone considers him a saint, and in my opinion he is one and has been one all his life.

4. The inhabitants of the city sent the previous nuncio[96] a long report informing him of what was happening and of the harm that the friars of the cloth[97] were doing, and he responded by giving orders under pain of excommunication that the confessors be restored to their house (for the Calced friars had driven them from the city heaping abuse on them and causing great scandal). And he also ordered that no friar of the cloth under pain of excommunication go to the Encarnación for business purposes, to say Mass, or to hear confessions, but only the Discalced friars and secular clergy.[98] As a result, everything ran smoothly until the nuncio died. Then the Calced friars returned without demonstrating by what right they did so, and the disturbances started up again.

5. And now a friar[99] who came to absolve the nuns has really upset them, for he acted so arbitrarily and unjustly that he left them deeply distressed and still bound by the same penalties as before, according to what I have been told. And worst of all, he has taken away their confessors. (They say that he has been made the vicar provincial, and this is probably true because he is more capable than the others of making martyrs.) And he is holding these confessors captive in his monastery after having forced his way into their cells and confiscating their papers.[100]

6. The whole city is truly scandalized, since he is not a prelate nor did he show any evidence of the authority on which he acted. (These confessors are subject to the apostolic commissary.)[101] Those friars were so brazen, even though this city is very close to where your majesty resides, that it doesn't seem they fear either the law or God.

7. I am deeply troubled to see these [Discalced] confessors in their hands. The Calced have been wanting to seize them for days. I think [these confessors] would be better off if they were held by Moors, who perhaps

would show them more compassion. And this one friar who is so great a servant of God is so weak from all his suffering that I fear for his life.

8. I beg your majesty for the love of our Lord to issue orders at once for the friars of the cloth to set him free, and command them not to subject these poor Discalced friars to so much hardship. The Discalced just suffer and keep silent, and by doing so gain a great deal.[102] But the people are scandalized by what is being done to them.

9. This past summer in Toledo, without any reason, the same superior took prisoner Fray Antonio de Jesús—a blessed old man, who was the first Discalced friar.[103] They go around saying that they have orders from Tostado[104] to destroy them all.

10. May God be blessed! Those who should be vehicles for preventing offenses against God have become the cause of so many sins, and each day it gets worse. If your majesty does not provide us with some remedy, I don't know where things will end up, because we have no other help on earth.

11. May it please our Lord that for our sake you live many years. I hope in him that he will grant us this favor. He is so alone, for there are few who look after his honor. All these servants of your majesty's and I ask this of him continually.

Written in Ávila, in the convent of San José, 4 December 1577.

Your majesty's unworthy servant and subject,

Teresa de Jesús, Carmelite

6

A la M. María de San José. Sevilla
Valladolid, 22 de julio de 1579

1. Jesús. La gracia del Espíritu Santo sea con vuestra reverencia, hija mía, y ¡con cuánta razón la puede llamar así! Porque aunque yo la quería mucho, es ahora tanto más, que me espanta, y así me dan deseos de verla y abrazarla mucho. Sea Dios alabado, de donde viene todo el bien, que ha sacado a vuestra reverencia de batalla tan reñida con victoria. Yo no lo echo a su virtud, sino a las muchas oraciones que por acá se han hecho en estas casas por ésa. Plega a Su Majestad que seamos para darle gracias de la merced que nos ha hecho.

2. El padre provincial me envió la carta de las hermanas, y el padre Nicolao la suya, por donde he visto que está ya vuestra reverencia tornada a su oficio, que me ha dado grandísimo consuelo; porque todo lo demás era no acabar de quietarse las almas.

3. Vuestra reverencia tenga paciencia. Pues le ha dado el Señor tanto deseo de padecer, alégrese de cumplirle en eso, que ya entiendo no es pequeño trabajo. Si hubiésemos de andar a escoger los que queremos y dejar los otros, no sería imitar a Nuestro Esposo, que con sentir tanto en la oración

del huerto su Pasión, el remate era: «Fiat voluntas tua». Esta voluntad hemos menester hacer siempre, y haga Él lo que quisiere de nosotros.

4. Al padre Nicolao he pedido dé a vuestra reverencia los avisos que entiende que conviene, porque es muy cuerdo y la conoce, y así me remito a lo que su reverencia la escribiere. Sólo le pido yo que procure el menor trato que ser pueda fuera de nuestros descalzos (digo para que traten esas monjas ni vuestra reverencia sus almas); no se les dé mucho de que les hagan falta alguna vez; no siendo las comuniones tan a menudo, no se le dé nada, que más importa no nos ver en otra como la pasada.

5. De los frailes, si quisiera mudar algunas veces alguna monja, no se lo quite.

6. Tengo tan poco lugar que aun no la pensé escribir.

7. A todas me encomiende muy mucho y les agradezca de mi parte el buen conocimiento que han tenido. El acertar a darme contento también les agradezco. La Virgen se lo pague y me las dé su bendición y haga santas.

8. Creo no han de poder dejar de tomar a la hija mayor de Enrique Freile, porque se le debe mucho. Hará en esto conforme a lo que la dijere el padre Nicolao, a quien lo remito. La más chica en ninguna manera conviene ahora, así por la edad como porque en ningún monasterio están bien tres hermanas juntas, cuánto más en nuestros que son de tan pocas. Váyalo entreteniendo diciendo que por la edad, no los desconsuele.

9. Cuando pudiere ir pagando a mi hermano, sepa que tiene necesidad, porque ha tenido muchos gastos juntos; ya ve que se lo deben. ¡Oh, pues lo que ha sentido sus trabajos! Dios la dé el descanso que más le conviene para contentarle.

10. Escríbame largo de todo, en especial de esas dos pobrecitas, que me tienen con mucho cuidado. Muéstrelas gracia y procure por los medios que le pareciere si pudiese se viniesen a entender.

11. Yo me partiré de aquí un día después de Santa Ana, Dios queriendo. Estaré en Salamanca algunos de asiento. Pueden venir sus cartas a Roque de Huerta.

12. Todas estas hermanas se le encomiendan mucho, y a todas. Harto las deben.

13. Están estos monasterios que es para alabar al Señor, de todo. Encomienden a Su Majestad lo de Malagón y el negocio a que voy a Salamanca, y no olviden a todos los que debemos, en estos tiempos en especial.

Es hoy día de la Magdalena.

14. Las ocupaciones de aquí son tantas, que aun no sé cómo he escrito ésta; ha sido en algunas veces, y a esta causa no escribo al padre fray Gregorio, que lo pensé hacer. Escríbale ella un gran recaudo por mí, y que estoy contenta que le haya cabido tan buena parte de esta guerra, que así le cabrá del despojo.

15. Dígame cómo está nuestro buen padre el prior de las Cuevas, para que vea cómo le he de escribir en estos negocios.

De vuestra reverencia sierva

Teresa de Jesús

To Mother María de San José, Seville
Valladolid, 22 July 1579

1. Jesus. The Holy Spirit be with your reverence, my daughter, and I truly can call you "my daughter"! Because, although I've always loved you, now I love you so much that it amazes me, and I want so much to see and hug you. Praise God, from whom all blessings come and who has led you through a terrible battle to victory.[105] I don't attribute this to your virtue, but to the countless prayers these many convents have offered up for yours. Please His Majesty that we may thank him sufficiently for everything he has done for us.

2. Father Provincial[106] sent me a letter from the sisters, and Father Nicolao[107] sent me yours, from which I learned that your reverence has been reinstated as prioress. This has given me great joy, since everything that happened was enough to make wrecks of all our souls.

3. Your reverence should be patient. Since the Lord gave you such desire to suffer, delight in the fact that your request has been granted. I understand that you've been through a lot, but if we got to pick and choose which trials to suffer and which to avoid, we wouldn't be imitating our Spouse, who, after suffering from his Passion in the garden,[108] closed with the words: "Fiat voluntas tua."[109] We need to do God's will always, and let him do whatever he wants with us.

4. I asked Father Nicolao to give you whatever instruction he thinks suitable. He is very shrewd, and he knows you, so I go along with whatever he writes to you. All I ask of him is that he try to manage things so that you have as little to do as possible with those who aren't our Discalced friars. (I mean with respect to the souls of the nuns and your reverence.) Don't worry if there aren't always Discalced friars available because you don't have to take communion so frequently. What's more important is that we don't get into another mess like the last one.

5. If a nun wants to consult some other friar, you should let her go ahead and do it.

6. I have so little time that I didn't think I was even going to be able to write to you.

7. Give my best regards to all the nuns and give them my thanks for their excellent conduct. Also express my gratitude to them for the joy they give me. May the Virgin reward them and bless them and make them holy.

8. I don't think you can avoid taking the older daughter of Enrique Freile,[110] since we owe him so much. With regard to this, do whatever Father Nicolao tells you. I leave it to him. However, by no means would

it be suitable for you to accept the youngest girl now, not only because of her age but also because it's not good for three sisters to be together in any monastery, and especially not in ours, where there are so few nuns. You can put him off by saying that she's too young, but don't discourage them.

9. When you can, begin paying back my brother. You should know that he's in need because he has had a lot of expenses all at one time. You know you owe him this money. He has suffered so much because he has taken on your troubles. May God give you the respite you need so that you can give him satisfaction.

10. Write to me at length about everything, especially about those two poor little things.[111] They have me so worried. Be kind to them and see if you can get them to understand, by whatever means seem right to you.

11. I'm leaving here the day after the feast of Saint Anne,[112] God willing. I'll be staying in Salamanca a few days. You can send your letters for me to Roque de Huerta.

12. All these [Valladolid] sisters send their regards to all of you. You owe them a lot.

13. These monasteries are doing so well they make you want to praise God. Pray to His Majesty for Malagón[113] and my business in Salamanca.[114] And don't forget all those to whom we are indebted, especially during these [difficult] times.

Today is the feast of the Magdalene.[115]

14. There is so much to do here that I still don't know how I've managed to write this letter. I had to write it in snippets. That's why I'm not writing to Father Gregorio,[116] although I intended to. Write to him and send him my warmest greetings. Tell him I'm happy he played such a big role in this war; he'll get his share of the spoils.[117]

15. Let me know how our good father the prior of Las Cuevas[118] is doing so I'll know what to write to him about these affairs.

Your reverence's servant

Teresa de Jesús

7

A la Madre María de San José. Sevilla
Burgos, 17 de marzo de 1582
Para la madre priora de San José de Sevilla.

1. En gracia me ha caído qué autorizada está con su campanario, y si campea tanto como dice, tiene razón. Yo espero en Dios que ha de ir muy adelante esa casa, porque han pasado mucho.

2. Vuestra reverencia lo dice tan bien todo que, si mi parecer se hubiera de tomar, después de muerta la eligieran por fundadora, y aun en vida muy de buena gana, que harto más sabe que yo y es mejor; esto es decir verdad. Un poco de experiencia la hago de ventaja; mas de mí hay ya que hacer poco caso, porque se espantaría cuán vieja estoy y cuán para poco, etcétera.

To Mother María de San José, Seville
Burgos, March 17, 1582
To Mother Prioress, San José, Seville

1. I'm amused by what an authoritative presence your bells have given you, but if they get people going, as you say, then you're right. I hope in God that your house will continue to make progress, because you've been through a lot.

2. You are so well spoken that, if my opinion counted for anything, after my death they would elect you foundress. And even if I were still living, I would be delighted, for you know much more than I do, and you're a better person. This is the truth. The only advantage I have over you is a little more experience, but no one should pay much attention to me anymore, for you would be shocked to see how old I've gotten and how incapable I am of anything, etc.

Notes

PREFACE

1. *Religion Bookline, Publishers Weekly Online*, 24 January 2007.
2. Among them, *Women's Letters across Europe, 1400–1700*, edited by Jane Couchman and Ann Crabb; *Per lettera*, edited by Gabriella Zarri; *Die Frau im Dialog: Studien zu Theorie und Geschichte des Briefs*, edited by Anita Runge and Lieselotte Steinbrügge; and *A History of Women's Writing in Italy*, by Letizia Panizza and Sharon Wood, which contains a perceptive article on letter-writing by Maria Luisa Doglio. Two dissertations on Teresa's letters exist: Sandra Loueen Dunn, *Teresa of Ávila and the Written Self* (Cornell University, 1998) and Constance Marina, *The Business of Courtesy: An Examination of the Letters of Teresa of Avila* (Harvard University, 1993).

INTRODUCTION

1. The Low Countries are composed of Holland, Belgium, and Luxembourg.
2. Mendicants are religious granted the privilege of begging in their own dioceses, since they are vowed to corporate as well as personal poverty. The terms "conventuals" and "observants" were first applied to the Franciscan order. As the order evolved from its itinerant lifestyle and friars began living in convents, their communities increased, leading to certain modifications of the original rule of Saint Francis. As the order grew laxer and more decadent, some friars wished to return to the original observance of the rule. Those who preferred the mitigations as they were practiced in the convents came to be called the "conventuals," while those who wanted reforms were called the "observants."
3. Marcel Bataillon writes that Erasmus was read more in Spain than in any other country.
4. The English edition of Teresa's works used here is *Collected Works of St. Teresa of Avila*, 3 vols., translated by Kieran Kavanaugh and Otilio Rodríguez (hereinafter cited as *CWST*).
5. Lehfeldt uses "convent" to refer only to female religious houses, although technically the term can refer to a community of either men or women.
6. Tomás Gálvez Campos elucidates the details of the Crown's efforts to impose reform.
7. See Smet 1:71–75.
8. In Catholicism, an "indulgence" is a partial remission of purgatorial atonement

(a reduction of the time one must spend in purgatory before going to heaven) that is due for sins the individual has committed on earth.

9. See Parker 80–81.

10. My thanks to Carole Slade for his observation.

11. The BAC edition of *Obras de San Ignacio de Loyola* contains 180 letters. For a discussion of the importance of correspondence in maintaining the cohesiveness of the Jesuits, see O'Malley 62–63.

12. See Chapter 1 for a discussion of the magnitude of Teresa's correspondence.

13. Jodi Bilinkoff asserts that Teresa "deeply envied male priests" because they had the freedom to preach and proselytize. In Bilinkoff's view, Teresa saw founding convents as a means of achieving an apostolate, which she had long yearned for but, as a woman, had been denied ("Woman" 296). Carole Slade points out that Teresa aspired to model herself after Mary Magdalene, whom she saw as an apostle working tirelessly to bring Christ souls ("Social Reformer" 95).

14. The picaresque novel, which reached its apogee in Spain in the seventeenth century, is a first-person narrative in which a *pícaro* (rogue) recounts his adventures traveling from one place to another, trying to survive however he can. It is the prototype of the "on-the-road" adventure story. In the first Spanish picaresque novel, *Lazarillo de Tormes* (1554), the protagonist, Lazarillo, learns to live by his wits, often lying, stealing, and cheating. The novel is constructed as a confession: Lazarillo recounts his life to a judge or confessor, identified only as *Vuestra Merced* (Your Mercy), after being apprehended for marrying the mistress of an archpriest to provide a cover for the illicit relationship. By controlling the information he provides, the narrator is able to portray himself in a favorable light. Through Lazarillo's observations, the anonymous author of the novel exposes corruption at every level of society in sixteenth-century Spain.

15. See George Shipley, "The Critic as Witness for the Prosecution." Shipley shows how Lázaro de Tormes frames his story to validate his actions.

16. See Anne Cruz, *Discourses of Poverty* (5–6), and Alexander Blackburn, *The Myth of the Pícaro*. See also Harry Sieber, *Language and Society in* La vida de Lazarillo de Tormes.

17. Antonio Pérez-Romero calls Lazarillo "a whore in a whore's world," since the *pícaro* learns to adapt to society's depraved norms. *Subversive Tradition in Spanish Renaissance Writing*, 212–13.

18. On Teresa's relationship with her confessors, see Weber, "Three Lives," and also Mujica, "Paul the Enchanter."

CHAPTER 1

1. Since the mid-twentieth century, two main currents of thought have dominated discussions of the influence of minority cultures on medieval Spain. Américo Castro popularized the view that Spanish identity was the result of cross-cultural interaction among Christians, Jews, and Muslims living and working together. Claudio Sánchez Albornoz countered this view, arguing that Jews and Muslims had minimal effect on Spain's development. For a discussion of views on the Jewish presence in Spain, see Ray, "Beyond Tolerance."

2. Henry murdered Peter on 23 March 1369 and succeeded him as king. Two other examples are Elionor of Sicily (1349–1375) and María de Luna (1396–1406), queens of Aragón who were instrumental in protecting the Jewish community of Morvedre, to the north of Valencia. As Mark Meyerson has shown, both queens

acted out of self-interest. Morvedre was an important source of revenue for them. See Meyerson.

3. Ferrer was canonized in 1455 and is currently the patron saint of the Community of Valencia. He was made a saint because he was considered a moving orator who instilled devotion to Christ in his followers, but he was viciously anti-Semitic.

4. See Martz (24–36) for a fuller description of events.

5. For a detailed explanation of Jewish and *converso* participation, see Baer (2: 307).

6. Alexander VI and Ximénez de Cisneros represented two opposing approaches to clerical authority. When reports of the latter's austerity reached Alexander, the pontiff reprimanded him for neglecting the external splendor of his rank. However, Ximénez agreed to wear episcopal dress only in such a way that his friar's habit would show underneath.

7. These "edicts of grace" permitted the accused to wipe clean their slates by making a payment to the inquisitors (Kamen, *Spanish Inquisition* 58).

8. The first were in Córdoba, Jaén, and Cuidad Real. Others were then set up farther north, in Toledo, Ávila, Medina del Campo, Segovia, Valladolid and Sigüenza. For a concise overview, see Edwards.

9. For a more complete discussion of the expulsions, see Kamen, *Spanish Inquisition* (18–24).

10. Teófanes Egido reproduces the testimony of Pedro de Cepeda and other pertinent legal documents in *El linaje judeoconverso de Santa Teresa*.

11. We do know the names of the children who later settled in Ávila with him: Alonso, Pedro, Ruy, Elivira, Lorenzo, and Francisco (Efrén de la Madre de Dios and Steggink 7).

12. In 1520 Francisco Pérez testified, "I, Francisco Pérez, scribe and public notary by royal and apostolic authority, and officer in charge of confidential information of the Holy Office of the Inquisition of the city and archbishopric of Toledo and surrounding areas, swear and certify, that according to the books and records of the Holy Office, on 28 June, 1485, Juan Sánchez, merchant, son of Alonso Sánchez, inhabitant of Toledo,collation of Santa Leocadia, swore and confessed to the inquisitors who at the time were conducting the investigation that he had committed many serious crimes of heresy and apostasy against our holy Catholic faith" (Egido 189, my translation).

13. Pedro de Cepeda's wife, Catalina del Águila, was the sister of Ana del Águila, Pajares's wife (Egido 15–17). Pajares's daughter, María del Águila, was Teresa's godmother.

14. See, for example, Egido (142–54); Alonso Cortés (85–110); and Bilinkoff, *Ávila* (110).

15. On Teresa's education and pedagogical influence on other women, see Howe, *Education and Women in the Early Modern Hispanic World*, 59–90.

16. In *La perfecta casada* (*The Perfect Wife*) Fray Luis de León writes of the danger of books of chivalry, which ignite the imaginations of ladies and keep them away from their spinning (1:278). In *Los nombres de Cristo* Fray Luis asserts that people who read such books "all day and all the time" are poisoning their minds (1: 406).

17. Death in childbirth was not uncommon, and infant mortality rates were high. Between a fifth and a third of newborns could be expected to die before their first birthday. In Valencia between 40 and 50 percent of children failed to reach adulthood (Casey 31–32). See also King (3–6) and Vigil (129).

18. Modern visitors can view some of the exquisite silverware and religious objects used by aristocratic nuns in the museum sections of the Encarnación and Descalzas Reales convents in Madrid.

19. Medieval abbesses had sometimes wielded tremendous power, directing double monasteries for men and women with huge agrarian holdings. Some even heard the confessions of their nuns, presumed to preach, and issued licenses to priests to say Mass in their churches. Hildegard of Bingen (1098–1179), from a German noble family, grew so prominent that she exerted influence over bishops, popes, and kings—in addition to producing major works of theology and visionary writings and composing music. Finally, the church took steps to limit the power of women. In 1220 Pope Innocent III issued an inhibition on the Cistercian abbesses of Burgos and Palencia known as the "Monastieum Cisterciense," condemning their sacramental and political activities as "unheard of, most indecorous, and highly preposterous" (Thomassin, part 1, lib. 3, chap. xlix, paragraph 4). Furthermore, social and economic conditions had changed, depriving female religious of much of their power.

20. See Sampson Vera Tudela on Spanish nuns in the Americas.

21. By "that path," Teresa means the path of the prayer of recollection.

22. The illuminative stage (*via illuminativa*) stressed meditation on Christ's life and Passion, leading to a greater identification with Jesus. The unitive stage (*via unitiva*) achieved the soul's transformation through union with God by means of mental prayer. This highest stage required quieting the senses and intellect in order to transcend the images and thoughts that had served as guides in the illuminative stage. The purgative stage (*via purgativa*) guided the individual toward self-knowledge through examination of conscience and vocal prayer.

23. My thanks to Carole Slade for this observation.

24. "Contemplatives, who claimed to have direct, unmediated experience of God, and not necessarily during the Mass, constituted a distinct challenge to the church insofar as it was centered upon ritual and run by priests. As a *converso*, Alonso was already marginal, and probably somewhat anticlerical, so he would have been relatively comfortable in this 'church within a church' " (Flinders 168).

25. "Conversion" in the theological sense does not refer to a change of religion, but to "the profound transformation of mind, will, and heart toward God" (*Encyclopedia of Catholicism* 366). At this time Teresa underwent a personal renovation marked by a new and profound awareness of God's awe-inspiring presence.

26. Teresa describes the four degrees of prayer in her *Life* in the chapters on "the four waters" (chapter 11ff.) However, she is so imprecise that scholars have not been able to reach any agreement on the definition of each. Kavanaugh and Rodríguez identify them as meditation, prayer of quiet, recollection (characterized by the numbing of the intellect, faculties, and senses), and union (*CWST* 1:38, 514). The first two are active stages, that is, they require some effort on the part of the individual such as reading an inspirational passage or gazing at a crucifix. The second two are passive stages, for the soul is completely under the power of God. For Tietz each of the four levels occurs *after* the active or meditative phase. Tietz identifies them as recollection, prayer of quiet, union, and mystical marriage (967).

27. The verse that Teresa notes is Ps 119:137.

28. Ultimately, the *Exercises* "prepare and dispose the soul to rid itself of all its disordered affections and then, after their removal, to seek and find God's will in the ordering of one's life for the salvation of one's soul" (Ignacio de Loyola 221).

29. It is probable that at some point Teresa made the *Spiritual Exercises*, either with Cetina or with her next Jesuit confessor, Juan de Prádanos, because she describes using the imagination to recreate mentally scenes from the New Testament in a fashion similar to that recommended by Ignatius. On the possible influence of the *Exercises* see my article, "Beyond Image."

30. Once one of the most powerful men in Spain, Borja had been the Marquis of Lombay and the Duke of Gandía. Upon witnessing the decomposing corpse of the Empress Isabel of Portugal, once reputedly the most beautiful woman in the world, he vowed never again to serve a mortal being. After the death of his wife, he took vows and became a Jesuit.

31. The erotic dimensions of the Bernini sculpture have long intrigued art historians. In his BBC series, *The Power of Art*, Simon Schama remarks: "No wonder when art historians look at this sculpture they tie themselves in knots to avoid saying the obvious, that is, that we're looking at the most intense convulsive drama of the body that any of us experience." www.bbc.co.uk/arts/powerofart/bernini.shtml.

32. Justification by faith or works was a dominant theme in theological discussions of the sixteenth century. The central theological principle of Lutheranism is justification by grace through faith, with no need for good works. In *Of the Bondage of the Will (De Servo Arbitrio)*, art. xviii, Luther writes: "Now that God has taken my salvation out the control of my own will, and put it under the control of His, and promised to save me, not according to my working or running, but according to His own grace and mercy, I have the comfortable certainty that He is faithful and will not lie to me, and that He is also great and powerful, so that no devils or opposition can break Him or pluck me from Him. . . . Thus it is that, if not all, yet some, indeed many, are saved; whereas, by the power of free-will none at all could be saved, but every one of us would perish. Furthermore, I have the comfortable certainty that I please God, not by reason of the merit of my works, but by reason of His merciful favor promised to me; so that, if I work too little, or badly, He does not impute it to me, but with fatherly compassion pardons me and makes me better."

33. See Bataillon (572–77).

34. Magdalena de la Cruz was so highly esteemed that the Empress Isabel of Portugal, wife of Charles V, gave her a portrait of herself and the baptismal garment of her infant son, the future Philip II. Even the inquisitor general, Alonso Manrique, fell under her spell and traveled from Seville to Córdoba to see her.

35. Black-veiled or choir nuns were responsible for chanting the Office and carrying out administrative duties, while white-veiled nuns performed menial labor. Although in her early foundations, which were very small, all nuns were required to perform all tasks, as the reform grew, Teresa accepted *frailas* or white-veiled sisters.

36. The next several paragraphs are adapted from my article, "Was Saint Teresa a Feminist?"

37. Teresa referred to all Protestants as Lutherans.

38. Each major city had its own Inquisitional Tribunal. Teresa's *Life* had already been sent to the Inquisition in Toledo. The Toledo tribunal still hadn't reached a decision on Teresa's book, and there was no reason to believe the Valladolid censors would work any faster.

39. In 1564 the Carmelites declared themselves observants and denounced conventualism in a general chapter. Therefore, the mitigated Carmelites were

officially observants, as opposed to the unmitigated Carmelites, known as Discalced or—as Rubeo preferred to call them—Contemplatives.

40. See my article "Paul the Enchanter."

41. As I have argued in "Paul the Enchanter," Gracián could not have forced Teresa to found in Seville. It is possible that at this point in her career she wanted to expand the reform into the south.

CHAPTER 2

1. Efrén de la Madre de Dios and Steggink include some communications to Teresa in their collection of her letters, but these are too few to allow for an analysis of two-way correspondence. Except for one, the letters of María de San José were destroyed. The extant letters of Gracián include no letters to Teresa.

2. Some of the better known manuals by men designed to dictate the conduct of women are *The Education of a Christian Woman* (1521), by Juan Luis Vives; *The Institution of Marriage* (1526), by Erasmus; and *La perfecta casada* (1583), by Fray Luis de León.

3. Examples are the October 1578 note to "the Discalced Carmelite Mothers of Beas," the January 1579 letter to "the Discalced Carmelite Mothers of Seville," the May 1579 letter to "the Prioress and Sisters of the Valladolid Monastery," the 6 October 1580 note to "the Discalced Carmelite Mothers of Malagón," and the 7 October 1580 letter to "the Discalced Carmelites of San José, Ávila."

4. My translation.

5. My translation.

6. Esperanza is an unidentified nun.

7. This translation of the passage is not from *Letters*, but my own. The first sentence of the passage is ambiguous because Teresa omitted some words. The original Spanish is as follows: "A las cartas de nuestro padre pondré sin cubierta, y para vuestra reverencia el sobreescrito y dos cruces o tres." Kavanaugh translates: "I will put the letters for our *padre* in an envelope without an address and with your name on it and two or three crosses." Peers translates: "I shall not put my letters for our Father into a separate cover, but shall address the cover to you, and (I shall mark anything for him with) two or three crosses." Since no envelopes existed at the time, it seems likely she placed the letter in some sort of wrapping along with those meant for María de San José and marked those for the priest with crosses. Peers notes that he has supplied the words in parentheses in order to clarify the meaning.

8. Peers, *Letters* 2:636.

9. See, for example, her letter to Padre Pablo Hernández, 4 October 1578.

10. A Spanish *legua* was roughly 5.5 kilometers. Twenty leagues were about 110 kilometers or 68.3 miles.

11. The Taxis (or Tassi) were an Italian family that had previously organized the postal system of Burgundy (Kamen, *Spain* 51–52).

12. "A Credo" is the time it takes to recite the Apostles' Creed.

13. She names all four of them in the letter: Juan Pedro de Espinoza, Varrona, Antonio Morán, and Alonso Rodríguez.

14. For a detailed description of the development of epistolary art in the Middle Ages, see Trueba Lawand (35–41).

15. See Trueba Lawand for a description of these books.

16. See Concejo. In "The Business of Courtesy: An Examination of the Letters of Teresa of Avila," Marina points out the differences between recommended usage and Teresa's.

17. Faith Beasley notes that between 1640 and 1715 alone, more than 220 women participated in the literary scene in France, their participation greatly influencing the development of French letters. Madame de Sévigné, one of the most famous intellectuals of the period, left over 1,500 extant letters.

18. See Jensen, "Male Models of Feminine Epistolarity."

19. See Carrera (69–86).

20. Carrera examines Teresa's readings and how they contributed to her sense of self in *Teresa of Ávila's Autobiography* (42–59).

21. Luxury editions of books still used vellum until the end of the sixteenth century (Jardine, *Worldly Goods* 145–46).

22. One of the most influential Spanish printing houses was the one run by Jacopo Cromberger and his son Juan, in Seville. The Crombergers produced prayers, religious woodcuts, and other devotional material. Until 1520 the Crombergers imported paper; after that, they began buying directly from the mills (Jardine, *Worldly Goods* 163).

23. See Man for a detailed description of printing and paper in early modern Europe. Man discusses the difference between paper used for correspondence and that used for printing (135).

24. *IHS* stands for Jesus (Greek IHΣ, short for IHΣOYΣ). Other interpretations are Jesus Savior of Men (Latin, *Iesus Hominum Salvator*) and In This Sign (the Cross) You Shall Conquer (Latin, *In HΣc SaΣs*). In the letter to Lorenzo Teresa was referring to the legend of Ignatius of Antioch, on whose heart the initials IHS were found imprinted in gold after his martyrdom.

25. Teresa wrote two versions of *Way of Perfection*. The first, the autograph of which is conserved in the Library of the Royal Monastery of El Escorial, was probably composed in 1566. The second, whose autograph is at the Discalced Carmelite Convent in Valladolid, was probably composed in 1566–1567 and is identified in this book as *WPV*. The Valladolid version was revised by Teresa and approved by García de Toledo.

26. Lehfeldt asserts that even after the reform, the convent remained a permeable space. She argues that for Teresa tension existed between the ideal of enclosure and the need to travel and to interact with secular persons in her role as foundress.

27. On the controversy over whether or not Philip and Teresa actually ever met, see Slade, "Teresa of Avila and Philip II."

28. On the conflict between Philip II and Rome, see the introduction.

29. Teutonio de Braganza (1530–1602) was the son of the duke of Braganza, a rich and powerful aristocrat. He joined the Jesuits in 1549 but left the order after a falling out with Ignatius of Loyola. He met Teresa in 1574 and committed large sums of money for her foundations. He paid for the publication of her *Way of Perfection* in 1583, a year after her death.

30. Deborah Tannen discusses modern women's use of these strategies in conversation in *You Just Don't Understand*. My thanks to Maureen Russo for this observation.

CHAPTER 3

1. Teresa recognizes the paradox created by the image of the soul, which both *is* the castle and travels inward *through* the castle: "It seems I'm saying something foolish, for if this castle is the soul, clearly one doesn't have to enter it since it is within oneself. . . . But you must understand that there is a great difference in the ways one may be inside the castle. . . . You have already heard in some books on prayer that the soul is advised to enter within itself; well that's the very thing I'm advising" (*CWST* 2, *The Interior Castle* I, 1:5).

2. See Ahlgren, *Entering Teresa of Ávila's Interior Castle* (31–35).

3. See, for example, her letters to Mariano, 12 December 1576: 1; Braganza, 16 January 1578: 5; Dávila, 14 February 1578: 5; Roque de Huerta, 8–12 March 1578: 1.

4. See Wilson, "Saint Teresa de Ávila's Martyrdom."

5. See Efrén de la Madre de Dios and Steggink (293–97).

6. A visitator is an official who visits different monasteries to make certain the rules of the order are being followed. See Moriones, *Teresian Carmel* (ch. 6), for a more detailed description of these developments.

7. A noted historian, Smet is a member of the Order of Carmelites, not the Discalced Carmelites.

8. This letter has not survived. Smet refers to it in the history of the order (2:62).

9. As we shall see later in this chapter, Rubeo had written to Teresa in 1571, broadening her authority to found houses anywhere in Spain.

10. Beas was in the civil jurisdiction of Castile, but in the ecclesiastical jurisdiction of Andalusia. At the time she made the foundation, Teresa thought the town was in both the civil and ecclesiastical jurisdiction of Castile. Teresa states her dislike for Andalusians in several letters, but Tomás Álvarez argues that in spite of her bad experiences in the south of Spain and her dislike of the heat, she loved the beautiful landscape (699).

11. She is referring to the archbishop of Seville.

12. The Carmelites, or Order of Our Lady of Mt. Carmel, were founded in the twelfth century on Mt. Carmel, in the current state of Israel. The order is believed to be under the special protection of the Virgin Mary, and Marian devotion is therefore an important element of Carmelite spirituality.

13. The papal brief *Pia consideratione* was issued on 11 June 1580.

14. By "down here" Teresa is referring to Seville.

15. This will be discussed more fully in the next chapter.

16. In her letter of 18 June 1575, she had written: "Both of them have asked me to write to you and present their excuses, for they don't dare do so themselves."

17. By "Council" Teresa means the Council of Trent and the pope. *Moto proprio* is "the name given to certain papal rescripts on account of the clause *motu proprio* (of his own accord) used in the document. The words signify that the provisions of the rescript were decided on by the pope personally, that is, not on the advice of the cardinals or others, but for reasons which he himself deemed sufficient" (*Catholic Encyclopedia CD Rom*).

18. For a description of these reforms, see Smet (2:74–75).

19. Teresa is probably referring to the king when she says "the one you mention." Tostado still had not received permission from the royal council to assume the position of visitator.

20. This letter is not included in Gracián's *Cartas*.

21. For a more detailed description of events, see Smet (2:80).

22. Translations of Gracián's letters are my own, unless otherwise noted.

23. Kieran Kavanaugh mentions that Teresa is probably referring to an account of her illnesses made by one of the nuns in Toledo (*Letters* 1:512n1).

24. In early modern theater, the lasting consequence of a charge, even when the accused successfully defends himself, is a *topos*. See, for example, the case of Don Juan in Calderón's *A secreto agravio, secreta venganza*. See also the discussion of this play in Mujica, *Calderón's Characters*.

25. See Gracián, *Peregrinación de Anastasio* 37.

26. Smet says fifty-four nuns voted for Teresa.

27. See Chapter 6.

28. Recall that the Carmelites are the order of Our Lady of Carmen.

29. For a brief overview of scholarship on these letters, see Slade, "Teresa of Avila and Philip II."

30. "Paul" is code for Gracián. "Ángela" is code for Teresa.

31. Romero was a friar from Santo Tomás, the Dominican monastery in Ávila. A *presentado* is a theologian who has completed his studies and is awaiting the conferral of his master's degree. "Faculties" means license or authorization.

32. See Cixous and Irigaray.

33. Sega called her "a restless gadabout, a disobedient and contumacious woman." Peers, *Complete Works* 3:150n2, and *Letters* 2:125.

34. Peers identifies the recipient of this letter as Roque de Huerta, but Martínez and Egido argue convincingly that it must have been meant for Pedro de los Ángeles, who had been designated at Almodóvar as the representative of the order to go to Rome (*Epistolario* 569). Kavanaugh does not identify the recipient, but simply calls the document a memo for Rubeo (Introductory Note in *Letters* 2:126).

35. Curiously, Teresa tells Beatriz's story with much compassion in *Foundations*, where she describes the young woman as "holy and virtuous" (26:9).

36. "Your charity" is the equivalent of "you."

37. All translations from Efrén de la Madre de Dios and Steggink are mine.

38. Doria had cleverly managed to keep out of jail and stayed in Madrid managing Discalced affairs apparently without Sega suspecting what he was up to. Teresa had wanted Doria to go to Rome, but he had made himself so indispensable to the nuncio that he was not allowed to leave.

39. This letter exists only in fragmented form. Rodríguez Martínez and Egido date this letter 10 February with Doria as the addressee, as does Kavanaugh. Efrén de la Madre de Dios and Steggink date it 20 February (820). Peers dates it 20 February and believes it was destined for Gracián, but this is obviously an error, since Teresa refers to the possibility of the addressee going to Rome, and Gracián was in prison at the time.

40. See Kavanaugh's introduction to Teresa's 12 March 1579 letter to Roque (*Letters* 2:164).

41. "Father Vicar General" refers to the vicar general of the entire order, Calced and Discalced. Teresa was careful to show submission to the authorities in an effort to obtain their goodwill toward the petition for a separate province.

42. Her main concern in this letter seems to be that a war might break out between Spain and Portugal. She writes to Braganza to beg him to do all he can to prevent it.

CHAPTER 4

1. Parts of this section were published as "Paul the Enchanter: Saint Teresa's Vow of Obedience to Gracián," in *The Heirs of Saint Teresa*, Ed. Christopher Wilson, and are included with permission of the editor and publisher. For a more complete discussion of Teresa's vow to Gracián, readers are directed to the article.

2. As we saw in earlier chapters, the Andalusian Carmelites were notoriously lax, and Rubeo, Carmelite general, was trying to impose reforms on them. The papal nuncio, Nicolás Ormaneto, had written to the pope's secretary that it would be necessary to exert pressure on the Andalusian Carmelites to keep them under control. For that reason, visitations were necessary. However, the apostolic visitator, the Dominican Francisco Vargas, did not "have the stomach" for the job (Smet 2:64), so Ormaneto appointed Vargas and Gracián to serve *in solidium*.

3. Martínez and Egido attribute this letter to Inés de Jesús, prioress of Medina, but Álvarez and Kavanaugh attribute it to Isabel de Santo Domingo, who had been prioress of the Carmel in Pastrana, where Gracián entered the order.

4. Auclair, a French biographer writing in the forties, comments, "Teresa of Jesus was so excited that she almost seemed like Doña Teresa de Ahumada again" (258). Peers writes that "the effect which the charm and apparent saintliness of this young man had on the woman of nearly sixty was almost incredible . . . she could not put Fray Jerónimo out of her thoughts" (*Mother of Carmel* 122). Smet notes: "It is an interesting insight into the femininity of St. Teresa that this personable, intelligent but imprudent young man should have so completely captivated her" (2:65). Pedra comments that Teresa was undergoing all kinds of problems at the time she met the young visitator, not the least of which was the princess of Eboli's denunciation of *Life* to the Valladolid Inquisition. "Why," asks Pedra, "would she write, with the enthusiasm of a young girl, that her time in Beas was the happiest in her life? Because that's where she met Father Gracián in person" (46–47, translation mine). All of these scholars describe Teresa's meeting with Gracián as something of a thunderbolt.

5. In fact, there are many examples of close friendships between nuns and their confessors or spiritual directors, among them those of Saint Francis of Assisi (1181?–1226) and Saint Clare (1194–1253), the Blessed Angela of Foligno (d. 1309) and Fra Arnaldo, and Ana María de San José (d. 1632) and Martín García (d. 1640). See Jane Tar, "Angela of Foligno."

6. The confessor-penitent relationship could be extremely complex, as Bilinkoff points out, involving issues of sex, class, gender, and age. ("Confession, Gender, Life-Writing" 180–81).)

7. As Tar has shown, women often assumed positions of authority in heterosexual spiritual friendships. See "Angela of Foligno" and "Spiritual Counsel."

8. In the sixteenth century, many people, not just religious, made vows of obedience. Since the will of God was identified with the institutional form of authority, submission to a priest was seen as a means of spiritual purification that freed the individual from the interference of the ego. However, the conditional nature of this submission meant that those who made vows of obedience still had use of their judgment and consciences.

9. Although Teresa does not explicitly say she made the *Spiritual Exercises*, her description in *Life* of how her Jesuit spiritual director taught her to enter a prayerful state by imagining Christ on the cross suggests that she was exposed to them. Ignatius of Loyola lays out guidelines for priests directing the *Spiritual*

Exercises that promote cooperation between director and directee. Annotation 15 of the instructions for spiritual directors states that the director "ought not to move the one receiving [the Exercises] more to poverty or to any particular promise than to their contraries," that is, the director ought not try to influence the directee unduly (286). The very first line of the instructions for the first week of the Exercises refers to the priest-directee relationship as a collaboration and suggests that both approach the experience with goodwill and an open mind: "So that the director and the exercitant may collaborate better . . . it must be presupposed that any good Christian has to be more ready to justify than to condemn a neighbor's statement" (289). In his letters on obedience, Ignatius stresses that one is never obligated to follow a command he believes to be contrary to God, and in his *Reminiscences* and letters he warns against excessive scrupulosity.

10. Such role reversal was not uncommon. See Tar's articles on Angela of Foligno and Ana María de San José listed in the bibliography.

11. Matins is an early morning prayer.

12. See Cammarata, "*Epístola consolatoria.*"

13. Antonio de San José relates that the Calced have spread the rumor that Gracián was thinking of becoming an Augustinian, but that his mother opposed the move vehemently (Peers, *Letters* 2:618). Kavanaugh suggests that Gracián himself may have told Teresa that he was being encouraged to change orders, but that the accusation that he wanted to become an Augustinian was false (*Letters* 2:119n1).

14. Since the Carmelites were the order of Our Lady of Carmen, to abandon the order would constitute a betrayal of the Virgin.

15. Concerned about the formation of cliques in her convents, Teresa was averse to accepting too many nuns from one family into a single Carmel.

16. Teresa's letter to María Bautista is quoted in Chapter 3.

17. In 1581, one year before Teresa's death, King Philip II had a brief issued separating the Calced and Discalced into separate provinces. From this time on, the Calced (or Mitigated) and Discalced (or Unmitigated) were separate orders and their names written with capitals.

18. By "those others" she means the Calced.

19. Juan de la Roca, who was then in Madrid preparing for his journey to Rome, was prior in Mancera. Gracián had written to Teresa that he planned to go to Peñaranda.

20. Reverend Padre Rioja was a Calced Carmelite in Castile (Kavanaugh, *Letters* 2:95n21).

21. Since women did not ordinarily travel unaccompanied, Fray Julián, a Discalced Carmelite, usually accompanied Teresa on her journeys.

22. Gracián, *Pereginación* 168.

23. See Weber, "Spiritual Administration."

24. The stipulation is found in *CWST* 3, *Constitutions* 40. Teresa believed that true wisdom came from God, not books. She disparaged learned men who presumed to judge her without ever having had a mystical experience. See my article, "Skepticism and Mysticism in Golden Age Spain." For more on Teresa's support for female literacy, see Chapter 5.

25. The letter was written to Gaspar Villanueva, in Malagón.

26. For more on the calumnies, see Chapter 3 and below.

27. I analyze María's language in my next volume. See also "María de San José: Priora y 'letrera' " in Mujica, *Women Writers of Early Modern Spain*.

28. The letters addressed to María de San José in Gracián's *Cartas* are meant for his sister, María de San José Dantisco, not for María de San José Salazar.

29. See Chapter 3.

30. See Chapter 3.

31. Casilda de Padilla escaped from her mother and sister on a visit to the Valladolid Carmel and refused to leave the convent, insisting she wanted to serve God there. Her mother, along with her confessor Domingo Báñez and the prioress, finally convinced her to wait until she was of age because, Teresa tells us in *Foundations*, she was not yet twelve years old. One day she convinced her grandmother (who was supposed to become her future mother-in-law) to let her go to the country. While she was out she escaped from her governess and servants and snuck into the convent, refusing to come out even when her fiancé and relatives came to the grille and begged her. Finally, the fiancé and relatives obtained a court order to remove her by force. Once she was back at home, her mother made arrangements for her to join a lax convent where Casilda's sister was a nun. One day, while she was at church with her mother, Casilda ran off to the Valladolid Carmel while her mother was busy saying her confession. At this point, the nuns gave her the habit immediately. "And thus she fulfilled the good inspirations the Lord had placed within her. His Majesty began very shortly to repay her with spiritual favors, and she to serve Him with the greatest happiness, humility, and detachment from everything" (*CWST* 3, *Foundations* 11:11). This series of events is probably what Teresa is referring to by "what has already been done." I have supplied my own translation of Teresa's letter rather than using that of Kavanaugh or Peers.

32. Casilda proved to be a disappointment. In 1581 she obtained a brief from Rome allowing her to withdraw from her convent and join the Franciscans.

33. The translation of this material is not from *Letters*, but my own. The English versions of Kavanaugh and Peers obscure the ambiguities in this letter, which I have tried to preserve.

34. Teresa uses the plural *les* when she writes "all you" in the phrase "I don't like it one bit that all you think. . . ." She seems to be referring to all the Valladolid nuns, but it is also possible that in her haste she wrote *les* instead of *le*, in which case she would be referring only to María. Peers has translated the word "all of you," while Kavanaugh has translated it "you." The translation appearing here is my own.

35. The passage is quoted above, in the section on Gracián.

36. María de San José described the episode in *Book for the Hour of Recreation* (147).

37. By "bad humor" Teresa is referring to the humors that were believed to govern people's moods.

38. Teresa mentions this letter in a communication to Roque de Huerta, dated October 1578.

39. Padre Nicolao is Doria, Teresa's financial manager.

40. Rodrigo's participation is not certain.

41. Brother of the conquistador Francisco.

42. When María was belittled at the convent for her visions and extreme ascetic practices, her brothers rushed to her defense. After she died in 1617, Lorenzo, the surviving brother, tried unsuccessfully to maneuver her canonization. Sisters could also support their male siblings in spiritual matters. For example, the Carmelite nun Cecilia del Nacimiento wrote a treatise in support of the beatification of her brother, Friar Antonio Sobrino.

43. Doña Luisa is Teresa's friend Luisa de la Cerda. For an account of Teresa's encounters with the Inquisition, see Ahlgren, *Teresa of Ávila and the Politics of Sanctity*. See also Medwick, *Teresa de Ávila: The Progress of a Soul* (146–47). The Inquisition did not return Teresa's manuscript, and it was not until 1580, two years before her death, that the Grand Inquisitor Gaspar de Toledo told her he had read her *Life* and found her teachings acceptable.

44. On the issue of mysticism and sensuality see Bataille (224–25).

45. The age stipulation can be found in *CWST* 3, *Constitutions* 21.

CHAPTER 5

1. My translation.

2. Carrión points out that Teresa often refers to the soul as a "palace." Carrión defines the "palace" as an *alcázar*, a walled compound in which a woman can seek refuge, a space governed by God, into which not even her father or confessor can intrude (188). Carrión also notes that Teresa's detailed descriptions of her illnesses and physical deterioration serve to undermine the image of woman as an "alabaster temple," replacing it with another of woman as a spiritual being.

3. See Carrera for an exposition of the writings of the principal opponents of mental prayer (69–89).

4. "The nature of women is weak," she laments in *Foundations* (4.2); in *The Interior Castle* she comments on "our womanly dullness of mind" (2.6). In *Life* she says that she finds being a woman depressing (10.8). On Teresa's misogynistic language, see Weber's *Teresa de Ávila and the Rhetoric of Femininity*. Teresa builds on the notion of spiritual androgyny (the idea that the soul is neither male nor female) to argue that any soul can strive for perfection. She shrewdly turns women's limitations into an advantage by arguing that since God favors the weak ("the last shall be first" [Mt 20:16]), women's frailty is a blessing. Basing her argument on the widely held notion that females are spiritually gifted, she notes that the Lord "lets His magnificent riches show forth in us weak, little women" (*Foundations* 12.10) and that "there are many more women than men to whom the Lord grants these favors" (*Life* 40.8). Thus, for Teresa, women's inferiority was a help rather than a hindrance in the quest for spiritual perfection.

5. At the time Doria was still a secular priest, that is, one not associated with any order; thus, the title "Señor." Teresa was unhappy with Mariano, who disobeyed Rubeo's instructions about founding monasteries in Andalusia. See Chapter 2.

6. Teresa uses this same tactic in *Way of Perfection*. See Mujica, "Was Saint Teresa a Feminist?"

7. Encarnación was being renovated.

8. María de San José's financial problems are discussed in Chapter 4.

9. In 1577 made Nicolás Doria financial manager for the friaries.

10. Doña Luisa (de la Cerda) is the sponsor.

11. See Mujica, *Women Writers* (liii, lxxvi–lxxvii), and Taggard, "Art and Alienation in Early Modern Spanish Convents."

12. Rubeo ordered that the habits should be brown.

13. Worsted wool protected against fleas. See *Un rincón del cielo* (111–12).

14. Kavanaugh has pointed out that this letter may have been tampered with

(Introductory Note in *Letters* 1:55). However, with regard to the modifications Teresa made for Malagón, the information is correct. She agreed to found the convent on Doña Luisa's estate and to accept Doña Luisa's patronage. She also agreed to let the women eat meat, since fish was hard to come by in that area.

15. Foucault argues that the medicalization of deviant religious experience created an alliance between medicine and the church. In his view, the association that sixteenth-century thinkers made between madness and the body made possible a policy of exclusion of those deemed possessed or deviant, which reinforced the power of the church. See *Histoire de la folie* (187) and also *Religion and Culture* (34–36).

16. See Schiesari's discussion of witchcraft (251–52).

17. Isabel was the oldest of the nuns (Kavanaugh, Biographical Sketches in *Letters* 1:627).

18. The requirements in the Middle Ages were quite diverse. Fasting could mean refraining from food altogether, limiting oneself to a single meal per day, or eliminating certain foods from the diet. See Bynum, *Holy Feast and Holy Fast* (37).

19. The statue was probably destined for Valladolid, but it wound up in Seville.

20. There is some doubt about the recipient of this letter. (See Kavanaugh, *Letters* 1:444.)

21. This story appears in Yepes and is recounted by Walsh (558).

22. "Discernment of spirits" is also central to Ignatius of Loyola's *Spiritual Exercises*. He describes the process in the introduction to the *Exercises* and in a 1536 letter to the nun Teresa Rejadell.

23. See Kavanaugh, *Letters* (1:519). Teresa was writing from Toledo, in Castile. Isabel de San Jerónimo had been in Castile before going south to Andalusia.

24. Teresa is also distraught that one of Isabel's confessors told her to write down her spiritual experiences. One of the pages was mislaid and might have fallen into the wrong hands (*Letters* 1, 1–2 March 1577: 6). In a Spain where the Inquisition aggressively pursued false visionaries, the consequences could have been catastrophic for the whole convent.

25. The eight points may have been part of the letter quoted below in which Teresa comments on vicars, or part of a different letter she sent to the commissary or the chapter. See Kavanaugh, *Letters* (2:390).

26. See Weber, "Introduction to María de San José" (7–9).

27. My translation.

28. My translation.

29. The University of Salamanca was founded in 1218.

30. Beatriz de la Madre de Dios and a lay sister, Margarita de la Concepción, brought charges against María de San José before the Inquisition. Beatriz then replaced María as prioress. After María was cleared, Isabel de San Jerónimo took over as prioress. See Chapter 3.

31. "Beatriz de la Madre de Dios . . . tells me that for more than a year they spanked, punished, and made her sleep on the floor so that she would confess that she had planned to do something so evil" (*CWST* 3, *Foundations* 26:4).

32. Since all of the convent confessors were of the unmitigated rule, giving Beatriz a choice presented no danger.

33. Quotes are my own translations.

34. On the importance Teresa attaches to obedience, see *Foundations*, Prologue: 2, 5:11, 18:13.

35. Daza was a local Ávila priest to whom Teresa gave an account of her spiritual

experiences. Daza was doubtful with respect to Teresa's visions and raptures, and he caused her considerable grief by spreading rumors about her. However, he eventually came to support the reform, and when Teresa founded San José in Ávila, the bishop commissioned Daza to give the habit to the four first Discalced Carmelite nuns.

36. As mentioned earlier, although Teresa does not actually name the *Spiritual Exercises*, the new emphasis she gives at this time to the humanity of Christ and her description of how she prays by imagining Christ on the cross suggest that she had experience with them.

CHAPTER 6

1. See Chapter 2.
2. Conversation with Teófanes Egido, O.C.D., at the Benedictine monastery in Valladolid (June 2006).
3. For more on these two extraordinary sisters see Arenal and Schlau.
4. My translation.
5. This oft-quoted condemnation appears in nearly every modern biography of Teresa.
6. See Jordan.
7. See Ahlgren, "Negotiating Sanctity" 381.
8. Attributed to Velázquez.
9. The "fifty-year rule," which stipulated that proceedings for canonization could not begin until fifty years after the death of the candidate, was established by Urban III (1568–1644) after Teresa's canonization.
10. See Delooz.
11. A "good shepherd" is someone such as a bishop responsible for a flock of souls.
12. The Transverberation is the vision Teresa describes in *Life* in which an angel pierces her heart with a flaming arrow.
13. Not to be confused with Hieronymous Wierex, his brother. Both men were members of the renowned Wierex family, which produced many fine engravers.
14. The exact date of composition is unknown. The work was first published in *Revista Agustiniana* 5 (1883) and is a copy of an autograph found in the Discalced Carmelite convent in Salamanca.
15. I wish to thank Dr. Christopher Wilson for sharing the Collaert and Galle images with me.
16. Tyre was a Phoenician city known for its production of red dye.
17. See Dassbach.
18. For an analysis of this play, see my article, "Performing Sanctity."
19. His name was Juan de Ovalle, not del Valle. In real life Juan de Ovalle bought the house that Teresa transformed into San José, in Ávila.
20. "Your Reverend Father" is equivalent to "you." (This is a courteous way of addressing ecclesiastics.)
21. My translation. All translations in this chapter are mine unless otherwise indicated.
22. Saint Pammachius was a Roman senator who died around A.D. 409. He and Saint Jerome were friends who maintained a vigorous correspondence throughout their lives. When the one-time monk Jovian was condemned for heresy for holding, among other false doctrines, that virginity was not a superior state to that of marriage, Jerome wrote two books attacking him.

Pammachius wrote to Jerome criticizing his books on prudential grounds, and Jerome responded with two letters thanking him and vindicating the book. After Pammachius became a monk, he and Jerome continued to exchange letters on theological matters. Several of Jerome's commentaries on Scripture were dedicated to Pammachius.

23. The reference is surely to Saint Erasmus (d. 303), also known as Saint Elmo, who was Bishop of Formiae, Campagna, Italy, and fled to Mount Lebanon due to the persecutions of Diocletian. He was known for his great eloquence, through which he converted many pagans. Eventually, he was martyred by disembowelment. A famous painting by Matthias Grünewald, *The Meeting of St. Erasmus and St. Maurice*, c.1520–1524, shows him in a disputation with the Roman saint Mauritius. An early triptych of the martyrdom of Saint Erasmus includes an image of Saint Jerome in one panel and Saint Bernard in another, as though witnessing the execution. Fray Diego cannot be referring to Desiderio Erasmus (1466–1536), who lived centuries after Jerome. My thanks to Héctor Campos and Mauro E. Mujica for clarifying this reference.

24. See Chapter 1 on the seals Teresa used.

25. See Chapter 1 for a description.

26. In *Life* Teresa writes of deriving great strength from Jerome: "Reading the *Letters of Saint Jerome* so encouraged me that I decided to tell my father about my decision to take the habit" (*CWST* 1, 3:7). She mentions Jerome again in *Life* 11:10 and 38:1, and in *The Way of Perfection* (*CWST* 2, 5:2).

27. See Alvarez de Toledo.

28. Translations are mine. Because numerous editions of the work exist, I have identified the quotes by section or letter number rather than by page number.

29. See Efrén de la Madre de Dios and Steggink (761).

30. See Efrén de la Madre de Dios and Steggink (851).

31. On Teresa's obedience to spiritual directors, see my article, "Paul the Enchanter," and Weber, "The Three Lives of the *Vida*."

CONCLUSION

1. See Rodríguez Martínez and Egido (58).

APPENDIX

1. "Your mercy" is equivalent to "you."

2. The merchants Espinosa and Varrona were two of Lorenzo's messengers.

3. Teresa's friend Guiomar de Ulloa, who gave her money for the first foundation.

4. Un cuento de renta: one million maravedís (Rodríguez Martínez and Egido 64n3).

5. Because the Carmelite provincial Ángel de Salazar opposed the foundation, Teresa put the new convent under the jurisdiction of the bishop.

6. A friend of Lorenzo's who served as his messenger.

7. In reality the foundation was not made until 24 August 1562.

8. Don Alonso Rodríguez, from Trujillo, Perú, also served as Lorenzo's messenger to his sister.

9. María de Guzmán, Teresa's older widowed sister.

10. Juan de Ovalle, the husband of Teresa's younger sister Juana, was threatening a

lawsuit in order to obtain a larger share of his father-in-law's estate. (See Chapter 4.)

11. Part of Don Alonso's estate. He inherited the houses from his wife.

12. Don Alonso's housemaid.

13. Possibly Lorenzo's oldest son, who died in 1563.

14. Note that this is the only time Teresa mentions this document in her writing.

15. Apparently a statue that Lorenzo sent.

16. The letter is dated 24 December. In Ávila the new year began on 25 December until 1564, when it was changed to January 1 (Rodríguez Martínez and Egido 68n12).

17. Their younger brother, who was returning to Spanish America from Spain.

18. Two of their brothers.

19. This paragraph appears in the Álvarez edition. Rodríguez Martínez and Egido include it not in the main body of the text but in a footnote.

20. The text reads *un*, although in modern Spanish *una* would be used.

21. Teresa is apparently referring to a nun who is transferring to another convent. The nun can travel with the three who are going from Segovia to Caravaca to make a foundation.

22. Code name for the Calced Carmelites.

23. Rubeo.

24. Weather conditions—excessive heat, for example—were one reason nuns used for requesting transfers.

25. For example, if a particular house had too few nuns and needed more.

26. Teresa had taken nuns from Malagón to send to Beas, Seville, and Caravaca.

27. The Jesuits were Teresa's main source of novices in Valladolid. (See Chapter 6.)

28. This paragraph appears in the Álvarez edition. Rodríguez Martínez and Egido include it not in the main body of the text but in a footnote.

29. Teresa's name for John of the Cross.

30. Father Juan Evangelista, subprior of the Seville Carmel.

31. Francisco Arias, rector of the Seville Jesuits. Rodrigo Álvarez, also a Jesuit, was Teresa's spiritual director.

32. Teresa refers to Antonio de Jesús (Heredia), who had made the first male foundation with John of the Cross in Duruelo. Fray Antonio had worked with Pedro Fernández, the visitator in Castile, who in 1571 sent him to be prior at the Calced monastery in Toledo. Fray Antonio held several other positions until the end of 1575, when he accompanied Gracián to Seville. He was supposed to help Gracián by making visitations to smaller convents, but Teresa notes that he did not accomplish as much as she had hoped.

33. The Calced Andalusian Carmelites.

34. Juana Dantisco, Gracián's mother.

35. Dr. Alonso Velázquez. (See Chapter 6).

36. Discalced Carmelite nuns were supposed to keep their faces covered when speaking to those who were not family members. (Recall the discussion of this issue in Chapter 5.) It is a sign of trust that Gracián tells Teresa to uncover her face for his mother.

37. Gracián's sister Juana was at a school for young noblewomen in Toledo.

38. Gracián's little sister Isabel entered the order at age seven and received the habit from Teresa herself in 1576.

39. Wife of a well-known grammarian, Blas de la Serna. Gracián's relatives stayed in Doña Ana's house.

40. María Dantisco, another of Gracián's sisters. She professed as María de San José in Valladolid. (See Chapter 5.)

41. Still another of Gracián's sisters.

42. One of Gracián's brothers.

43. Another of Gracián's brothers. He was married to one of Doña Ana de Zurita's daughters.

44. Code name for Teresa. She speaks of herself in the third person in this paragraph.

45. Code name for Jesus.

46. Teresa is referring to the chapter meeting that took place during the first few days of September 1576 in Almodóvar del Campo.

47. A convent official whose job it is to promote monastic observance.

48. Juan de Jesús (Roca), who was to be in charge of overseeing observance of the rule in the Discalced monasteries.

49. Rubeo.

50. Rubeo.

51. Pedro de los Ángeles, prior of La Peñuela, and Ambrosio Mariano were selected to go to Rome. Fray Pedro apparently was on good terms with Rubeo. After Fray Pedro came back from Rome, he returned to the Calced Carmelites (Pacho 1159).

52. Nicolás Ormaneto, the nuncio, who was very ill.

53. Possibly another code name for the nuncio Ormaneto.

54. See note 32.

55. Ángel Salazar, the provincial.

56. Official in charge of inspecting convents.

57. Agustín Suárez, provincial of the Carmelites in Andalusia.

58. In January 1576 Gracián relieved Miguel de Ulloa of his duties as prior of the Seville monastery, which had made so many problems for the reform, and replaced him with Juan Evangelista.

59. Brianda de San José. The Malagón convent was undergoing terrible problems. Several nuns were sick, the house was in grave disrepair, and there was bickering among some of the sisters. Doña Luisa, on whose property the convent had been founded, had badly neglected it. Teresa wrote to Gracián and María de San José about the possibility of disbanding the house, but decided against it. She moved the nuns out so a new monastery could be built and entrusted the affair to her friend Antonio Ruiz, a local merchant.

60. Juana Bautista Baena, one of the Malagón nuns.

61. Beatriz was the daughter of Teresa's cousin, Francisco de Cepeda. She turned out to be a fine prioress, as Teresa writes to her second cousin, Don Luis de Cepeda: "Sister Beatriz is now in charge of governing the house in Malagón, and she is very busy. She is doing extremely well, glory to God, for I didn't think she was capable of so much" (*Letters* 1, 26 November 1576: 1).

62. Isabel de Jesús (Gutiérrez) had been in Encarnación in Ávila.

63. Gaspar de Villanueva, the Malagón chaplain.

64. Perhaps the unreformed nuns in Seville, who participated in the gossip campaign against Gracián.

65. Code for the Calced Carmelites.

66. Possibly Rubeo.

67. Code for Tostado, who was in Portugal.

68. Teresa had become ill from exhaustion caused by overwork.

69. Luisa de la Cerda's overseer or administrator, Juan Huidobro de Miranda (Rodríguez Martínez and Egido, *Epistolario* 426).

70. Teresa had to wear a garment of higher-quality material because of her health.

71. Used as an air freshener.

72. Orange blossom in hot water was believed to relieve anxiety.

73. Leonor de Valera, mother of Blanca de Jesús María (Rodríguez and Egido, *Epistolario* 426).

74. On February 28, 1577, Teresa had written to María de San José that she was exhausted from so much work and about the problems she was having with the very trying Isabel de San Jerónimo.

75. Beatriz de la Madre de Dios, who had caused considerable turmoil with her claims to mystical visions. (See Chapters 4 and 5.)

76. In Castile.

77. She had left to go to Paterna.

78. A confessor had told Isabel to write down her prayer experiences. The page was mislaid, but found by the prioress of Paterna, Isabel de San Francisco. Teresa was worried that it could have fallen into the hands of the Inquisition. Because Isabel de San Jerónimo claimed to have mystical experiences and such claims by women were always suspect, things could have gone badly for her. (See Chapters 4 and 5.)

79. Gracián.

80. Ana de Jesús.

81. Beatriz's "mystical language."

82. The Jesuit Diego de Acosta.

83. Apparently the nuns who went to Paterna demanded more than what was required by the Constitutions.

84. Luisa de la Cerda.

85. Guiomar Pardo de Tavera, Doña Luisa's daughter.

86. Gracián's little sister, Isabel Dantisco, who was living in the Toledo Carmel.

87. She probably means *tacamaca,* or balsam, a resin used as a sedative.

88. The question was concerning the words, "Seek yourself in me." "Once in a prayer Teresa heard the words, 'seek yourself in me.' In awe over the meaning they might contain, she sent them to her brother Don Lorenzo so that he might reflect on them" (*CWST* 3, Introduction, "A Satirical Critique" 357). Lorenzo consulted many learned persons and they decided to write out their reflections and send them to the nuns at San José in Ávila for judgment. However, the bishop of Ávila, Don Álvaro de Mendoza, suggested they send them to Teresa.

89. Nicolás Doria.

90. Bartolomé de Jesús was a Discalced friar in Seville.

91. The Carmelites are the Order of Our Lady of Carmen (or Carmel).

92. Teresa had been prioress of the Convent of the Encarnación from 1571 until 1574. The nuns attempted to reelect her in 1577, but unreformed (Calced) Carmelite authorities blocked the move and the nuns who voted for Teresa were excommunicated.

93. The Calced confessors were insensitive to the kind of spirituality that Teresa taught, which stressed recollection and mental prayer, and so she insisted that the nuns have access to Discalced confessors.

94. Pedro Fernández, who had appointed her prioress at Encarnación. (Kavanaugh, *Letters* 1:581n2).

95. Teresa is referring to John of the Cross (Juan de la Cruz), her friend and disciple,

whom she selected as confessor for the nuns of the Encarnación. The companion was Germán de San Matías.

96. Nicolás Ormaneto, who had died earlier in the year.

97. That is, the unreformed (Calced) confessors.

98. That is, priests who do not belong to an order.

99. "Hernando Maldonado, prior of the monastery in Toledo. He went there for the purpose of absolving those who voted for Teresa from the excommunication imposed on them" (Kavanaugh, *Letters* 1:581n6).

100. John of the Cross had been arrested the night before by Calced friars and imprisoned in Toledo, where he was held in a tiny cell and deprived of food and communion. He escaped nearly a year later, on August 15, 1578.

101. Teresa's friend and confessor, Jerónimo Gracián.

102. They "gain a great deal" because suffering brings the individual closer to Jesus.

103. Recall that Antonio de Jesús (Heredia) and John of the Cross were the first two friars to join Teresa's reform. They occupied the first male convent in Duruelo on November 28, 1568.

104. Jerónimo Tostado, visitator and commissary general of the Spanish provinces, had the power to smother the reformed convents.

105. The prioress-ship had just been returned to María de San José after the terrible episode in which Beatriz de la Madre de Dios and Margarita de la Concepción had accused her to the Inquisition. (See Chapters 4 and 5.)

106. Ángel de Salazar, who at that time was actually the vicar general, was the one who reinstated María de San José as prioress.

107. Doria. This letter shows the great esteem in which Teresa held Nicolás Doria, her financial manager.

108. A reference to Jesus's agony in the Garden of Gethsemane.

109. Thy will be done.

110. His name was actually Enrique Freire. He already had one daughter in the Seville Carmel. Teresa's was reluctant to accept more than two from one family into a single convent, and Freire had two more daughters who wanted to profess in Seville. The eldest, who was already a nun, was María de San José (Freire). The next one became Isabel de San Fabronio. The youngest, Blanca de Jesús, was only admitted to the Seville Carmel after one of her sisters transferred to Lisbon.

111. Beatriz de la Madre de Dios and Margarita de la Concepción. See notes 30 and 105.

112. The feast of Saint Anne is July 26, but Teresa did not actually leave Valladolid until July 30.

113. See note 59.

114. Teresa was buying a new house in Salamanca.

115. July 22.

116. Gregorio Nacianceno, vicar of Los Remedios, the Discalced Carmelite friary in Seville.

117. She means the "war" against the Calced, for which he will be rewarded in heaven.

118. Hernando de Pantoja, the Carthusian prior who befriended Teresa when she first went to Seville.

Bibliography

PRIMARY SOURCES

Ana de San Bartolomé. *Obras Completas*. Ed. Julián Urkiza. Monte Carmelo: Burgos, 1988.

Francisco Javier. *Cartas y escritos*. Ed. Félix Zubillaga, S.J. Madrid: Bibliotecta de Autores Cristianos, 1996.

Gracián, Jerónimo de la Madre de Dios. *Cartas*. Ed. Juan Luis Astigárraga. Roma: Teresianum, 1989.

———. *Peregrinación de Anastasio*. Roma: Teresianum, 2001.

Ignacio de Loyola. *Obras*. Madrid: Biblioteca de Autores Cristianos, 1991.

Juan de la Cruz. *Obras Completas*. Ed. Lucinio Ruano de la Iglesia. Madrid: Biblioteca de Autores Cristianos, 1994.

Luis de León. *Obras completas castellanas, I*. Madrid: Biblioteca de Autores Cristianos, 1991.

Luther, Martin. *Discourse on Free Will*. Ed. Ernst F. Winter. New York: Continuum, 1997.

María de San José. *Escritos espirituales*. Roma: Postulación General, 1979.

Quevedo, Francisco de. *Contra el Patronato de Santa Teresa de Jesús*. In *Obras completas: Obras en verso*. Ed. Felicidad Buendía. Madrid: Aguilar, 1964. 449–453.

Teresa de Jesús. *Camino de perfección*. Ed. P. Tomás de la Cruz. 2 vols. Rome: Tipografía Poliglotta Vaticana, 1965.

———. *Cartas*. Ed. Tomás Álvarez. Burgos: Monte Carmelo, 1983.

———. *Epistolario*. Ed. Luis Rodríguez Martínez and Teófanes Egido. Madrid: Espiritualidad, 1984.

———. *Libro de las fundaciones*. Buenos Aires: Espasa-Calpe, 1951.

———. *Libro de la vida*. Ed. Dámaso Chicharro. Madrid: Cátedra, 1993.

———. *Las moradas del castillo interior*. Ed. Dámaso Chicharro. Madrid: Biblioteca Nueva, 1999.

———. *Obras completas*. 10th ed. Ed. Tomás Álvarez. Burgos: Monte Carmelo, 1998.

———. *Obras completas*. Ed. Enrique Llamas et al. Madrid: Espiritualidad, 1994.

———. *Obras completas*. Edición manual. Ed. Efrén de la Madre de Dios and Otger Steggink. Madrid: Católica, 1962.

TRANSLATIONS

Gracián, Jerónimo. *Just Man, Husband of Mary, Guardian of Christ: An Anthology of Readings from Jerónimo Gracián's* Summary of the Excellencies of St. Joseph *(1597)*. Ed. and trans. Joseph F. Chorpenning. Philadelphia: Saint Joseph's University Press, 1993.

María de San José. *Book for the Hour of Recreation.* Intro. Alison Weber. Trans. Amanda Powell. Chicago: University of Chicago Press, 2002.

Teresa of Ávila. *The Collected Letters of St. Teresa of Ávila.* Trans. Kieran Kavanaugh. 2 vols. Washington, D.C.: Institute of Carmelite Studies, 2001, 2007.

———. *The Collected Works of Saint Teresa of Ávila.* Trans. Kieran Kavanaugh, O.C.D., and Otlio Rodríguez, O.C.D. 3 vols. Washington, DC: Institute of Carmelite Studies, 1980–1987.

———. *The Complete Works of Saint Teresa of Jesus.* Ed. and trans. E. Allison Peers. 3 vols. London: Sheed and Ward, 1946.

———. *The Letters of St. Teresa of Jesus.* Trans. E. Allison Peers. 2 vols. London: Burns, Oates and Washbourne, 1951.

SECONDARY SOURCES

Ahlgren, Gillian. *Entering Teresa of Avila's Interior Castle.* Mahwah, NJ: Paulist Press, 2005.

———. "Negotiating Sanctity: Holy Women in Sixteenth-Century Spain." *Church History* 64.3 (Sept. 1995): 373–88.

———. *Teresa de Avila and the Politics of Sanctity.* Ithaca: Cornell University Press, 1996.

Alonso Cortés, Narciso. "Pleitos de los Cepedas." *Boletín de la Real Academia Española* 15 (1946): 85–110.

Álvarez, Tomás, ed. *Diccionario de santa Teresa*, 2nd ed. Burgos: Monte Carmelo, 2006.

Álvarez de Toledo, Cayetana. *Politics and Reform in Spain and Viceregal Mexico: The Life and Thought of Juan de Palafox 1600–1659.* Oxford: Oxford University Press, 2004.

Arenal, Electa, and Stacey Schlau. " 'Leyendo yo y escribiendo ella': The Convent as Intellectual Community." *Journal of Hispanic Philology* 13 (1989): 214–29.

Arenal, Electa, and Stacey Schlau, eds. *Untold Sisters: Hispanic Nuns in Their Own Words.* Trans. Amanda Powell. Alburquerque: University of New Mexico Press, 1989.

Asín Palacios, Miguel. "El símil de los castillos y moradas en la mística islámica y en Santa Teresa". *Al-Andaluz* 11 (1946): 263–74.

Auclair, Marcelle. *Saint Teresa of Avila.* Trans. Kathleen Pond. Petersham, MA: St. Bede's, 1988.

Baer, Yitzhak. *A History of the Jews in Christian Spain.* 2 vols. Philadelphia: Jewish Publication Society of America, 1966.

Bataille, Georges. *Erotism: Death and Sensuality.* Trans. Mary Dalwood. San Francisco: City Lights, 1986.

Bataillon, Marcel. *Erasmo y España.* Trans. Antonio Alatorre. Mexico City: Fondo de Cultura Económica, 1982.

Beasley, Faith. "Altering the Fabric of History: Women's Participation in the Classical Age." *A History of Women's Writing in France.* Ed. Sonya Stephens. Cambridge: Cambridge University Press, 2000. 64–83.

Bell, Rudolph M. *Holy Anorexia.* Chicago: University of Chicago Press, 1985.

Bilinkoff, Jodi. *The Avila of Saint Teresa: Religious Reform in a Sixteenth-Century City.* Ithaca: Cornell University Press, 1989.

———. "Confession, Gender, Life-Writing: Some Cases (Mainly) from Spain." *Penitence in the Age of Reformations.* Ed. Katharine Jackson Lualdi and Anne T. Thayer. Aldershot: UK, 2000. 169–83.

———. "Confessors, Penitents, and the Construction of Identities in Early Modern Avila." *Culture and Identity in Early Modern Europe (1500–1800).* Ed. Barbara B. Diefendorf and Carla Hesse. Ann Arbor: University of Michigan Press, 1993. 83–100.

———. "Teresa of Jesus and the Carmelite Reform." *Religious Orders of the Catholic Reformation. Essays in honor of John C. Olin on His Seventy-fifth Birthday.* Ed. Richard De Molen. New York: Fordham University Press, 1994. 166–86.

———. "Woman with a Mission: Teresa of Avila and the Apostolic Model." *Modelli di santità e modelli di comportamento.* Ed. Giulia Barone, et al. Turin: Rosenberg and Sellier, 1994. 295–305.

Blackburn, Alexander. *The Myth of the Pícaro: Continuity and Transformation of the Picaresque Novel, 1554–1954.* Chapel Hill: University of North Carolina Press, 1979.

Boulay, Shirley du. *Teresa of Avila: An Extraordinary Life.* New York: BlueBridge: 2004.

Burke, Peter. "How to Be a Counter-Reformation Saint." *Religion and Society in Early Modern Europe 1500–1800.* Ed. Kaspar von Greyerz. London: German Historical Institute / George Allen and Unwin, 1984. 45–55.

Bynum, Caroline Walker. *Fragmentation and Redemption: Essays on Gender and the Human Body in Medieval Religion.* New York: Zone, 1991.

———. *Holy Feast and Holy Fast: The Religious Significance of Food to Medieval Women.* Berkeley: University of California Press, 1987.

Cammarata, Joan. "*Epistola consolatoria* y *contemptus mundi*: El epistolario de consuelo de Santa Teresa de Avila." *Actas del XIII Congreso de la Asociación Internacional de Hispanistas.* Vol. 1, *Medieval: Siglo de Oro.* Ed. Florencio Sevilla and Carlos Alvar. Madrid: Castalia, 2000. 301–8.

———. "El discurso femenino de Santa Teresa de Avila, defensora de la mujer renacentista." *Actas Irvine 92,* Asociación Internacional de Hispanistas. Irvine, CA: University of California Irvine, 1994. 58–65.

———. "Mystical Psychagogue, Cultural Other: St. Teresa of Avila." *Homenaje a Bruno Damiani.* Ed. Filippo María Toscano. Lanham, MD: University Press of America, 1994. 31–42.

Cammarata, Joan, ed. *Women in the Discourse of Early Modern Spain.* Gainsboro: University of Florida Press, 2003.

Canons and Decrees of the Council of Trent. Trans. H. J. Schroeder. St. Louis: B. Herder, 1941.

Carreño, Antonio. "*El libro de la Vida* de Santa Teresa: los trances de su escritura." *Ínsula* 430 (Sept. 1982): 1.

Carrera, Elena. *Teresa of Avila's Autobiography: Authority, Power and the Self in Mid-Sixteenth-Century Spain.* Oxford: Legenda / Modern Humanities Research Association, 2005.

Carrión, María. *Arquitectura y cuerpo en la figura autorial de Teresa de Jesús*. Barcelona: Anthropos, 1994.

Casey, James. *Early Modern Spain: A Social History*. London: Routledge, 1999.

Castro, Américo. *Teresa la Santa y otros ensayos*. Madrid: Alfaguara, 1972.

Catholic Encyclopedia CD Rom. New Advent, 2003.

Chartier, Roger, Alain Boureau, and Cécile Dauphin, eds. *Correspondence: Models of Letter-Writing from the Middle Ages to the Nineteenth Century*. Trans. Chistopher Woodall. Cambridge, UK: Polity, 1997.

Cilveti, Angel L. *Introducción a la mística española*. Madrid: Cátedra, 1974.

Cirlot, Juan Eduardo. *Diccionario de símbolos*. Madrid: Siruela, 1997.

Cixous, Hélène. "The Laugh of Medusa." *Signs* 1.4 (1975): 875–93.

Conde, C. "Sobre la escritura de Santa Teresa y su amor a las letras." *Revista de Espiritualidad* 22 (1963): 348–58.

Concejo, Pilar. "Fórmulas sociales y estrategias retóricas en el epistolario de Teresa de Jesús." *Santa Teresa y la literatura mística hispánica: Actas del I Congreso Internacional sobre Santa Teresa y la Mística Hispánica*. Ed. Criado de Val. Madrid: EDI-6, 1984.

Couchman, Jane, and Ann Crabb, ed. *Women's Letters across Europe, 1400–1700*. Aldershot, UK: Ashgate, 2005.

Covarrubias, Sebastián de. *Tesoro de la lengua castellana*. Madrid: Castalia, 1995.

Criado de Val, M. "Santa Teresa de Jesús en la gran polémica española: mística frente a picaresca." *Revista de Espiritualidad* 22 (1963): 376–84.

Criado de Val, M., ed. *Santa Teresa y la literatura mística hispánica: Actas del I Congreso Internacional sobre Santa Teresa y la Mística Hispánica*. Madrid: EDI-6, 1984.

Crisógono de Jesús Sacramento. *Santa Teresa de Jesús. Su vida y su doctrina*. Barcelona: Labor, 1936.

———. *Santa Teresa, madre y doctora*. Madrid: Espiritualidad, 1970.

Cruz, Anne J. *Discourses of Poverty: Social Reform and the Picaresque Novel in Early Modern Spain*. Toronto: University of Toronto Press, 1999.

Curtius, Ernst Robert. *European Literature and the Latin Middle Ages*. Trans. Willard R. Trask. New York: Harper and Row, 1963.

Dassbach, Elma. *La comedia hagiográfica del Siglo de Oro español: Lope de Vega, Tirso de Molina y Calderón de la Barca*. New York: Peter Lang, 1997.

Delooz, Pierre. "Towards a Sociological Study of Canonized Sainthood in the Catholic Church." *Saints and Their Cults: Studies in Religious Sociology, Folklore, and History*. Ed. Stephen Wilson. Cambridge: Cambridge University Press, 1983.

Deneuville, D. *Santa Teresa y la mujer*. Barcelona: Herder, 1966.

Derrida, Jacques. *L'Ecriture et la différence*. Paris: Seuil, 1967.

Doglio, Maria Luisa. "Letter Writing, 1350–1650." *A History of Women's Writing in Italy*. Ed. Letizia Panizza and Sharon Wood. Cambridge: Cambridge University Press, 2000. 13–24.

———. *Lettere e Donna: Scrittura epistolare femminile tra Quatro e Cinquecento*. Roma: Bulzoni, 1993.

Dolan, Frances E. *Whores of Babylon: Catholicism, Gender, and Seventeenth-Century Print Culture*. Ithaca, NY: Cornell University Press, 1999.

Dunn, Sandra Loueen. *Body, Soul, Text: Teresa of Avila and the Written Self*. Dissertation Abstracts International, Section A (Humanities and Social Sciences). (59:7) 1999 Jan., 2535. Cornell University, 1998. DA9900047.

Edwards, John. *Inquisition*. Stroud, Gloucestershire, UK: Tempus, 2003.

Efrén de la Madre de Dios. *La herencia teresiana*. Madrid: Espiritualidad, 1975.

———. *Santa Teresa por dentro*. Madrid: Espiritualidad, 1973.

Efrén de la Madre de Dios, and Otger Steggink. *Tiempo y vida de Santa Teresa*. 3rd ed. Madrid: Biblioteca de Autores Cristianos, 1996.

Egido, Teófanes. *El linaje judeoconverso de Santa Teresa*. Madrid: Espiritualidad, 1986.

Eisenstein, Elizabeth L. *The Printing Revolution in Early Modern Europe*. Cambridge: Cambridge University Press, 1983.

Enyclopedia of Catholicism. Ed. Richard P. McBrien. New York: HarperCollins, 1995.

Erasmus, Desiderius. *The Collected Works of Erasmus*. Trans. Craig R. Thompson. Toronto: University of Toronto Press, 1997.

———. *Opera omnia*. Amsterdam: North-Holland, 1969–.

Fernández de Alarcón, Cristobalina. "A santa Teresa de Jesús en su beatificación." *Tras el espejo la musa escribe: Lírica femenina de los Siglos de Oro*. Eds. Julián Olivares and Elizabeth S. Boyce. Mexico City: Siglo XXI, 1993.

Flinders, Carol Lee. *Enduring Grace: Living Portraits of Seven Women Mystics*. San Francisco: HarperSanFrancisco, 1993.

Foucault, Michel. *Histoire de la folie à l'âge classique*. Paris: Gallimard, 1972.

———. *Religion and Culture*. Ed. Jeremy R. Carrette. New York: Routledge, 1999.

Fumerton, Patricia. "Introduction: A New New Historicism." *Renaissance Culture and the Everyday*. Ed. Patricia Fumerton. Philadelphia: University of Pennsylvania Press, 1999. 1–20.

Galle, Cornelio, and Adrián Collaert. *Estampas de la vida de la Santa Madre Teresa de Jesús. Grabadas por los famosos artistas Cornelio Galle y Adrián Collaert, impresas en Amberes en 1613, ahora reproducidas en facsímil y publicadas por Carlos Sanz, en ocasión de la conmemoración del IV centenario de la reforma de la Orden Carmelitana*. Madrid, 1962.

Gallagher, Catherine, and Stephen Greenblatt. *Practicing New Historicism*. Chicago: University of Chicago Press, 2000.

Gálvez Campos, Tomás. "La 'reforma' de los conventuales durante el reinado de los Reyes Católicos. El caso de Calatayud." *Paz y Bien*. 25 Dec. 2004. *http://pazybien.org/centenario/documentos/cursillo/tomas.doc*.

García de la Concha, Víctor. *El arte literario de Santa Teresa*. Barcelona: Ariel, 1978.

———. Introducción. *Libro de las fundaciones*. By Teresa de Jesús. Buenos Aires: Espasa-Calpe, 1951.

García Valdés, O. *Teresa de Jesús*. Barcelona: Omega, 2001.

García-Villoslada, Ricardo. *Martín Lutero*. 2 vols. Madrid: Católica, 1973.

Giles, Mary, ed. *The Feminist Mystic, and Other Essays on Women and Spirituality*. New York: Crossroads, 1982.

Gitlitz, David. "Inquisition Confessions and Lazarillo de Tormes." *Hispanic Review* 68.1 (2000): 53–75.

Goldsmith, Elizabeth C. "Authority, Authenticity, and the Publication of Letters by Women." In *Writing the Female Voice*. Ed. Elizabeth Goldsmith. Boston: Northeastern University Press. 46–59.

Goldsmith, Elizabeth, ed. *Writing the Female Voice*. Boston: Northeastern University Press, 1989.

Gross, Francis L., Jr. "Teresa de Avila's Body: Symbol of Her Life." *Studia Mystica* 18 (1997): 134–43.

Guillén, Claudio. "Notes toward the Study of the Renaissance Letter." *Renaissance*

Genres: Essays on Theory, History, and Interpretation. Ed. Barbara Kiefer Lewalski. Cambridge: Harvard University Press, 1986. 70–101.

Hatzfeld, Helmut. *Santa Teresa de Ávila.* New York: Twayne, 1969.

Howe, Elizabeth Teresa. *Education and Women in the Early Modern Hispanic World.* Aldershot, UK: Ashgate, 2008.

———. *Mystical Imagery: Santa Teresa de Jesús and San Juan de la Cruz.* New York: Peter Lang, 1988.

Huarte de San Juan, Juan. *Examen de ingenios para las ciencias.* Ed. Guillermo Serés. Madrid: Cátedra, 1989.

Irigaray, Luce. *This Sex Which Is Not One.* Trans. Catherine Porter and Carolyn Burke. Ithaca, NY: Cornell University Press, 1985.

Jantzen, Grace M. *Power, Gender, and Christian Mysticism.* Cambridge: Cambridge University Press, 1995.

Jardine, Lisa. *Erasmus, Man of Letters.* Princeton: Princeton University Press, 1993.

———. *Worldly Goods.* New York: Doubleday, 1996.

Jensen, Katharine. "Male Models of Feminine Epistolarity: Or, How to Write like a Woman in Seventeenth-Century France." *Writing the Female Voice.* Ed. Elizabeth Goldsmith. Boston: Northeastern University Press, 1989. 25–45.

Jordan, Constance. *Renaissance Feminism.* Ithaca: Cornell University Press, 1990.

Kamen, Henry. *Philip of Spain.* New Haven: Yale University Press, 1997.

———. *Spain 1469–1714.* London: Longman, 1991.

———. *The Spanish Inquisition.* New Haven: Yale University Press, 1998.

Katz, Stephen T. "Mystical Speech and Mystical Meaning." *Mysticism and Language.* Ed. Steven T. Katz. Oxford: Oxford University Press, 1992. 3–41.

Kavanaugh, Kieran. Introduction. *Book of Her Life.* By Teresa de Ávila. *The Collected Works of Saint Teresa of Ávila.* Vol. 1. 2nd ed. (revised). Washington, DC: Institute of Carmelite Studies, 1987. 15–51.

Kavanaugh, Kieran, trans. Introduction. *The Collected Letters of St. Teresa of Ávila.* 11–27. 2 vols. Washington, DC: Institute of Carmelite Studies, 2001, 2007.

King, Margaret L. *Women of the Renaissance.* Chicago: University of Chicago Press, 1991.

Lázaro Carreter, Fernando. Lazarillo de Tormes *en la picaresa.* Barcelona: Ariel, 1983.

Lehfeldt, Elizabeth. *Religious Women in Golden Age Spain: The Permeable Cloister.* Aldershot, UK: Ashgate, 2005.

Levy-Navarro, Elena. "The Religious Warrior: Luisa de Carvajal y Mendoza's Correspondence with Rodrigo de Calderón." *Women's Letters across Europe: 1400–1700.* Ed. Jane Couchman and Ann Crabb. Aldershot, UK: Ashgate, 2005. 263–73.

Lincoln, Victoria. *Teresa: A Woman.* Albany: State University of New York Press, 1984.

López, Josefina C. "Voz y sumisión del alma: *Moradas del castillo interior.*" *Bulletin of Spanish Studies* 85.1 (2008): 1–9.

Luti, Mary. " 'A Marriage Well Arranged': Teresa of Avila and Fray Jerónimo Gracián de la Madre de Dios." *Studia Mystica* (1989): 32–46.

MacCulloch, Diarmaid. *The Reformation: A History.* New York: Viking, 2004.

MacLean, Katie. "The Mystic and the Moor-Slayer: Saint Teresa, Santiago and the Struggle for Spanish Identity." *Bulletin of Spanish Studies* 83.7 (2006): 887–910.

Maiorino, Giancarlo. *At the Margins of the Renaissance: Lazarillo de Tormes and the Picaresque Art of Survival.* University Park: Pennsylvania State University Press, 2003.

Man, John. *Gutenberg*. New York: John Wiley and Sons, 2002.

Marco Merenciano, F. "Psicoanálisis y melancolía en Santa Teresa." *Ensayos médicos y literarios*. Madrid: Cultura Hispánica, 1958. 497–535.

Marichal, Juan. "Santa Teresa en el ensayismo hispánico." *La vountad de estilo*. Madrid: Taurus, 1958. 89–98.

Marina, Constance. *The Business of Courtesy: An Examination of the Letters of Teresa of Avila*. Dissertation Abstracts International (54:6) 1993 Dec., 2168A. Harvard University, 1993. DA9330984.

Martz, Linda. *A Network of Converso Families in Early Modern Toledo: Assimilating a Minority*. Ann Arbor: University of Michigan Press, 2003.

McAlister, Lyle N. *Spain and Portugal in the New World, 1492–1700*. Minneapolis: University of Minnesota Press, 1984.

McBrian, Richard P., ed. *Encyclopedia of Catholicism*. San Francisco: Harper Collins, 1995.

Medwick, Cathleen. *Teresa de Avila: The Progress of a Soul*. New York: Knopf, 1999.

Menéndez Pidal, Ramón. "El estilo de santa Teresa." *La lengua de Cristóbal Colón y otros estudios sobre el siglo XVI*. 6th ed. Madrid: Espasa Calpe, 1978.

Menocal, María Rosa. *The Ornament of the World: How Muslims, Jews, and Christians Created a Culture of Tolerance in Medieval Spain*. New York: Little, Brown, 2002.

Meyerson, Mark. "Defending Their Jewish Subjects: Elionor of Sicily, María de Luna, and the Jews of Morvedre." *Queenship and Political Power in Medieval and Early Modern Spain*. Ed. Theresa Earenfight. Aldershot, UK: Ashgate, 2005. 55-77.

Miller, Naomi, and Naomi Yavneh, eds. *Sibling Relations and Gender in the Early Modern World: Sisters, Brothers and Others*. Aldershot, UK: Ashgate, 2006.

Mir, M. *Santa Teresa de Jesús*. Madrid: Jaime Ratés, 1912.

Moriones, Ildefonso. *El Carmelo teresiano y sus problemas de memoria histórica*. Vitoria: El Carmen, 1997.

———. *El P. Doria y el carisma teresiano*. Roma: Orden de los Padres Carmelitas Descalzos, 1994.

———. *Teresian Carmel: Pages of History*. Trans. S. C. O'Mahony. Rome: Order of the Discalced Carmelites, 2003. *www.ocd.pcn.net/histo_1.htm*.

Morón Arroyo, C. "Mística y expresión: la originalidad cultural de Santa Teresa." *Crisis* 20 (1973): 211–41.

Moura Sobral, Luís de. "Josefa de Óbidos and her Use of Prints: Problems of Style and Iconography." *The Sacred and the Profane: Josefa de Óbidos of Portugal*. Washington, DC: National Museum of Women in the Arts, 1997.

Mujica, Bárbara. "Beyond Image: The Apophatic-Kataphatic Dialectic in Teresa de Avila." *Hispania* 84.4 (2001): 741–48.

———. "Paul the Enchanter: Gracián and Saint Teresa's Vow of Obedience." *The Heirs of Saint Teresa*. Ed. Christopher Wilson. Washington, DC: Institute of Carmelite Studies, 2006. 21–44.

———. "Performing Sanctity: Lope's Use of Teresian Iconography in *Santa Teresa de Jesús*." *A Companion to Lope de Vega*. Ed. Alexander Samson and Jonathan Thacker. London: Tamesis, 2008. 183–98.

———. "Skepticism and Mysticism in Golden Age Spain: Teresa de Avila's Combative Stance." *Women in the Discourse of Early Modern Spain*. Ed. Joan Cammarata. Gainesville: University of Florida Press, 2002. 54–76.

———. *Teresa de Jesús: Espiritualidad y feminismo*. Madrid: Ediciones del Orto, University of Minnesota Press, 2006.

———. "Was Saint Teresa a Feminist?" *Approaches to Teaching Teresa of Avila and the Spanish Mystics*. Ed. Alison Weber. New York: Modern Language Association, 2009.

———. *Women Writers of Early Modern Spain: Sophia's Daughters*. New Haven: Yale University Press, 2004.

Netanyahu, B. *The Origins of the Inquisition in Fifteenth-Century Spain*. New York: Random House, 1995.

Nicolás, Antonio T. de. Introduction. *Teresa, a Woman: A Biography of Teresa of Avila*. By Victoria Lincoln. Albany: State University of New York Press, 1984. xi–xxi.

O'Malley, John, S.J. *The First Jesuits*. Cambridge: Harvard University Press, 1995.

Orozco Díaz, E. *Mística, plástica y barroco*. Madrid: Anaya, 1970.

Osuna, Francisco de. *Tercer abecedario espiritual*. Madrid: Biblioteca de Autores, 1998.

Pacho, E., ed. *Diccionario de San Juan de la Cruz*. Burgos: Monte Carmelo, 2000.

Panizza, Letizia, and Sharon Wood, eds. *A History of Women's Writing in Italy*. Cambridge: Cambridge University Press, 2000.

Parker, Geoffrey. *The Grand Strategy of Philip II*. New Haven: Yale University Press, 1998.

Pedra, José Alberto. *Jerónimo Gracián de la Madre de Dios: o herdeiro exilado*. Curitiba: Artes e Textos, 2003.

Peers, E. Allison, trans. Introduction. *The Complete Works of Saint Teresa of Jesus*. 3 vols. London: Sheed and Ward, 1944–1946.

———. Introduction. *The Letters of St. Teresa of Jesus*. 2 vols. London: Burns, Oates and Washbourne, 1951.

———. *Madre del Carmelo: retrato de Santa Teresa de Jesús*. Madrid: C.S.I.C., 1948. Trans. of *Mother of Carmel: A Portrait of St. Teresa de Jesús*. Gorham, NY: Morehouse, 1946.

———. "Saint Teresa's Style: A Tentative Appraisal." *Saint Teresa de Jesus and Other Essays and Addresses*. London: Faber and Faber, 1953. 81–135.

———. *Studies of the Spanish Mystics*. London: Macmillan, 1951.

Pérez, Joseph. *The Spanish Inquisition*. Trans. Janet Lloyd. New Haven: Yale University Press, 2005.

Pérez-Romero, Antonio. *The Subversive Tradition in Spanish Renaissance Writing*. Lewisburg, PA: Bucknell University Press, 2005.

Poutrin, Isabelle. *Le Voile et la plume: autobiographie et sainteté féminine dans l'Espagne moderne*. Madrid: Casa de Velázquez, 1995.

Ray, Jonathan, "Beyond Tolerance and Persecutions: Reassessing Our Approach to Medieval *Convivencia*." *Jewish Studies* 11.2 (Winter 2005): 1–18.

———. *The Sephardic Frontier: The Reconquista and the Jewish Community in Medieval Iberia*. Ithaca, NY: Cornell University Press, 2006.

Rico, Francisco. *La novela picaresca y el punto de vista*. Barcelona: Seix Barral, 1979.

Rivers, E. "The Vernacular Mind of Saint Teresa." *Carmelite Studies*. Washington, DC: Institute of Carmelite Studies, 1984. 113–29.

Rodríguez, O. *Leyenda áurea teresaiana*. Madrid: Espiritualidad, 1970.

Rodríguez Martínez, Luis, and Teófanes Egido. Introducción. *Epistolario*. Ed. Luis Rodríguez Martínez and Teófanes Egido. Madrid: Espiritualidad, 1984. 7–60.

Rossi, Rosa. *Teresa de Ávila: Biografía de una escritora*. Trans. Marieta Gargatagli. Barcelona: Icaria, 1984.

Runge, Anita, and Lieselotte Steinbrügge, eds. *Die Frau im Dialog: Studien zu Theorie und Geschichte des Briefs*. Stuttgart: J. B. Metzlersche, 1991.

Ruiz, Alfonso. "La correspondencia de Gracián y santa Teresa vista desde el epistolario teresiano." *El Padre Gracián: Discípulo, amigo, provincial de santa Teresa*. Burgos: Monte Carmelo, 1984.

Sampson Vera Tudela, Elisa. *Colonial Angels*. Austin: University of Texas Press, 2000.

San José de Ávila: Rinconcito de Dios, paraíso de su deleite. Burgos: Monte Carmelo, 1998.

Sánchez Lora, José L. *Mujeres, conventos y formas de la religiosidad barroca*. Madrid: Fundación Universitaria Española, 1988.

Schama, Simon. *The Power of Art*. BBC Television Series. *www.bbc.co.uk/arts/powerofart/bernini.shtml*.

Schiesari, Juliana. *The Gendering of Melancholia*. Ithaca, NY: Cornell University Press, 1992.

Schlumpf, Heidi. "A Mystic for Our Times." *Religion BookLine, Publishers Weekly*. 24 Jan. 2007. *www.publishersweekly.com/article/CA6409698.html*.

Shipley, George. "The Critic as Witness for the Prosecution: Making a Case against Lázaro de Tormes." *PMLA* 97 (March 1982): 179–94.

Sieber, Harry. *Language and Society in* La vida de Lázarillo de Tormes. Baltimore: Johns Hopkins University Press, 1978.

Silverio de Santa Teresa. *Vida de Santa Teresa de Jesús*. 5 vols. Burgos: Monte Carmelo, 1935–1937.

Slade, Carole. "The Relationship between Teresa of Avila and Philip II: A Reading of the Extant Textual Evidence." *Archive for Reformation History* 94 (2003): 223–42.

———. *St. Teresa of Avila*. Berkeley: University of California Press, 1995.

———. "St. Teresa of Avila as a Social Reformer." *Mysticism and Social Transformation*. Ed. Janet K. Ruffing. Syracuse: Syracuse University Press, 2001. 91–103.

Smet, Joachim. *The Carmelites: A History of the Brothers of Our Lady of Mount Carmel*. Vols. 1 and 2. Darien, IL: Carmelite Spiritual Center, 1985.

Soufas, Teresa. *Melancholy and the Secular Mind in Spanish Golden Age Literature*. Columbia: University of Missouri Press, 1990.

Steggink, O. *Experiencia y realismo en Santa Teresa y San Juan de la Cruz*. Madrid: Espiritualidad, 1974.

———. *La reforma del Carmelo español*. Roma: Institutum Carmelitanum, 1965.

Surtz, Ronald. *Writing Women in Late Medieval and Early Modern Spain: The Mothers of Saint Teresa of Avila*. Philadelphia: University of Pennsylvania Press, 1995.

Swietlicki, Catherine. *Spanish Christian Cabala: The Works of Luis de León, Santa Teresa de Jesús, and San Juan de la Cruz*. Columbia: University of Missouri Press, 1986.

Taggard, Mindy Nancarrow. "Art and Alienation in Early Modern Spanish Convents." *South Atlantic Review* 65.1 (Winter 2000): 24–40.

Tannen, Deborah. *You Just Don't Understand: Women and Men in Conversation*. New York: Morrow, 1990.

Tar, Jane. "Angela of Foligno as a Model for Franciscan Women Mystics and Visionaries in Early Modern Spain." *Magistra: A Journal of Women's Spirituality in History* 11.1 (Summer 2005): 83–105.

———. "Spiritual Counsel and the Bonds of Affection: A Study and Translation of

Four Letters by a Seventeenth-Century Franciscan Woman Mystic." *Magistra: A Journal of Women's Spirituality in History* 14 (Summer 2008): 3–33.

Thomassin, Louis. *Vetvs et Nova Ecclesia Disciplina circa Beneficia et Beneficiarios, in Tres Partes Distribvta, Variisqve Animadversionibvs Locupletata*. Mainz: Svmtibvs Societatis Typographicae, 1787.

Tietz, Manfred. "Teresa de Jesús." *Diccionario de la mística*. Ed. Peter Dinzelbacher. Trans. Constantino Ruiz-Garrido. Burgos: Monte Carmelo, 2000. 963–8.

Trueba Lawand, Jamile. *El arte epistolar en el renacimiento español*. Woodbridge, UK: Tamesis, 1996.

Valdés, Juan de. *Diálogo de doctrina cristiana*. Madrid: Editora Nacional, 1979.

Vega y Carpio, Lope. *Santa Teresa de Jesús, monja descalza de Nuestra Señora del Carmen. Obras*. Madrid, 1890. 5: 467–503.

Vigil, M. *La vida de las mujeres en los siglos XVI y XVII*. Madrid: Siglo Veintiuno, 1986.

Vives, Juan Luis. *The Education of a Christian Woman*. Ed. Charles Fantazzi. Chicago: University of Chicago Press, 2000.

Vollendorf, Lisa. *The Lives of Women: A New History of Inquisitional Spain*. Nashville: Vanderbilt University Press, 2005.

Vollendorf, Lisa, ed. *Recovering Spain's Feminist Tradition*. New York: Modern Language Association, 2001.

Walsh, William. *Saint Teresa of Avila*. Rockford, IL: Tan, 1943.

Weber, Alison. " 'Dear Daughter': Reform and Persuasion in St. Teresa's Letters to the Prioresses." *Women's Letters across Europe, 1400–1700: Form and Persuasion*. Ed. Ann Crabb and Jane Couchman. Aldershot, UK: Ashgate, 2004. 217–36.

———. "Introduction to María de San José." *Book for the Hour of Recreation*. By María de San José. Trans. Amanda Powell. Chicago: University of Chicago Press, 2002. 1-26.

———. "María de San José (Salazar): Saint Teresa's 'Difficult' Daughter." *The Heirs of Saint Teresa of Avila*. Ed. Christopher Wilson. Washington, DC: ICS Publications, 2006. 1–20.

———. "Spiritual Administration: Gender and Discernment in the Carmelite Reform." *Sixteenth Century Journal* 31 (2000): 127–50.

———. *Teresa of Avila and the Rhetoric of Femininity*. Princeton: Princeton University Press, 1990.

———. "The Three Lives of the *Vida*: The Uses of Convent Autobiography." *Women, Texts and Authority in the Early Modern Spanish World*. Ed. Marta V. Vicente and Luis R. Corteguera. Aldershot, UK: Ashgate, 2003. 107–25.

Weissberger, Barbara F. *Isabel Rules: Constructing Queenship, Wielding Power*. Minneapolis: University of Minnesota Press, 2004.

Welch, J. *Spiritual Pilgrims: Carl Jung and Teresa de Avila*. New York: Paulist Press, 1982.

Wilson, Christopher C. "Masculinity Restored: The Visual Shaping of St. John of the Cross." *Archive for Reformation History* 98 (2007): 134–66.

———. "Saint Teresa of Ávila's Martyrdom: Images of Her Transverberation in Mexican Colonial Painting." *Anales del Instituto de Investigaciones Estéticas* 74–75 (1999): 211–33.

Ynduráin, Domingo. "Las cartas en prosa." *Estudios sobre Renacimiento y Barroco*. Madrid: Cátedra, 2006. 179–212.

Zarri, Gabriella, ed. "Introduzione." *Per lettera: La scrittura epistolare femminile tra archivio e tipografia: secoli XV–XVII*. Roma: Viella, 1999. ix–xxix.

Index